Antique Stock Certificate Almanac 2014

Antique Stock & Bond Price Guide

Fred Fuld III

No part of this book may be reproduced, stored in a retrieval system, or transmitted by any means in whole or in part without the express written permission of the author.

All trademarks, registered trademarks, service marks, and registered service marks are owned by their respective trademark, registered trademark, service mark, and registered service mark owners. Images of certificates are shown for educational purposes.

Copyright © 2013 Fred Fuld III

All rights reserved.

ISBN-13: 978-1492748557
ISBN-10: 1492748552

CONTENTS

Chapter		
	Introduction	i
1	Definitions	Pg 1
2	Parts of a Certificate	Pg 3
3	Where to Find	Pg 5
4	Speculation	Pg 7
5	Topics	Pg 9
6	Famous Signatures	Pg 11
7	Aviation & Aircraft Certificates	Pg 13
8	Automobile Certificates	Pg 19
9	Bank, Financial, & Insurance Certificates	Pg 31
10	Beverage Certificates	Pg 50
11	Entertainment Certificates	Pg 56
12	Government Certificates	Pg 69
13	Mining Certificates	Pg 84
14	Miscellaneous Certificates	Pg 129
15	Oil and Gas Certificates	Pg 181
16	Railroad Certificates	Pg 189
17	Ship Certificates	Pg 212
18	Telecommunications Certificates	Pg 218

INTRODUCTION

This is the 2014 edition of the Antique Stock Certificate Almanac, originally developed by Investment Research Institute® back in 1993. This edition is completely updated with various articles about old certificates, along with definitions, and collecting tips.

Collecting antique stock certificates is one of the most fascinating of all hobbies. The collecting of old stock and bond certificates is called scripophily, from the Latin words scrip (document) and phily (love of). The hobby first became popular during the 1960's, primarily in Europe and to a small extent in the United States. In the last twenty years, the hobby has taken off with collectors all over the world and regular auctions held throughout the year.

The collecting of antique stocks has been compared to the collecting of coins and stamps. The advantages of collecting certificates over numismatics and philately are numerous:
- They are large enough to be framed and hung on your wall
- Despite their large size, hundreds can be stored in one album
- Most have unique certificate numbers
- Because of unique numbers, there is little chance of the certificate being stolen and resold publicly
- There is financial history behind every certificate
- Many certificates have signatures of famous individuals
- There are numerous types of certificate topics that can be collected (see our chapter on topics)
- Certificates are currently undervalued compared to coins and stamps

The certificates in this almanac are listed by type: Aircraft, Automobile, Bank, Beverage, Entertainment, Government, Mining, Miscellaneous, Oil, Railroad, Ship and Telecommunications. If you can't find a certificate in a specific topic category, try the Miscellaneous category.

This almanac was not designed to be the be-all and end-all of every certificate in existence; we tried to include as many certificates as possible that have been featured in catalogs and auctions over the past few years. If there are any certificates you would like to see listed that you did not see, or you see any glaring errors, please let us know. By the way, the certificates contained in this book do not represent the certificates we have for sale. We have numerous certificates in inventory, but they make up only a very small portion of what is in the guide.

Happy Collecting!

Fred Fuld III
Investment Research Institute®
5100 Clayton Road, Suite B1-405
Concord CA 94521 USA
925-914-9148
www.antiquestocks.com   www.stockmarkettrivia.com   www.investmenttrivia.com

CHAPTER 1 - DEFINITIONS

Allegorical - a Greek or Roman individual appearing in the vignette of the certificate.

Bearer Bond - a bond which is not registered to any individual or entity, but is owned by whoever has the bond, just like currency.

Bond - a loan by an investor to a corporation or governmental entity, which can be bought or sold.

Ca - approximately, around the era of.

Cancelled (also spelled Canceled) (abbrev: C) stamped with an ink stamp or hole punched, indicting that the certificate has been sold or redeemed.

Certificate (abbrev: cert) - a document representing ownership of a stock or bond.

Coupon - a very small certificate, usually appearing in multiples on a sheet, that represents interest payment on a bond (also, it can also represent dividend payments on a stock, usually on European certificates)

CUSIP - the unique number that is assigned to all modern stocks and bonds.

Debenture - an unsecured bond that is backed only by the full faith and credit of the company.

Facsimile signature - a signature that is printed onto a certificate by machine and not handsigned.

Foxing - staining or spotting on paper, which can be caused by fungus, humidity, acid in the paper, or iron in the paper.

Intaglio - the printing process that creates the fancy borders with raised ink on certificates.

Issued (abbrev: I) - the name of the shareholder is filled out, the certificate Is dated and signed by the officers, and the number of shares is filled in on a stock certificate.

Issued and cancelled (abbrev: IC) -fully filled out and cancelled.

Issued and uncancelled (abbrev: IU) - fully filled out with no cancellation mark.

Partially issued (abbrev: PI) - the certificate is partially filled out but not completely. In other words, it may be missing the owner, the date, or the number of shares.

Partially issued and cancelled (abbrev: PIC) - the certificate is partially filled out and cancelled.

Scripophilist - collector of antique stock and bond certificates.

Scripophily - the collecting of antique stock and bond certificates.

Specimen (abbrev: SP) - unissued certificate with has the word *Specimen* either stamped, printed, or hole punched into it. These are genuine certificates which are used by banknote salespeople to show as example of their products. These certificates are rare, usually in extremely fine condition, and are highly desired by collectors.

Stock - a share of ownership in a corporation.

Stock Certificate - a printed paper document representing ownership of a specified number of shares of a corporation.

Toning - change in the color of parts of the certificate paper, usually a brown color.

Uncancelled (also spelled uncanceled) - no cancellation marks of any kind.

Unissued (abbrev: U) - nothing is filled in on the certificate.

Unissued Cancelled (abbrev: UC) - never filled out and cancelled. Occasionally found on leftover unissued certificates of companies.

Void (abbrev: V) - stamped with the word *Void*. Sometimes found on leftover unissued certificates of modern companies or on certificates that were issued in error.

CHAPTER 2 - PARTS OF A CERTIFICATE

Border - the fancy, usually engraved section around the edge of a certificate.

Certificate number - the unique assigned number of the certificate.

CUSIP - the unique number that is assigned to all modern stocks and bonds.

Date - the date the certificate was issued.

Incorporation - the state that the company was incorporated in.

Indenture - the legal contract between the bond owner and bond issuer, specifying what the terms of the agreement are.

Owner - the owner of the shares of the company.

Printer - the banknote printer that printed the certificate.

Registrar - the company that keeps track of all the shareholders.

Seal - the circular section of the certificate, sometimes attached, usually embossed, which shows the date and state of incorporation.

Shares - the number of shares that are issued by the certificate.

Transfer agent - the company that redeems sold shares and issues new shares.

CHAPTER 3 - WHERE TO FIND CERTIFICATES

Old stock and bond certificates can be found in numerous places. They can be purchased through auction houses, from Internet sellers, and through online auctions, of course. But certificates can also be found in many unlikely places. Collectors have found certificates in coin shops, stamp shops, antique stores, coin and stamp shows, and old postcard shows. They have occasionally been found at book fairs and estate sales. You can also ask stockbrokers if they ever come across old worthless stock certificates that their clients want to get rid of for tax purposes. Your parents, grandparents, aunts, and uncles may even have old worthless stock certificates.

Keep your eyes open and ask around, and you may find certificates in laces you never even thought of.

CHAPER 4 - SPECULATION

There is a relatively new sector in the scripophily market called Speculation. I would never recommend that anyone consider antique stocks and bonds as investments. Collectors should collect because they enjoy the hobby, the visual appeal of the certificates, and the history behind the documents.

There are some collectors who like to acquire bonds (and occasionally stocks) that have been issued by a government or corporation that, if a company, has either gone out of business, or if a government, has for some change in government, is no longer considering such bonds acceptable for redemption.

These collectors buy these documents with the consideration that at some point in the future, the bond may be redeemed. Every few years, another type of bond pops up as a speculation. This started many years ago with some of the German and China bonds. Now these speculations have become more common.

Because of this, some of these certificates have reached outrageous prices, far above their collectible value, only to drop in price later when the bubble bursts.

Some of the certificates that have been subject to speculation include:

German Dawes bonds
German Young bonds
Chinese Reorganization 1913 bonds
Chinese Government bonds
Chicago Saganaw and Canada Railroad bonds
Republic of Mexico bonds
Mexican Government bonds
Banco Central Mexicano
Estados Unidos Mexicanos
Banco de Londres y Mexico
National Railways of Mexico
United States of America Santa Anna bonds
Republica dos Estados Unidos do Brazil
Peruvian bonds

CHAPTER 5 - TOPICS

Topics refer to the various types of certificates that collectors choose to collect. This is just a small list of the numerous types of certificate collecting specialization.

Business

Aviations (Aircraft, Airplane, Airline, Blimps, Balloons)
Automobile (Bus, Truck, Trailer, Tire, Rubber, Bicycles)
Cemetery
Computer and Technology
Financial (Bank, Insurance, Investment, Real Estate, Construction)
Beverage (Beer, Wine, Liquor, Soft Drinks)
Canals, Bridges, Tunnels
Chemicals
Colonies
Firearms (Guns, Rifles, Gunpowder, Ammunition)
Fisheries
Food (Agriculture, Restaurant)
Entertainment (Motion Pictures, Television, Theaters, Gambling, Casino, Horse Racing, Photo, Zoo, Sports, Music, Tourism)
Glass
Government (State Bonds, Chinese Bonds, Russian Bonds, Mexico Bonds)
Hotels
Manufacturing
Mining (Gold, Silver, Coal, Diamond)
Music
Perfume
Petroleum (Oil, Gas, Pipeline)
Printing
Utilities
Railroad (Tramways, Trolley, Streetcar)
Religious
Ship (Navigation, Boats, Maritime, Whaling)
Telecommunications (Telephone, Telegraph)
Textile
Tobacco (Cigarettes, Cigars)
Wood (Lumber, Paper)

Incorporation

States
Territorials (certificates issued by companies in territories before they became a state)
Countries

Famous People

Autographs
Issued to Famous People

Printers
American Banknote, Security Colombian Banknote, De La Rue, Jefferson, etc.

Vignettes
Unique
Unusual
Multicolor
Native American Indians
Animals
Women
Erotica
Cars
Airplanes
Trains
Mining Scenes

Dates
19th Century
18th Century
17th Century
1929 (year of the great stock market crash)

Denominations
High denomination stocks (e.g. 1,000,000 shares)
High denomination bonds (e.g. $1,000,000)
Low denominations (e.g. 1/10 of a share)

Certificate Numbers
Low Certificate Numbers
Certificate Number 1
Certificate Number 7
Certificate Number 8

Issues
Stocks (common, preferred, preference)
Bonds
Bearer versus Issued versus Unissued

Scams
Scams
Swindles
Scandals

CHAPTER 6- FAMOUS SIGNATURES

Signatures of the following individuals have been found on stock certificates, either as an officer of the company or as a shareholder.

Konrad Adenauer	Thomas Drayton	Mary Henry
Oakes Ames	Felix du Pont	Conrad Henslee
Oliver Ames	H.A. du Pont	James Hill
W.C. Andrews	Philip du Pont	Alex Holland
Walter Annenberg	Dumont	Johns Hopkins
Benjamin Augustine	Dunlap	Harry Houdini
Steven Austin	AP Durham	Sam Houston
Wm. Badger	John Echols	Elbert Hubbard
Bernard Baruch	John Ecols	C.P. Huntington
Alfred Beit	Charles Edison	Collis P. Huntington
Melville Bell	Thomas Edison	CP Huntington
August Belmont	Edward Everett	Clarence Hyde Cooke
Jacob Beringer	James Fargo	Samuel Insull
Ch. Bialik	William Fargo	John Jarvis
Nicholas Biddle	H. Farnam	Marshall Jewell
William Bingham	Henry Farnam	Egbert Judson
Henry Blackwell	Thomas Fawick	John E. W. Keely
G.L. Bossard	Gov.R.E. Fenton	John Kelly
JH Brown	Marshall Field III	Kirk Kerkorian
Charles Buckalew	Millard Fillmore	Alexander Kinloch
David Buick	F.J. Fisher	Robert Kinnier
Ambrose Burnside	John Forbes	Ivar Krueger
Jim Butler	Nathan B. Forrest	Charles Krug
John Butterfield	M.J. Foster	Wm. Ladd
T.A. Campbell	J. Fremont	E. Ladenbrug
George Cannon	Henry Frick	Lafarge
J.R. Carpentier	Sheriff Garret	Simon Lake
Daniel Carroll	J.W. Gates	Gazaway Lamar
Henry Caulfield	J. P. Getty	MA Leach
Charles Chaplin	Bernard Gimbel	Emanuel Lehman
Charlie Chaplin	Jay Gould	Henry Leland
Peter Colt	H.J. Grant	Wilfred Leland
Jay Cooke	W. T. Grant	Mervyn LeRoy
Frank Cooper	W.T. Grant	Robert Lincoln
Austin Corbin.	Edward H R Green	Jacob Lit
Erastus Corning	Galusha Grow	Huey Long
Jonathan Dayton	Murry Guggenheim	John Long
Alphonse de Rothschild	Walter Haas	Pierre Lorillard
Antonio Lopez de Santa Anna	Frank Hague	Jacob Luden
P.R. Delling	Halifax	Charles Ludwig
John Delorean	Alexander Hamilton	William Mahone
Denfert-Rochereau	F.B. Hamlin	Bernard Manischewitz
Devereux	E.H. Harriman	David McKay
Bill DeWitt	George Harriman	William McKinley
Arthur Dickerson	George Hartford	Andrew Mellon
Walt Disney	Frederick Heinze	David Moffat

Alfred Moisant
J.R. Moon
J. Morgan
JP Morgan
"Henry Morgenthau, Jr."
Robert Morris
Joe Namath
Van Ness
Tasker L. Oddie
James Oglethorpe
Ransom Olds
Walter Olen
Leon Orban
Fred Pabst
Frederick Pabst
Gustave Pabst
Victor Page
William Paine
Guy Park
GH Parsons
George Peabody
Fred Pearson
Daniel Phoenix
Mary Pickford Rogers
 Porterfield
C. Pratt
F.A. Pratt
George Pullman
E. Remington
RS Reynolds
John Rigney

Victor Ringhoffer
JD Rockefeller
John Rockefeller
"John Rockefeller, Jr."
H. Rogers
Henry Rogers
Henry Rogers
James Rolph Jr.
EH Romano
W.W. Rose
Nathan Rothschild
Russell Sage
Antonio Lopez de Santa Anna
Charles Savage
Charles Schwab
Thomas Scott
William Sharon
Henry Sibley
George Smith
Joseph Smith
Lorenzo Snow
Louis Sonnenberg
Claus Spreckels
Rudolph Spreckels
Leland Stanford
Frederick Stanley
Abram Stevens Hewitt
William Stewart
Henry Strong
Gloria Swanson
John Taylor

John Taylor
Moulton Taylor
Mark Ten Suie
J. Thompson
J. W. Thompson
Preston Tucker
Preston Tucker
Florence Twombly
Felix van den Peerenboom
Mr. Van Nylen
George W. Vanderbilt
Jacob Vanderbilt
William Vanderbilt
Leonard Volk
C. von Linde
H.C. Warmouth
W.S. Webb
Henry Wells
David Werblin
E. White
George Wingfield
Arthur Winslow
Major Wood
Jonah Woodruff
Wilford Woodruff
W.W. Wrigley
Ed Wynn
Brigham Young
John Young
Newton Zant

CHAPTER 7 - AVIATION & AIRCRAFT CERTIFICATES

Aviation certificates can include everything from airlines, airplane and jet manufacturers, balloon companies, airports, aerospace companies, and blimp, zeppelin, and dirigible companies.

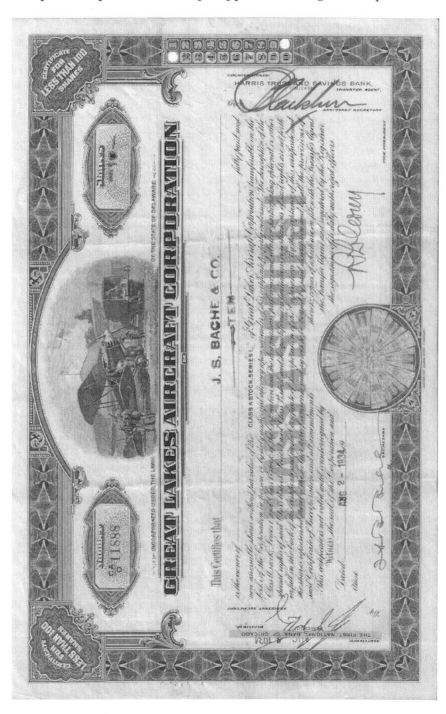

Name	IU	Date	State	Vignette	Signed by	Value	Category
Aero. Pour L'Expl. des Ballons	IC	1880's	Belgium			560	Aviation
Aeronautical Corp. of America	IC	1940's	OH	Logo		300	Aviation
Aeronca Aircraft	IC	1940's	OH	Woman, globes		250	Aviation
Aeronca Aircraft	IC	1940's	OH	No vignette	Walter A. Haas	250	Aviation
Aerospace-Science Fund	I	1960's		Eagle		35	Aviation
Air Canada	IC	1920's	Canada	Maple leaf logo of the airline.		120	Aviation
Air T	I	2001		Company logo		50	Aviation
Aircraft Acceptance Corp.	I	1960's	OH	Eagle		35	Aviation
Aireon Manufacturing Corporation	IC	1940's	CA, KS	Male figure & two aircraft.		240	Aviation
Airship International Ltd.	IC	1980's	NY, FL	Airship.		80	Aviation
America West Airlines	IC	1990's	DE	Company logo.		130	Aviation
America West Holdings	I	2001				75	Aviation
American Airlines	IC	1960's		Mercury & airport		35	Aviation
American Airlines	IC	1970's		Mercury & airport		30	Aviation
American Airlines $1000 bond	IC	1960's		Airplane		35	Aviation
American Airlines $1000 bond	IC	1970's		Airplane		30	Aviation
American Airports Corporation	U	1920's	DE			260	Aviation
American Eagle Aircraft Corp of Del	IC	1930's	DE	Eagle.	Porterfield	200	Aviation
American Eagle Aircraft of Delaware	IC	1930's	DE	Roaring eagle.		176	Aviation
Amtran	I	2001		Multicolor vignette of a large passenger jet		125	Aviation
Apache Arial Transportation	IU	1909	AZ	Apache airplane		975	Aviation
Ateliers de Const. Mecan.	IC	1900's	France	Decorative border.		52	Aviation
Autoplane Development Co. of Nev	I	1930's		Flying eagle		295	Aviation
Aviation Corp.	I	1940's		Eagle & map of United States		45	Aviation
Aviation Sales Co	I	2001		Two pilots watching plane		75	Aviation
Aviation Shares	I	1960's		Steamship, trains, & old factory		95	Aviation
Aviation-Electronics-Electrical	I	1960's		Eagle		35	Aviation
Aviator S.A.	IC	1900's	Belgium			150	Aviation
Bach Aircraft Co.	IU	1929	DE	Bach logo		350	Aviation
Baldwin Airship	I	1906	ME	Orange.	J.R. Carpentier	650	Aviation
Baldwin Airship	I	1900's	ME	Orange. Issued to/signed by	J.R. Carpentier	750	Aviation
Bendix Helicopter, Inc.	U	1940's	DE			160	Aviation
Berlin Doman Helicopters	I	1968-9		Green		75	Aviation
British Airways PLC	IC	1980's	NY	Globe, female & male figures.		100	Aviation
Broadband.com Angel Technologies	SP	1998		Two unusual airplanes		45	Aviation
Butler Aviation	IC	1972		Blue (no vignette)		25	Aviation
CargoLifter AG	U	2004	Germany	Blimp		35	Aviation
Central Airport, Incorporated	IC	1930's	DE	Aircraft flying past hangar.		220	Aviation
Chicago Helicopter Industries, Inc.	IC	1980's	DE, IL			130	Aviation
City of Fort Wayne	I	1929	IN	Brown. Spirit of St. Louis.		195	Aviation
Coastal Aeroplane & Motor	IU	1910's	NY			200	Aviation
Coastal Airways	IU	1929	DE	Seaplane		975	Aviation

Company	Type	Date	Location	Description	Signature	Price	Category
COLON Transaerea	I	1928	Spain	Airship		150	Aviation
Continental Airlines, Inc.	IC	1970's	NV	Allegorical heroic figures, airline logo.		70	Aviation
Cornelius Aircraft Corporation	I	1932		Eagle	V. L. Cornelius	58	Aviation
Curtiss-Wright Corp.	IC	1983		Man, three women/ tools, winged wheel		35	Aviation
Curtiss-Wright Corporation	IC	1920's	DE			200	Aviation
Danville Flying Service, Inc.	U	1930's	VA	Plane, blimp, tri-motor, bi-plane		450	Aviation
Delta Airlines, Inc.	U	1967		Woman		60	Aviation
Detroit Aircraft	IU	1930's	MI	Plane, blimp		695	Aviation
Douglas Aircraft	SP	1958	DE	Biplanes, globe		495	Aviation
Douglas Aircraft	SP	1900's		Globe separated by two allegoricals		750	Aviation
E-Systems, Inc.	IC	1960's	DE	Beautiful girl.		48	Aviation
Eastern Airlines	SP			Kneeling man with Co. logo		250	Aviation
Expreso Aereo Inter-Americano	IU	1947	Cuba			250	Aviation
ExpressJet Holdings	I	2003		Passenger jet		85	Aviation
Ezekiel Air Ship	IU	1902		Unusual airship		2,900	Aviation
Fairchild Engine & Airplane Corp.	I	1950's		Man, woman, & winged horse		35	Aviation
Fairchild Engine and Airplane Co.	IC	1950's	MD	Classical figures, company logo.		124	Aviation
Flyworm Corp. of America	I	1920's	NV	Large eagle		75	Aviation
Glenn L. Martin Co.	IC	1950's	MD			56	Aviation
Grand Express Aeriens	IU	1922	Paris	Viking ship in the middle of a winged logo		295	Aviation
Gray Goose Airways, Inc.	U	1930's	NV	Goose, company logo.		296	Aviation
Great Lakes Aircraft	PI	1923	DE	Men loading packages in early biplane		295	Aviation
Great Lakes Aviation	I	2002		GA logo		50	Aviation
Harriman Aeromobile	U	1900's	ME	Aerocar	G. W. R. Harriman	990	Aviation
Hawaiian Airlines	I	2001		Logo		35	Aviation
International Aviators	IU	1911	NY	Clouds	Alfred Moisant	750	Aviation
JetBlue Airways	I	2002		JetBlue logo		75	Aviation
Keit Agency Inc.	U	1900's		Small plane & blimp. (Blue)		45	Aviation
Kinner Airplane & Motor	U	1920's	CA	Single Propeller Aircraft		350	Aviation
Kinner Airplane & Motor	IU	1930's	CA	Plane		350	Aviation
La Revue de L' Aviation	IC	1900's	France	Art noveau design.		110	Aviation
Le Moter Laviator S.A.	IC	1900's	France	Aircraft.		190	Aviation
Lincoln Aircraft Co.	I	1920's		Portrait of Lincoln		175	Aviation
Longren Aircraft Corporation	I	1915	KS	Woman	Longren	67	Aviation
Lucht. Antwerpen	IC	1970's	Belgium			380	Aviation
Martin-Marietta Corporation	IC	1960's	MD			52	Aviation
Mexican Central Airways	IU	1930	AZ	Plane, hangers		875	Aviation
Moore Aircraft Corp.	I	1930's	NV	Flying eagle		75	Aviation
New York City Airport, Inc.	SP			Old airport with old flying transport plane		175	Aviation
New York Rio & Buenos Aires Line	IU	1930	DE	Airplane & flying fish		350	Aviation
North American Aviation, Inc.	SP			Flying Mercury with transport plane		175	Aviation

Name	Type	Date	State	Description	Price	Category
Orbital Sciences	SP			Multi-color vignette of outer space	250	Aviation
Pan Am Airlines	U	1975			250	Aviation
Pan Am World Airways debenture	IC	1970's		Two men either side of two globes	35	Aviation
Pan American Airways	U	1945	NY		46	Aviation
Pan American World Airways	I	1966-78	NY	Registered Bond. Spread eagle.	35	Aviation
Pan-American World Airways	I	1950's		4.75% bond, eagle, two hemispheres, allegoricals	35	Aviation
Pan-American World Airways	I	1950's		Eagle, two hemispheres, allegorical figures	35	Aviation
Peekskill Hydro-Aeroplane Co.	U	1910's		Airplane	250	Aviation
Pickwick Airways.	I	1920's		Standing woman on mountain with two flying planes	350	Aviation
Pinnacle Airlines	I	2004		Logo	50	Aviation
Pioneer Aviator	I		CA		128	Aviation
Resort Airlines	I			Eagle	45	Aviation
Rigid Airship USA	I	2001			100	Aviation
Robinson Airlines Corp.	IU	1940's	NY		100	Aviation
Robinson Airlines Corp.	U	1940's	NY		50	Aviation
San Francisco Airport Bond	IC	1949	CA	Early four engine passenger plane. (Green).	150	Aviation
Saturn Airways, Inc.	IC	1960's	FL	Planet Saturn with its rings.	110	Aviation
Seaboard Airways, Inc.	IC	1930's	DE	Eagle.	300	Aviation
Sperry	IC	1950's		Biplane, cockpit, ship	85	Aviation
State of Hawaii Airport Bond	IC	1980's	HI	Blue. Man & woman, Hawaiian seal.	45	Aviation
Swanson Aircraft	I	1920	VA		48	Aviation
Tradewinds Airlines	U	1950's		Puerto Rico (Blue).	35	Aviation
Tradewinds Airlines	U	1950's		Eagle	35	Aviation
Trans World Airlines, Inc.	U	2001	DE	Company initials	66	Aviation
Transcontinental & Western Air	U			Specimen, perched eagle by bay	195	Aviation
Transcontinental Aerial Navigation	IU	1888	IL	Blimp flying over farm	1,750	Aviation
Transcontinental Air Transport	IU	1930	DE	Planes, trains, stagecoach	975	Aviation
Translntl. Airlines	U	1900's	NV	Specimen, Co. logo	125	Aviation
Transworld Airlines	I			Eagle & plane	50	Aviation
U.S. Airlines	IU	1950's	FL	Brown	75	Aviation
U.S. Airlines	IU	1950's	FL	Green	75	Aviation
United Aircraft	IC	1960's		Woman holding plane, planes overhead	35	Aviation
United Aircraft Corp.	I	1960's		Bond, planes, skyline	35	Aviation
United Airlines	IC	1950's		Mercury	35	Aviation
United Airlines	I	1960's		Bond, winged Mercury with winged wheel	35	Aviation
United Airlines	IC	1960's		Man with winged wheel	35	Aviation

Universal Aero-Transportation Co.	U	1910's	AZ	Eagle & early aircraft	195	Aviation
Universal Airlines	IU	1970's		Woman holding globe, modern airport terminal	75	Aviation
Vickers Ltd.	IC	1900's	GB	Warship, army & naval guns.	640	Aviation
Western Air Lines	U	1980	CA	Woman	100	Aviation
Whitehead Aircraft	IU	1918	GB	Orange/Blk. Airport with hangers, two biplanes	750	Aviation
Whitehead Aircraft	IU	1918	GB	Green/Blk. Airport with hangers, two biplanes	750	Aviation
Whitehead Aircraft Ltd.	IC	1900's	GB	Factories, fighters.	480	Aviation
Whitehead Werke A. G.	IC	1920's	Austria		152	Aviation
Wilcox Rich	SP	1929	MI	Plane, boat, truck, car	950	Aviation
WTC Air Freight	IC	1960's	CA	Logo & aircraft.	80	Aviation
Zeebrugge Aeronautical Construction	IC	1920's	Belgium	Two seat fighter biplane.	150	Aviation

CHAPTER 8 - AUTOMOBILE, TRUCK, TRACTOR, TIRE CERTIFICATES

There are plenty of sub-categories in the automobile category, including trucks, buses, motor homes, tractors, tires, rubber, auto parts, and motorcycles. Even bicycles are sometimes included in this category.

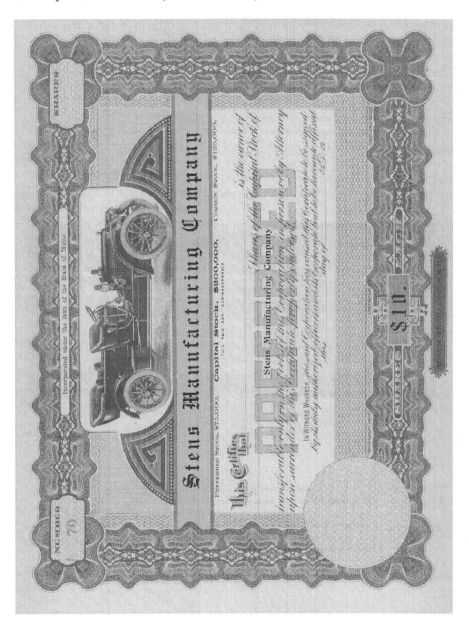

Name	IU	Date	State	Vignette	Signed by	Value	Category
ACF-Brill Motors	I	1955		Orange. Two men, large car wheel.		75	Auto
Acme Motor & Power	IC	1900's	SD	Electric horse carriage.		187	Auto
Aerocar Inc.	IU	1951	WA	Dome	Moulton B. Taylor	1,250	Auto
Ajax Rubber Co.	I	1920's	NY	Two allegorical figures		20	Auto
Alpen. Karo.-Fabrik	IC	1920's	Austria	Arms of Graz.		168	Auto
American Automotive Accessories	U	1931	NV			25	Auto
American La France Fire Engine	SP	1900's	NY	Horse drawn fire truck		795	Auto
American La France Fire Engine	I	1920's	NY	Eagle		395	Auto
American Motors	IC	1974	MD	Men & woman, large winged wheel. 6% Bond		35	Auto
American Motors	IC	1974	MD	Men & woman, large winged wheel		35	Auto
American Motors Corp.	I	1960's		Winged wheel with two men & woman		35	Auto
American Motors Corporation	U			Two god-like figures		50	Auto
American-La France Fire Engine	SP	190-		Horses pulling steam powered firetruck		495	Auto
Anglo-American Rapid Vehicle Co.	IC	1900's	NY	Train.		600	Auto
Armstrong Rubber Co.	SP			Workers & storage tanks		35	Auto
Arsenal Motor Co.	I	1920's	PA	Dealership		20	Auto
Assoc. Commerc Indust. Franco Ital	IC	1920's	France	Car		160	Auto
Atelifers Gillet S.A.	IC	1950's	Belgium	Motorcycle.		70	Auto
AUDI	U	1932	Germany	Logo		59	Auto
Augustine Automatic Rotary Engine	I	1921	NY	Orange. Spread eagle.	Ben. Augustine	75	Auto
Augustine Automatic Rotary Engine	U	1921	NY	Orange. Spread eagle.		45	Auto
Auto Bus Beiges	U	1920's		Old busses in front of buildings		45	Auto
Auto-Train Corp.	I	1970's	FL	Co. logo, seal		15	Auto
Automobile Advertising Co.	U	1900's	ME	Early little car with four poles & sign		95	Auto
Automobile Shares	I	1940's		Eagle with ship & factory		40	Auto
Automobile Shares	SP			Ship, train, eagle		50	Auto
Automobiles & Moteurs Henriod S.A.	IC	1890's	France		Victor Ringhoffer	56	Auto
Automobiles Belgica	IC	1900's	Belgium	Belgica Car		200	Auto
Baker Steam Motor Car	I	1920				47	Auto
Baker Steam Motor Car	I	1920's	AZ	Allegorical		350	Auto
Baker Steam Motor Car & Manuf.	I	1923	AZ	Orange underprint of vintage touring convertible.		300	Auto
Banner Motor Car Co.	I			Winged Mercury with steering wheel		45	Auto
Beggs Motor Car Co.	I	1910's				100	Auto

Company	Type	Date	State/Country	Description	Signature	Price	Category
Belmont Motors	IC	1920's	DE	Woman with cape, gold shield.		198	Auto
Belmont Motors Corp.	U	1900's		Lady		100	Auto
Ben-Hur Motor Car Co.	IU	1910's		Logo of car plus gladiator & chariot		350	Auto
Ben-Hur Motor Car Co.	IU	1910's		Western hemisphere		300	Auto
Bessemer-American Motors	I	1923	DE	Orange. Title in ornate scroll.		125	Auto
BMW M5 certificate	U	1992	IL	BMW logo		30	Auto
Bonner Motor Car	I	1920's		Driver with winged helmet		150	Auto
Budd Wheel Co.	IC	1930's	PA	Two nude men		35	Auto
Cadillac Automobile Co.	I	1920's	MA			125	Auto
Carbiz (Carbiz.com) Inc.	I	2004		Silver over print name		35	Auto
Carrosserie Automobile Grand Luxe	IC	1900's	France	Art noveau border & flowers.		60	Auto
Checker Motors	SP	1920's	NJ	Car in circle flanked by man.		220	Auto
China Motor Co.	U		Panama			35	Auto
Chrysler Corp.	SP	1997	DE	Two women Chrysler hood ornament		100	Auto
Chrysler Corp.	SP			Goddesses, radiator cap, cars, trucks		100	Auto
Co. Generale des Omnibus de Paris	IU	1855	France	Blue, yellow. Cathedral of Reims, Arras, Verdun		70	Auto
Columbia Wagon Co.	I	1890's	PA			100	Auto
Comp Generale des Omnibus de Paris	I	1855	France	Cathedral of Reims, Arras and Verdun, workers below.		70	Auto
Consolidated Motors Corporation	I	1917		Eagle		75	Auto
Continental Lines S.A.	IC	1960's	Belgium			22	Auto
Continental Motors Corp.	I	1920's		Automobile motor		75	Auto
Continental Motors Corp.	I	1960's		Automobile motor		50	Auto
Cooper Tire & Rubber Co.	U			Specimen, Co. logo, figures		25	Auto
Cornfield Wheel Co.	I	1910's	MI	Seal		40	Auto
Crawford Motor Co.	I	1920's	PA	Three allegorical figures		50	Auto
Daimler Benz bond	IU	1942	Germany	Logo		500	Auto
Daimler-Benz A.G.	IC	1940's	Germany	Mercedes star logo.		100	Auto
DaimlerChrysler	I	2003		Old automobiles		75	Auto
Darracq & Cie	SP	1890's	France	Darracq factory, border of thistles.		390	Auto
Delling Motors	IC	1920's	NJ	Eagle on rock.	P.R. Delling	132	Auto
Delling Steam Car	I	1928		Eagle		112	Auto
Delorean	SP			Blue.	Facsimile	1,000	Auto
Delorean Motors Corp.	IC				John Delorean	4,950	Auto
Detroit & Canada Tunnel Co.	I	1920's		Flag-covered ladies		35	Auto
Detroit & Canada Tunnel Co.	I	1930's		Flag-covered ladies		35	Auto
Detroit & Canada Tunnel Corp.	SP	1927	MI	Woman sitting on throne		75	Auto
Diamond T Motor Car	SP	19--	IL	Logo, two men		500	Auto
Dill Tractor	I	1920's	AK	Eagle		50	Auto
Dort Motor Car	IC	1920's	DE	Reclining women.		154	Auto
Dort Motor Car Co.	I	1922	DE	Women		75	Auto
DTirant-Motors	I	1920's		Five-star shield, factory		225	Auto

Name	Type	Date	State	Description	Signer	Price	Category
Duesenberg Automobile	IU	1920's	DE	Woman, globes		950	Auto
Duesenberg Automobile	IU	1920's		Yellow. Allegoricals. Preferred.		1,850	Auto
Duesenberg Automobile	IU	1920's		Brown. Allegoricals. Common.		1,250	Auto
Duesenberg Automobile & Motors	IU	1922	IN	Eagle		595	Auto
Duesenberg Automobile & Motors	IU	1921-3	DE	Red, green. Eagle.		500	Auto
Dunlop Rubber	IC	1964		Pink. No vignette. Large		10	Auto
Dunlop Rubber	IC	1964		Pink. No vignette. Small		10	Auto
Duplex Tire Co.	I	1910's	AZ	No		15	Auto
Durant Motor	I	1923		Dragon		56	Auto
Durant Motors	I	1920-3	DE	Company logo flanked by winged allegorical figures.		75	Auto
Durant Motors	I	1920's		Two figures with Co. logo D		125	Auto
Eagle-Macomber Motor Car	I	1916	DE	Green. Eagle on globe.		200	Auto
Eagle-Macomber Motor Car	I	1916	DE	Green. Eagle on globe.		200	Auto
Electric Road Carriage	U	1890's	ME	Gray/Black	Le Roy Carter	407	Auto
Elgin Motor Car Corp.	I	1920's				150	Auto
Emerson Motors	IC	1916	DE	Green borders, security underprint.	T.A. Campbell	110	Auto
Empire Tire & Rubber Corp.	I	1910's	VA	Plantation worker at rubber tree		35	Auto
Engrenages Citroen, S.A. Des	IC	1900's	France	Different sets of gears.		200	Auto
European Auto Classics	IC	1981	DE	Logo of famous expensive cars		65	Auto
Excelsior	IC	1920's	Belgium			80	Auto
F.A.L. Motor	IC	1900's	IL	Model M-35-40		297	Auto
Fabrica Automobili Isotta Fraschini	IC	1900's	Italy	Factory, girl running with the company flag.		440	Auto
Fabrica Automobili Isotta Fraschini	IC	1940's	Italy	Company's marquee.		100	Auto
Falls Motor Corp	.I	1910's				100	Auto
Fawick Motor Car	U	1900's	SD	None	Thomas Fawick	286	Auto
Fisher Body Ohio	IC	1921	OH	Three figures	F. J. Fisher	250	Auto
Fisk Rubber Co.	IU	1932		Man extracting rubber from tree		45	Auto
Flint Motor	I	1924	MI	Purple. Two women and mills flank the Flint logo.		250	Auto
Flint Motor Corp.	I	1920's	MI	Two women, factory		295	Auto
Ford Foreign Motor Co.	I	1930's		Investment trust certificate, gold seal		150	Auto
Ford International Capital bond	IC	1969	DE	Early car		39	Auto
Ford International Capital Corp.	IC	1969		Pink. Ford with early car.		35	Auto
Ford International Capital Corp.	IC	1960's		Bond, Henry Ford & antique car		45	Auto
Ford Motor	I	2002		Man standing by early Ford automobile		45	Auto

Company	Type	Year	State	Description	Price	Category
Ford Motor	IC	1970's		Green. Henry Ford with Old Ford Car	65	Auto
Ford Motor	IC	1980's		Blue. Old Ford Car.	65	Auto
Ford Motor Co.	IC	1960's		Red. Henry Ford with Old Ford Car	100	Auto
Ford Motor Co.	IC	1970's		Orange. Henry Ford with Old Ford Car	100	Auto
Ford Motor Co.	SP			Green. Henry Ford with Old Ford Car	195	Auto
Ford Motor Co. of Berlin	I	1920's			150	Auto
Ford Motor Company of Canada	I	1906	Ontario		2,200	Auto
Ford S.A. Francaise	IC	1940's	France	Ford radiator & shield.	60	Auto
Four Wheel Drive Auto Co.	IC	1929		Walter A. Olen	75	Auto
Four Wheel Drive Auto Co.	IC	1959		Blue. Two men with tools, logo	35	Auto
FOX MOTOR CAR COMPANY	I	1921			100	Auto
FOX MOTOR CAR COMPANY	I	1921			68	Auto
Franklin Automobile	I	1921		Woman	50	Auto
Fulton Motor Truck	I	1919	DE	Grey, gold. Eagle.	75	Auto
Fulton Motor Truck	I	1919	DE	Grey, gold. Eagle.	75	Auto
General Electric Automobile	U	1890's	WV	Woman, eagle.	209	Auto
General Motors	I	1916		Allegorical woman, lion, ships. Rubber stamp cancelled.	100	Auto
General Motors	I	1916		Olive. Allegorical woman, lion, ships	100	Auto
General Motors	SP	1920's	NJ	Woman, lion, ships.	121	Auto
General Motors	IC	1931	DE	Logo, man & woman	125	Auto
General Motors $5 preferred	SP	1981		Car, truck, train	95	Auto
GENERAL MOTORS COMPANY	I	1916		Woman and lion	46	Auto
General Motors Corp.	I	1950's		Bond, train, truck, & car	35	Auto
General Motors Corp.	IC	1950's		Two figures with GM logo	75	Auto
General Motors Corp.	SP			Two figures with GM logo	150	Auto
General Motors Corp. Bond	IC	1954		Car, Truck, Train (green)	35	Auto
General Motors Corp. Bond	IC	1954		Car, Truck, Train (green)	35	Auto
General Motors Corp.-Stock	IC			Car, Truck, Train (orange)	25	Auto
General Motors Corp.-Stock	IC			Car, Truck, Train (green)	25	Auto
General Motors Corp.-Stock	IC			Car, Truck, Train (blue)	25	Auto
General Motors Fuel	I	1920's		Six percent bond	35	Auto
General Tire & Rubber Co.	I	1970's		Three seated figures with chemistry	25	Auto
Goodrich, B.F.	I	1960's	NY	Two men & Co. logo	35	Auto
Goodrich, B.F.	I	1970's	NY	Two men & Co. logo	30	Auto
Goodrich, B.F.	I	1970's		9.75% note, $1,000	35	Auto

Name	Type	Date	State	Description	Price	Category
Goodrich, B.F.	I	1970's		Nine & three-quarters% note, $100,000	35	Auto
Gove Motor Car Co.	I	1920's	ID	Truck manufacturing, eagle	125	Auto
Grant Motor Car	I	1920's		Winged Mercury, horn of plenty, books	300	Auto
Grant Motor Car I		1910's		Winged Mercury, horn of plenty, books	350	Auto
Greenwich Rubber Co.	I	1920's	OH	Eagle	25	Auto
Greyhound	IC		AZ	Greyhound dog	85	Auto
Greyhound	SP		AZ	Greyhound dog	225	Auto
Greyhound Motors Corp.	I	1920's		Factories, machinery, gold seal	100	Auto
Gros Camionnage De Paris, Comp	IC	1870's	France	Fine action scenes.	480	Auto
Grummer	IC	1920's	France	Car.	220	Auto
H.H. Franklin Manufacturing	I	1921	NY	Woman seated, train, mill behind.	175	Auto
H.H. Franklin Manufacturing	I	1921	NY	Woman seated, train, mill behind.	175	Auto
Halladay Motor Corp.	I	1920	OH		64	Auto
Hamlin Motor	IC	1920's	DE	Eagle with spread wings. F.B. Hamlin	121	Auto
Harley Davidson	SP		WI	Man, wheel, hammer anvil	175	Auto
Harroun Motors	I	1917	DE	Brown borders and security underprint.	125	Auto
Harroun Motors	I	1920	DE	Brown borders and security underprint.	75	Auto
Harroun Motors Corp.	I	1920's			350	Auto
Hawkeye Cord Tire Co. of Iowa	I	1920's		Green seal	25	Auto
Hawkeye Tire & Rubber	I	1910's	IA	Eagle, gold seal	35	Auto
Hawkeye Tire & Rubber	I	1920's	IA	Eagle, gold seal	25	Auto
Herschell-Spillman Motor	I	1919	MA	Orange	250	Auto
Herschell-Spillman Motor	I	1919	MA	Green	250	Auto
Higley Automatic Sulky	U			Gold seal, eagle	35	Auto
Hispano Suiza Fabrica de Automobiles	IU	1918	Spain	Woman, car	350	Auto
Hispano Suiza Fabrica de Automoviles	SP	1900's	Spain	High Society Woman, car in background.	297	Auto
Honda Motor Co.	SP	1996	Japan	Man and women in front of huge winged gear	135	Auto
Hudson Automobile	U	1951			48	Auto
Hudson Motor Car	IC	1920's		3 factories	150	Auto
Hudson Motor Car Co.	I	1920's		Three different factory	150	Auto
Hudson Motor Car Co.	I	1930's		Three different factory	100	Auto
Hudson Motor Car Co.	I	1940's		Three different factory	90	Auto
Hudson Motor Car Co.	I	1950's		Three different factory	85	Auto
Hutsell Motor Co.	I	1920's	WA	Eagle with flag	120	Auto
ICN Pharmaceuticals	SP	1977	CA	Woman holding beaker and globe	50	Auto

Name	Type	Date	State	Description	Signer	Price	Category
Industria Nacional de Taxi.	IC	1930's	Spain	Taximeter, busy street.		70	Auto
Industrial Motors Corp.	I	1920's	DE	Beautiful lady, two seminude men		50	Auto
Italiana Segnaiator Avtomatico bond	IU	1911	Italy	Early automobile		750	Auto
Jaguar Cars, Limited	I	1970's				95	Auto
Jaguar Racing Club	I			Jaguar		60	Auto
Jones Motor Car	IU	1919	KS	Early convertible car		675	Auto
Kaiser Frazer	IC	1940's		brown		35	Auto
Kaiser Frazer	IC	1940's		brown		20	Auto
Kaiser Frazer	IC	1940's		blue		35	Auto
Kaiser Frazer	IC	1940's		blue		20	Auto
Kaiser-Frazer	IC	1940's	NV	Maroon borders, security underprint.		45	Auto
Kardell Tractor & Truck Co.	I	1920's				75	Auto
Keely Motor	I	1887	PA	Woman, unusual engine, globe, anvil	Keely	750	Auto
Keely Motor Co.	I	1880's	PA	Woman, unusual engine, globe, anvil, hammer		350	Auto
Kerosene Burning Carburetor Co.	I	1910's	MI			85	Auto
Kinnier Taxi-Cab & Touring	U	1900's	MD	Convertible sedan.	Robert Kinnier	297	Auto
L'Auto	IC	1930's	France	Border of many different sports.		220	Auto
L'Bleriot	IU	1919	France	Early automobile		700	Auto
Laurel Motors Corporation	I	1921		Car		191	Auto
Leach-Biltwell Motor Car Co.	IC	1920's	CA		MA Leach	280	Auto
Lincoln Motor	IC	1918	MI	Eagle	Henry Leland	1,750	Auto
Lincoln Motor Co.	IC	1920's		Temporary certificate-orange	Wilfred C Leland	100	Auto
Lincoln Motor Co.	IC	1920's		Temporary certificate-green	Wilfred C Leland	100	Auto
Lincoln Motor Co.	IC	1920's		Orange. Goes.	W Leland, Nash	100	Auto
LINCON MOTOR COMPANY	U	1920				59	Auto
Liquid Air, Power & Automobile	U	1900's	WV	Columbia with flag, shield & eagle		330	Auto
Lomer Armored Tire	IC	1922	MA	Eagle on dome		50	Auto
Mack Financial	IC	1970's	OH	Old truck		35	Auto
Macomber Motors	U	1900's	CA	Eagle.		154	Auto
Maibohm Motors	IC	1920's	OH	Woman with helmet.		165	Auto
Maibohn Motors	I	1920	OH	Olive. Woman with globe and child.		250	Auto
Maibohn Motors	I	1920	OH	Olive. Woman with globe and child.		250	Auto
Manufactured Rubber Co.	U	1900's		Lady with two children		35	Auto
Marmon Motor Car	U	1920's	IN	Man holds tools.		365	Auto
Marmon Motor Co.	I	1930's				350	Auto
Maxim Motor	I	1920	NV	Smiling portrait of Victor Maxim.		425	Auto
Maxim Motor	I	1920	NV	Smiling portrait of Victor Maxim.		425	Auto
McPhee Motor Co.	U	1900's	VA	Winged Mercury holding steering wheel		50	Auto
Merchants Union Express Co.	IC	1860's	NY	Horse drawn wagon.		180	Auto

Company	Type	Date	State/Country	Description	Vignette	Price	Category
Metropolis Motor Co.	I	1910's		Winged Mercury holding steering wheel		250	Auto
Mitchell Lewis Motors of Illinois	I	1910's		Bond		50	Auto
Mohawk Rubber	SP			Indian Chief		75	Auto
Mohawk Rubber	IU			Indian Chief		75	Auto
Monos. Fahrzeug-A.G.	IC	1920's	Austria			120	Auto
Moon Motor Car	I	1930	DE	Brown. Woman in circle holds MOON placard.		250	Auto
Moon Motor Car	I	1930's		Woman with moon tablet		350	Auto
Moon Motor Car	U			Specimen, woman with moon tablet		395	Auto
Moon Motor Car Co.	U	1930's	DE	Topless goddess, company marquee.		160	Auto
Morris Motors Ltd.	IC	1930's	GB			150	Auto
Moteurs et Automobiles	IC	1900's	Belgium	Car, transmission system.		140	Auto
Motocyclettes Durandal S.A.	IC	1920's	France	Motorcycle, ornate border.		130	Auto
Motor Vehicle Speed Alarm Co.	U	1900's		Woman and head of an eagle.		35	Auto
Nash Kelvinator Corp.	I	1950's		Allegorical figure & factories		65	Auto
Nash Motors	U	1900's		Two ladies & child		85	Auto
Nash Motors	I	1910's		Two ladies & child		125	Auto
Nash Motors	I	1930's		Two ladies & child		95	Auto
Nash-Pittsburgh Motors	I	1920's	PA	Dealership		35	Auto
New London Ship & Engine	I	1912	CT	Blue. Large engine.		35	Auto
New London Ship & Engine	I	1912	CT	Blue. Large engine.		35	Auto
Nissan Motor Co.	I	2003		Very early automobile		65	Auto
Northway Motors	IU	1919	MA			175	Auto
Northway Motors	I	1920's		Woman's portrait		25	Auto
Oester. Daim.-Motoren	IC	1920's	Austria			52	Auto
Olds-Fayette Motor Co.	I	1920's	PA	Child on globe		250	Auto
Omnibus De Paris, Cie Generale S.A.	IC	1910's	France	Many fine views of Paris from 1855.		80	Auto
Packard	I	1942		Woman and two men		65	Auto
Packard Motor Car	I	1920's				950	Auto
Packard Motor Car	SP	1930's	MI	Woman with semi-nude men.		385	Auto
Packard Motor Car	U	1930's	MI	Three allegorical figures.		550	Auto
Pan Motor Co.	I	1920's		Automobile		295	Auto
Pan Motor Company	I	1918		Car	SC Pandolfo	53	Auto
Peerless Motor Car	I	1929		Seated woman		77	Auto
Peerless Motor Car	I	1927-29	VA	Brown. Allegorical figures, beehive, factories.		85	Auto
Peerless Motor Car Co.	I	1920's		Train, building, & two allegorical figures		100	Auto
Peerless Motor Car Company	IC	1928		Two People		65	Auto
Peerless Motor Car Corporation	I			Man and woman		50	Auto

Peerless Truck & Motor	I	1923-2	VA	Women, beehive, train and factories beyond.		100	Auto
Peerless Truck & Motor	I	1923-25	VA	Women, beehive, train and factories beyond.		100	Auto
Pennsylvania Electric Vehicle	U	1900's	NJ	Man, woman.		265	Auto
Piedmont Motor Car Co.	IC	1900's	VA	Female figure.		200	Auto
Pierce Arrow Motor Car	I	1935		Man		433	Auto
Pierce Arrow Motor Car Company	I	1934		Man		150	Auto
Pierce-Arrow Motor Car	I	1935	NY	Muscular man reclining, machinery beyond.		350	Auto
Pierce-Arrow Motor Car	U	1920's		Reclining man		325	Auto
Pierce-Arrow Motor Car	IU	1930's	NY	Man, logo		750	Auto
Plainfield Auto-Bus	I	1909	NJ	Women sides. Arm and hammer below.		150	Auto
Plainfield Auto-Bus	I	1909	NJ	Women sides. Arm and hammer below.		150	Auto
Portsmouth Automobile & Machine	I	1910's	OH	Early model auto		395	Auto
Princess Motor Car Corporation	I	1917		Torch		125	Auto
Rambler Auto Co. of New England	U	1910's	MA	State buildings		65	Auto
Rambler Auto Co. of New York	U	1900's		Two ladies, train, & steamboat		75	Auto
Reflex Auto-Light Corp.	I	1920's	IN	Lady with shield		25	Auto
Reliance Taxi-Cab Co., Ltd.	IC	1900's	GB	Taxi-cab in London.		130	Auto
Reo Motor Car	IC	1916	MI	Logo, two women	Ransom E. Olds	500	Auto
Reo Motor Car Co.	I	1920's		Females with winged logo	Scott	200	Auto
Reo Motor Car Company	I	1952	MI	Two men		70	Auto
Reo Motors	SP	1900's	MI	Logo between two seminude men		250	Auto
Revere Motor Car	IC	1920's	DE	Torch.	Newton Van Zant	198	Auto
Revere Motor Car Co.	I	1910's		Torch		150	Auto
Revere Motor Car Co.	I	1920's		Torch		125	Auto
Richard Auto Manufacturing Co.	I	1910's	WV	Touring car & eagle		450	Auto
Rickenbacker Motor Co of Michigan	I	1926	MI	Gods		100	Auto
Rickenbacker Motor Co.	I	1920's				275	Auto
Ringhoffer	IC	1920's	Czech			160	Auto
Roamer Motor Car	I	1923	MI	Green.		20	Auto
Roamer Motor Car	I	1923	MI	Green.		200	Auto
Rolls-Royce	SP	1967		Blue. Famous double R logo.		100	Auto
Rolls-Royce	SP	1967		Blue. Famous double R logo.		95	Auto
Rolls-Royce	SP		UK	Black. Company's logo.		95	Auto
Rolls-Royce	SP		UK	Blue. Company's logo.		100	Auto
Rolls-Royce of America	I	1930's		Seated warrior with sword		2,995	Auto
Ruggles Automobile	U	1905	MA	Silos		112	Auto
S.E.A.C.	IC	1920's	France	Car.		96	Auto
S.S. Cars Ltd.	IC	1930's	GB			360	Auto

Company	Type	Date	State	Vignette	Signature	Price	Category
Sanitary Dungcart Co. S.A.	IC	1910's	Cuba	Horse drawn dungcart, dustbin. Colorful.		88	Auto
Sebring Tire & Rubber Co.	I	1910's	OH	Winged Mercury with steering wheel		35	Auto
Severin Motor Co.	I			Winged Mercury with steering wheel		35	Auto
Sinclair Engine &.Foundry	I	1920's		Eagle		30	Auto
Sinclair Motors	I	1920's		Two allegorical		100	Auto
Sound Rubber Co.	IU	1921	WA	Sound rubber tire		100	Auto
Speedway Motorsports	SP			Automobiles racing around a racetrack		75	Auto
St. Charles Car Company	I	1887		Train		139	Auto
Stanard Automobile Mfg	I	1914		Open touring car		400	Auto
Star Motors	I	1924		Star		52	Auto
Star Motors	I	1920's		Star in front of factories & train		295	Auto
State of Missouri Road bond	IC	1932		Road. brown variety	Henry S. Caulfield	35	Auto
State of Missouri Road bond	IC	1936		Road. blue variety	Guy B. Park	25	Auto
Steinmetz Electric Car Co.	I	1920				50	Auto
Steinmetz Electric Motor Car Co.	I	1920's		Eagle		250	Auto
Steinmetz Electric Motor Car Corp.	IC	1920's	MD			340	Auto
Sterling Engine Co.	I	1940's		Eagle on rock		15	Auto
Stevens Duryea, Inc.	I	1920's		Co. logo		100	Auto
Studebaker	IC	1940's	NJ	Blacksmith shop		89	Auto
Studebaker	IU	1940's	NJ	Blacksmith shop		150	Auto
Studebaker Brothers Manufacturing	U	1900's	IN	Large auto production plant		150	Auto
Studebaker Corp.	IC	1950		Old blacksmith's shop		45	Auto
Studebaker Corp.	I	1920's		Blacksmith shop		200	Auto
Studebaker Corp.	I	1930's		Blacksmith shoeing horse		175	Auto
Studebaker Corp.	SP			Three auto worker vignettes		100	Auto
Studebaker Corporation	U	1920's	NJ	Blacksmith's workshop.		180	Auto
Studebaker Packard	IC	1960's	MI	Man, factory, office		20	Auto
Studebaker Packard	IC	1960's	MI	Man, factory, office	Kirk Kerkorian	500	Auto
Stutz Motor Car Co. Of America, Inc.	U	1930's	NY	Heroic ladies, company logo.		640	Auto
Stutz Motor Car of America	SP	1900's	NY	Two women, Stutz logo		495	Auto
Templar Motors Corp.	I	1910's		Eagle		200	Auto
The Church Motor Car	I	1914			Edmund Church	200	Auto
The Willys-Overland Company	I	1926		Man and woman		69	Auto
Tire Mileage Recording Device Co.	U	1900's	CA	Eagle		25	Auto
Tractor Supply Co.	I	1960's		Female		15	Auto
Tucker	IU	1947	NY	Tucker name logo		350	Auto
Tucker	IC	1940's	DE	Tucker logo.	Preston Tucker	1,018	Auto
Tucker	I	1947-48	DE	Stylized TUCKER corporate logo	Facsimile	295	Auto
Tucker Automobile	U	1946			Prestin Tucker	80	Auto
Tucker Car Auto Co	I	1947				203	Auto
Tucker Corp.	SP	1947	MI	orange		750	Auto
Tucker Corp.	IU	1947	MI	green		295	Auto
Tucker Corp.	IU	1947	MI	brown		295	Auto
Tucker Corp.	SP	1947	MI	green		500	Auto

Company	Type	Year	State	Description	Signature	Price	Category
Tucker Corp.	SP	1947	MI	brown		500	Auto
Tucker Corp.	IU	1947	MI	blue		750	Auto
Tucker Corp.	SP	1947	MI	blue		750	Auto
Tucker Corp.	IU	1947	MI		Preston Tucker	5,000	Auto
Tucker Corp.	IU	1947	MI		Preston Tucker	5,000	Auto
Tucker Corp.	I	1940's				250	Auto
Tucker Corporation	I	1947				89	Auto
Tucker Corporation	I	1947				120	Auto
Tucker Corporation	I	1947				99	Auto
U.S. Automotive Corp.	I	1920's		Minuteman with rifle		200	Auto
Union Electro Motor	I	1875	NY	Liberty holds lightning as she flies on eagle's back.		90	Auto
Union Electro Motor	I	1875	NY	Blue-green underprint. Liberty holding lightning		90	Auto
United Motor Clubs, Inc.	U	1920's				15	Auto
United States Motor Company	U	1911	NJ	Eagle		70	Auto
USA Tonka Toys, Inc.	U					50	Auto
Velie Motor	IC	1900's	MO	Woman with starred cap.		330	Auto
Victor Motors	IC	1920's	DE	Truck, city in distance.		176	Auto
Victor Page Motors	U	1920's	DE	Seated allegorical woman, factory	Victor Page	253	Auto
Voit. Elect. Paris.	IC	1900's	France	Several types of the Company's cars.		180	Auto
Voitures Du Grand Hotel S.A., Cie.	IC	1890's	France			320	Auto
W. E. Hendricks	U	1900's	CO	Man on bicycle		70	Auto
Walker-Johnson Truck Co.	I	1920's		Eagle, Capitol		100	Auto
White Motor Co.	IC	1910's				45	Auto
White Motor Corp.	IC	1977		Woman / globe / winged wheel.		20	Auto
White Motor Corp.	IC	1977		Woman / globe / winged wheel.		20	Auto
Willy's Corp.	IC	1920's				25	Auto
Willys Corp.	I	1920's		Certificate of deposit		35	Auto
Willys Corp.	I	1930's		Fractional share		35	Auto
Willys-Overland	I	1936	OH	Brown borders and underprint. Spread eagle.		200	Auto
Willys-Overland Co.	I	1920's		Two seated figures with Co. logo		250	Auto
Willys-Overland Co.	I	1930's		Two figures with Co. logo		200	Auto
Winslow Motor Carriage	I	1900	DE	Green, gold. State arms. Preferred		350	Auto
Winslow Motor Carriage	U	1900's	DE	State arms.	Arthur Winslow	187	Auto
Woods MOBILETTE	I	1916	AZ	Car		47	Auto
Woods Mobilette	IC	1900's	AZ	1916 Model S	John C. Long	297	Auto
Woods Mobilette	IC	1910's	AZ	Narrow two-door automobile		395	Auto
World's Fair Autocar Co.	I	1910's		Double-decker bus, gold seal		450	Auto
World's Fair Autocar Co.	I	1930's		Fraction share		100	Auto
Yellow Truck & Coach Manufacturing	SP			Woman, city skyline		65	Auto

CHAPTER 9 - BANK, FINANCIAL & INSURANCE CERTIFICATES

This category includes everything from stock exchanges to real estate companies to mortgage lenders to savings and loan companies.

ANTIQUE STOCK & BOND PRICE GUIDE 2014

Name	IU	Date	State	Vignette	Signed by	Value	Category
Africanine Banque D'Etudes D'Enterp	IC	1890's	BelCongo	Elephant tusks breaking through the canvas.		100	Bank
Albany Insurance	SP	1904	NY	New York City arms, pier scene, train on bridge		50	Bank
Albany Insurance	I	1904-22	NY	Grey. New York City arms, pier scene, train on bridge		50	Bank
Algemeene Brugsche Kredietbank	IC	1930's	Belgium			90	Bank
All City Insurance	I	1870's	NY	United States map		15	Bank
America, Bank of	I	1850's		Eagle, ship, & old train		125	Bank
America, Bank of	I	1930's		Eagle, ship, & old train		75	Bank
American Bank	IU	1860				95	Bank
American Continental Corp	IU	1988	AZ	Red white & blue logo		100	Bank
American Express	I	1866		Eagle	Wells & Fargo	995	Bank
American Express	I	1878	NY	Dog	WM Fargo	278	Bank
American Express	I	1888		Dog	James C Fargo	150	Bank
American Express	IC	1860's	NY	Blue borders.	Wells, W. Fargo	1,550	Bank
American Express	IC	1860's	NY		Wells, W. Fargo	1,660	Bank
American Express	U	1860's	NY		Wells, Fargo	1,210	Bank
American Express	IC	1880's	NY	Dog in a circle.	James C. Fargo	275	Bank
American Express Company	I	1972		Man		89	Bank
American General Insurance	IC	1960's	TX	Multi-colored. George Washington on horseback.		35	Bank
American General Insurance	IC	1970's	TX	George Washington.		25	Bank
American General Insurance Co.	IC	1960's	TX	Multi-colored. George Washington on horseback.		60	Bank
American General Insurance Co.	IC	1970's	TX	Multi-colored. George Washington on horseback.		45	Bank
American Intl. Savings & Loan	I	1960's				15	Bank
American Merchants Union Express	I	1869		Horse and carrige		78	Bank
American Merchants Union Express	IC	1860's	NY	Express car leaves port warehouse.	William G. Fargo	198	Bank
American Merchants Union Express Company	I	1864		Dock		130	Bank
American Trust Co.	I	1920's		Eagle, seal		15	Bank
Andover National Bank	IC	1913	MA	Government building		65	Bank
Andover National Bank, The	I	1890's		Capitol building with horses & carriages		75	Bank
Anglo London Paris National Bank	IC	1929	CA	Two women, logo		45	Bank
Anglo- Californian Bank Limited	I	1900's		Ornate embossed seal. British format and style.		15	Bank

Antique Bank of America	I	1857		Eagle	129	Bank
Aradmeguei Takar.	IC	1900's	Hungary		52	Bank
Arkansas, Real Estate Bank of	I	1830's		Copy of certificate	350	Bank
Associates Investment Co.	IU			Bond, Co. logo	15	Bank
Assurances De Paris Contre Risques	IC	1870's	France	Train, steamship, arms of Paris, decorative border.	320	Bank
Asylum Life Insurance	IU	1824	GB		250	Bank
Atalntic Avenue Bank	I	1920's			15	Bank
Atlanta National Bank	IC	1873	GA	Eagle	300	Bank
Atlanta National Bank	I	1870's	GA	Eagle	100	Bank
Atlanta, Lowry National Bank of	I	1910's	GA	Eagle, embossed seal	35	Bank
Atlantic Bank of the City of New York	U	1860's	NY	Ships of various types, also a sailor.	360	Bank
Atlantic Mutual Fire & Marine Insur	I	1870's		Sailing ship, with stamp	175	Bank
Atlantic Mutual Insurance Co.	I	1870's	TX	Eagle with ships, revenue stamp	175	Bank
Augusta Bank	IU	1817	ME		295	Bank
Austro-Hollandische Bank	IC	1920's	Austria		56	Bank
Auto City Brewing	SP		MI	Two seated ladies with eagle	50	Bank
Azores Dairy Bank	I	1928	CA	Grey. Western Litho.	25	Bank
Azores Dairy Bank	I	1928-29	CA	Grey. Western Litho.	25	Bank
Azures Dairy Bank	I	1920's		Embossed seal	25	Bank
Baltimore American Insurance	IC	1929		Knight on horse.	20	Bank
Baltimore American Insurance	IC	1929		Knight on horse.	20	Bank
Baltimore American Insurance Co.	I	1920's		Knight on horseback	20	Bank
Baltimore American Insurance Co.	I	1930's		Co. logo	15	Bank
Baltimore, Drovers & Mechanics Bank	I	1930's		Arm & hammer, & cow	75	Bank
Baltimore, National Marine Bank of	I	1920's	MD	Early steamboat with sails	35	Bank
Banca Agricola Risparmi Conti Corr.	IC	1920's	Italy	Agricultural scenes, Coat of Arms Lucca, Tuscany.	60	Bank
Banca Comerciala Din Buzau S.A.	IC	1920's	Romania	Farmer & woman in traditional dress.	190	Bank
Banca Cooperativa Torinese S.A.	IC	1900's	Italy	Arms of Torino, & a lovely lady.	156	Bank
Banca Cooperative Credito L'Unione	IC	1900's	Italy	Decorative border.	100	Bank
Banca Mercur Buzau S.A.	IC	1900's	Romania	Mercury, train & ship.	100	Bank
Banca Moldovei De Jos Din Barlad	IC	1920's	Romania	Woman, agriculture, industry.	160	Bank
Bancal Tri-State Corp.	SP		CA	Cowboy panning for gold	195	Bank
Banco Camogliese F. Bertolotto E.C.	IC	1870's	Italy		90	Bank
Banco Central Mexicano	IU	1903	Mexico	Eagle, snake, Inca shield, green	6,123	Bank
Banco Central Mexicano	IU	1905	Mexico	Eagle, snake, Inca shield, green	4,995	Bank
Banco Central Mexicano	IU	1908	Mexico	Eagle, snake, Inca shield, green	4,995	Bank

Name	Type	Year	Location	Description		Price	Category
Banco Central Mexicano	IU	1908	Mexico	Eagle, snake, Inca shield, blue		9,950	Bank
Banco Central Mexicano	IU	1908	Mexico	Eagle, snake, Inca shield, brown		9,950	Bank
Banco de Cartagena	I	1900	Spain	Mercury & Argos		45	Bank
Banco de Durango Mexico	U	1904	Mexico	Train		52	Bank
Banco de Guanajuato	IU	1906	Mexico			1,650	Bank
Banco de San Luis Potosi	IU		Mexico			16,633	Bank
Banco Hipotecario De Chile	IC	1930's	Chile	Arms of Chile.		52	Bank
Banco Londres y Mexico	IU	1905	Mexico			1,260	Bank
Banco Peninsular Mexicano	U	1908	Mexico	Women		1,495	Bank
Banco Popular Portuguez	IC	1920's	Portugal	Portuguese cross, Coat of Arms of Portugal.		70	Bank
Banco Ruquijo Catalan S.A.	IC	1900's	Spain	Architectural & classical border, Coat of Arms		60	Bank
Bank Hapoalim	I	1923	Palestine			110	Bank
Bank Leumi Le-Israel	I	1980	Israel	Bright red seal		35	Bank
Bank of America	I	1853	NY	Grey/Black. Eagle, shield, early train, sailing ships.		40	Bank
Bank of America	IC	1856	NY	Eagle		100	Bank
Bank of America	IC	1930		Dark Blue. Train, eagle & ship.		50	Bank
Bank of America	IC	1930		Dark Blue. Train, eagle & ship.		50	Bank
Bank of America Capital Trust Shares	SP	1930		Woman between pillars		75	Bank
Bank of Catasauqua	IC	1862	PA	Miners, women, farmer, train		175	Bank
Bank of Charleston	IU	1863	SC	State seal		125	Bank
Bank of Charleston	I	1873	SC	Palm tree island vignette		100	Bank
Bank of Charleston	I	1880	SC	Palmetto tree, cotton bale, barrel, steamboat		85	Bank
Bank of Germantown	I	1815	PA			53	Bank
Bank of Gettysburg	IU	1858	PA	Man, Liberty, Commerce		195	Bank
Bank of Gettysburg	U	1850's	PA	Allegorical women, produce.		143	Bank
Bank of Italy warrant	IC	1926	CA			65	Bank
Bank of Kentucky	I	1864	KY			175	Bank
Bank of New Orleans	I	1860	LA	Neptune		142	Bank
Bank of New York	I	1870's		Check. Blue with large GOLD underprint.		15	Bank
Bank of North America	U	1780's	PA			2,310	Bank
Bank of North America	I	1780's	PA			36,300	Bank
Bank of North Carolina	I	1860-4	NC	Harvest scene. Allegorical women.		150	Bank
Bank of North Carolina	I	1860-4	NC	Harvest scene. Allegorical women		150	Bank
Bank of Pennsylvania	I	1790's	PA			5,060	Bank
Bank of Pennsylvania	U	1850's	PA	Train, ship.		165	Bank
Bank of the United States	I	1841	PA	Woman with spear, eagle, ship.	Dunlop	250	Bank
Bank of the United States	I	1841	PA	Woman with spear, eagle, ship	Dunlop	250	Bank

Name		Year	Location	Description	Signature	Price	Category
Bank of the United States	I	1929	NY	Blue. Eagle, bank monogram.		12	Bank
Bank of the United States	I	1929	NY	Blue. Eagle, bank monogram.		12	Bank
Bank of the United States	I	1930		Second cert attached		75	Bank
Bank of the United States of America	IU	1840's		Liberty, eagle, shield		500	Bank
Bank of the United States of Pennsyl	I	1830's	PA		Nicholas Biddle	176	Bank
Bank of the United States of Pennsyl	I	1830's	PA		Nicholas Biddle	363	Bank
Bank of the United States of Pennsyl	I	1830's	PA		Nicholas Biddle	242	Bank
Bank of the United States of Pennsyl	I	1830's	PA		Nicholas Biddle	660	Bank
Bank of the United States of Pennsyl	I	1830's	PA		Nicholas Biddle	330	Bank
Bank of the United States of Pennsyl	I	1830's	PA		Dunlap	198	Bank
Bank of the United States of Pennsyl	I	1840's	PA		Dunlap	248	Bank
Bank of the United States of Pennsyl	I	1850's	PA		Wm. Badger	308	Bank
Bank of the United States of Pennsyl	I	1850's	PA			319	Bank
Bank of Wilmington	IU	1862	NC	Ships, sailor, blacksmith, etc.		250	Bank
Bank Polskich Kupcow	IC	1920's	Poland	Eagle on rock, classical lady.		64	Bank
Bankers Trust Co. of Philadelphia	IU	1929	PA	State seal		65	Bank
Bankers Trust, New York	I			Reclining lady in front of mountain		15	Bank
Bankers Trust, New York Corp.	I			Reclining woman		15	Bank
Bankokentucky	IU	1930	KY	Woman with globe		95	Bank
Banque Coloniale De Belgique, S.A.	IC	1890's	BelCongo	African scenes, train & river steamer.		400	Bank
Banque Commerciale & Viticole S.A.	IC	1920's	France	Naked man reading book, topless woman		280	Bank
Banque Credit Populaire	IC	1920's	Belgium			36	Bank
Banque De Rose, S.A.	IC	1900's	Bulgaria	Harvesting & distilling of roses.		260	Bank
Banque des Etats-Unis	IU	1859	France			475	Bank
Banque Des Etats-Unis	IC	1850's	USA/Paris		AlphonseRothschild	320	Bank
Banque Diamantaire	IC	1930's	Belgium			70	Bank
Banque Generale Belge S.A.	IC	1920's	Belgium			60	Bank
Banque Generale Des CDF	IC	1880's	France	City of Lyon, trains, globe, factories.		280	Bank
Banque Hellenique Pour Commerce	IC	1920's	Greece	Gods, ship, factory.		96	Bank
Banque Industrielle de Chine	I	1913	China	Bright yellow with brown, pagoda		45	Bank
Banque Industrielle de Chine	I	1913	China	Bright yellow Pagoda. Printed in French and Chinese		140	Bank
Banque Industrielle de Chine		1919	China	Castle		120	Bank
Banque Intermediaire De Belgique	IC	1890's	Belgium	Map of Europe.	Felix Peerenboom	120	Bank
Banque J-B Joany & Cie.	IC	1900's	France	Classical ladies, reclining.		120	Bank

Banque Meuse Et Campine S.A.	IC	1900's	Belgium	Decorative border.	150	Bank
Banque Nationale de Grece	I	1913	Greece	Pink with blue revenue stamp.	25	Bank
Banque Nationale de Grece	I	1913	Greece	Pink with blue revenue stamp.	25	Bank
Barnstable Bank	IU	1861	MA		95	Bank
Barnstable Bank	I	1850's	ME		100	Bank
Barnstable Bank	I	1860's	ME		50	Bank
Barnstable Bank,	I	1830's	ME		125	Bank
Barnstable Bank,	I	1840's	ME		100	Bank
Bath, First National Bank of, Maine	I	1900's		State seal	75	Bank
Bath, Lincoln National Bank of	I	1880's	ME	Capitol building	100	Bank
Bath, Lincoln National Bank of	I	1900's	ME	Capitol building	75	Bank
Beaver Creek Distillery	IC	1960		Barrel Dripping	35	Bank
Berlinische Feuer-Versicherungsunst	IC	1900's	Germany	Germania.	24	Bank
Bethel, National White River Bank	I	1870's	VT	Pedestrians, horses, carriages, & capitol building	100	Bank
Boston National Union Bank of	I	1880's	MA	Large capitol building	100	Bank
Boston National Union Bank of	I	1890's	MA	Large capitol building	50	Bank
Boston Personal Property Trust	I	1960's	MA	Eagle	15	Bank
Boston, Atlantic National Bank of	I	1930's	MA	Sailing ships	75	Bank
Boston, Investment Trust of	I	1960's	MA	State building	15	Bank
Boston, Rockland-Atlas National Bank	I	1950's	MA	Man with world on his back	35	Bank
Boston, Second National Bank	I	1920's	MA		35	Bank
Boston, Second National Bank of	I	1900's	MA	Capitol building, Indian maiden, & seated lady	75	Bank
Boston, Second National Bank of	I	1910's	MA	Capitol building, Indian maiden, & seated lady	45	Bank
Boston, Second National Bank of	I	1920's	MA	Capitol building, Indian maiden, & seated lady	35	Bank
Bourse Industrielle De Belgique Coop	IC	1920's	Belgium		45	Bank
Brewers Malting Corp.	I	1910's		Six percent gold bond, eagles	35	Bank
Bridgeton Saving Fund & Building	I	1860's		With revenue stamp	100	Bank
Briggs National Bank & Trust Co.	I	1930's	NY	Eagle & gold seal	15	Bank
Briggs National Bank & Trust Co.	I	1940's	NY	Eagle & Id seal	15	Bank
Briggs National Bank of Clyde	U	1870's		Two (old sailing ship)	35	Bank
Broadway Bank & Trust	I	1920	CT	State arms.	10	Bank
Broadway Bank & Trust	I	1920	CT	State arms.	10	Bank
Broadway National Bank of Boston	I	1890's			35	Bank
Brooklyn, First National Bank of	I	1860's		Woman with eagle, also seated lady	75	Bank

Brownville, First National Bank of	U	1870's		Cows & girl	35	Bank
Builders Loan & Fund Corp.	U	1850's		of large house	75	Bank
Builders Loan & Fund Corp.	U	1860's	MA	Old bank building	50	Bank
Bullion & Exchange Bank	I	1880's	NV		175	Bank
Bullion & Exchange Bank	U	1880's	NV		35	Bank
Bullion & Exchange Bank	I	1890's	NV		125	Bank
Bullion & Exchange Bank	I	1900's	NV		100	Bank
Burlington Bank	Proof	1800's	NJ	Milkmaid, cows, farmer	165	Bank
Caisse Generale Des Warrants Ltd.	IC	1900's	Guernsey	House on fire, ship sinking	120	Bank
Caisse locale Credit Agricole Mutuel	IC	1930's	France	Agriculture & industry	72	Bank
California, Bank of	I	1870's	CA	Small certificate	50	Bank
Carbon Building & Loan Assoc	I	1910's		Three	15	Bank
Carbon Building & Loan Assoc	I	1920's		bid house	15	Bank
Carlo Darwin Insurance	I	1920's	NC	Eagle	15	Bank
Carnegie Life Insurance of America	I	1920's	NC	Females & co. logo	15	Bank
Carolina Insurance Co.	I	1920's	NC	Stamps	15	Bank
Carolina Savings Bank	U	1870's	SC	Dog in front of safe	50	Bank
Carrollton Bank	IU	1836	LA		195	Bank
Carson City Savings Bank	U		NV	Eagle	35	Bank
Carson City Savings Bank of Amer	I			Train	50	Bank
Centerville National Bank	I	1860's		Eagle with shield	15	Bank
Central National Bank	IC	1905	DC	Capitol building	85	Bank
Chandler, Bank of	I	1920's	AZ	Eagle	15	Bank
Charleston, Bank of	I	1830's		Two women, palm tree, sailing ships, & seal	225	Bank
Charleston, Bank of	I	1840's		Two women, palm tree, sailing ships, & seal	175	Bank
Charleston, Bank of	I	1850's		Two women, palm tree, sailing ships, & seal	125	Bank
Charleston, Bank of	I	1860's		Two women, palm tree, sailing ships, & seal	100	Bank
Charleston, Bank of	I	1870'S		Palm trees	100	Bank
Chester Bank & Saving Fund	I	1880's			35	Bank
China Agency & Trading Co.	I	1910's	CA	Chinese characters	75	Bank
China Industrial Bank	U	1913			60	Bank
China Mutual Insurance Co.	I	1920's		Chinese junks, ship, & sailor	125	Bank
Citizen's Trust & Deposit Co. of Ball	I	1890's		Dog in front of large safe	100	Bank
City Bank Farmer's Trust	I	1950's		Eagle, ship, train & tank cars	25	Bank
Commercial Bank of Keokuk Iowa	I	1872	IA	25 cent BLUE revenue stamp attached	195	Bank
Commercial Bank of Keokuk Iowa	I	1872	IA	25 cent RED revenue stamp attached	195	Bank
Commercial National Bank of Raleigh	IU	1924	NC	Sir Walter Raleigh	195	Bank

Commercial State Bank of Waterloo	IC	1920	IL	Woman, cornucopia	40	Bank
Compt International Banque Change	IC	1900's	Belgium	Classical ladies, factory, winged wheel.	120	Bank
Comptoir D'Escompte De Paris	IC	1880's	France	DenfertRochereau	52	Bank
Concord Bank	U	1807			170	Bank
Concord Bank	I	1807			160	Bank
Concord Bank	I	1807			140	Bank
Concord Bank	I	1807			116	Bank
Concord Bank	I	1807			109	Bank
Concord Bank	I	1812			116	Bank
Concord Bank	I	1812			100	Bank
Concord Bank	I	1813			100	Bank
Concord Bank	IU	1846	MA		100	Bank
Connecticut Fire Insurance Co., The	I	1870's		State seal, eagle	50	Bank
Connecticut Fire Insurance Co., The	I	1890's		State seal, eagle	35	Bank
Connecticut Fire Insurance Co., The	IU	1900's		Co. logo	15	Bank
Connecticut Fire Insurance Co., The	I	1960's	CT		15	Bank
Connecticut Insurance Co.	I	1906		To Hartford Orphan Asylum	35	Bank
Connecticut Ntl Bank of Bridgeport	IC	1901	CT	Cowboys, horses	60	Bank
Continental Insurance Co.	IC	1860's	NY	Globe, patriotic lady.	176	Bank
Continental Trust Co.	IC	1901	MD	Continental soldier	30	Bank
Continuous Transit Securities Co.	IU	1920's			15	Bank
Cooperstown, First National Bank	I	1920's		Lady with flag, hunter with rifle, eagle	15	Bank
Cooperstown, First National Bank	I	1930's		Lady with flag, hunter with rifle, eagle	15	Bank
Corporation Securities of Chicago	I	1931	IL	Olive. Allegorical figure, eagle, factory and dam.	25	Bank
Corporation Securities of Chicago	I	1932	IL	Olive. Allegorical figure, eagle, factory and dam.	25	Bank
Corroon-Reynolds	I	1930's		Two kneeling women with two globes	15	Bank
Credit Agricole d'Egypte	IU	1934	Egypt	Egyptian figures	30	Bank
Credit Commercial Congolais S.A.	IC	1890's	BelCongo	Congolese smelting metal, lady.	140	Bank
Credit Cooperatif Francais S.A.	IC	1880's	France	Border with classical ladies & a beehive.	96	Bank
Credit Foncier du Bresil	I	1928		Nude woman, horn of plenty, woman's head of snakes	35	Bank
Credit Foncier S.A.	IC	1900's	Belgium		24	Bank
Credit Mutuel Ivria Soc.Coop.Banque	IC	1930's	Belgium		44	Bank
Culver City, First National Bank of	I	1920's	CA	Allegorical figures	35	Bank

Cumberland, Second National Bank o	U	1900's		Seated lady	15	Bank
Dallas, State Savings Bank	I	1870's	TX	Indian maiden with star on rock, gold seal	125	Bank
De Eigenaarsbond, Naamlooze Verzed	IC	1920's	Belgium	Company arms, & ornate border.	32	Bank
Dean Witter Reynolds, Inc.	U	1978	NY	City drawing	50	Bank
Delaware County Trust Co.	I	1930's	PA	Two horses & eagle	15	Bank
Delaware County Trust, Safe Dep	I	1890's		Ships, plus Pennsylvania	35	Bank
Delaware County Trust, Safe Dep	I	1890's			15	Bank
Delaware County Trust, Safe Deposit	IC	1893	PA	State seal	65	Bank
Delaware Mutual Safety Insurance	I	1870's	PA	Riverboat & sailing ship, Indian warrior, & portrait	225	Bank
Detroit Mortgage Corp.	I	1920's		Embossed seal	15	Bank
Dime Savings Institution	I	1860's		Dog	50	Bank
Disconto-Bank Van Antwerpen S.A.	IC	1930's	Belgium	Shipping, unloading in the port of Antwerp	110	Bank
Doylestown National Bank & Trust	I	1940's	PA	Grey/black. Eagle on shield.	10	Bank
Doylestown National Bank & Trust	I	1940's	PA	Grey/black. Eagle on shield.	10	Bank
Eastman College Bank	I	1880's	NY	of large old college building & carriage	175	Bank
Empire Loan & Trust Co.	I	1890's		One thousand dollar bond	50	Bank
Emporia Mutual Loan & Savings As	I	1880's			35	Bank
Ensle Land	I	1902	AL	Brown. Sphinx.	75	Bank
Ensley Land	I	1902-04	AL	Brown. Miners, mining community. Sphinx.	35	Bank
Equitable Trust Co.	I	1870's		Seven% mortgage bond, seated female	50	Bank
Estonian Land Credit Association	IC	1930's	Estonia	Arms of the bank.	70	Bank
Eureka Casualty	IU	1928	CA	Calif. Seal	50	Bank
Exeter Bank	I	1850's		Train	75	Bank
Fame Mutual Insurance Co.	I	1850's	PA	Angel, eagle & seal	175	Bank
Fame Mutual Insurance Co.	I	1860's	PA	Angel, eagle & seal	150	Bank
Farmers & Exchange Bank	I	1850's	SC	Overseer on horse in cotton field	225	Bank
Farmers & Mechanics Bank	IC	1862	PA	State seal	80	Bank
Farmers Deposit National Bank	I	1906	PA	Green. Dog named PRINCE.	150	Bank
Farmers Deposit National Bank	I	1906	PA	Green. Dog named PRINCE.	150	Bank
Farmers Deposit National Bank	I	1916	PA	Dog	68	Bank
Farmers Deposit National Bank	U	1900's		Prince the Dog	75	Bank
Farmers Deposit National Bank	U	1900's		Prince the Dog	75	Bank
Farmers Deposit National Bank	IC	1910's	PA	Large vignette of dog Prince	125	Bank
Farmers Deposit National Bank	U	1910's	PA	Large vignette of dog Prince	85	Bank

Name	Type	Date	State	Description	Price	Category
Farmers Loan & Trust	I	1900's			35	Bank
First American Bank & Trust	I	1924		Great Indian vignette	85	Bank
First Charter Financial	IC	1960		Topless woman	35	Bank
First Charter Financial	IC	1970		Topless woman	35	Bank
First Charter Financial Corp.	I		CA	Large, bare-breasted lady, covered wagon	35	Bank
First National Bank City of Brooklyn	I	1865-71	NY	Liberty, shield. Woman with eagle.	75	Bank
First National Bank City of Brooklyn	I	1865-71	NY	Liberty, shield. Woman with eagle.	75	Bank
First National Bank Hermosa Beach	I	1950	CA	Torch	76	Bank
First National Bank of Bath	IC	1911	ME	State seal	65	Bank
First National Bank of Bozeman	I	1875	MT	All purple.	95	Bank
First National Bank of Bozeman	I	1875	MT Terr	All purple.	95	Bank
First National Bank of Brooklyn	I	1863-71	NY	Columbia, shield, sailing ship. Allegorical woman	75	Bank
First National Bank of Cooperstown	I	1890's	NY	Leatherstocking statue, Liberty, state arms, eagle.	55	Bank
First National Bank of Cooperstown	I	1890's	NY	Leatherstockin statue, Liberty, state arms, eagle.	55	Bank
First National Bank of Parkton	U	1900's	MD	Ladies harvesting wheat.	80	Bank
Four States Life Insurance Co.	IU	1911	AR	Seals of OK,TX,AR,LA	95	Bank
Franklin Fire Insurance Co.	IC	1939		Benjamin Franklin.	35	Bank
Franklin Fire Insurance Co.	IC	1939		Benjamin Franklin.	35	Bank
Franklin Fire Insurance of Philadelp	I	1930's		Portrait of Benjamin Franklin	35	Bank
Franklin-American Trust	I	1930's	MO	Embossed seal	15	Bank
Freeland Ville Bank	I	1920's		Large eagle, green or orange seal	15	Bank
Fresno Building Corp. & Bank	I	1920's	CA	Eagle	251	Bank
Frontier National Bank	I	1880's		Eastport, Maine, Capitol building	50	Bank
Garfield National Bank	Proof	1900's	NY	Two cherubs.	165	Bank
Gastonia, Citizens National Bank of	U		NC	Eagle	15	Bank
Germania Fire Insurance Co.	I	1880's	NY	Woman with sword in front of king's chair	75	Bank
Germania Fire Insurance Co.	I	1900's	NY	Woman with sword in front of king's chair	50	Bank
Globe National Bank	I	1890's	ME	Globe	35	Bank
Grossbard Securities	I	1970's	NY	Blue. Bull and bear.	25	Bank
Grossbard Securities	I	1970's	NY	Blue. Bull and bear.	75	Bank
Guaranty Trust Co. of Detroit	I	1920's		Gold bond, of bank building	15	Bank
Guardian Detroit Union Group	IU	1930	MI	Ship, woman, factories	125	Bank
Harmonia Fire Insurance	IC	1915	NY	State seal	35	Bank
Harmonia Fire Insurance Co.	I	1910's	NY	State seal, green seal, with many stamps	35	Bank

Name		Date	State	Description	Signer	Price	Category
Hatfield National Bank & Trust	U			Warrant		15	Bank
Helena, First National Bank of	U	1890's	MT			35	Bank
Hoboken, First National Bank of	I	1860's		Capitol building with revenue stamp		100	Bank
Hoboken, First National Bank of	I	1860's		Capitol building		100	Bank
Hoboken, First National Bank of	I	1880's		Capitol building		75	Bank
Hoboken, First National Bank of	I	1890's		Capitol building		35	Bank
Hoboken, First National Bank of	I	1920's		Capitol building		35	Bank
Hoboken, First National Bank of	I	1930's		Capitol building		15	Bank
Hoffe Insurance Co.	IU	1867		Blue rev stamp. Mother bird in nest, four babies		35	Bank
Hollywood, Bank of	U	1920's		Embossed seal		35	Bank
Home Bank	I	1923	TN	Building	S.M. Alexander	52	Bank
Home Fire Security	I	1931	NY	Green. House on island in circle, cherubs.		20	Bank
Home Fire Security	I	1931	NY	Green. House on island in circle, cherubs.		20	Bank
Home Insurance Co.	I	1880's	NY	Three people & pyramid		75	Bank
Home Insurance Co.	I	1930's	NY	Three engineers		35	Bank
Home Insurance Co.	I	1960's		Fireman, family, & woman		15	Bank
Home Insurance Company	I	1867	CT	City scenery		50	Bank
Home National Bank	I	1921	TX			49	Bank
Homestead Fire Insurance Co., The	I	1930's		House & old car		15	Bank
Hope Insurance	IU	1807	GB	Woman, London		1,250	Bank
Hypothekenbank Landes Vorarlberg	IC	1920's	Austria	Arms of Vorarlberg, & the main towns		84	Bank
Illion Bank	IU	1852	NY	Sunset, eagle, man with axe	E. Remington	595	Bank
Independence Trust Shares	I	1930's		Independence Hall & Liberty Bell		15	Bank
Independence Trust Shares	I	1940's		Independence Hall & Liberty Bell		15	Bank
Industrial Finance Corp. Morris Pla	I	1920's-30's		Two seated figures with tools, world globe		15	Bank
Insurance Co.	I	1864	CT	Legendary bird rises from the ashes.		45	Bank
Insurance Securities	I	1929	LA	Brown.		10	Bank
Insurance Securities	I	1929	LA	Brown.		10	Bank
International Insurance	IC	1860's	NY	Four Allegorical Women		319	Bank
Invincible Building & Loan Associate	I	1920's	NJ	Family home		15	Bank
Iroquois Trust	IU	1929		Indian Chief		85	Bank
Irving Bank	IC	1920's	NY	Woman, train, sailing vessels.	Edward HR Green	330	Bank
Irving Trust	I	1929-33	NY	Green. Commerce, train, ships beyond.		20	Bank
Irving Trust Co.	IC	1930's		Woman, hole in safe, coins		35	Bank

Irving Trust Co.	IC	1930's		Woman, hole in safe, coins	45	Bank
Irving Trust Co.	IC	1940's		Seated woman, old train, & paddle steamer	25	Bank
Irving Trust Co.	IC	1950's		Seated woman, old train, & paddle steamer	15	Bank
Jamaica, West River National Bank	I	1870's	VT	Three including boy on a horse	100	Bank
Jamestown, Bank of, Jamestown,	I			Specimen, of bank building	35	Bank
Jaysour Mortgage Bank Ltd.	IC	1960's	Israel		32	Bank
Jersey, State Bank of	I	1950's		Eagle on rock holding arrows	15	Bank
Kensington National Bank of Philadel	I	1870's		Three with revenue stamp	75	Bank
Kensington Natl Bank of Phila.	I	1872	PA	Sinking ship	65	Bank
Kent Fire Insurance Office	IC	1800's	GB	Firefighters & fire engine. White horse	640	Bank
Kentucky, Bank of	I	1840's	KY	Two portraits, two scenes of children, woman	175	Bank
Kentucky, Bank of	I	1860's	KY	Woman with eagle, blacksmith, & seated lady	125	Bank
Kompass Allgemeine Kredit- Und Gar	IC	1920's	Austria		40	Bank
La Salvadora, Seguros Maritimos, Av	IC	1850's	Spain	Arms of Spain, anchor, barrel	480	Bank
Lancaster, Farmer's Bank of	I	1810's			350	Bank
Land Bank of Eqypt	IC	1905	Egypt	Farmer, cattle	95	Bank
Landesbank Fur Mahren	IC	1930's	Czech	Peasant girls at work.	80	Bank
Langdon Bank	I	1850's	NH	Embossed seal	125	Bank
Latvijas Tautas Bankas	IC	1920's	Lativa	Banks head office, logo.	120	Bank
Latvijas Valsts Kreditzime	IC	1930's	Lativa	Road beside a river, Arms of Latvia.	100	Bank
Lebanon Valley Savings & Loan	IU	1925	PA	Panoramic vignette of farms	95	Bank
LH Hershfield	I	1866	MT	Traveler	50	Bank
Liberty National Bank	SP	19--	NY	Statue of Liberty	375	Bank
Lincoln National Bank of Bath	IC	1867	ME	Government building	100	Bank
Lloyd Bank	I	1923	Hungary	Wreaths & cherubs done in copperplate engraving.	125	Bank
Lloyd Bank	I	1923	Hungary	Swags of wreaths & cherubs	125	Bank
Long Island National Bank of New	I	1920's		Eagle, many stamps	15	Bank
Louisiana Purchase Exposition	U	1904	LA	Palace	362	Bank
Love Joy's Wharf Trust	I	1920's	MA		15	Bank
Lowry National Bank of Atlanta	IC	1912	GA	Eagle	50	Bank
Lowry National Bank of Atlanta	I	1910's		Large eagle	35	Bank
Lynn Central National Bank of	I	1930's	MA	Eagle, teepee with squaw, & ship	50	Bank

Lynn, Manufacturer's National Bank	I	1890's	MA	Horses, carriages, & banks	50	Bank
Lynn, Manufacturer's National Bank	I	1910's	MA	Horses, carriages, & banks	35	Bank
Magdeburgische Land-Feuersozietat	IC	1910's	Germany	Arms of Magdeburg.	24	Bank
Manufacturer's & Trader's Bank	I	1890's		Vignettes	175	Bank
Manufacturer's & Trader's Bank	I	1900's		Vignettes	100	Bank
Manufacturer's National Bank	I	1910's	MA	Large old bank building with horse & carriages	50	Bank
Manufacturers & Traders Bank	IC	1890's	NY	Woman drawing water from well, shipbuilding	120	Bank
Marine National Bank	I	1880's	NY	Ship in heavy seas	175	Bank
Marine Securities	I	1927	CA	Reddish brown. Anchor in circle.	15	Bank
Marine Securities	I	1927	CA	Reddish brown. Anchor in circle.	15	Bank
Maryland Trust Co.	U	1900's		State seal	35	Bank
Maryland, Farmers Bank of	I	1800's		Embossed seal	500	Bank
Massachusetts Investors Trust	I	1940's		Old state building	15	Bank
Massachusetts Investors Trust	U			Old state building	15	Bank
Massachusetts Securities	I	1902	MA	5% Gold Coupon Note. Brown. State arms.	19	Bank
Massachusetts Securities	I	1902	MA	5% Gold Coupon Note. Brown. State arms	19	Bank
Mechanics Bank of Burlington	IC	1865	PA	Man, two eagles	150	Bank
Merchant's Mutual Insurance Co.	I	1860's			125	Bank
Merchants & Manufacturer's Bank	I	1860's	CT	Portrait of woman, antlered deer	125	Bank
Merchants Dispatch Transportation	IC	1870's	MA	Five story building. Fargo, Holland	506	Bank
Methuen, The National Bank of	I	1890's	MA	Capitol building with stagecoach & riders	75	Bank
Methuen, The National Bank of	I	1900's	MA	Capitol building with stagecoach & riders	50	Bank
Methuen, The National Bank of	I	1910's	ME	Capitol building	35	Bank
Metropolin Bank Ltd.	IC	1930's	Israel	Dome of the Rock, Star of David.	440	Bank
Miner's & Merchant's Bank	U		SC		35	Bank
Mitten Bank Securities Corp.	I	1920's	PA		35	Bank
Mitten Bank Securities Corp.	I	1930's	PA		35	Bank
Monarch Life Insurance Co.	I	1960's	MA	Lions & Co. logo	5	Bank
Monarch Royalty	I	1930	DE	Dark blue. Lion. Western Bank Note. Preferred.	15	Bank
Monarch Royalty	I	1930	DE	Dark blue. Lion. Western Bank Note. Preferred.	15	Bank
Monte Napoleone	IC	1810's	Italy	Arms.	408	Bank
Morrellville Deposit Bank	IU	1926		Eagle on dome	65	Bank
Morris Canal & Banking Co.	I	1840's		Certificate	125	Bank
Morris Canal & Banking Co.	I	1850's	NJ	Canal scenes, seal	100	Bank

Morris Canal & Banking Co.	I	1860's		Topless women, seated women, & canal boat	175	Bank
Morristown National Bank	IC	1914	NJ	Farmer plowing field	75	Bank
Mortgage Bank & Financial Admini	I	1960's		Bond, girl	15	Bank
Mutual Benefit Life Insurance	I	1860's		Pelican with little birds in nest	125	Bank
Mutual Benefit Life Insurance Co.	IU	1867		Blue rev stamp. Mother bird in nest, four babies	35	Bank
Mutual Contra Maestros Albaniles Bar	IC	1900's	Spain	Border of thistles.	32	Bank
Nakanomachi Bank	IU	1940's	Japan		75	Bank
National Bank Chicago	I	1865	IL	Eagle	69	Bank
National Bank Wilmington Brandywn	IC	1884	DE	Woman carrying baby, govt. building	150	Bank
National Liberty Insurance	IC	1936		Woman holding logo next to torch.	20	Bank
National Liberty Insurance	IC	1930's		Woman holding logo next to torch.	20	Bank
National Liberty Insurance Co.	IC	1940's		Co. logo	20	Bank
National Rockland Bank of Boston	SP	19--	MA	Santa Claus on sleigh	2,500	Bank
Nevada Freehold Properties Trust	I	1869		British and American flags.	55	Bank
Nevada Freehold Properties Trust	I	1869		2 Pounds British and American flags.	55	Bank
Nevada National Bancorporation	SP		NV	Train on bridge	100	Bank
New England Mutual Marine Insuran	I	1870's		Scrip, old sailing ships, sailors on dock	225	Bank
New Haven, Second National Bank	I	1930's		Bank Building	15	Bank
New York, City of, Insurance Co.	I	1920's	NY	Skyline	15	Bank
New York, First Fulton National Bar	I	1860's	NY	Man sitting against statue, ship & city	175	Bank
Norfolk, First National Bank of	I	1870's		Seated woman, old sailor, & anchor	125	Bank
North Eastern Insurance Co. of Ha	I	1950's		Eagle on rock	15	Bank
North Pennsylvania Bank	U			Eagle	15	Bank
Oakland Mortgage & Finance Co.	IU	1930's	CA	Large three-story home	15	Bank
Occidental Finance & Mortgage Co.	I	1910's	CA	Eagle, seal	15	Bank
Oesterreichische Nationalbank	IC	1920's	Austria	Arms of Austria, snowflake medallions.	35	Bank
Ohio Union Loan	I	1860's	OH	Ben Franklin & safe	350	Bank
Ohio Valley Improvement & Contract	I	1889	KY	Brown, green. Gold seal. Train in snowstorm.	60	Bank
Ohio Valley Improvement & Contract	I	1889-90	KY	Brown, green. Gold seal. Train in snowstorm.	60	Bank
Old Colony State Bank	U	1920's	NY	State seal	15	Bank
Old Colony State Bank	I		NY	State seal	15	Bank
Old Wild West Bank	I	1801	MT		59	Bank

Omni Bank	SP	1979	CA	Gold lettering		65	Bank
Oriental Bank	IU	1910's	NY	Figure with globe, steamship, sailing ship		50	Bank
Oriental Fire & Marine Insurance	U	1800's	CA	Seated woman		35	Bank
Pajaro Valley Bank	I	1880's	CA	Bank logo		50	Bank
Pajaro Valley Bank	I	1890's	CA	Bank logo		35	Bank
Pajaro Valley National Bank	I	1910's		Co. logo & name in clouds		35	Bank
Pajaro Valley National Bank	I	1920's		Co. logo & name in clouds		35	Bank
Palisades Trust Co.	I	1950's		Certificate of deposit, Palisades & Hudson River		15	Bank
Palisades Trust Co.	U	1950's		Certificate of deposit, Palisades & Hudson River		15	Bank
Parker Nat. Metro Bank Wash. DC	I	1909	VA			51	Bank
Paypal	I	2002		Logo		150	Bank
Pennsylvania Insurance	I	1790's	PA			154	Bank
Pennsylvania Insurance	I	1790's	PA			154	Bank
Pennsylvania Safe Deposit & Trust	U	1880's		City of Philadelphia		35	Bank
Pennsylvania, Bank of	IU	1850's	PA	State seal, William Penn, train & harbor canal		175	Bank
Peoples Bank	IC	1892	PA	State seal		95	Bank
Peru Bank	U					60	Bank
Philadelphia	I	1780's	PA			473	Bank
Philadelphia	I	1790's	PA			462	Bank
Phoenix Insurance	I	1864	CT	Legendary bird rises from the ashes.		45	Bank
Phoenix Insurance Co.	I	1850's	CT	Phoenix rising from fire		85	Bank
Phoenix Insurance Co.	I	1860's	CT	Phoenix rising from fire		75	Bank
Phoenix Insurance Co.	I	1930's	CT	Eagle		15	Bank
Phoenix Insurance Co.	I	1950's	CT	No		15	Bank
Pioneer Real Estate	I	1899-1	NY	Black/Green. Eagle.		15	Bank
Pioneer Real Estate	I	1900's	NY	Black/Green. Eagle.		15	Bank
Pordand National Bank	I	1900's	ME	State seal of Maine		15	Bank
Powow River National Bank	IU	1888	MA	Building, eagle		185	Bank
Prudential Insurance Co.	U	1901	NY	Cliff		110	Bank
Puerto Rico Bank/Agriculture	U	1895	PR	Woman		50	Bank
Reliable Loan, Mortgage & Security	I	1926	NJ	Orange. Eagle.		10	Bank
Reliable Loan, Mortgage & Security	I	1928	NJ	Orange. Eagle.		5	Bank
Republic Insurance	IC	1860's	IL	Eagle, train.		83	Bank
Republic Life Insurance Co.	I	1870's	IL	Large community building		100	Bank
Roger Williams Bank	IU	1804	RI	Roger Williams & Indian Chief		1,500	Bank
Rossia Insurance Co.	I	1920's	CT	Eagle on rock		20	Bank
Rossia Insurance Co.	I	1930's	CT	Eagle on rock		15	Bank
Royal National Bank of New York	I	1960's		Bank logo, seal		15	Bank

Sachsische Bank Zu Dresden	IC	1870's	Germany	Border of Mercury, goddess & the Arms of Saxony.		220	Bank
Seaboard National Bk	I			Specimen, large four-funnel ship		75	Bank
Second Bank of the United States	I	1800's	PA			2,640	Bank
Second Bank of the United States	I	1820's	PA		Nicholas Biddle	165	Bank
Second National Bank of Cooperstown	IC	1925	NY	City view		65	Bank
Second Street Trust, State Street	I	1950's		Old courthouse with clock		15	Bank
Security Pacific bond	IC	1970's	CA			25	Bank
Security Pacific bond	IC	1980's	CA			25	Bank
Seminole Land & Investment	I	1909	FL			50	Bank
Skowhegan, First National Bank of	I	1890's	ME			35	Bank
South Carolina Loan & Trust	I	1860		Embossed seal		125	Bank
South Carolina Loan & Trust	I	1870's		Soldier & state seal		125	Bank
South Carolina Loan & Trust	I	1880's		Allegorical figures, seal		125	Bank
South Carolina Loan and Trust	I	1871		3 vignettes		125	Bank
South Danvers National Bank	I	1860's	MA	Portrait plus revenue stamp		175	Bank
South Side Trust Svgs Bank Chicago	IU	1929				85	Bank
Springfield, First National Bank of	I	1870's		Train & farmer		125	Bank
Springfield, First National Bank of	I	1880's	KY	Three of train, river, farmer, & sheep		100	Bank
State Bank of Indore	I	1961	India			50	Bank
State Street Bank & Trust Co.	I	1960's		Old courthouse with clock		15	Bank
Stissing National Bank of Pine Plains	IC	1869	NY	Dog and safe		150	Bank
Stissing National Bank of Pine Plains NY	I	1877	NY	Boy and dog		75	Bank
Straus Safe Deposit Co.	I	1920's	IL	Bond, woman with child, seal		35	Bank
Stroudsburg Bank	IC	1868	PA	Bull, cattle		295	Bank
Stuart Central Farmer's Bank	I	1920's		Eagle with shield		15	Bank
Stuart Central Farmers Bank	IU	1929	FL	Eagle		50	Bank
Sutro Mortgage Investment Trust	I	1970's		Co. logo, seal		15	Bank
The Anglos London Paris National Bank	I	1927	CA			89	Bank
The Bank of Pittsburgh	I	1919	IL	Woman	Harrison Nesbit	85	Bank
The Delaware Cnty Trust, Safe Dep	I	1885		Two horses		25	Bank
The Delaware County Trust, Safe Dep	I	1885		Two horses		25	Bank
The First National Bank of Parkton	I	1932	MD	Two women		60	Bank
The Franklin Fire Ins. Co. of Phila	IC	1939	PA	Ben Franklin		35	Bank
The Franklin Fire Ins. Co. of Philad	IC	1939	PA	Ben Franklin		35	Bank
The Metropolin Bank Ltd.	I	1932	Israel	Orange, Jerusalem showing the Dome of the Rock		100	Bank

The Metropolin Bank Ltd.	I	1932	Israel	Jerusalem, Dome of the Rock	100	Bank
Third National Bank of Sandusky	U	1880's	OH	Farmer, blacksmith, train, riverboat.	72	Bank
Thomaston Geor es National Bank	I	1910's	ME	Maine state seal	50	Bank
Thomaston National Bank	I	1870's	ME	Deer & dog	100	Bank
Thomaston National Bank	I	1900's	ME	Deer & dog	75	Bank
Thomaston National Bank	I	1910's	ME	Pine tree & seal	50	Bank
Times Fire Assurance Co.	IC	1850's	GB	Very decorative piece, with border.	170	Bank
Times Square Trust	I	1930's	NY	Eagle	15	Bank
Tioga National Bank & Trust Co.	I	1920's		State seal of Pennsylvania	15	Bank
Tioga National Bank & Trust Co.	I	1930's		State seal of Pennsylvania	15	Bank
Trapshooter Development	I	1922	TX	Green. Large eagle and shield.	25	Bank
Trapshooter Development	I	1922	TX	Green. Large eagle and shield.	25	Bank
Troy, National Bank of	I	1880's	NY	Eagle with flag, gold seal	35	Bank
Uncas National Bank of Norwich	IC	1900's	CT	Indian, sail/steamship, blacksmith.	80	Bank
Union Deposit & Trust	I	1910's	CO		20	Bank
Union Deposit & Trust	I	1920's	CO		15	Bank
Union Des Mutuelles S.A.	IC	1910's	France	Three lovely ladies.	120	Bank
Union Mutual Insurance	I	1864-69	NY	Eagle and flag. Sailor, sailing ship.	45	Bank
Union Mutual Insurance Co.	I	1870's	NY	Eagle, ship, & sailor	100	Bank
Union National Bank	IC	1866	PA	Eagle, statues, woman	100	Bank
Union National Bank	I	1860's	PA	Eagle & lad	100	Bank
Union National Bank	I	1870's	PA	Eagle widespread wings. Statues of Columbia	60	Bank
Union National Bank	I	1870's	PA	Eagle. Statues of Columbia at sides. Ship.	60	Bank
Union National Bank	I	1870's	PA	Eagle & seated lady	100	Bank
Union National Bank	I	1880's	PA	Eagle & lady	75	Bank
United States Bank of,	I	1920's		Eagle & seal	35	Bank
United States Bank of,	I	1930's		Eagle & seal	15	Bank
United States Casualty	U	1936		Dark blue, eagle on top of globe.	20	Bank
United States Casualty	U	1936		Dark blue, eagle on top of globe.	20	Bank
United States National Bank	U	1920's	CA	Capitol, seal	15	Bank
United States National Bank	I	1930's	CA	Capitol, seal	15	Bank
United States, Bank of	I	1920's	NY	Large eagle	35	Bank
United States, Bank of	I	1930's		Eagle with logo	35	Bank
Valle Thrift Corp., The	I	1930's		Green embossed seal	10	Bank
Venice, First National Bank of	I	1920's	CA		35	Bank
Victoria Bond Holders	I	1930's	NY	Capitol building	15	Bank
Wachovia Bank & Trust Company	U		NC	Logo of fruits and vegetables	65	Bank
Walthan National Bank	IC	1880	MA	Eagle	85	Bank
Washington Mutual	I	2003	WA	Logo	50	Bank

Name		Date	Location	Vignette	Price	Type
Washington Square National Bank NY	IU	1929	NY	Washington Square monument	395	Bank
Waverly Co-operative Bank	I		MA	House	125	Bank
Wayne Building Loan Accumulating	IU	1897	NY	General Anthony Wayne	195	Bank
Wells Fargo & Co.	I		CA	Stagecoach	195	Bank
Wells Fargo Bank & Union Trust	V	1951		Cowboy on horse	195	Bank
West Hollywood, Bank of	I	1930's			35	Bank
Westeuropeesche Beleggingsbank	IC	1920's	Netherlands		70	Bank
Westminister, First National Bank o	I	1870's	MD	Eagle & farmers	125	Bank
Williamson Securities	U		NY	State seal	15	Bank
Williamson, State Bank of	I	1910's	NY	Sailing ship, eagle	35	Bank
Wilmington & Brandywine Ntl. Bank	IU	1880's	NY-DE	Large capitol building, woman, flying eagle	100	Bank
Wilshire National Bank	I	1920's	CA	Embossed seal	35	Bank
Zemska Banka	IC		Czech	Border of leaves, lady, Arms of Bohemia.	80	Bank
Zurcher Depositenbank	IC	1900's	Switzerland		120	Bank

CHAPTER 10 - BEVERAGE CERTIFICATES

Beverage certificates include beer, wine, liquor, soft drinks, and water.

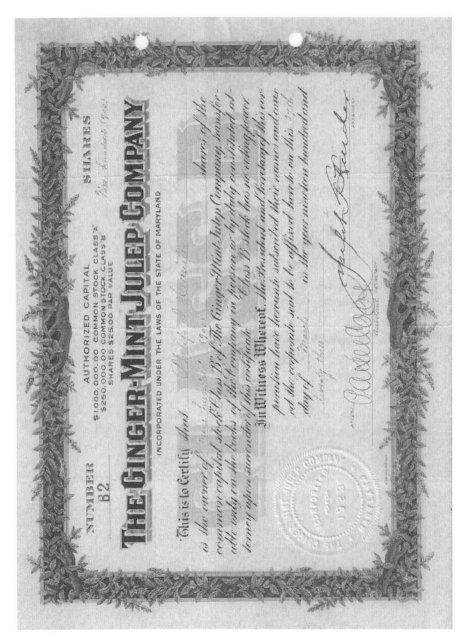

Name	IU	Date	State	Vignette	Signed by	Value	Category
A & P Tea Co., The Great,	I	1970's	MD	Two winged ladies with Co. logo		15	Beverage
Aktien-Brauerei Malmedy A.G.	IC	1940's	Belgium			70	Beverage
Aktienbrauerei In Smichow	IC	1930's	Czech	Brewery, hops, brewing scenes, King with beer.		200	Beverage
Arthur Guinness Son & Co. Ltd.	IC	1890's	GB			640	Beverage
Beaver Creek Distillery	IC	1960		Barrel Dripping		25	Beverage
Bergner & Engel Brewing	U	1920's	PA	Black eagle, gold medal.		132	Beverage
Brasserie De L'Union Assesse S.A.	IC	1900's	Belgium	King enjoying a glass of beer.		70	Beverage
Brasserie De Staceghem, S.A.	IC	1890's	Belgium			70	Beverage
Brasserie-Malterie Moulin Branchon	IC	1910's	Belgium	Decorative border.		100	Beverage
Centrale Des Grands Vins De France	SP	1930's	Belgium	Colorful.		36	Beverage
Charles Jacquin et Cie Inc.	UV		PA	photo vignette of three bottles of liquor		125	Beverage
Chateau & Verreries De Quiquencr	IC	1840's	France	Chateau & glassworks, Coats of Arms, Portraits		110	Beverage
City of Chicago Brewing & Malting	I	1893				35	Beverage
City of Chicago Brewing & Malting	I	1910's	UK			35	Beverage
Cleveland & Sandusky Beer Brewery	U	1932	OH	Woman		77	Beverage
Co-op Pure Milk Association	U			Farm scene & house		15	Beverage
Coca Cola	IC	1929	DE	Script logo		1,000	Beverage
Coca Cola	I	2003		Woman with book and lamp		75	Beverage
Coca Cola	IC	1940's	DE	Woman with book and lamp		195	Beverage
Coca Cola	SP		DE	Reclining woman holding book magic lamp		150	Beverage
Coca Cola Beverages	I	2000	UK	Logo		35	Beverage
COCA COLA BOTTLING	U		OH			239	Beverage
Coca Cola Femsa	I	2002		Wan with scroll, logo		50	Beverage
Coca-Cola	I	1929	DE	Blue borders.		750	Beverage
Coca-Cola	I	1929	DE	Blue borders.		750	Beverage
Coca-Cola	U	1930	MO			50	Beverage
Coca-Cola Bottling of NY	SP	1920's	DE	Women flank small globe.		220	Beverage
Coco Cola Bottling	I	1922	OH	Eagle		65	Beverage
Coffeetone Manufacturing Co.	IU	1917	SD	Genie holding a cup of coffee		125	Beverage
Cortina Vineyards	U	190-	CA	Bunch of grapes		75	Beverage
Cresta Blanca Wine Co.	U	1900's	CA			150	Beverage
Cresta Blanca Wine Co.	U	1900's	CA			150	Beverage
Dayton Breweries	U	1904		Man	Adam Schantz	225	Beverage
Dick & Brothers Quincy Brewery	IC	1934	IL	Large brewery buildings		95	Beverage
Diedrich Coffee	SP	1996	DE	Logo		45	Beverage

Distilleries Du Craonnais, S.A. Des	IC	1920's	France	Border of apples.		60	Beverage
Elizabeth Brewing	IU	1932	NJ	Man with strange apparatus		150	Beverage
Elizabeth Brewing Corp.	I	1930's	NJ			35	Beverage
Erie Brewing	SP	1899	PA	Green. Woman, beehive, grain.		300	Beverage
Erie Brewing	SP	1899	PA	Green. Woman, beehive, grain.		300	Beverage
F. & M. Schaefer Corp.	I	1970's	NY	Seminude man, globe, mountains & city skyline		10	Beverage
Frank Fehr Brewing Co.	I	1940's		Woman		35	Beverage
Goebel Brewing	IU	1964	MI	Two men on either side of beer barrel		65	Beverage
Goebel Brewing Co.	I	1960's		Two men with Co. logo		45	Beverage
Goebel Brewing Co.	SP			Train & eagle with beer barrel		75	Beverage
Grands Crus De Chateauneuf	IC	1930's	France	Ornate border of leaves.		80	Beverage
Great Atlantic & Pacific Tea Co.	I	1960's		Horn of plenty, & Co. logo		15	Beverage
Heidelberg Brewing Co.	U	1880's	KY	Specimen, of brewery		50	Beverage
Holland's Far East, Tea, Coffee	I	1920's		Asian vignette		15	Beverage
Horlacher Brewing	I	1943			F.B. Franks, Jr.	50	Beverage
Horlacher Brewing	I	1994				100	Beverage
Industria Cervecera Eugenio Josenha	IC	1900's	Spain	Brewery & company logo, list of all products		40	Beverage
Isker Soda and Lemonade Joint Stock	IC	1900's	Bulgaria	Grapevines, vineyard workers, cherubs		341	Beverage
Kansas City Grape Sugar Company	I	1883	KS	Large building		78	Beverage
Kentucky Brewing Co.	SP	1880's	KY	Logo between two women		75	Beverage
La Salle Wines & Champagne	IC	1960's	MI	Vineyard purple		100	Beverage
La Salle Wines & Champagne	IC	1960's	MI	Vineyard green		100	Beverage
La Salle Wines & Champagne	IC	1960's	MI	Vineyard		100	Beverage
La Salle Wines and Champagne	IC	1963	MI	Vineyard blue		100	Beverage
La Vinicole Forezienne S.A.	IC	1890's	France	Vineyards, bottles of wines.		184	Beverage
Les Distilleries Francaises S.A.	IC	1930's	France	Cutting grapes, pressoir, distillation, etc.		80	Beverage
Liebman Breweries	U	1900's				35	Beverage
Lucky Breweries	U	1953	CA	Lucky Lager logo		95	Beverage
Maryland & Sandusky Brewing Co.	I	1930's	OH	Seated woman		75	Beverage
Napa & Sonoma Wine Co.	PI	1872	CA	Wine bunch, two women	Jacob Beringer	1,000	Beverage
Napa & Sonoma Wine Co.	PI	1872	CA	Wine bunch, two women	C.Krug, JBeringer	4,500	Beverage
Napa & Sonoma Wine Co.	PI	1872	CA	Wine bunch, two women	C.Krug, JBeringer	4,500	Beverage
Napa & Sonoma Wine Co.	PI	1872	CA	Wine bunch, two women	Jacob Beringer	1,000	Beverage
Napa & Sonoma Wine Co.	U	1872	CA	Wine bunch, two women		150	Beverage

Company	Type	Year	State/Country	Description	Signature	Price	Category
Napa & Sonoma Wine Co.	U	1872	CA	Wine bunch, two women		150	Beverage
National Tea Co.	I	1920's		Reclining lady		15	Beverage
National Tea Co.	I	1950's		Factory		15	Beverage
Northhamption Brewery	I	1937		Woman		69	Beverage
Old Kentucky Distillery Inc.	IC	1900's	KY	Large plan of the distillery.		44	Beverage
Old Tyme Distillers Corp.	I	1930's		Two seated men & distillery		75	Beverage
Pabst Brewing	IU	1889	WI	Brewery	Fred Pabst	695	Beverage
Pabst Brewing	IC	1915	WI	Hops leaf and Pabst logo		85	Beverage
Pabst Brewing Co.	I	1900's		Large Co. brewery	Pabst	195	Beverage
Pabst Brewing Co.	U	1900's		Large Co. brewery		50	Beverage
Pabst Brewing Co.	IC	1940's	DE	Brewery, field, lady, aerial view of Brewery.		128	Beverage
Paul Ruinart & Cie, S.A., Ets.	IC	1920's	France	Girl picking grapes.		300	Beverage
Pepsi Cola Co.	Proof		DE	Original Pepsi Cola bottle		175	Beverage
Pepsi-Cola Company	I	1955		Man and Woman		115	Beverage
Pepsi-Cola United Bottlers	I			Seminude woman, world globe, Pepsi		35	Beverage
Phillip Best Brewing	IC	1873	WI	Two breweries	Frederick Pabst	395	Beverage
Phillip Best Brewing	IC	1880's	WI	Empire Brewery, South Side Brewery		100	Beverage
Playtime Distillers	I	1930's				15	Beverage
Pop Shoppes International	IU	1979	Ontario	24 bottle case of Pop Shoppe beverages		85	Beverage
Prunus-A. Centrale Zadruga Za	IC	1910's	Croatia	Plums growing on a tree.		52	Beverage
Ravenswood Winery	U	1999	CA	Unusual circular logo		80	Beverage
Red Bell Brewing	SP	1993	PA	Horse drawn cart pulling barrels of beer		150	Beverage
Red Bell Brewing	I	2002		Horses pulling large beer cart		75	Beverage
Red Bell Brewing Company	U	2001		Carriage and horse		125	Beverage
Romania Azuga Brewery	U	1923	Romania			50	Beverage
Samuel Adams Boston Beer	I	2004		Samuel Adams holding a beer		65	Beverage
Schaeffer, F. M. Corp.	I	1960's		Man with globe, mountains, & city view		35	Beverage
Schaeffer, F. M. Corp.	I	1970's	NY	Man with globe in city		30	Beverage
Starbucks Coffee Corp.	U	2006		Starbucks logo		50	Beverage
Thanksgiving Coffee	I	2001	CA	Victorian men		75	Beverage
Uniao Dos Vinicultores De Portugal	IC	1900's	Portugal	Border with flowers.		90	Beverage
United Importing & Bottling Co.	IC	1920's	Belgium			44	Beverage
Viticole Et Vinicole D' Egypte, Egypt	IC	1930's	Egypt	Scenes of harvesting grapes & making wine		140	Beverage
Vollmer Brewing Corp	I	1933				85	Beverage
Welch Grape Juice	I	1940's		Large eagle		45	Beverage

CHAPTER 11 - ENTERTAINMENT CERTIFICATES

This is a fun category that has drawn a lot of interest during the last several years. It includes many sub-categories, including motion picture studios, television, casinos, toys, computer games, horse racing, sports, recreational boating, auto racing, golf, tennis, baseball, soccer, skiing, circuses, and amusement parks.

Information about the Disney War Bonds

During World War II, the Disney company issued "War Bonds" which, although they were not true bonds themselves, were given to investors who bought U.S. Treasury War Bonds. The certificates feature 22 different Disney characters making up the border of the certificate, including Mickey Mouse, Donald Duck, Goofy, and Pluto. The Disney certificates were given out by banks and war finance committees. These are available in the collectors' market in both issued and unissued form.

There were only two authorized printers: the U.S. Government Printing Office and the Homer H. Boelter Printing Company. There were also two different types of war bonds, one in multi-color and one in black and white, where dot and line patterns were used in place of colors. The black and white variety is extremely rare.

If you collect Disney War Bonds, be careful of color photocopy fakes that are being sold. There are several ways to check if a war bond is genuine or not:

1. For the certificates printed by the Government Printing Office, if you hold the paper up to the light, you will see that the paper has a watermark depicting an eagle, about three inches high by three inches wide. All Disney War Bonds printed by the U. S. Government Printing Office have an eagle water mark. If it says it is printed by the Government Printing Office and it doesn't have an eagle watermark, it is a fake. Certificate printed by the Boelter company do not have an eagle watermark but they do have the watermark of the paper company that manufactured the paper.

2. The certificate has a light beige background. If it has a yellow background, it is a color photocopy. Even if the paper was left in the sun for a long time, it would not have a yellow background, it would have a darker beige background.

3. Look very closely at the background of Donald Duck's eyes. They are made up of very tiny light blue dots (use a magnifying glass if necessary). If the eyes are a solid dark blue or solid purple, the certificate is a photocopy fake.

Name	IU	Date	State	Vignette	Signed by	Value	Category
A. G. Spaulding & Sons	IU	1959	DE	Logo, two figures		325	Entertain
Abilene Hotel Co.	IC	1890's	TX	Hotel, flowers & seal with the Lone Star of Texas.		220	Entertain
AC Gilbert Toy Company	I	1954				145	Entertain
Actual Bruxelles S.A.	SP	1930's	Belgium			32	Entertain
Adams Golf	I	2000		Adams logo		75	Entertain
Admiral Corp.	IC	1970's		Man and woman turning on radio, orchestra		35	Entertain
All England Lawn Tennis Ground Ltd.	IC	1930's	GB			220	Entertain
American Film Co.	IC	1920's	Greece	Theatre stage within a theatre stage.		380	Entertain
American League Base Ball Club Chi.	IC	1950's	IL	Embossed seal.	John D. Rigney	440	Entertain
American League Baseball Club	IC	1940's	IL	Eagle, harbor city.		517	Entertain
American League Baseball St. Louis	I	1940's		(Old Saint Louis Browns)	Bill DeWitt	1,000	Entertain
American Skiing	I	2004		Family on skis		39	Entertain
Anderson Baseball Association	IC	1950's	SC	Eagle, globe.	AP Durham	250	Entertain
AOL Time Warner	U	2002			Steve Case	95	Entertain
AOL Time Warner	I	2004		Entertainment logos		95	Entertain
Arena N.M., S.A.	SP	1930's	Belgium			48	Entertain
Atlantic City Racing Association	I	1940's		Bond	John B. Kelly	250	Entertain
Atlantic City Racing Association	IC	1950's	NJ		John B. Kelly	100	Entertain
Atlantic City Racing Association	IC	1950's	NJ		John B. Kelly	100	Entertain
Audio Color Motion Pictures	IU	1934	NY	Seal		195	Entertain
Auto-Photo Co. Ltd.	IC	1900's	GB			32	Entertain
Baird Television Ltd.	IC	1930's	GB			300	Entertain
Baltimore Baseball Club	SP		MO	Oriole logo		695	Entertain
Baltimore Orioles	I	1964	MD			173	Entertain
Baltimore Orioles	U	1964	MD	Orioles logo		399	Entertain
Baltimore Orioles	I	1968	MD	Baseball		97	Entertain
Baltimore Orioles, Inc.	I	1980's		Ball, bats & bird		200	Entertain
Barnum's Museum	Proof	188-	NY	P. T. Barnum		650	Entertain
Bay Area Ghosts	IC	2003	CA	Two ghosts & full moon		95	Entertain
Bay Area Ghosts	SP	2003	CA	Two ghosts & full moon		175	Entertain
Beacon Films	IU	1931	NY			50	Entertain
Billings Golf and Country Club	IC	1900's	MT	Woman wearing French liberty cap.		220	Entertain
Bingo King Company, Inc.	IC	1900's	DE	Bingo card.		40	Entertain
Bioscoopmaatschappij Palace N.V.	U		Netherlands			56	Entertain
Bonshommes Guillaume, Soc. De	IC	1890's	France	Border of rosettes.		100	Entertain
Bordellos Inc. (Li'l Darlin's of West)	U	1988	NV	Woman in silhouette		25	Entertain
Boston American League Baseball Clb	IC	1900's	NJ	State Arms.	John I. Taylor	341	Entertain
Boston Red Sox Stock	U		NJ	Women and horse		430	Entertain
Boston Red Stockings	U	1877	MA			255	Entertain

Boyd Gaming Corporation	IC	1990's	NV	Boyd, roulette wheel, slot machine, chips, dice, cards		90	Entertain
Brewster Color Film	IU	1930	NJ			100	Entertain
Brewster Color Pictures	IU	1924	DE			75	Entertain
Brighton Aquarium Co.	IC	1870's	GB			200	Entertain
British Lion Film Corporation Ltd.	IC	1930's	GB	Lion logo.		60	Entertain
Broadway Joe's	IC	1969	FL	Joe Namath of NY Jets. Green		50	Entertain
Broadway Joe's	IC	1969	FL	Joe Namath of NY Jets. Green	Joe Namath	750	Entertain
Broadway Joe's	IC	1969	FL	Joe Namath of NY Jets. Blue		50	Entertain
Broadway Joes	IC	1969	FL	Joe Namath of NY Jets. Green		35	Entertain
Broadway Joes	IC	1969	FL	Joe Namath of NY Jets. Blue		35	Entertain
Brooklyn Majestic Theatre	IC	1920's	NY	Embossed seal, dog.		154	Entertain
Caesars World	IC	1976	FL	Woman with globe		35	Entertain
California Acclimatizing Society	U	1870's	CA	Fish, pelican, ducks.		720	Entertain
California Chinese Fireworks	IC	2004	CA	Dragon with fireworks and flags		95	Entertain
California Chinese Fireworks	SP	2004	CA	Dragon with fireworks and flags		175	Entertain
Capital Theater	I	1921	NJ	Eagle		52	Entertain
Carolco Pictures Inc.	IC	1980's	CA/DE	Elegant lady, globe & cinema film.		28	Entertain
Cartridge Television	IU	1970's		Three-color logo		35	Entertain
Casino Ceretano	IC	1890's	Spain			110	Entertain
Casino De Palavas-Les-Flots Fermiere	IC	1920's	France			52	Entertain
Casino Des Bains De Mer De Dieppe	IC	1920's	France			40	Entertain
Casino Des Deux Luxembourgs S.A.	UI	1900's	Belgium			88	Entertain
Casino Des Fleurs Beaulieu Surmer	IC	1920's	France	Casino with gardens, elegant lady with her dog		220	Entertain
Casino et Concerts Paganini	IU	1837	France	Composer's names in border		5,000	Entertain
Casino Grands Hotels Ouistreham-Riv	IC	1920's	France			48	Entertain
Casino Municipal Cannes, Fermiere	IC	1940's	France			40	Entertain
Casino Municipal De La Ville De Nice	IC	1880's	France	Nice, showing the casino.		320	Entertain
Casino-Gesellschaft Basel	IC	1900's	Switzerland			200	Entertain
Cavalier Motion Picture Co.	I	1920's		Mounted rider, gold seal		100	Entertain
Cercle Des Regates	IC	1900's	Belgium			60	Entertain
Chaplin Studios	IC	1918	CA	State seal	Charlie Chaplin(3)	15,000	Entertain
Chaplin Studios	IC	1918	CA	State seal	Charlie Chaplin	9,000	Entertain
Chaplin Studios	I	1900's	CA	State Arms of CA	CChaplin,SChaplin	7,920	Entertain
Chicken Club	UC	1992	WY	Topless woman		100	Entertain
Churchill Downs	SP	1998	KY	Horses racing around track		175	Entertain
Cineac Bruxelles-Centre S.A.	SP	1930's	Belgium			40	Entertain
Cinemas Du Quesnoy S.A., Les	IC	1940's	Belgium			20	Entertain

Cinematographe Automobile S.A.	IC	1900's	France		60	Entertain
Cinematographes Theophile Pathe	IC	1900's	France		110	Entertain
Cinematographiques	IC	1920's	Belgium	Colorful.	40	Entertain
Civilization Film	IU	1917	NJ	Statue of Liberty	200	Entertain
Cleveland Professional Basketball Co.	U	1970	OH	Eagle	95	Entertain
Colonial Downs Holding	SP	1996	VA	Head of horse	55	Entertain
Columbia Broadcasting System	IC	1975	NY	Woman atom	39	Entertain
Columbia Broadcasting System, Inc.	IC	1970's	NY	Columbia.	98	Entertain
Columbia Graphophone Manuf.	I	1920's		Angels, Co. logo & seal	75	Entertain
Columbia Pictures	IC	1950's	NY	Woman with torch - purple	45	Entertain
Columbia Pictures	IC	1950's	NY	Woman with torch - orange	45	Entertain
Columbia Pictures	IC	1950's	NY	Woman with torch - brown	45	Entertain
Columbia Pictures Corp.	IC	1960's		Famous Columbia statue: woman holding torch	35	Entertain
Columbia Pictures-brown	IC	1950's		Woman with torch	45	Entertain
Columbia Pictures-orange	IC	1960's		Woman with torch	45	Entertain
Continental Broadcasting	IU	1930	DE		195	Entertain
Cosmos S.A. Pour	IC	1900's	Belgium		28	Entertain
Courses Du Lude Soc. Des	IC	1930's	France		160	Entertain
De Forest Photofilm	IU	1925	DE		85	Entertain
Dick Clark Productions	I	2002		dc logo	150	Entertain
Dick's Sporting Goods	SP	2002	DE	Men holding fishing poles, equipment	125	Entertain
Doncaster Golf Co.	IC	1920's	GB	Crossed golf clubs.	120	Entertain
Dorson Sports	U	1945		Golfers	35	Entertain
Dorson Sports	U	1945		Golfers	35	Entertain
Dover Downs Entertainment	SP	1994	DE	Horse, slot machine, race car	225	Entertain
Dover Downs Entertainment	SP	1994	DE	No vignette	35	Entertain
DSI Toys Inc.	SP		TX	DSI logo	35	Entertain
Dunes Hotels and Casinos	U			Woman and globe	65	Entertain
E. Dubois Fils & Cie., Ass. En Partic	IC	1910's	Belgium		52	Entertain
Edison Bell, Ltd.	IC	1930's	GB		36	Entertain
Edison Phonograph	U				129	Entertain
Edison Phonograph Works	IC	1880's	NJ	Thomas Edison	3,500	Entertain
Edison Phonographs LTD	U				150	Entertain
Edison Phonographs Ltd.	U	1900's		Eagle	50	Entertain
Edison's Kinetoscope Francais S. A.	IC	1890's	Belgium		76	Entertain
Educational Pictures	IU	1938	DE	Two women, logo	125	Entertain
Elkhart Opera House Co.	I	1900's	IN	Scene of running bull, gold seal	195	Entertain
Enfield Golf Club, Ltd.	IC	1930's	GB		100	Entertain
Esquire	I	1969	DE	Olive. Semi-nude man, quill, scroll.	35	Entertain
etoys.com	U	1996		Toy computer	395	Entertain
eToys.com	U				96	Entertain
Fallon Amusement Corp.	U	1920's	NV	Goddess	50	Entertain
Farnsworth Television & Radio	I	1945		Seated Male holding Antennas	193	Entertain

Farnsworth Television & Radio	I	1946	DE	Man	150	Entertain
Farnsworth Television & Radio	U	1949		Man holding antennae	50	Entertain
Films for Television	IU	1954	DE		125	Entertain
First German Target Club	I	1860's	OH	Hunter, dog and stag.	550	Entertain
Fort Wayne Rink	I	1873	IN	Ice skaters under an arched iron roof.	75	Entertain
Fort Wayne Rink	I	1873	IN	Ice skaters under an arched iron roof.	100	Entertain
Four Star Television	IC	1965	CA	Woman with TV equipment	35	Entertain
Fox Entertainment Group	I	2003		Fox monument	50	Entertain
Fox Theatres	I	1929	NY	Woman	60	Entertain
Freedom Golf Corp.	I	2002		Eagle	95	Entertain
FreeGolfStats.com	I	2003			95	Entertain
Gaylord Entertainment	SP	1980's	DE	Minnie Pearl	250	Entertain
General Radio	IC	1920's	Belgium		48	Entertain
Glen Summit Hotel and Land Co.	U	1880's	PA	Arms of Pennsylvania.	60	Entertain
Gloria Game Co	U	1950's	CA	Eagle with shoreline	25	Entertain
Golden Books Family Entertainment	I	2002		Cartoon train	150	Entertain
Goldwin Pictures	SP	1924	DE		110	Entertain
Golf Trust of America	I	2003		Half golf ball half globe	35	Entertain
GolfRounds.com	I	2002	DE	Golf ball	45	Entertain
Grand Casino Municipal Ville Biarritz	IC	1900's	France	Casino, lady in swimsuit on beach, Biarritz Arms	220	Entertain
Grand Hotel Du Casino De La Plage	IC	1930's	France		72	Entertain
Grand Panorama National Francais	IC	1880's	France	Famous monuments of Paris.	108	Entertain
Grands Hotels S.A., Cie Internationale	IC	1890's	Belgium		100	Entertain
Grands Restaurants A Bruxelles, S.A.	IC	1920's	Belgium	Decorative border.	32	Entertain
Green Bay Packers	I	1919			Miller	389	Entertain
Green Bay Packers	I	1919			Miller	389	Entertain
Green Bay Packers	I	1919			Miller	389	Entertain
Green Bay Packers	U	1924			Miller	2,495	Entertain
Green Bay Packers	U	1997		Green Bay logo	73	Entertain
Green Bay Packers	U	2011		Packers logo	54	Entertain
Haagsche Voetbalvereeniging V.U.C.	IC	1940's	Netherlands		36	Entertain
Harvey Comics	SP	1993		Casper the Friendly Ghost	395	Entertain
Heuck's Opera House Co.	I	1880's	KY	Seal	75	Entertain
Highland Golf Club of Shelton	I	1927	CT	Blue. Improvement Certificate of Indebtedness.	75	Entertain
Holiday Inns, Inc.	IC	1970's	TN	Watchman, old inn stage-coach & modern Holiday Inn.	60	Entertain
Hollywood Turf Club	IC				Mervyn LeRoy	500	Entertain
Hotel Arcadia	IC	1880's	CA	Hotel beside the Pacific Ocean at Santa Monica.	180	Entertain

Name	Type	Date	Location	Description	Signature	Price	Category
Hotels Des Thermes D'Amelie Bains	IC	1920's	France	Waterfall.		80	Entertain
Hoteluri Romania, Marilor-Grossen	IC	1940's	Romania	Colorful.		36	Entertain
Houdini Picture Corp.	I	1921	NY	Eagle	Harry Houdini	4,300	Entertain
Houdini Picture Corp.	I	1920's	NY	Eagle	Harry Houdini	5,995	Entertain
Ice Skating & Supply Co. Ltd.	IC	1890's	GB	Skate & skating rink.		150	Entertain
Indianapolis Indians Baseball	I	1955	IN	Eagle	Owen J. Bush	104	Entertain
International Radio	IU	1922	DE	Mercury, globe		125	Entertain
Internationale Tobis Maatschappij	IC	1930's	Netherlands			50	Entertain
Jackpot Enterprises	IC	1980's		Blue. No vignette.		20	Entertain
Jackpot Enterprises	IC	1980's		Blue. No vignette.		20	Entertain
JAKKS Pacific Inc.	SP	1985	DE	JAKKS logo		35	Entertain
JAMES DEAN	U				James Dean	1,275	Entertain
Jardim Zoolllogico d'Acclimacao Port	IC	1900's	Portugal	Zebra, ostrich, lioness, bear and wolf.		198	Entertain
Jardin Zoologicoe	IU	1904	Portugal	Animals		600	Entertain
Jardin Zoologique De Bruxelles S.A.	IC	1930's	Belgium			260	Entertain
Jugoslavije Tvornice Filmova Zagrebu	IC	1920's	Jugoslavia	Girl on a globe with film around it.		130	Entertain
Kansas City Baseball Club	IC	1930's	MO	Title in fancy scroll.		143	Entertain
Kansas City Baseball Club, Inc.	I	1930's		Transferred from Tris Speaker		500	Entertain
Keenan Productions	U	1930's	NY	Eagle	Ed Wynn	975	Entertain
Keller Dorian Color Film Corporation	U	1930's	DE	Eagle		100	Entertain
Keller-Dorian Colorfilm Corporation	IC	1930's	DE/NY	Film-camera & an eagle.		100	Entertain
Keystone Theatre Co.	U	1910's		Lady & theatrical masks		15	Entertain
Kitsap County Central Fair	IU	1923	WA	Passenger ship on choppy waters		110	Entertain
Kittyhawk Television	I	1970	OH	Green. State arms.		25	Entertain
Kittyhawk Television	I	1970	OH	Green. State arms.		25	Entertain
La Fauvette, Soc.	IC	1900's	France	Cylinder-type phonograph.		240	Entertain
Lake Geneva Lanes	I	1950's	WI	Eagle		35	Entertain
Leon Volterra Et Theatre Marigny	IC	1920's	France	Theatre characters.		180	Entertain
Lion Country Safari, Inc.	I	1980's	CA	Car & lions in animal park		125	Entertain
Lion Country Safari, Inc.	SP	1980's	CA	Car & lions in animal park		950	Entertain
Lionel	I	1951		Boy		48	Entertain
Lionel	I	1960		Boy	Roy Cohn	52	Entertain
Lionel Corp.	IC	1950's		Boy with trains-old style		100	Entertain
Lionel Corp.	IC	1960's		Boy with two trains-new style		85	Entertain
Loew's Boston Theaters	I	1920's	MA	Two seated ladies, many stamps on reverse		35	Entertain
London Gigantic Wheel Co., Ltd.	IC	1890's	GB	Scrollwork at left.		220	Entertain
Long Beach Bath House Amusement	I	1930's	CA	Deep yellow textured paper.		100	Entertain

Name	Type	Date	State	Description	Signer	Price	Category
Long Beach Bath House Amusement	I	1940's	CA	Deep yellow textured paper.		85	Entertain
Louisiana Purchase Exposition Co.	IC	1900's	MO	Lake, fountains, statues, gardens.		890	Entertain
Madison Park	I	1909	VA	Green underprint.	Henry W. Farnam	70	Entertain
Madison Square Garden	IC	1975	MI	Madison Square Garden		35	Entertain
Magic, Soc. Internationale	IC	1910's	Switzerland	Company logo surrounded by light bulbs.		160	Entertain
Majestic Radio & Television	IU	1947		Eagle on rock.		25	Entertain
Majestic Radio & Television	I	1940's		Eagle		35	Entertain
Manufacture Des Pianos Guillot S.A.	IC	1900's	France			60	Entertain
Martin Johnson African Expedition	I	1930	NY	Brown. Preferred.		25	Entertain
Martin Johnson African Expedition	I	1930	NY	Brown. Preferred.		50	Entertain
Martin Johnson African Expedition	U	1920's		Common		45	Entertain
Martinsburg Baseball Club	IC	1920's	WV	Eagle, ship.		250	Entertain
Marvel Spider-Man Kid's Stock	U			Spiderman		39	Entertain
Marvel Spider-Man Kid's Stock	U			Spiderman		49	Entertain
Maryland Telecommunications	IC	1966	MD	movie/TV cameras and monitors		25	Entertain
Mattel	I	2004		Children playing with Mattel toys		95	Entertain
Mattel	IC	1970's		Brown. Man and woman, Matty Mattel logo.		50	Entertain
Mattel Inc.	SP	2000	DE	Children playing with toys		110	Entertain
Mattel, Inc.	I	1970's		Two children at play, Co. logo		60	Entertain
Mayflower Hotel Co.	IC	1920's	DE	Hotel, busy street.		56	Entertain
MCA	SP		NY	Two men, globe		125	Entertain
Meadowood Country Club	U	19--	OH	No vig.		30	Entertain
Merton Park (Wimbledon) Golf Club	IC	1920's	GB			100	Entertain
MGM Grand Hotel Finance Corp.	IC	1990's	NV	MGM Lion, classical man & woman.		80	Entertain
Midwest Saints, Inc.	I	1970's	MN	Cartoon of winged angel, hockey player		50	Entertain
Milton Bradley Co.	SP			Figures with world lobe		50	Entertain
Mirage Resorts, Incorporated	IC	1990's	NV	Man (Steve Wynn?) in pirate costume.		120	Entertain
Monmouth Park Jockey Club	IC	1950's			David Werblin	250	Entertain
Monmouth Park Jockey Club	IU	1950's			David Werblin.	250	Entertain
Montana Phonograph Co.	U	1800's	MT	Old phonographs		195	Entertain
Mount Rushmore National Memorial	SP			Engraving of George Washington		75	Entertain
Multiprises, Inc.	U	1930's	NY	Eagle.	Gloria Swanson	950	Entertain
Mustang Ranch	SP		NV	Logo		1,995	Entertain
Narragansett Racing Association	U		RI	Indian chief at racetrack & horses		45	Entertain
Nashua Fair Association	I	1900	NH	Woman		100	Entertain

Name		Year	Location	Description	Signature	Price	Category
Newark Athletic Club	I	1922	NJ	Pink, orange underprint. State seal.		40	Entertain
Norfolk Hotel Co.	IC	1860's	VA	The Elegant Hotel, Arms of Virginia, Eagle.		184	Entertain
North American Phonograph	I	1890's		Bond, of phonograph	Samuel Insull	1,500	Entertain
Officine Meccaniche Zanotta	IC	1910's	Italy	Lovely lady with a film projector.		72	Entertain
Orpheum Circuit Inc.	I	1922				36	Entertain
Orpheum Circuit, Inc.	I	1920's		Temporary certificate		15	Entertain
Orpheum Circuit, Inc.	I	1920's		Female with lion		35	Entertain
Pacific Leisure Enterprises	IU	1970	DE	Hawaiian Islands		50	Entertain
Palestine Theatre Limited	IC	1920's	Israel	Theater mask at top.	Ch. N. Bialik	374	Entertain
Palmengarten-Gesellschaft	IC	1900's	Germany	Garden.	E.Ladenbrug	1,280	Entertain
Panavision	I	2002		Motion picture film camera		35	Entertain
Panoramas De Londres, S. A. Des	IC	1870's	GB	Panorama of London from the River Thames.		200	Entertain
Paramount	IC	1960's	NY	Paramount logo - green		39	Entertain
Paramount	IC	1960's	NY	Paramount logo - brown		39	Entertain
Paramount	IC	1960's	NY	Paramount logo - blue		39	Entertain
Paramount - blue	IC	1950's		Paramount logo		45	Entertain
Paramount - green	IC	1950's		Paramount logo		45	Entertain
Paramount Pictures	IC	1960's	NY	Two women, logo		40	Entertain
Paris Gigantic Wheel	IU	1898	GB	Ferris Wheel		750	Entertain
Paris Gigantic Wheel &Varieties	I	1898	France	Ferris wheel		495	Entertain
Paris Gigantic Wheel &Varieties Co.	I	1898	France	Ferris wheel at top center, Fortune at left.		500	Entertain
Paris-Tennis, Soc. Immobiliere	IC	1920's	France			80	Entertain
Park Place Company	U	1800's	OH	Park trees fountain		25	Entertain
Pathe Film Corp.	IU			Bare-breasted women, rooster		75	Entertain
Pathe Freres Phonograph	U	1920's	DE	Pathe Rooster Logo		88	Entertain
Pathe Industries	IU	1967	DE	Red rooster logo		45	Entertain
Paxson Communications	I	2003		Lion and large P on crest		25	Entertain
Penthouse International	I	2003				100	Entertain
Pequea Fishing Club	I	1910	PA	Eagle.		60	Entertain
Philadelphia Hockey Club	U	1920's	PA	Eagle.		225	Entertain
Phonograph Corp. of Indiana	I	1920's			Thomas Edison	2,000	Entertain
Phonographs Ltd.	IC	1817	NJ	Eagle	Thomas Edison	1,950	Entertain
Photo-Tampon, Cie. Internationale	IC	1900's	Switzerland	Arms of seven countries		28	Entertain
Pixar	I	2000			Steve Jobs facs.	345	Entertain
Pixar	I	2002		Toy Story Characters	Steve Jobs facs.	202	Entertain
Pixar	I	2005		Toy Story Characters	Steve Jobs facs.	153	Entertain
Pixar	I	2006		Toy Story characters	Steve Jobs facs.	250	Entertain
Pixar	I	2006		Toy Story Characters	Steve Jobs facs.	200	Entertain

Pixar	I		Toy Story Characters		500	Entertain
Planet Hollywood	SP		PlanetHollywood building		295	Entertain
Planet Hollywood	I		PlanetHollywood building		150	Entertain
Playboy	SP	1974	Willy Rey Playboy bunny Green		395	Entertain
Playboy	I	2002	Woman holding globe	Hugh Hefner fac	95	Entertain
Playboy	SP		Willy Rey Playboy bunny Blue	Hugh Hefner fac	495	Entertain
Playboy	SP		Willy Rey Playboy bunny Brown		495	Entertain
Playboy Enterprises	SP	1970's	DE	Nude woman	450	Entertain
Playboy Enterprises, Inc.	U	2006	DE	Woman holding globe	95	Entertain
Playboy Enterprises, Inc.	I	1980's		Green. Reclining nude. Playboy bunny below.	395	Entertain
Playboy Enterprises, Inc.	SP	1980's		Brown. Reclining nude. Playboy bunny below.	475	Entertain
Playboy Enterprises, Inc.	SP	1980's		Blue. Reclining nude. Playboy bunny below.	495	Entertain
Playboy Enterprises, Inc.	SP			Green. Reclining nude. Playboy bunny below.	450	Entertain
Playboy Enterprises, Inc.	U			Woman with globe	75	Entertain
Portland Baseball Club	I	1955		Baseball man	125	Entertain
Prag-Film A.G. In Prag	IC	1940's	Czech		35	Entertain
President Hotel Co.	U	1930's	NJ	Photovignette of the Hotel on a popular beach.	44	Entertain
Presidio Motion Pictures	U	1900's			35	Entertain
Presidio Motion Pictures Corp.	U	1920's	NV		15	Entertain
Prestbury and Upton Golf Club, Ltd.	IC	1920's	GB		120	Entertain
Prince of Wales Hotel Co.	IC	1940's		Blue.	25	Entertain
Prince of Wales Hotel Co.	IC	1940's		Blue.	25	Entertain
Providence Bowling Club	I	1840's	RI		225	Entertain
Radio Telephone	I	1908	NJ	Eagle. DeF logo, red.	60	Entertain
Radio Telephone	I	1909		Title in red and purple, red seal.	20	Entertain
Red Fish Boat	I	1962	TX	Red. A futuristic fiberglass speedboat.	35	Entertain
Renaissance Entertainment Corp.	SP		CO	Red flag logo	30	Entertain
Resorts International	IC	1970's		Green. No vignette.	20	Entertain
Resorts International	IC	1970's		Green. No vignette.	20	Entertain
Revere Racing Association, Inc.	I	1960's	MA	Nude runner with sash	45	Entertain
Ringling Bros	U			Circus	395	Entertain
Ringling Bros	U			Circus	395	Entertain
Ringling Bros	U			Circus	395	Entertain
Ringling Bros Barnum & Bailey	SP		DE	Circus characters	595	Entertain

Ringling Bros.	I	1969		Circus		400	Entertain
Ringling Bros. - Barnum & Bailey	U	1969		Circus		395	Entertain
Ringling Bros. Barnum & Bailey	IC	1971		Green. Clowns, animals acrobats, horse drawn carriages		600	Entertain
Ringling Bros. Barnum & Bailey	IC	1971		Red. Circus parade		795	Entertain
Ringling Bros.- Barnum & Bailey	IC	1970's	DE	Multicolored inner frame.		528	Entertain
Ringling Bros.-Barnum & Bailey	I	1960's	DE	Multi-colored circus figures.		600	Entertain
Ringling Bros.-Barnum & Bailey Co.	SP		DE	Multi-colored circus figures.		995	Entertain
Ringling Bros., Barnum & Bailey	IU			Circus parade		850	Entertain
Ringling Bros., Barnum & Bailey	SP			Circus parade		950	Entertain
Ringling BrosBarnum & Bailey Shows	SP	1960's	DE	Multi-color		792	Entertain
Ringling BrosBarnum & Bailey Shows	SP		DE	Blue.		1,100	Entertain
Ringling Brothers-Barnum & Bailey	IU	1960-7	DE	Multi-colored circus figures.		975	Entertain
Roulette de Monte Carlo bond	I		France	Cert #1	M Duchamp	1,082,500	Entertain
Roulette de Monte Carlo bond	I		France		M Duchamp	447,500	Entertain
Royal Italian Opera Covent Garden	IC	1880's	GB	Classical ladies, masks of tragedy & comedy.		240	Entertain
Rubber Streets and Tennis Courts	IC	1920's	GB			80	Entertain
S. Hurok Amusement	IC	1920's	NY	Eagle on shield.		143	Entertain
Safety Cinematogr Photographic Films	IC	1920's	Belgium	Cine-camera.		110	Entertain
Saint-Andre S/Mer, S.A. Immobiliere	IC	1920's	Belgium			140	Entertain
Santa Anita Realty Enterprises	SP	1979	DE	Racetrack Dr. Charles H. Strub		75	Entertain
Saugatuck Recreation Co.	IU	1930's	MI	Eagle & gold seal		35	Entertain
Sentinel Radio	IC			Allegorical & lightning		30	Entertain
Societe Micro-Phonographes Bettini	IC	1900's	France	Early gramaphone at bottom.		253	Entertain
Societe Royale Zoolocie Horticulture	IC	1870's	Belgium	Garden gate, animals.		264	Entertain
Soutenco Manufacture Souliers Tennis	IC	1920's	Belgium			100	Entertain
South Carol. Interstate W. Indian Expo	IU	1901	SC	Woman, train, ships, field		395	Entertain
Southern Hotel Co.	IC	1980's	MO	Hotel, with busy street, horse-trams & buses		90	Entertain
Sportsworld 2000 Inc.	IU	1992	FL	Huge sports stadium		150	Entertain
St. Louis American League Baseball	I	1909				360	Entertain
St. Louis Exposition and Music Hall	IC	1900's	MI	Grizzly bear, miniature allegorical scenes.		160	Entertain
St. Paul Base Ball Club	IU	1925	MN	State seal		1,000	Entertain
Stan Lee Media	I	2002		Stan Lee		85	Entertain

Name	Type	Date	State	Description	Signature	Price	Category
State of Connecticut note	I	1780	CT	Fancy border	Peter Colt	275	Entertain
Steppenwolf Inc.	U	1969	CA	Dome		65	Entertain
Steppenwolf Productions Inc.	U	1960's	CA	Screaming eagle		65	Entertain
Stratfield Amusement Co.	IU	1920's	NY	Waterfront, Indians, & teepees		100	Entertain
Tacony Driving Park	U	1880's	PA	Man with two fast trotters.		286	Entertain
Television Indus.	IC	1966		TV transmission tower.		15	Entertain
Television Indus.	IC	1966		TV transmission tower.		10	Entertain
Ter Rivieren Wielerbaan N.V.	IC	1930's	Belgium			52	Entertain
The Greenbrier Hotel	U		WV			150	Entertain
Theatre Et Le Cinema S.A.E.	IC	1920's	Egypt	Decorative border.		48	Entertain
Thorsen & Cassedy	IU	1895	IL	Guns, fishing rods, bicycle		1,495	Entertain
Toledo Mudhens Baseball Club	I	1952	OH	Ohio		90	Entertain
Triangle Film Corp	IU	1917	NY	Fancy border		150	Entertain
Triangle Film Corp	U	1918	NY			60	Entertain
Triangle Film Corporation	IC	1920's	NY			55	Entertain
Tru-Tone Phonograph, Inc.	U		NY	State seal		15	Entertain
Twentieth Century Fox bond	SP	1978	DE	Attractive woman running through valley		75	Entertain
Twentieth Century-Fox Film Corp	SP		DE	Figures with masks of tragedy & comedy.		120	Entertain
Tyco Toys	SP	1993	DE	Woman, rocket ship		85	Entertain
Unique Theatre Co. of Boston	U	1900's		Eagle with train		15	Entertain
United Artists Theatre Circuit	I	1956			MaryPickfordRogers	525	Entertain
United Artists Theatre Circuit	I	1930's	MD	Or. Allegorical female.		35	Entertain
United Artists Theatre Circuit	I	1940's	MD	Or. Allegorical female.		15	Entertain
United Artists Theatre Circuit	IC	1950's	MD		MaryPickfordRogers	660	Entertain
United Cinema	IU	1928	DE			95	Entertain
United Picture Productions	IU	1919	DE	Eagle		110	Entertain
United Radio	IC	1970's		Orchestra, Man and woman turning on radio		35	Entertain
United States Treasury	IC	1940's	CA	Disney Characters.		720	Entertain
US Treasury Disney War Bond	U	1944		Disney characters printed in color		450	Entertain
US Treasury Disney War Bond	U	1944		Disney characters printed in color		450	Entertain
US Treasury Disney War bond	IU	1940's		22 Disney characters		350	Entertain
US Treasury Disney War bond	U	1940's		22 Disney characters		350	Entertain
Velodrome D' Anvers, S.A. Du	IC	1890's	Belgium			100	Entertain
Velodrome De Mondesir-Bordeaux	IC	1890's	France	Start of a race in the velodrome.		280	Entertain
Velodromes Reunis S.A.	IC	1900's	Belgium			48	Entertain
Velodroom Van Herenthals N.M.	IC	1920's	Belgium	Racing cyclists.		72	Entertain
Vereeniging Toneelgebouw Groningen	IC	1920's	Belgium			64	Entertain
Vermont Teddy Bear	IC	1994	NY	Green. Teddy bear, IN BEARS WE TRUST		35	Entertain

Victor Talking Machine	SP	1927	NJ	Dog and phonograph		1,500	Entertain
Walt Disney	U	1992	DE	Disney characters		46	Entertain
Walt Disney	U			Disney Characters		60	Entertain
Walt Disney Co	I	2004		Disney & characters		100	Entertain
Walt Disney Co	SP			Disney & characters		395	Entertain
Walt Disney Co. Go.com	I	2000	DE/CA	Walt Disney		150	Entertain
Walt Disney Inc.	IC	1950's	CA	Eagle	Walt Disney (1)	55,000	Entertain
Walt Disney Inc.	IC	1950's	CA	Eagle	Walt Disney (2)	80,000	Entertain
Walt Disney Inc.	U	1950's	CA	Eagle		950	Entertain
Walt Disney Productions	U	1988		Walt Disney		81	Entertain
Walt Disney Productions	V		CA	Walt Disney, Mickey & Other Disney characters		150	Entertain
Walt Disney Productions	SP		CA	Walt Disney, Mickey & Other Disney Chars		395	Entertain
Walt Disney Productions	U			Woman		100	Entertain
Walt Disney Productions	U			Woman		100	Entertain
Washington Target Shooting Assoc	I	1880	DC	Red seal with crossed target, rifles, bullseye		150	Entertain
Washington Target Shooting Assoc	IC	1860's	DC	Sharpshooter. Crowd around clubhouse		528	Entertain
Welte Co., Inc.	U	1920's	DE/NY	Allegorical lady reclines with Cupid.		190	Entertain
Western Publishing Group	I	1998	DE	Cartoon train pulling animals		110	Entertain
Western Television Corporation	U	1930's	DE/NY	Design of a classical lady between TV towers		240	Entertain
Whip Amusement Co	IU	1935	TN	Eagle on cliff	J.R. Moon	50	Entertain
Women's Golf Unlimited	I	2003		Stylistic eagle		255	Entertain
Woodbridge Hills Country Club	I	1934	CT	Green.		15	Entertain
World's Columbian Exposition	IU	1892	IL	Woman, wheel, eagle		350	Entertain
Wospag	IC	1920's	Austria	Trotting horse race.		90	Entertain
Wotan, Deutsche Film-A.G.	IC	1920's	Germany			96	Entertain
Zackey Talking Machine Co.	U	1900's				35	Entertain

CHAPTER 12 - GOVERNMENT CERTIFICATES

The government category includes federal, state, and local government bonds, and includes government bonds from around the world.

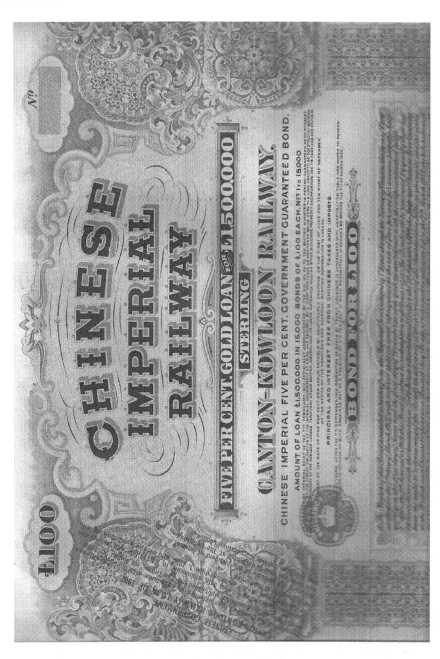

ANTIQUE STOCK & BOND PRICE GUIDE 2014

Name	IU	Date	State	Vignette	Signed by	Value	Category
Alachua County	I	1930's	AL	5.5% road & bridge bond, tree, Indian maiden, ship		100	Govt
Albany, City of	I	1810's		Bond, embossed seal		500	Govt
Altoona, City of	I	1880's		Bond, city by river, old train		75	Govt
Altoona, City of	I	1890's		Bond, city by river, state seal		50	Govt
America, Confederate States of	I	1860's		8% bond, portrait & old city scene, reclining woman		75	Govt
America, Confederate States of	I	1860's		Fifth series 6% bond, mounted soldier, 2 females		50	Govt
America, Confederate States of	I	1860's		8% bond, 3 figures surround portrait		125	Govt
America, Confederate States of	I	1860's		8% bond, 2 ladies with sailing ship		100	Govt
America, Confederate States of	I	1860's		8% bond, 2 ladies with sailing ship		100	Govt
America, Confederate States of	I	1860's		7% bond, portrait of General Lee		75	Govt
America, Confederate States of	I	1860's		4% bond, sailing warships		100	Govt
America, Confederate States of	I	1860's		8% bond, portrait		125	Govt
Antonio Lopez de Santa Anna bond	IC	1860's	NY-Mexico	Santa Anna & his palaces.	A.L. Santa Anna	24,950	Govt
Arkansas State Levee Bond	I	1870's		7% bond, riverboats on Mississippi River, seal		350	Govt
Arkansas State Levee Bond	I	1870's		7% bond, sidewheeler & log raft		500	Govt
Arkansas, State of	I	1860's		7% RR bond (Memphis & Little Rock Railroad)		225	Govt
Arkansas, State of	I	1860's		8% war bond state seal		75	Govt
Atlantic City, City of	I	1890's		5% water gold bond, state seal, train & ship		125	Govt
Avondale School Bond	UC	1989	MI	Eagle		10	Govt
Bridgeport, City of	I	1950's	CT	2 & 3-tenths% school bond, large eagle		15	Govt
Bristol, Borough of	I	1960's	PA	3 & 3-4ths% general fund bond, state seal		15	Govt
Broome County, War Loan	I	1860's	NY	7% war bond, eagle		225	Govt
Bundeshauptstadt	IC	1920's	Austria	Panorama of Vienna, & underprint of Austrian eagle.		48	Govt
Chamber of Commerce of Chicago	I	1891		Chamber of Commerce Building. Train. Eagle. Steamship		200	Govt

Name	Type	Date	Location	Description	Price	Category
Chamber of Commerce of the City	I	1891		Chamber of Commerce Bldg. Train. Steamship.	200	Govt
Chinese Central Government	I	1912	China		42,579	Govt
Chinese Government	I	1912	China	Blue decorative scroll work, brown security underprint.	45	Govt
Chinese Government	I	1912	China	Blue decorative scroll work	100	Govt
Chinese Government	I	1913	China	Blue. Mercury. Farmers. Pagoda.	4,995	Govt
Chinese Government	I	1913	China	Russian Issue. Brown.	495	Govt
Chinese Government	I	1913	China	Green.	495	Govt
Chinese Government Reorg	I	1913	China	Orange	995	Govt
Chinese Imperial Government	I	1877	China	100 pound bond 8%	53,224	Govt
Chinese Imperial Government	I	1911	China	Green, purple. Train.	35	Govt
Chinese Imperial Government	I	1911	China	Green, purple. Train.	50	Govt
Chinese Imperial Government	I	1911	China	Red, purple. Train.	95	Govt
Chinese Imperial Government	I	1911	China	Red, purple. Train.	125	Govt
Chinese Imperial Government	IC	1890's	China	Loan Certificate.	99	Govt
Chinese Imperial Government	IC	1890's	China	Loan Certificate.	242	Govt
Chinese Imperial Government	IC	1890's	China	Gold Loan.	143	Govt
Chinese Province of Petchili bond	IU	1913	China		19,600	Govt
City of Albany	IC	1840's	NY	City and State Arms.	176	Govt
City of Barnaul	IC	1910's	Russia		320	Govt
City of Duisburg, Germany	IC	1920's	Germany	Female, arm on globe, industrial complex.	99	Govt
City of Frankfurt	I	1907	Germany	Decorative borders. Bavarian arms on top.	125	Govt
City of Frankfurt	IU	1907	Germany	Blue. Text in German. Bavarian arms on top.	125	Govt
City of Frankfurt-Betriebs-Anleihe	I	1908	Germany	Ornate blue underprint. Prussian emblem.	60	Govt
City of Frankfurt-Betriebs-Anleihe	IU	1908	Germany	Text in German, blue underprint. Prussian emblem.	60	Govt
City of Karkhof	IC	1900's	Russia	Local buildings in the four corners.	462	Govt
City of Karkhof	IC	1900's	Russia	Local buildings in the four corners.	682	Govt
City of Los Angeles	I	1940	CA	City seal. Bond	25	Govt
City of Los Angeles	IC	1940	CA	City seal.	15	Govt
City of Moscow	IC	1900's	Russia		120	Govt
City of Munich	IC	1920's	Germany	Monk.	130	Govt
City of Pittsburgh	I	1870	PA	Woman representing Commerce, ships, train.	60	Govt
City of Pittsburgh	I	1870	PA	Woman representing Commerce, ships, train.	60	Govt

Name	Type	Date	Location	Description	Price	Category
City of San Paulo Improve&Freehold	IC	1930's	Brazil		72	Govt
Colony of Connecticut	I	1700's	CT		121	Govt
Colony of Connecticut	I	1700's	CT		121	Govt
Colony of Georgia	I	1700's	GA	James Oglethorpe	5,720	Govt
Colony of New Jersey	I	1760's	NJ		440	Govt
Colony of Pennsylvania	I	1750's	PA		2,090	Govt
Colorado Springs, City of	I	1900's	CO	Public improvement gold bond, allegorical figure	75	Govt
Colorado Springs, City of	I	1900's	CO	4% refunding bond	75	Govt
Colorado Springs, City of	I	1920's	CO	6% pavin & improvement gold bond	35	Govt
Commonwealth of Massachusetts	I	1770's	MA		3,410	Govt
Commonwealth of Massachusetts	I	1780's	MA		231	Govt
Commonwealth of VA, Warrant Land	I	1850's			396	Govt
Commonwealth of Virginia	IC	1870's	VA	Charles Ludwig	1,155	Govt
Connecticut, State of	I	1780's	CT	Interest-bearing note	100	Govt
Connecticut, State of	I	1780's	CT	6% bond	350	Govt
Connecticut, State of, U.S. Loan Of	I	1790's	CT	Certificate of loan	500	Govt
County of New York	IU	1865	NY	Jacob H. Vanderbilt	1,200	Govt
Cumb & County Power & Light	U	1920's	ME	4 & one-half% gold bond, specimen	100	Govt
Delaware, State of	I	1900's	DE	6% water improve. old bond, state seal	35	Govt
Denver, City & County of	I	1920's	CO	Moffat Tunnel gold bond, state seal	15	Govt
Edison County War Bond	I	1860's		7% bond, state seal	175	Govt
Essex Count Volunteer War Bond	I	1860's	NY	7% bond, red seal	125	Govt
Essex County Volunteer War Bond	I	1860's	NY	7% bond, blue seal	125	Govt
Etat Belge	IC		Belgium		22	Govt
Fallon, City of	I	1911	NV	Sewer bond	125	Govt
Flemish United States Bond Consort	I	1790's	Belgium		253	Govt
Fort Wayne, City of	I	1920's	IN	P.B. Aviation bond, buffalo & hunter	75	Govt
Fort Wayne, City of	I	1930's	IN	4 & one-4th% bond, buffalo & hunter	15	Govt
Fourth Liberty Loan	I	1918	WA	Green, underprint, red treasury seal	425	Govt
Fourth Liberty Loan	I	1918	WA	Green underprint, red treasury seal.	425	Govt
Free State of Saxony	IC	1920's	Germany	Lady cutting wheat, mining.	100	Govt
Georgia, State of	I	1870's	GA	7% old bond, 2 portraits & several figure	350	Govt
Georgia, State of, County of Baldwin	U	1860's	GA	Bond	75	Govt
Golden Gate Bridge-Highway Dist.	I	1930's		Gold bond, Golden Gate Bridge	100	Govt

Govt of UK \Great Britain Ireland	SP	1900's	GB			688	Govt
Grand River Dam Authority	U	1930's		Specimen, four% bond		125	Govt
Imperial Chinese Government	IC	1900's	China	Hukuang Railroad.		385	Govt
Imperial Chinese Government	IC	1900's	China	Hukuang Railroad.		385	Govt
Imperial Chinese Government	IC	1900's	China			1,408	Govt
Imperial Gov of Russia 3% Gold Bond	I	1894		Brown. 4 languages. Double headed eagle.		35	Govt
Imperial Gov. of Russia Gold Bond	IU	1894	Russia	Brown. 4 languages. Double headed eagle.		35	Govt
Imperial Government of China	I	1900	China	5% Gold bond		42,579	Govt
Imperial Government of Russia	I	1893	Russia	Brown, orange underprint. Russian arms.		18	Govt
Imperial Government of Russia	IU	1893	Russia	Brown, orange underprint. Russian arms.		20	Govt
Imperial Russian Three Per Cent Loan	IC	1850's	Russia			240	Govt
Importing & Exporting Co of Georgia	IC	1860's	GA	Ship.	Gazaway B. Lamar	1,232	Govt
Indiana, State of, County of Shelby	I	1860's	IN	6% bond, portrait, stamps		125	Govt
Indianapolis	I	1920's	IN	4 & one-half% hospital bond, old seal		20	Govt
Indianapolis	I	1930's	IN	2% city hall refunding bond		15	Govt
Indianapolis	I	1950's	MS	One & 3-quarters% airport bond, eagle		15	Govt
Jasper, County of	I	1910's	MS	Bond, Mossville School District, Eagle		15	Govt
Jasper, County of	I	1920's	MS	Road bond, eagle		15	Govt
Jasper, County of	I	1930's	MS	5 & 3-quarters% school bond, eagle		15	Govt
Jasper, County of	I	1940's	MS	3 & one-half% school bond, eagle		15	Govt
Jersey City Municipal Bond	I	1930's			Frank Hague	75	Govt
Jersey City, City of	IC	1880's	NJ	6% funded debt bond, passenger steamer	Frank Hague	125	Govt
Jersey City, City of	IC	1910's	NJ	School gold bond		15	Govt
Jersey City, City of	IC	1930's	NJ	Bond	Frank Hague	75	Govt
Jersey City, City of	IC	1940's	NJ	Street assessment bond		15	Govt
Kansas, State of	I	1870's	KS	Bond, scenic		350	Govt
Kingdom of Bulgaria	I	1926	Bulgaria	Blue. Farmers resting.		50	Govt
Kingdom of Bulgaria	I	1926	Bulgaria	Blue. Farmers resting		50	Govt
Kingdom of Bulgaria	I	1928	Bulgaria	Allegorical woman holding a wheat sheaf, farm		50	Govt
Kingdom of Spain	IC	1790's	Spain	Arms at top, fighting swans.		297	Govt

Name	Type	Date	State	Description	Signature	Price	Category
L.A. Department of Water & Power	SP	1963	CA	Olive. Woman, transmission lines, skyline.		20	Govt
Lakeshore City	I	1960's	NM	Sanitation district bond		35	Govt
Lawrence City	I	1950's	AL	Gas tax anticipation bond		15	Govt
Lawrence County	I	1950's	AL	Tax warrant		15	Govt
Letchfield, Town of	I	1860's		Volunteer fund bond with stamps		100	Govt
Lewisboro, Town off	U	1860's	NY	7% military bond, eagle with national shield		125	Govt
Lincoln, County of	I	1930's	OR	6% refunding gold bond, large eagle		15	Govt
Loan of the City of Philadelphia	I	1850's		Independ. Hall, train, Wm Penn, Franklin, Washington		75	Govt
Loan of the City of Philadelphia	I	1860's	PA	Independence Hall, steam locomotive		75	Govt
Los Angeles Department of Water	SP	1954	CA	Green.		20	Govt
Los Angeles Department of Water	SP	1962	CA	Blue.		20	Govt
Los Angeles Department of Water	SP	1963	CA	Olive. Woman, transmission lines, skyline.		20	Govt
Los Angeles Dept of Water & Power	SP	1954	CA	Green.		20	Govt
Los Angeles Dept of Water & Power	SP	1962	CA	Blue. Similar to the preceding item.		20	Govt
Los Angeles Water Bond	IC	1930's	CA	LA Seal		25	Govt
Los Angeles Water Works	IC	1930's	CA	Woman above LA seal flag, bear, eagle & lion		25	Govt
Los Angeles Water Works Muni Bond	IC	1930's	CA	Blue. Woman. LA seal flag, bear, eagle & lion.		25	Govt
Los Angeles, City of	I	1920's	CA	4% waterworks, 2 women city seal, ships, waterfall		125	Govt
Los Angeles, City of	I	1920's	CA	Sewage disposal bond, large city official seal		35	Govt
Los Angeles, City of	I	1920's	CA	Street improvement bond		50	Govt
Los Angeles, City of	I	1930's	CA	Bond, waterworks		50	Govt
Louisiana	I	1892	LA	Green, gold seal. Eagle.	Huey Kingfish Long	200	Govt
Louisiana	I	1892		Green, gold seal. Eagle.	Huey Kingfish Long	200	Govt
Louisiana Baby Bond	IC	1875	LA	Baby		20	Govt
Louisiana bond	I	1870's	LA	8% bond for railroad	Gov H.C.Warmouth	500	Govt
Louisiana, State of	I	1880's	LA	4% bond, riverboats		350	Govt
Louisiana, State of	I	1890's	LA	Consolidated 4% bond, building & trees	Gov. M.J. Foster	100	Govt
Louisiana, State of	I	1890's	LA	Consolidated bond, state building		75	Govt

Louisiana, State of	I	1890's	LA	Baby bond	25	Govt
Maryland, State of	I	1770's	MD	6% bond	525	Govt
Maryland, State of	I	1890's	MD	6% bond, barrels & pail	125	Govt
Massachusetts Bay	I	1770's	MA	6% note bond, war committee	595	Govt
Massachusetts Bay	I	1770's	MA	6% note bond	510	Govt
Massachusetts Bay, State of	I	1770's	MA	6% bond, soldier with sword	725	Govt
Massachusetts Bay, State of	I	1770's	MA	6% bond, pine tree	650	Govt
Massachusetts, Commonwealth	Proof	1860's	MA	Eagle, liberty cap, soldiers.	253	Govt
Massachusetts, Commonwealth	Proof	1870's	MA	George Washington, flags.	220	Govt
Massachusetts, Commonwealth of	I	1780's	MA	6% bond	650	Govt
Massachusetts, Commonwealth of	I	1950's	MA	8 & one-half% highway flood relief bond, eagle	15	Govt
Massachusetts, Commonwealth of	I	1950's	MA	August & October bond, eagle	15	Govt
Massachusetts, Commonwealth of	I	1950's	MA	Capital outlay loan, eagle	50	Govt
Miami Beach, City of	U	1960's	FL	Improvement bond, eagle, city seal	15	Govt
Military Loan 8%	IC	1910's	China	Red chop seal.	48	Govt
Minnesota, State of	I	1890's	MN	6% bond, farming	175	Govt
Minnesota, State of	U	1920's	MN	4 & 3-quarters% bond, specimen, state seal	100	Govt
Mississippi, State of	I	1830's	MS	5% bond, 2 seated ladies, 2 eagles, & ships	500	Govt
Mississippi, State of	I	1870's	MS	State capitol building	225	Govt
Missouri Defense Bond	I	1860's	MS	Red on blue	225	Govt
Missouri Defense Bond	I	1860's	MS	Red on tan	350	Govt
Monroe, County of	I	1860's	NY	Indebtedness bond, female	75	Govt
Montana State Warrant	I	1890's	MT	Standing lady	75	Govt
Montana Territory bond	I	1860's	MT	Sailor	225	Govt
Mossville, Mississippi	I	1930's	MT	4% bond	15	Govt
Munich City Loan Certificates	IC	1920's	Germany	Loan.	242	Govt
Municipalidad De Valparaiso Bond	Proof	1870's	Chile	Chilean arms, Columbus sights land.	363	Govt
Muskegan, City of	I	1950's		3 & 3-4ths% highway bond, eagle	15	Govt
Nashville, City of	I	1860's	TN	8% bond, state capitol building	175	Govt
Nevada State Bond	I	1870's	NV	Train & mountain scene	175	Govt
Nevada State Warrant	I	1880's	NV	Orphan home fund	75	Govt
Nevada, State of	I	1880's	NV	State controllers warrant, train & miners	75	Govt
New Bergen, Township of	I	1940's	NJ	Refunding bond, state seal	15	Govt
New Hampshire, State of	I	1780's	NH	Loan office certificate	500	Govt

New York	I	1866		Green. State seal. Columbia. Liberty.	75	Govt
New York	I		NY	Green. State seal. Columbia. Liberty.	75	Govt
New York City	IC	1860's	NY	Court House	220	Govt
New York City & County	I	1863	NY	Sailor, Indian, windmill blades on shield	20	Govt
New York City & County	I	1863		Sailor, Indian, windmill blades on shield, NY City arms	20	Govt
New York City Street Improve. Fund	I	1860's		Colored embossed paper seal. City Hall. City arms.	40	Govt
New York City Street Improvement	I	1860's	NY	Colored embossed paper seal. City Hall. City arms.	40	Govt
New York City Volunteer Soldiers	I	1865	NY	Eagle, train, ship, cannon balls. Gunther as Mayor	75	Govt
New York State Canal Department	I	1857-73	NY	Canal Rev Cert. State arms. Washington, Clinton	55	Govt
New York State Canal Department	I	1857-73		Canal Revenue Cert. State arms. Washington, Clinton	55	Govt
New York State Canal Department	I	1860's		Three women, bust of Washington. Two men, Eagle	65	Govt
New York State Canal Department	I	1870's	NY	Three women, bust of Washington. Eagle below.	65	Govt
New York State Municipal Bond	IC	1940's	NY	NY seal: Two women, shield, sun rising over mountains	25	Govt
New York State Municipal Bond	IC	1940's	NY	NY seal: Two women, shield, sun rising over mountains	25	Govt
New York, City of	I	1850's	NY	Central Park assessment fund, city seal	175	Govt
New York, City of	I	1860's	NY	Tax repayment bond, city hall, red seal	125	Govt
New York, City of	I	1860's	NY	Assessment fund bond, city hall	175	Govt
New York, City of	I	1860's	NY	Revenue bond, of city hall	225	Govt
New York, City of	I	1870's	NY	Indian & merchant with canoe & ships Major Wood	175	Govt
New York, City of	I	1870's	NY	City parks improvement stock seal	100	Govt
New York, City of	I	1870's	NY	Improvement & assessment bonds	100	Govt
New York, City of	I	1870's	NY	Revenue bond, of city hall	175	Govt
New York, City of	I	1890's	NY	Hotel license, excise certificate	175	Govt

Name	Type	Date	State	Description		Price	Category
New York, City of	I	1890's	NY	Saloon liquor license		225	Govt
New York, City of, Insurance Co.	I	1920's	NY	Skyline		85	Govt
New York, County of	I	1860's	NY	Revenue bonds, city hall		125	Govt
New York, County of	I	1860's	NY	7% bond, red seal		125	Govt
New York, State	I	1810's	NY	7% stock bond		350	Govt
New York, State of	I	1830's	NY	Chenago Canal 5% bond, 2 figures with eagle		350	Govt
New York, State of	I	1830's	NY	Chenango Canal 5% bond, 2 cherubs		350	Govt
New York, State of	I	1830's	NY	Erie Canal improvement 5% loan		350	Govt
New York, State of	I	1830's	NY	5% stock, Black River Canal		350	Govt
New York, State of	I	1840's	NY	5 & one-half% stock, comptrollers office		350	Govt
New York, State of	I	1840's	NY	7% canal department stock debt		350	Govt
New York, State of	I	1850's	NY	6% canal revenue certificate		350	Govt
New York, State of	I	1860's	NY	7% stock bond, comptroller's office		225	Govt
New York, State of	I	1860's	NY	Certificate of indebtedness	Gov.R.E. Fenton	75	Govt
New York, State of	I	1860's	NY	7% civil war bounty bond		175	Govt
New York, State of	I	1960's	NY	General revenue bond, Power Authority		15	Govt
Newark Ohio Waterworks	I		OH	6% bond, prehistoric scene & water tower		75	Govt
Newbury County (South Carolina)	U	1880's	SC	2 & 9-tenths% road bond, eagle		15	Govt
Norfolk, City of	I	1870's		8% street paving bond		100	Govt
North Bergen Township of, State of	I	1920's		Improvement note, state seal		15	Govt
North Carolina State of	I	1860's	NC	6% bond, state capitol building		225	Govt
North Carolina State of	U	1900's	NC	4% bond specimen, 2 seated figures/seal		125	Govt
North Danville, Town of	U	1880's	VA	Train & landscape		125	Govt
NY City Volunteer Soldiers Fam. Aid	I	1865	NY	New Yor arms, eagle, train, ship, cannon balls. Gunther		75	Govt
NY Railroad Crossing Bond	IC	1934	NY			25	Govt
NY Railroad Crossing Bond	IC	1935	NY			25	Govt
Oklahoma, State of	U	1910's	OK	Building fund bond, state seal		35	Govt
Ontonagon Town Site Co.	U	1880's	MI	State seal		35	Govt
Orange, City of	I	1950's		Bond, housing authority, woman with houses		15	Govt

Name	Type	Era	State	Description	Price	Category
Owensboro Waterworks	I	1880's	KY	5% bond, eagle	75	Govt
Panama Pacific Exposition Bond	I	1910's		Waterfront scene with winged messenger	125	Govt
Passaic, Count of, Board of Educe	I	1950's	NJ	Bonds	15	Govt
Passaic, County of	I	1930's	NJ	Road, bridge, & building bond, figure, winged wheel	15	Govt
Pennsylvania, Commonwealth of	I	1790's	PA	Unfunded debt	500	Govt
Pennsylvania, Commonwealth of	I	1790's	PA	3% bond	520	Govt
Pennsylvania, Commonwealth of	I	1850's	PA	5% bond; portraits, man & woman figures, & seal	500	Govt
Pennsylvania, Commonwealth of,	I	1850's	PA	6% bond, woman with anchor & gears, train & harbor	500	Govt
Pens lvania State Treasurer Warra	I	1850's	PA	Farm scene, 2 corner figures	100	Govt
Philadelphia, City of	I	1850's	PA	5% bond, Indians, embossed seal	125	Govt
Philadelphia, City of	I	1850's	PA	Washington & Franklin, train	175	Govt
Philadelphia, City of	I	1850's	PA	6% bond, many	125	Govt
Philadelphia, City of	I	1860's	PA	6% bond, Independence Hall, embossed seal	125	Govt
Philadelphia, City of	I	1870's	PA	6% bond, Independence Hall, embossed seal	100	Govt
Philadelphia, City of	I	1880's	PA	4% bond, city hall & portraits	220	Govt
Philadelphia, City of	I	1880's	PA	4% bond, city hall & portraits	225	Govt
Philadelphia, City of	I	1890's	PA	Sewer & repaving bond	75	Govt
Philadelphia, City of	I	1900's	PA	3% bond, portrait plus 2 seated figures	225	Govt
Philadelphia, City of	I	1910's	PA	City hall & portrait	75	Govt
Pommern Konvolut Anleihen	IC	1900's	Germany		60	Govt
Poplar Bluff, City of	I	1910's		5% funding bond, eagle	15	Govt
Poughkeepsie, City of	I	1860's	NY	6% bond, Women, soldiers, & eagle	100	Govt
Poughkeepsie, City of	I	1870's	NY	7% sewer bond, Indian women & eagle	75	Govt
Poughkeepsie, City of	I	1870's	NY	7% water bond	100	Govt
Poughkeepsie, City of	I	1880's	NY	4 & one-half% second bounty bond Mayor E. White	100	Govt
Providence Plantations	U	1800's		Old city	100	Govt
Providence, City of	U	1880's	RI	State capitol	50	Govt
Providence, City of	I	1890's	RI	Pilgrims & Indians, plus 2 additional at sides	100	Govt
Providence, City of	I	1900's	RI	Bond, pilgrims & Indians	75	Govt

Name	Type	Date	Location	Description	Signature	Price	Category
Providence, City of	I	1910's	RI	Bond, pilgrims & Indians		50	Govt
Providence, City of	I	1930's	RI	2 & 3-4ths% bond. pilgrims & Indians		35	Govt
Province of Lower Austria	IC	1920's	Austria	Beautiful woman, by a hydro-electric plant.		100	Govt
Province of Saskatchewan	IC	1982	Canada	Buffalo, Indian, beaver and farmer.		25	Govt
Province of Saskatchewan	IC	1982		Buffalo, Indian, beaver and farmer.		25	Govt
Rawlins County	I	1920's	KS	4 & 3-4ths% school bond		15	Govt
Rensselaer Count Toll Road Bond	I	1900's		3% bond, eagle with flag		50	Govt
Rensslaer, Count of	I	1900's		3 & one-half% highway improve, bond, 2 ladies		75	Govt
Repubilca de Cuba	SP	1870's	Cuba	Cuban map, woman with shield.		220	Govt
Repubilca Mexicana 1859 Act Bonds	IC	1850's	Mexico	Republic eagle at center.		121	Govt
Republic of Bolivia	I	1870		Bond. Blue. Justice. Man with book and globe.		25	Govt
Republic of Bolivia	I	1870		Female allegory representing Art. Safe, below.		20	Govt
Republic of Bolivia	I	1870		1000 Pesos. Green. Female allegory Commerce.		30	Govt
Republic of Bolivia	I	1870		500 Pesos. Female allegory representing Art. Safe		20	Govt
Republic of Bolivia	I	1870		1000 Pesos. Green. Female allegory Commerce.		30	Govt
Republic of Bolivia	I	1870		Bond. Justice. Man with book		25	Govt
Republic of China	IC	1930's	China			120	Govt
Republic of China $1000 bond	IU	1937	China	Pagoda		600	Govt
Republic of Estonia	I	1927	Estonia	City of Tallinn with its many spires		70	Govt
Republic of Estonia	I	1927	Estonia	Blue. City of Tallinn		70	Govt
Republic of Estonia	IC	1920's	Estonia	Riga city view, Estonian Arms.		242	Govt
Republic of Mexico	IC	1860's	Mexico	Allegory of Monroe Doctrine, Portraits.		132	Govt
Republic of Nicaragua	IC	1850's				1,430	Govt
Republic of Poland	I	1920	Poland	Green. Crowned eagle.		10	Govt
Republic of Poland	I	1920	Poland	Green. Crowned eagle		25	Govt
Republic of Texas	IC	1830's	TX		Steven F. Austin	1,320	Govt
Republic of Texas	IC	1830's	TX		Sam Houston	3,575	Govt
Republica Argentina	Proof	1880's	Argentina	Arms.		440	Govt
Republica Mexicana 1000 bond	IU	1885	China	(Black Diamond)		27,878	Govt
Rhode Island, State of (Providence)	I	1890's	RI	4% highway loan bond, Indians & Pilgrims		75	Govt

Richmond Water Co.	I	1880's	ME	5% bond, water fountain with aqueduct		75	Govt
Rose Hill	I	1940's	MS	3 & one-4th % school bond, eagle with seal		15	Govt
Royal Siamese Government	IC	1930's	Thailand	Imperial arms flanked by Train and Rice Paddy scene.		121	Govt
Royaume De Belgique	IC	1920's	Belgium	Border has views of each of the provinces of Belgium		20	Govt
Russia-3.5% Schuldanleihe	IC	1900's	Russia			44	Govt
San Francisco Airport	I	1950's	CA	Bond, of 4 engined aircraft		200	Govt
San Francisco City Bond	I	1850's	CA	6% bond, city hall		500	Govt
San Francisco City Stock	I	1850's	CA	Ten% bond, Embarcadero waterfront		175	Govt
San Francisco Fire Protection	I	1900's	CA	8% bond, Warships in harbor		50	Govt
San Francisco Fire Protection Bond	I	1900's		Gold bond, sailing ships in bay		100	Govt
San Francisco Garbage System	I	1900's	CA	8% bond, ships in harbor		50	Govt
San Francisco Municipal Bond	I	1900's	CA	3 & one-half% bond		50	Govt
San Francisco School Bond	I	1870's	CA	$1000 dollar 7% bond, city hall		175	Govt
San Francisco School Gold bond	IC	1923	CA	The Thinker statue	James Rolph Jr.	75	Govt
San Francisco, City & County of	I	1850's	CA	$1000 dollar funded debt bond, courthouse		350	Govt
San Francisco, City & County of	I	1850's	CA	6% bond, city hall		175	Govt
San Francisco, City & County of	I	1860's	CA	5 hundred dollar bond, bay scene, unloading ship		300	Govt
San Francisco, City & County of	I	1860's	CA	$1000 dollar 7% bond, embossed seal		175	Govt
San Francisco, City & County of	I	1860's	CA	7% bond, sailing ships in Harbor		225	Govt
San Francisco, City & County of	I	1900's	CA	5% fire protection bond, large battleship scene		75	Govt
San Francisco, City & County of	I	1940's	CA	2 1/2% sewer bond, workers laying sewer lines		35	Govt
San Francisco, City & County of	I	1940's	CA	Airport bond, airplane		35	Govt
San Francisco, City & County of	I	1950's	CA	2 & one-4ths% hospital bond, Laguna harbor home		15	Govt
San Francisco, City & County of	I	1950's	CA	2 & 3-4ths% school bond, eagle		15	Govt
San Francisco, City of	I	1850's	CA	5 hundred dollar bond, San Francisco Bay	Van Ness	500	Govt

San Francisco, City of	I	1860's	CA	5 hundred dollar 7% bond, ships in harbor	225	Govt
San Francisco, City of	I	1860's	CA	One thousand dollar 7% bond, Mother Earth	175	Govt
San Francisco, City of	I	1900's	CA	Water supply & one-half% bond, water reservoir	35	Govt
San Francisco, City of	I	1900's	CA	4 & one-half% water bond, cascading water	50	Govt
San Francisco, City of	I	1910's	CA	5% street railway bond, trolley & early autos	50	Govt
San Francisco, City of	I	1910's	CA	4% water bond, waterfall & river	75	Govt
San Francisco, City of	I	1910's	CA	5% exposition bond, angel	35	Govt
San Francisco, City of	I	1920's	CA	5% school gold bond, The Thinker	35	Govt
San Francisco, City & County of	I	1940's	CA	Juvenile court bond, eagle	35	Govt
San Francisco, County of	I	1850's	CA	Bond, George Washington	350	Govt
Santa Clara, County of	I	1870's	CA	7% bond, of domed county building	350	Govt
Schuylkill Water Co.	U	1880's		Waterfalls, embossed seal	35	Govt
South Bend, City of	I	1950's		Sewage works revenue Bond, eagle	15	Govt
South Carolina	I	1830's	SC	5% steamer with seated woman	125	Govt
South Carolina	I	1830's	SC	5% bond	125	Govt
South Carolina	U	1860's	SC	6% stock certificate, error in printing: $30-$35	175	Govt
South Carolina	I	1860's	SC	6% bond, palmetto tree or of George Washington	125	Govt
South Carolina	I	1860's	SC	6% bond, palmetto tree	75	Govt
South Carolina	I	1870's	SC	Deficiency stock certificate, palm tree & farm	75	Govt
South Carolina	I	1870's	SC	6%a bond, Allegorical figures & cotton boll	100	Govt
South Carolina	U	1870's	SC	6% bond, Allegorical figures & cotton boll	50	Govt
South Carolina	I	1870's	SC	Fifty dollar deficiency bond, palm tree	100	Govt
South Carolina, State of	U	1800's	SC	Washington, sailing ship, cotton picker, & figures	75	Govt
South Carolina, State of	I	1800's	SC	6% loan, ships, woman, soldier & Washington	125	Govt

South Carolina, State of	U	1800's	SC	6% stock bond, seated women & cotton boll		50	Govt
Stamford, City of	I	1960's	CT	Bond specimen		15	Govt
State 6% Loan of 1936	IC	1930's	Russia	Arms of the Soviet Union.		60	Govt
State of Arkansas	U	1870	Arkansas	Train		47	Govt
State of Arkansas	IC	1830's	AR			231	Govt
State of Arkansas	IC	1870's	AR			110	Govt
State of Arkansas	IC		AR			209	Govt
State of Connecticut	I	1700's	CT			209	Govt
State of Connecticut	I	1780's	CT			143	Govt
State of Connecticut	I		CT			88	Govt
State of Georgia	IC	1870's	GA			330	Govt
State of Hamburg	I	1926	Germany	Female allegorical figure, with ship, globe, and anchor.		100	Govt
State of Hamburg	I		Germany	Blue. Female allegorical figure, with ship		100	Govt
State of Hawaii Genl. Airport Bond	IC	1980's	HI	Blue. Man & woman, Hawaiian seal.		75	Govt
State of Hawaii Genl. Obligation Bond	IC	1980's	HI	Blue. Man & woman, Hawaiian seal.		35	Govt
State of Maryland	I	1770's	MD			429	Govt
State of Maryland	I	1770's	MD			385	Govt
State of New York	IC	1840's	NY			908	Govt
State of New York	IC	1840's	NY			798	Govt
State of North Carolina	SP	1926	HI	Blue. State Arms.		65	Govt
State of North Carolina	SP	1926		Blue. State Arms.		65	Govt
State of North Carolina	I	1780's	NC			484	Govt
State of Tennessee	IC	1850's	TN			330	Govt
State of Vermont	I	1927	VT	Green. State arms.		55	Govt
State of Vermont	I	1927	VT	Green. State arms.		55	Govt
Tennessee Centennial Exposition Co.	IC	1890's	TN	Three Presidents.		1,980	Govt
Territory of Hawaii	U	1904-5	HI	Armed men		65	Govt
Texas, Late Republic of	I	1850's	TX	Public debt		175	Govt
Texas, Republic of	I	1840's	TX	Certificate of stock, 2 of man & woman		225	Govt
Texas, Republic of	I		TX	8% bond, cattle, steamboat, 5 stars at bottom		100	Govt
The City of Pensacola	IC	1880's	FL	City arms, coconut palm trees.		198	Govt
The County of San Francisco	IC	1850's	CA			220	Govt
The Greenbrier Hotel	I	1882	WV			150	Govt
Toledo, City of	I	1960's	OH	Bond, eagle		15	Govt
Township of North Bergen	I	1941	NJ	Blue. State arms.		10	Govt
Township of North Bergen	I	1941		Blue. State arms.		10	Govt
Treasury Opium Order Form	IU	1940's	US	Opium poppy, bank note paper		25	Govt
Treasury Opium Order Form	IU	1940's		Opium poppy, bank note paper		25	Govt
United States	I	1790's	US		Mary Henry	121	Govt
United States	I	1790's	US		Jonathan Dayton	187	Govt
United States	I	1800's	UK			165	Govt

United States Centennial Intl. Exhib	I	1870's	NJ	Famous people		1,250	Govt
United States Loan Office	I	1770's	CT			451	Govt
United States Loan Office	I	1770's	NJ			770	Govt
United States Loan Office	I	1780's	MA			429	Govt
United States Loan Office	I	1780's	NC			1,155	Govt
United States Loan Office	I	1780's	PA			429	Govt
United States Loan Office	I	1780's	SC			3,410	Govt
United States Loan Office	I	1790's	CT			341	Govt
United States North Carolina Loan	I	1790's	NC			2,145	Govt
United States of America	I	1780's	PA		Robert Morris	3,520	Govt
United States of America	I	1850's				506	Govt
United States of America 1st mtg bond	IU	1866	Mexico		A. L. Santa Anna	29,950	Govt
United States Registers Office	I	1790's	PA			990	Govt
United States South Carolina Loan	I	1790's	SC			1,265	Govt
United States Spanish Indemnity Bond	I	1840's	DC			1,155	Govt
United States, Treasury of	I	1790's	US	3% bond	Alex. Hamilton	1,600	Govt
USA, Bounty Land Dept. Interior-Pen	I	1850's				308	Govt
USA, Dept. of the Interior, Pensions	I	1850's				297	Govt
Vallejo City Water Co.	U	1860's	CA	Early of Vallejo, plus fountains & birdbath		50	Govt
Vereeniging Tot Bevordering	IC	1870's	Netherlands	Soldiers in camp, flags, guns, drums, armour		32	Govt
Ville De Kharkof	IC	1900's	Russia	View of the city in the four corners.		480	Govt
Wayne, Township of	I	1950's		State seal		15	Govt
West Hoboken	I	1890's		8% improvement bond, & beehive		75	Govt
Westport, Town of	I	1920's	CT	School bond		35	Govt
Wood County Bounty Fund	I	1867	OH	Eagle. Hen and chicks below.		75	Govt
Wood County Bounty Fund	I			Eagle. Hen and chicks below.		75	Govt
Yonkers, City of	I	1867		Consolidated bond, allegorical figures, eagle		100	Govt
Yonkers, City of	U	1890's		School bond		75	Govt
Yonkers, City of	I			Horses & coach		15	Govt

CHAPTER 13 - MINING CERTIFICATES

Mining is very popular scripophily topic, whether its gold, silver, copper, uranium, mercury, or any other type of mineral. Some collectors like to collect by the county, city, or town the operations were located in, such as Inyo County, California, and some like to collect by the mining district, such as the Cripple Creek mining district in Colorado.

Name	IU	Date	State	Vignette	Signed by	Value	Category
Abide Extension Mining	I	1940's	NV	Eagle		10	Mining
Abington Mining	I	1880's	ME	Working miners		48	Mining
Acacia Gold Mining	I	1900's				35	Mining
Acme Mines & Mill	IU	1930's	NV	Mines		10	Mining
Acme Mining	IU	1930's				20	Mining
Acme Uranium Mines	I	1950's	CA	Allegorical figures		10	Mining
Acme Uranium Mines	IU	1950's		Two men & one woman with stamp		10	Mining
Adventure Consol. Mining	IC	1910's		Michigan shield between two elks.		20	Mining
Adventure Consol. Mining	IC	1910's		Michigan shield between two elks.		20	Mining
Adventure Consolidated Copper	I	1900's	MI	Two elk & state seal		35	Mining
Adventure Consolidated Copper Co	I	1890's	MI	Two elk & state seal, revenue stamps		45	Mining
Adventure Copper	I	1860's	MI	State seal		35	Mining
Adventure Copper	I	1900's		State seal		35	Mining
Ahmeek Mining	I	1910's	MI	Two beavers at work		35	Mining
Ahmeek Mining	I	1920's	MI	Two beavers at work		30	Mining
Ajax Divide Mining	I	1910's	NV	Mining, gold seal		10	Mining
Ajax-Nevada Gold Mining	U	1900's	NV	Milling & mining		10	Mining
Alabama Gold & Copper Mining	I	1890's				1,500	Mining
Aladdin Gold Mining	I	1930's				60	Mining
Alameda Gold & Silver Mining	IC	1870's	CA	Prospectors shake hands.		121	Mining
Alaska Gold Fields	I	1890's	NV	Aladdin	Sheriff Garret	135	Mining
Alaska gold mine	I	1942	AK			50	Mining
Alaska Gold Mines	I	1910's		Eagle		35	Mining
Alaska Mexican Gold Mining	IU	1909	CA	Miners working above ground		125	Mining
Alaska Mildred	I	1900's	OR	Mountain & bay		50	Mining
Alaska Mines Development Co.	U	1900's		Woman holding light bulb with factories, fields, farms		45	Mining
Alaska Mines Development Co.	U	1900's		Woman, light bulb, factories, fields, farms & train		45	Mining
Alaska Mines Development Company	U	1900's	NV	Countryside, power station, lightbulbs		45	Mining
Alaska Mining	I	1883	KY	Gray, gold seal. Miners drill and shovel in a tunnel.		65	Mining
Alaska Mining	U	1883	KY	Gray, gold seal. Miners drill and shovel in a tunnel.		65	Mining
Alaska Treadwell Gold Mining	I	1890's		Mining & mountain		35	Mining
Alaska Treadwell Gold Mining	I	1930's		Snow capped mountains & miners		35	Mining
Alaska United Gold Mining	U	1895	AK	Miners		149	Mining
Alaska-Mexican Gold Mining	I	1900's	CA	Working miners		50	Mining
Alaska-Natazhat Consolidated Min	I	1910's		Figures & seal		35	Mining
Alaska-United Gold Mining	I	1890's	CA	Goddess & miners		50	Mining

Name		Year	State	Description	Price	Category
Albemarle Dixie Equipment Mining	U	1900's	AZ Terr		15	Mining
Albert Mining Co.	I	1866	Canada		159	Mining
Alden Coal Mining	I	1910's		Mining & mountain scene	15	Mining
Algoma Consolidated Corp.	I	1930's		Figures	15	Mining
Algomah Mining	I	1910's	MI	Miners using drills	25	Mining
Alhambra Flume & Mercantile	I	1880's	MT Terr		12	Mining
Alleghany Mini	U	1888	CO	Trees, mountains, cabins, mill.	40	Mining
Alleghany Mining	I	1888	CO	Trees, mountains, cabins, mill.	40	Mining
Alleghany Mining Co.	I	1880's		Large of mountain town	30	Mining
Allegheny Mining	IC	1840's	NJ	Eagle, shield, flags, canal scene.	275	Mining
Alma Lincoln Mining	I	1930's	CO	Eagle	15	Mining
Alpewa Mining	IU	1900's		Three mining scenes	16	Mining
Alta-Idaho-Gold & Copper Mining	I	1900's		Three mining scenes	20	Mining
Alvarado Mining & Milling	I	1910's	WA	Mining scene	30	Mining
Amador Coalition Mines	IU	1920's	NV	Eagle	10	Mining
Amalgamated Silver Mines	I	1920	MT	Gray, bright gold seal. Miners	15	Mining
Amalgamated Silver Mines	I	1925	MT	Gray, bright gold seal. Miners	15	Mining
Amazon Gold	I	1904	NY	Miners	60	Mining
Ambassador Mines	I	1930's	WA		10	Mining
American & Mexican Silver Mining	I	1860's		Bond, Mining, Geo. Washington	500	Mining
American Alkali	I	1900's		Mountain scene & eagle	12	Mining
American Coal Co. of Alleghany	I	1860's	MD	Train & ship	90	Mining
American Coal Co. of Alleghany	I	1870's	MD	Train & ship	85	Mining
American Metals & Mining	I	1850	VT	Indians, waters eagle	200	Mining
American Mining	I	1850	VT	Indians. Hebe waters eagle, center.	200	Mining
American Mining	I	1850's		Indian maiden, hunter & eagle	155	Mining
American Mining	IC	1870's	CA	Eagle on shield.	121	Mining
American Mining-Norwich Mine	I	1850's		Allegorical figures	56	Mining
American Reclamation Co.	U	1910's	AZ	Eagle, capitol building & Indian	75	Mining
American River Water & Mining	IU	1860's	CA	Bond	300	Mining
American Smokeless Coal	I	1900's		Gold bond, bold seal	35	Mining
American-Mexican Mining & Smelt	IU	1920's	AZ	Smelting scene	18	Mining
Amygdaloid Mining	I	1970's	MI	Lady, with stamp	40	Mining
Amygdaloid Mining Company	U	1870	IL	Woman	750	Mining
Anaconda	I	1960's			10	Mining
Anaconda Gold Mining	I	1890's	CO	Gold seal	50	Mining
Anaconda Gold Mining	IC	1890's	CO	David H. Moffat	295	Mining
Anchor Gold Mining & Milling	IU	1900's		Gold mining	15	Mining
Anglo-Californian Gold Mining	IU	1850's	CA		95	Mining
Annie C. Gold Mining	IU	1890's		Mining	35	Mining

Antelope Mining	I	1907	ID	Landscape	47	Mining
Apex Gold Mining & Milling	I	1900's	CO	Miners loading ore cars	15	Mining
Arato Mining & Development Co.	I	1880's		World globe	45	Mining
Arcadia Coal Company, Ltd.	I	1914	Canada	Miners	50	Mining
Arcadian Consolidated Mining	U	1920	MI	Miners	77	Mining
Arcadian Consolidated Mining	I	1920's		Working miners	20	Mining
Argentine Cobalt	I		ME	Train & ship	20	Mining
Argentine Tierra Del Fuego Explor.	IC	1900's	Argentina	Company's ship & the coast. Back:Tierra del Fuego.	160	Mining
Arizona Commercial Mining	I	1920's		Mining	15	Mining
Arizona Extension Silver Mines	I	1920's	NV	Miners working & jackhammer equipment	10	Mining
Arizona Mining	U	1860's	NY	Mill at base of mountain.	352	Mining
Arizona Patagonic Silver Mining	I	1920's		Lady	10	Mining
Arlington Mining	I	1900's	WA	Seven working miners	12	Mining
Arlington Mining	I	1910's	WA	Seven working miners	10	Mining
Arlington Mining	I	1920's	WA	Seven working miners	10	Mining
Arno Gold Mining	IU	1890's		Embossed seal	10	Mining
Arnold Silver & Gold Mining	IU	1886	CA		400	Mining
Arrow Gold Mining	IU	1900's	CO	Embossed seal, Co. logo	10	Mining
Arrowhead Development	IU	1920's		Three mine	10	Mining
Atlanta Mines	I	1900's	AZ Terr	Eagle	10	Mining
Atlantic & Pacific Mining & Tunnel	IU	1880's		Lad & moneybag	80	Mining
Atlas Consol. Mining	IC	1970's		Atlas holding world on his shoulders	25	Mining
Atlas Wonder Mining Co.	U	1910's	CA	State seal	10	Mining
Atrato Mining	I	1880's		Gold dredger, two state seals	50	Mining
Auburn & Rock Creek Gold Mining	IU	1880's	CA		45	Mining
Aurora Mining	I	1900's	AZ Terr	Allegorical figures	50	Mining
Ave-Maria Gold Quartz Mine	IU	1850's	CA		95	Mining
Ave-Maria Gold Quartz Mine	I	1880's		Certificate of proprietorship	85	Mining
Azteca Copper Mining	I	1920's		Seal	10	Mining
Bagdad Copper	I	1920's		Woman & generator	10	Mining
Bagdad Copper	I	1930's		Woman & generator	10	Mining
Baker Hansen Prospecting, Mining	I	1910's	AZ		10	Mining
Balbach-Hoornbeck Mines Syndica	IU	1910's		Bond, Eagle on shield, green seal	15	Mining
Bald Butte Gold Mines	I	1930's	MT		12	Mining
Bald Mountain Mining	I	1880	NY	Grey. Vignette of Fryerhill, Leadville, Colorado.	50	Mining
Bald Mountain Mining Co.	I	1880's	NY	Mining scene	100	Mining
Baldy Sour Mining	IU	1870's	NV	Flag & eagle, gold seal	100	Mining

Baltimore-Nova Scotia Mining Co.	I	1900's	WV	Bond, with stamps	10	Mining
Bandora Mining & Milling	I	1892	CO		86	Mining
Banker Mining & Milling	I	1900's	CO	Gold seal, mining scene plus six miners in border	18	Mining
Banner State Gold, Silver & Copper	U	1900's	CO	State seal, two of goddess & eagle	8	Mining
Bannock Ditch & Mining	U	1870's		Farmer	38	Mining
Barbarossa Mines	U			Two ore car mining & mountain scene	5	Mining
Barry-Hollinger Gold Mines	IU	1920's		No	5	Mining
Basic Resources	I	1960's	UT	Smaller certificate	5	Mining
Basic Resources	I	1960's		Eagle	5	Mining
Basin Gold & Copper	IU	1890's		Two mining	20	Mining
Basin Gold & Silver Mining	IU	1890's	UT	Mining	23	Mining
Basin Gold & Silver Mining	IU	1910's		Miners in mine	15	Mining
Basin Mine & Concentrate	U	1890's	MT	Large eagle with flag	8	Mining
Basin Montana Tunnel	I	1950's			5	Mining
Batchelor-Khedive Mines	U	1900's	CO	Eagle	5	Mining
Baundary Red Mountain Mining	IU	1922	WA	Elk	8	Mining
Bear Creek Development	IU	1920's		Two mining scenes plus large mountain	20	Mining
Beaver Head Hydraulics Mining	I	1880's		Hydraulic mining scene	125	Mining
Beaver Head Hydraulics Mining	I	1880's		Strip mining	75	Mining
Belcher Extension Consolidated Mir	IU	1920's	NV		7	Mining
Ben Franklin Mining & Reduction Co.	I	1902	CO	Woman	69	Mining
Ben Hur Mining	I	1907		Miners,	19	Mining
Ben Hur Mining	I	1910	MT	Miners.	19	Mining
Bendigo Goldfields Ltd.	IC	1890's	Australia	Mine at Bendigo.	200	Mining
Bertha & Edith Gold Mining Co.	IC	1878	MT	Miners working above ground with sluice boxes	75	Mining
Bertha & Edith Gold Mining Co.	IC	1878		Miners working above ground with sluice boxes	75	Mining
Big Canon Copper Mining	I	1860's		Mountain & river scene	200	Mining
Big Five Mining	I	1910's	WY	5 Logo	5	Mining
Big Giant Silver Mining of Colorado	IU	1879	IL	Eagle	750	Mining
Big Ledge Copper	I	1920's	AZ	Working miners	12	Mining
Big Smoke Uranium	IU	1950's			10	Mining
Big Vein Pocahontas Coal	U	1900's	WA	Large eagle, harbors, & ships scene	5	Mining
Bigbull Consolidated Mining	I	1890's	CO	Working miners	15	Mining
Bigbull Consolidated Mining	I	1900's	CO		12	Mining
Bingham Mary Copper	IU	1900's	UT	Working miners	32	Mining
Bismark Silver Mining Co.	I	1882			61	Mining
Black Bear Consolidated	I	1930's	NV	Co. logo	10	Mining
Black Bird Gold Mining Co	I	1904		Black Bird	96	Mining
Black Diamond Copper Mining	I	1901	WV	Miners. Embossed green seal.	15	Mining
Black Diamond Copper Mining	I	1902	WV	Miners. Embossed green seal.	13	Mining
Black Diamond Gold Mining	I		CO		52	Mining

Name		Year	State	Description	Signer	Price	Category
Black Hills & Denver Gold Mining	I	1902	SD	Brown. Mountain trails. Miners in circles.		25	Mining
Black Hills & Denver Gold Mining	I	1902	SD	Brown. Mountain trails. Miners in circles.		25	Mining
Black Hills Copper	I	1905	AZ Terr	Miners		18	Mining
Black Hills Copper	I	1905	AZ Terr	Miners		18	Mining
Black Mountain Copper CO.	I	1900's	AZ Terr	Workers in mine		35	Mining
Black Sulphuret Silver Mining	U	1880's	CO	Miners.		165	Mining
BLACKBIRD MINING CO	I	1909	WV	Bird		68	Mining
Blackfoot Mining & Milling	U	1880's	MT	Large mining scene, old ore train		45	Mining
Blacklick & Conemaugh Petroleum	U	1860's		Three mining scenes		35	Mining
Blue Jacket Copper	I	1910's	ID	Mining scenes, gold seal		35	Mining
Blue Mountain Gold & Silver Mining	IU	1887	AK	Miners, train		295	Mining
Bodie Bluff Consolidated Mining	U	186-	CA	Mountain	Leland Stanford	1,950	Mining
Bodie Bluff Consolidation Mining	U	1860's	CA	Mining Site.	Leland Stanford	1,675	Mining
Bodie Tunnel & Mining	I	1870's				75	Mining
Bohemian Coal Mining Co. Ltd.	IC	1850's	Austria	Unusual attractive blue paper.		70	Mining
Boise Basin Mines Merger Co.	U	1910's	WA	Mining camp with railroad tracks		35	Mining
BOISE COUNTY MINING CO	I	1893	ID			54	Mining
Bolivia Gold Exploration Co.	I	1910's	CA	Three mining scenes, gold seal		35	Mining
Bonanza Chief Mining	I	1880's	MT	Miners & Indian maiden		50	Mining
Bonanza Gold Mines	I	1930's	UT	Figures		10	Mining
Bondholder Mining	IU	1881	NY	Miners		295	Mining
Boston & Ely Consolidated Mining	I	1910's		No		5	Mining
Boston & Sonora Mining	U	1900's		Eagle at bottom		10	Mining
Boston Gold-Copper Smelting	I	1900's	ME	Red seal		12	Mining
Boston Montana Mining	I	1920's				7	Mining
Boston Occidental Mining	I	1900's	CO			20	Mining
Boston-Cobalt Mining	I	1906	MA	Miners. Gold seal.		15	Mining
Boston-Cobalt Mining	I	1906	MA	Miners. Gold seal.		15	Mining
Boulder Gold Silver New York	I	1881	CO	Miners		46	Mining
Boulder Smelting	U	1890's	MT	Large Co. too		10	Mining
Boundary Camp Mining & Milling	I	1900's	SD	Mining		23	Mining
Br&enburg Coal Mining	I	1910's				70	Mining
Braceville Coal	U	1800's	IL	Gold bond, large mining		15	Mining
Braceville Coal Co.	U	1800's				15	Mining
Branch Mint Mining & Milling	I	1900's				10	Mining
Branch Mountain Mining & Milling	I	1900's	SD			25	Mining
Braunkohlen Und Chemische Industrie	IC	1920's	Germany			70	Mining
Bre-X Minerals LTD	I	1997		Two men and the world		180	Mining
Brilliant Mining	IU	1879	CA	Wagons, mill		250	Mining

British Guiana Gold Concessions	IU	1900's	ME	Lion, unicorn with seal	35	Mining
British Guiana Gold Concessions	IU	1900's	ME	Lion	22	Mining
Brittenstene Silver Mining	IU	1880's	CO	Five working miners	75	Mining
Broken Hill South Silver Mining	I	1915	Australia	Blue.	35	Mining
Broken Hill South Silver Mining Co.	I	1915	Australia	Blue.	35	Mining
Brokers' Gold Mining Co.	U	1890's	CO	Miners in tunnel	12	Mining
Buck Mountain Coal Co.	I	1860's		Miners & elk	75	Mining
Buckeye Mining & Tunneling	I	1880	CO	Four miners in an oval. State arms below.	85	Mining
Buckeye Mining & Tunneling	I	1880	CO	Four miners in an oval. State arms below.	85	Mining
Buena Gold Mining	I	1881	CO	Diagram of mine shafts and creeks, underprinted in gold	120	Mining
Buena Gold Mining	I	1881	CO	Diagram of mine shafts & creeks, underprint in gold	120	Mining
Buffalo & Susquehana Coal & Coke	I	1900's			35	Mining
Buffalo Mines	I	1910's			15	Mining
Buffalo Placer Mining & Milling	I	1910's	CO	Gold bond	12	Mining
Bull Domingo Mining	U	1884		Mining men N. B. Stevens	270	Mining
Bull Hill Gold Mining & Tunnel	I	1899	CO	Gold, Prospectors, cabin, mountains.	85	Mining
Bull Hill Gold Mining & Tunnel	I	1901	CO	Gold. Prospectors, cabin, mountains.	75	Mining
Bull Hill Mining	I	1890	CO	Brown. Gold seal.	25	Mining
Bull Hill Mining	I	1890	CO	Brown. Gold seal.	25	Mining
Bull Valley Gold Mining	I	1910's	UT	Miners at work, also six miner on border	35	Mining
Bullfrog Golden Sceptre Mining	IU	1908	AZ Terr	Green frog on toadstool	495	Mining
Bullfrog Pioneer Extension Mines	I	1910's	AZ	Mining	75	Mining
Bullfrog Teddy Gold Mining	I	1907	NV	Miners	50	Mining
Bullion Gold & Silver Mining	I	1930's	CA		10	Mining
Bunker Hill Consolidated Mining Co	I	1920's	CA	Gold seal, eagle on rock	35	Mining
Bunker Hill Consolidated Mining Co	I	1920's	CA	Gold seal, eagle on rock	35	Mining
Burma Ruby Mines Ltd.	IC	1890's	Burma		200	Mining
Burro Burro Mining Co	I	1883	AZ	Workers	129	Mining
Butler Gold Mining	IU	1930's		Gold seal, three mining	35	Mining
Butte & Coeur D'Alene Development	IC	1927			35	Mining
Butte & Coeur D'Alene Development	IU	1927			35	Mining
Butte & London Copper Dev.	IU	1900's	MT	Gold seal, seven of miners	20	Mining
Butte & Yerin ton Copper	I	1900's	MT	Eagle	20	Mining
Butte & Yerington Copper	I	1910's	MT	Eagle	20	Mining
Butte Copper Consolidated Mines	IU	1920's	SD	Ornate Border	10	Mining

Name		Date	Loc	Description	Price	Category
Butte Copper Mining & Smelting	I	1900's		Elk	10	Mining
Butte Copper Mining & Smelting	IU	1900's		Elk	10	Mining
Butte Ramsdell Copper	I	1910's	MT	Mining	20	Mining
Butte Ramsdell Copper	I	1920's	MT	Mining	15	Mining
Butte-Corbin Mining	U	1900's	MT	Large mining scene, gold seal	35	Mining
Butterfly-Terrible Gold Mining	I	1870's		State seal	15	Mining
C-O-D Gold Mining	U		CO		10	Mining
Cabin Creek & Kanawha Coal Co.	I	1880's	WVa	Bond	130	Mining
Cabin Creek Kanawha Co.	I	1870's		State seal	50	Mining
Cactus Mining	I	1880's	UT	Eagle	110	Mining
Cadillac Consolidated Mining	I	1880's		Mining	35	Mining
Caladonia Mining	IU	1920's	ID	Working miners	10	Mining
Calaveras Water & Mining	I	1882	CA	Green. Fancy dies at center.	50	Mining
Calaveras Water & Mining	I	1882	CA	Green. Fanc dies at center.	50	Mining
Calaveras Water & Mining	IU		CA		85	Mining
Calaveras Water & Mining Co.	I	1889	CA		20	Mining
Calaveras Water & Mining Co.	I	1889	CA		20	Mining
Calaveras Water & Mining Co.	I	1880's	CA		35	Mining
Calaveras Water & Mining Co.	IU	1880's	CA		35	Mining
Calea, S.A. Pentru Exploatarea	IC	1920's	Romania	Quarry, breaking rock, transporting it. Crossed hammers.	220	Mining
California Consol. Mining & Mill	I	1900's	AZ Terr	Mining	30	Mining
California King Gold Mines	I	1902	CA	Crown	50	Mining
California Liberty Gold Mines	U	1900's	AZ	Mine	15	Mining
California Magnesia Co.	PI	1900's	CA	Cable car used to carry ore down a mountain	200	Mining
California-Ahumada Mining	I	1920's	AZ	Gold. Mountain trails. Miner in circles.	25	Mining
California-Ahumada Mining	I	1930's	AZ	Gold. Mountain trails. Miner in circles	25	Mining
California-Divide Mining	IU	1910's	NV	Miners sluicing for gold, gold seal	15	Mining
Californian Gold Mining	I	1850's			40	Mining
Callahan Mining	IC	1969		Nice vignette of gold weighing scale.	25	Mining
Callahan Mining	IC	1969		Nice vignette of gold weighing scale.	25	Mining
Calumet & Arizona Mining	I	1910's	AZ Terr	Mining	15	Mining
Calumet & Arizona Mining	I	1920's	AZ Terr	Mining	15	Mining
Calumet & Copper Creek Mining	I	1900's	NV	Bond, Mining scene	45	Mining
Calumet & Hecla, Inc.	SP	1900's		Indians around cooking campfire	35	Mining
Cambria County Coal	I	1910's	PA	Miners & coal cars	20	Mining
Cambria County Coal Co.	U	1910's		Two Mining	15	Mining
Cameron Gold & Silver Mining	IU	1880's	CO	Gold seal	50	Mining
Camp Summit Mining	IC	1880's	CO	Train, river, mountains, prospector.	187	Mining

Name	Type	Date	State/Country	Vignette	Price	Category
Cannon Ball Gold Mining	I	1900's	CO	Cannon & gold seal	20	Mining
Canterbury Mining	IU	1901	WT	Canterbury Cathedral	250	Mining
Capital Gold & Silver Mining	U	1888	OR	Soldier	225	Mining
Capuzaya Mining	IU	1900's		Mining	30	Mining
Carbonate Hill Gold Mining Milling	U	1890's		Mountain (Leadville)	449	Mining
Carboneras De Pelayo, Soc. Minera	IC	1850's	Spain	Miners, tools, fruit, flowers. Mining scenes.	640	Mining
Carolina Queen Consol. Mining	IU	1884	NH	Miners, tiger	250	Mining
Carp Lake Mining	IU	1861	MI	Lake, mine shaft	295	Mining
Carsons Creek Consolidated Mining	I	1850's	CA	Allegorical figure in chariot	60	Mining
Cascade Mining	I	1870's		Indian & sailor at harbor	35	Mining
Cascade Mining Co.	U	1880's	CO	Indian, sailor, ship, Zeepee & state seal	45	Mining
Cash Boy Consolidated Mining	IU	1910's	NV		10	Mining
Cash Boy Consolidated Mining	IU	1920's	NV		10	Mining
Cash Entr Mining	I	1910's		Co. logo	10	Mining
Casseler Braunkohlenbergbau A. G.	IC	1900's	Germany	Arms of the City of Cassel, flowers & leaves.	80	Mining
Castle Dome Mining & Smelting	I	1880's		Castle turret	60	Mining
Castle Rock Milling & Mines	U	1910's	CO	Working miners	35	Mining
Catalpa Mining	I	1880's		Working miners	60	Mining
Catalpa Mining	I	1900's		Working miners	50	Mining
Cataract Gold & Silver Mining	IC	1860's	CA	Woman by pillar. G. H. Parsons	341	Mining
Catherine Mining & Exploration	I	1900's		Nice mining	25	Mining
Cedar Hollow Lime Co.	I	1830's		Mountain scene	95	Mining
Cedar Tree Mining & Milling	I	1881	NY	Cedar Tree. Indians watch from cliff. Prospector	100	Mining
Cedar Tree Mining & Milling	I	1881	NY	Cedar Tree. Indians watch from cliff. Prospector in oval.	100	Mining
Centennial Claims	U	1930's	WA		10	Mining
Centennial Claims	U		ID	Gold seal	10	Mining
Centennial Mines	I	1930's	ID	Milling & smelting operation	10	Mining
Central El Dorado Gold Mining	IU	1910	AZ	Eagle	300	Mining
Chain O'Mines	I	1930's	NV	Gold bond	10	Mining
Chain O'Mines	I		NV	Voting trust certificate	10	Mining
Chance Silver Mining	U	1870's		Two miners	20	Mining
Chaparral Hill Gold Mining	I				10	Mining
Charbonnage De Belle-Vue	IC	1850's	Belgium		60	Mining
Charbonnage Du Paradis	IC	1850's	Belgium		56	Mining
Charbonnages Andre Dumont	IC	1900's	Belgium	Dumont	100	Mining
Charbonnages De Bray	IC	1870's	Belgium	Leon Orban	32	Mining
Charbonnages De Rety	IC	1870's	France	Border of leaves & flowers.	36	Mining
Charbonnages Du Levant De Mons	IC	1920's	Belgium		36	Mining
Charbonnages Prokhorow (Donetz)	IC	1890's	Russia	Three mining vignettes.	44	Mining

Charles H. Jacobs Mining Company	I	1887	Arkansas	Miners	50	Mining
Charleston Mining, Mfg & Improve	U	1890's		Red seal	12	Mining
Chicamonstone Copper Mining	U	1890's			15	Mining
Chico Gold & Silver Mining	IC	1860's	CA	Mining scene, mill.	341	Mining
Chico Gold & Silver Mining	U	1860's		Nevada mining scene	39	Mining
Chonchilula Gold Reef Mines of Calif	IC	1900's	SD/NY	Photovignette of a cliff.	200	Mining
Christmas Wonder Mining	PI	1907	AZ/NV	Santa Claus holding a gold nugget	250	Mining
Chrysolite Mining	Proof	1880's	NY	Capital, Miners underground.	253	Mining
Clara-Swansea Mining	I	1920's	NV	Working miners with ore car	35	Mining
Clara-Swansea Mining	U	1920's	NV	Working miners with ore car	25	Mining
Claremont Peak Grovel Gold Mine	I	1810's	CA		28	Mining
Clear Creek Mining & Development	U	1870's	CO		20	Mining
Cleary Mine	I	1920	Canada	Lion and horse head	69	Mining
Clememcau Minim	I	1940's	AZ	Portrait	30	Mining
Clinton Iron Co.	I	1870's		Seated woman	50	Mining
Clove Spring Iron Works	U	1870's		Allegorical figures	50	Mining
Co. Minera De Mina Grande Y Ane	IU	1911	Mexico	Orange. Miners.	10	Mining
Co. Minera Juanita Y Anexa	IU	1916	Mexico	Tan underprint, green border.	15	Mining
Coast Range Gold & Silver Mining	IC	1860's	CA	Sunset, mining scene. Frank Cooper	308	Mining
Cobalt Central Mines	I	1900's		Two miners	20	Mining
Coeur d'Alene Mining & Smelting	I	1911	ID	Stag.	50	Mining
Coeur d'Alene Mining & Smelting	I	1915	ID	Stag.	50	Mining
Coloma Gold Mining	IU	1905	AZ/CA	James W. Marshall	275	Mining
Colonial Silver Mines	IU	1900's		Three figures	15	Mining
Colorado Bar Gold Mining	I	1894	CO	Waterfall	137	Mining
Colorado Blue Bell Mining	I	1900's		Eagle	15	Mining
Colorado City & Manitau Mining	I	1900's		Working miners	35	Mining
Colorado Cripple Creek Gold Mining	I	1890's	CO	Miners at work	150	Mining
Colorado King Gold Mining Co.	I		CA	Miners	103	Mining
Colorado Tungsten Mines	U	1900's		Eagle, gold seal	10	Mining
Columbia County Iron Mining	IC	1871	NY	State Arms. Ornate green underprint. Red seal.	60	Mining
Columbia County Iron Mining	IU	1871	NY	State Arms. Ornate green underprint. Red seal.	60	Mining
Columbia Development Co.	IU	1880's	AZ Terr	Working miners with ore cars	35	Mining
Columbia Gold & Silver Mining	IC	1860's	NY	Underground mining scene.	209	Mining
Comet Mining	IU	1880's	UT Terr	Large vignette of miners & ore cars	295	Mining

Name	Type	Date	Location	Description	Price	Category
Commercial Coal	I	1900's	PA	Loaded coal car	20	Mining
Commercial Coal	I	1910's	PA	Loaded coal car	15	Mining
Commercial Gold Mining Co	I	1926	WY	Miners	145	Mining
Compania Minera De Mina Grande	I	1911	Mexico	Orange. Miners.	10	Mining
Compania Minera Juanita Y Anexa	I	1916	Mexico	Tan underprint, green border.	15	Mining
Companie de Ciment Unic	IU	1925	Montreal	Banknote style border	10	Mining
Companie Franc. Mines d'Or Canada	I	1929	Canada	Blue & Green	25	Mining
Companie Francaise des Mines d'Or	I	1929	Canada	Blue & Green	25	Mining
Comstock & Keystone Mining	I	1940's	Canada	Large eagle, with stamps	25	Mining
Comstock Limited	I	1930's	NV	Gold Bond with coupons & eagle	25	Mining
Comstock Tunnel & Drainage Gold	IC	1919		Miners drilling underground	95	Mining
Comstock Tunnel Co.	I	1880's	NY	Eagle	40	Mining
Concordia Virginia Mining Co.	I	1920's	NY	Three mining vignettes	35	Mining
Consolidated Arizona Smelting Co.	I	1910's		Large smelting works	35	Mining
Consolidated Chollar-Gould, Sava	I	1950's	CA		15	Mining
Consolidated Coal Co.	SP			Ore cars	25	Mining
Consolidated Esperanza Mining Co	I	1870's		Miners	175	Mining
Consolidated Gold Corp.	I	1920's		Embossed seal	10	Mining
Consolidated Gold Fields of S Africa	IC	1890's	So. Africa	Arms of South Africa.	280	Mining
Consolidated Mines & Smelting	I	1930's		Miners	20	Mining
Consolidated Nevada-Utah Mining	I	1910's		Miners working by lantern	20	Mining
Consolidated Republican Mountain	U	1870's	CO	Indian princess & state seal	35	Mining
Consolidated Republican Mountain	U	1880's	CO	Indian princess & state seal	20	Mining
Consolidated South Spring Hill Min.	I	1890's			32	Mining
Consolidated Virginia & Andes Corp.	I	1830's	NV	Gold seal, three of working miners at camp	35	Mining
Consolidated Virginia Mining	I	1930's	NV	Co. logo	15	Mining
Contact Gold Mining & Tunnel Co.	I	1890's	CO	Lady with star	28	Mining
Contact Gold Mining & Tunnel Co.	I	1900's	CO	Lady with star	24	Mining
Continental Consolidated Mines	I	1907	WY	Green seal.	15	Mining
Continental Consolidated Mines	IU	1907	WY	Green seal	15	Mining
Continental La Fiera Mines	IU	1965	Ontario		5	Mining
Continental Mining Co.	IU	1880's	WY	Three mining vignettes	50	Mining
Cook Gold Mining of Colorado	I	1860's			180	Mining
Copper Crown Mining	U	1900's	MI	Metallic copper title, and crown. Eagle.	627	Mining

Name		Date	Location	Description	Signer	Price	Category
Copper Giant Gold Mine Wyoming	I	1899	WY	Miners		77	Mining
Copper Giant Mining	I	1883	AZ	Men	John N. Goodwin	75	Mining
Copper Knob Mining	I	1880's		Cherub & mine		49	Mining
Copper Metals Co.	I	1910's	AZ Terr	Gold bond		30	Mining
Copper Plate Sheet & Tube	I	1928	NJ	Red. Snarling tiger.		15	Mining
Copper Plate Sheet & Tube	I	1928	NJ	Red. Snarling tiger.		15	Mining
Copper Range Co.	I	1910's	MI	Mining		18	Mining
Copper Range Co._	I	1950's	MI	Three bare-chested miners		18	Mining
Copper Range Company	U		MI	God-looking men		69	Mining
Copperfield Mining	I	1920's		Working miners		35	Mining
Corbin Copper Co.	I	1910's	MI	Ore cars at mine entrance		35	Mining
Corinth Silver-Lead Mines Co., Ltd.	I	1828	Canada	Mining scene		65	Mining
Cory Mine Co	IU	1930	CA	Trees, river, gold nugget		39	Mining
Cory Mine Limited	IU	1930's		Volcano		35	Mining
Corydon Mining	IC	1860's	NY	Miners above and underground.		440	Mining
Coulson Gold Mines	I	1946	Canada			56	Mining
Coulterville Virginia Mining	IU	1880's				75	Mining
Cracker Jack Mining	I	1900's	AZ	Two mining & smelting plant		45	Mining
Creede Contact Mining	I	1910's	CO	State seal		15	Mining
Crescant Mining	I	1900's		Large mining scene		45	Mining
Cresson Consolidated Gold Mining	I		CO			10	Mining
Cripple Creek Colorado Mining	I	1897	CO			88	Mining
Cripple Creek Consolidated Mining	I	1904	CO	Mountain		79	Mining
Cripple Creek Gold Temple Mining	I	1902	CO	Miners	F.F. Ash	74	Mining
Cripple Creek Mining & Milling	I	1936	Canada	Blue		10	Mining
Cripple Creek Mining & Milling	I	1936	Canada	Blue		10	Mining
Cripple Creel Gold Rock Mining	IU	1890's	CO	Mining		35	Mining
Cromwell Mining Development	I	1890's		Miners		35	Mining
Crown Chartered Gold Mining	I	1911	Montreal	Porccupine		75	Mining
Crown Chartered Gold Mining	I	1913	Montreal	Porcupine		100	Mining
Crown Mining	I	1880's		Mountain mining		125	Mining
Crusader Oil & Uranium Company	U	1958	CO	Mountain		75	Mining
Crystal Gold & Silver Mining	IC	1860's	CA	Tunnel, hills.		352	Mining
Crystal Mountain Mining & Drainage	I	1897	CO	Seven miners. Gold.		60	Mining
Crystal Mountain Mining & Drainage	I	1897	CO	Seven miners. Gold.		60	Mining
Cullman Coal & Coke	I	1900's	AL	Mining		30	Mining
Cumberland Consol. Gold Mining	IU	1900's	IA	Red seal		15	Mining
Curtis Minerals	IU	1960's	UT	Large eagle		10	Mining
Cusa-Mexicana Mining	IU			Miners		15	Mining
Cusi Mexicana Mining	I	1934-3	ME	Black. Prospectors, burro, mountains.		15	Mining

Cusi Mexicana Mining	I	1934-37	ME	Black. Prospectors, burro, mountains.	15	Mining
Cuyuna-Sultana Iron Co.	I	1910's		Miners panning for gold	35	Mining
Cyclone Mining	U	1900's	SD	Two mining & smelting plant	30	Mining
Daddy Mining	I	1920	MA	Green.	15	Mining
Daddy Mining	I	1920	MA	Green.	15	Mining
Dahl Mining	IU	1950's	WA	Large eagle	10	Mining
Dahlgren Mining	I	1880's		Mining	35	Mining
Dahlonega Gold Mining	I	1880's		Eagle &.flag	50	Mining
Daly Mining	I	1930's	UT	Three mining scenes	25	Mining
Darby Mine	I	1881	NY	Grey/Black. Miners underground. Eagle shield	60	Mining
Davenport Consolidated Gold Min	U	1910's	NV	Mining scene, six miners in border	35	Mining
Davidson Copper Mining	I	1867	NC	All blue. Factory.	35	Mining
Davidson Copper Mining	I	1867	NC	All blue. Factory.	35	Mining
Davidson Copper Mining	I	1860's		Embossed seal, milling plant	125	Mining
De Beers Consolidated Mines Limited	IC	1930's	So. Africa		176	Mining
De Lamar Mining Co. Ltd.	IC	1890's	ID	Smelter & village.	128	Mining
Deadwood-Terra Mining	I	1880	NY	Brown. Indians by campfire. Cherub below.	200	Mining
Deadwood=Terra Mining	I	1880		Brown. Indians by campfire. Cherub below.	200	Mining
Death Valley Arcalvada Consolidated	I	1900's	NY	Gold bond, large smelting scenes	50	Mining
Death Valley Big Bell Mining	U	1900's	AZ	Three mining	35	Mining
Death Valley Consolidated Mining	I		NV		30	Mining
DeBeers Consolidated Mines	IU	1921	GB	Coat-of-arms	200	Mining
Decatur Silver Mining Co.	I	1880's	CO	Mining	75	Mining
Deep River Copper Co.	I	1860's		Seminude woman	125	Mining
Deep Tunnel Mining	IU	1930's			35	Mining
Defender Gold Mining	I	1890's	CO	Three mining	50	Mining
Defense Metals	U		ID	Open pit mining & mill	20	Mining
Defiance Mining	I	1875	IN	Eagle (Inyo)	155	Mining
Del Norte Comstock Co.	I	1860's		Seated lady	200	Mining
Delaware Mining	I	1860's	MI	State Seal, embossed seal	75	Mining
Delaware Mining _	I	1860's	MI	of hunters, farmers, & pioneers, with stamp	75	Mining
Denbigh Mining	I	1920's		Two mining, plus woman with banner	35	Mining
Des Moines Gold Mining	IU	1890's	CO	Miners & mountains	25	Mining
Deseret Silver Mining	U	1870	MI	Landscape	69	Mining
Desert Gold Mines	IU	1910's	AZ	Miners	25	Mining
Dexter Mining Co.	I	1900's	WY	Bond, two miners pushing ore car	25	Mining
Diamond Black Butte Consol.	I	1900's		Mining	25	Mining
Diana Mining	IU	1882	AZ		300	Mining
Dinero Consol Mining & Tunnel	I	1900's	CO	Working miners & mountain scene	25	Mining

Dirigo Slate Quarry	Proof	1870's	ME	Men drill and split slate.	121	Mining
Divide City Mining	IU	1920's		Three mining, gold seal	25	Mining
Divide Extension Consolidated	I	1930's	NV	Co. logo with stamp	25	Mining
Dividend Gold Mining Company	U	1890	CO	Mining men	51	Mining
Dividend Mining & Milling	IC	1907	AZ	Light orange underprint. Eagle	15	Mining
Dividend Mining & Milling	IU	1907	AZ	Light orange underprint. Eagle	13	Mining
Dixie Extension Consolidated	I	1931's		Co. logo with stamp	25	Mining
Dona Carolina Gold & Silver Mining	IC	1860's	CA	Train.	341	Mining
Dona Louisa Copper & Gold	IU	1906	DE	Miners	75	Mining
Donna Louisa Mining	I	1900's	NV	Two mining, gold seal	35	Mining
Douglas Gold & Silver Mining	I	1864	NV	Power of Attorney revenue affixed, treasurer's initials.	150	Mining
Douglas Gold & Silver Mining	I	1864	NV Terr	Power of Attorney revenue affixed, treasurer's initials.	150	Mining
Douglas Mining & Leasing	IU	1920's		Elk	20	Mining
Eames Petroleum Gold & Silver Sm	IU	1880's			50	Mining
Eames Petroleum Iron	IU	1880's			45	Mining
Early Silver Mining Co.	U	1880's	CO	Working miners	25	Mining
East Blue Hill Gold & Silver Mining	I	1880	ME	Miners	69	Mining
East Divide Mining	IC	1920's	NV	Mining scene	25	Mining
East Divide Mining	IC	1920's	NV	Mining scene	25	Mining
Eastern Montana Mining & Smelt	I	1870's		Mining	175	Mining
Eastern Montana Mining & Smelting	U	1870's		Mining	35	Mining
Eastern Ore on Gold Mining	I	1890's		Bond	35	Mining
Eastern Oregon Gold Mining	IU	1880's			35	Mining
Economy Mining & Milling	IU	1930	CO	Woman, ship, train	60	Mining
Edna Gold Mining C_ o.	U	1890's	CA	Mining	35	Mining
Edwin Booth Gold Mining & Milling	U	1890's	CO	Engraving of Edwin Booth	198	Mining
Egypt Silver Mining	U	1899	ME	Miners working on side of hill.	35	Mining
Egypt Silver Mining	U	1899	ME	Miners working on side of hill.	35	Mining
El Dorado Gold & Silver Mining	IC	1860's	CA	Prosperity gestures at sunset.	352	Mining
El Paso Extension Gold Mines	U	1910's			20	Mining
El Picacho Gold & Silver Mining	I	1863	CA	Woman	92	Mining
El Salvador Silver Mines	I	1910's	CO	Eagle	15	Mining
Elba, S.A. Di Miniere E Di Alti Forni	IC	1920's	Italy	Blast-furnaces & mines. Underprint of logo.	128	Mining
Eldora-Grand Gold Mining	I	1901	CO	Gold borders. Mining camp. Picks and shovels.	45	Mining

Name	Type	Date	State	Description	Price	Category
Eldora-Grand Gold Mining	I	1901	CO	Gold borders. Mining camp. Picks and shovels.	45	Mining
Elizabeth Mining	I	1892	MT	1889 Morgan silver dollar	375	Mining
Elkhorn Coal Corp._	I	1910's		Coal train	20	Mining
Ellensburg h Mining, Milling & Smelt	I	1870's		Horse & man before smelting plant	20	Mining
Ely Consolidated Copper	IC	1917	UT	Brown. Eagle and shield, train, Indian camp.	15	Mining
Ely Consolidated Copper	IU	1917	UT	Brown. Eagle and shield, train, Indian camp.	15	Mining
Ely Consolidated Copper	I	1920's	NV	Eagle	25	Mining
Ely-Witch Copper	I	1900's		Head & wing, embossed seal	20	Mining
Ely-Witch Copper	IU	1900's		Head & wing, embossed seal	25	Mining
Empire Gold & Silver Mining	IC	1860's	CA	Miner with rail cart.	341	Mining
Empire Gold & Silver Mining	I	1860's		Bond, mining scenes	300	Mining
Empire Lee Mining	IU	1920's	CO	Co. logo, grey seal	15	Mining
Empire Lee Mining	I			Grey seal	15	Mining
Empire State Silver Mining	I	1860's		Scenic	175	Mining
Empress Gold Mining & Milling	I	1896	CO	Grey. Orange underprint. Eagle.	70	Mining
Empress Gold Mining & Milling	I	1896	CO	Grey. Orange underprint. Eagle.	70	Mining
Estella Gold Mining	I	1900	CO	Gold. Mine entrance at the foot of a mountain.	50	Mining
Ethel Consolidated Mines	IU	1900's	WA	Trees & buildings	35	Mining
Etowah Gold Mining	U	1900's		Three mining	15	Mining
Eudora Mining & Milling	I	1896-9	CO	Chocolate brown. Miners underground.	70	Mining
Eureka Climax Mining	U	1910's	NV	Large mining	10	Mining
Eureka Gold & Silver Mining	IC	1860's	CA	State arms.	303	Mining
Excelsior Coal	U	1870's		Mining	25	Mining
Excelsior Coal _	I	1870's		Mining	50	Mining
Excelsior Drift Gold Mining	U	1890's		Train & factory	25	Mining
Exchequer Gold & Silver Mining	I	1900's		Quality printing	15	Mining
Exchequer Mining	I	1900's	NV	Co. logo & miners	15	Mining
Fagan Consolidated Silver Mines	IU	1920's	NV	Eagle with flag	15	Mining
Fairbanks Gold & Silver Mining	I	1880's	CO	Bond, mining, state seal, gold seal	200	Mining
Fairview Gold Mining	I	1880's	CO	Mining	75	Mining
Fairview Golden Boulder Mining	U	1900's		Golden boulder	10	Mining
Farmer Jones Gold Mining	U	1900's		Large mining at bottom	10	Mining
Farmsville Coal & Iron	U	1890's		Mining scene with two factory	20	Mining
Farwell Consolidated Mining	I	1880's			50	Mining
Favorite Gold Mining	I	1890's	CO	Mountains, embossed seal	35	Mining
Favorite Gold Mining	I	1900's	CO	Mountains, embossed seal	35	Mining

Federal Hill Mining	U	1900's		Two mining, seal	15	Mining
Fidelity Gold & Silver Mining	U	1880's	PA	Miners shows sample.	176	Mining
Findley Gold Mining Co.	I	1900's	CO	Rust seal	35	Mining
First National Copper	I	1909	NV	Green. Eagle.	18	Mining
First National Copper	I	1909	NV	Green. Eagle.	18	Mining
First National Copper	I	1910-1	NV	Orange. Eagle.	18	Mining
First National Copper	I	1910-19	NV	Orange. Eagle.	18	Mining
First National Mining	U	1900's	NV	Ore carts with miners & two burros	35	Mining
Fisherman Gold Mines Co.	IC	1900's	AZ/CO	Underground mining, border in goldprint.	92	Mining
Flagstaff Gold Mining Co.	U	1920's	OR	Three of mining scene, mountains & valleys	15	Mining
Flint Creek Mining	I	189-	MT	Eagle. Miners. U.S. silver dollars as counters.	30	Mining
Flint Creek Mining	I	189-	MT	Eagle. Miners. U.S. silver dollars as counters.	30	Mining
Flora Bell Mining	I	1910's		Bond	35	Mining
Florence Divide Mining	I	1919	NV	Brown.	40	Mining
Florence Divide Mining	I	1919	NV	Brown.	40	Mining
Flusey Lead Co	I	1900's	WA	Miners	35	Mining
Fortune Dyke Gold Mining Co.	IC	1900's	CO	Underground mining, crossed pick, shovel, miners.	96	Mining
Fortunia, Intl Diamant Handelaarsver	IC	1910's	Belgium	Statue.	40	Mining
Four Aces Mining	I	1906	NV	Red, brown. Hand holds four aces.	400	Mining
Four Aces Mining	I	1906	NV	Red, brown. Hand holds four aces.	400	Mining
Fours A Coke De Chirokaia, S.A.	IC	1890's	Russia	Drawing of coke ovens.	70	Mining
Francaise & Americaine de San Fran.	IU	1850	France	Miners	1,000	Mining
France Shipping	U	1927		Island and bridge	48	Mining
Fredericksburg Mining	U	1860's		Indian & naked man	100	Mining
Free Coinage Gold Mining	I	1890's	CO	Train, ship & eagle	35	Mining
French Bob Gold Mining Co., Ltd	IC	1880's	So. Africa	Alfred Beit	240	Mining
Furnace Creek Copper	I	1900's	CA		35	Mining
Furnace Valley Copper Co.	I	1900's		Miners & horses working in tunnel, seal	50	Mining
G.V.B. Mining	I	1890's		Working miners	75	Mining
Gallia Szent Antal Gold Mining Co.	IC	1900's	Hungary		90	Mining
Game Ridge Consolidated Mines	I	1900's	CA	Train & smelter	75	Mining
Game Ridge Consolidated Mining	IU	1880's		Miners drilling in mine	75	Mining
Game Ridge Consolidated Mining	I			Trustee certificate	75	Mining
Garfield Consolidated Mining	I	1890's	WY		50	Mining
Garner Creek Gold Mining	I	1900's	CO	Large mining	35	Mining
Garner Creek Gold Mining	I	1920's	CO	Large mining	15	Mining

Name		Date	State	Description	Price	Category
Garnett Gold Mining	I	1896	WV	1st Mortgage 8% Gold Bond.Green.Red $500 underprint	75	Mining
Garnett Gold Mining	I	1896	WV	1 st Mortgage 8% Gold Bond. Green. Red	75	Mining
Gaston Mining	Proof	1870's	NC	Buildings, chimney, mule-drawn wagons.	286	Mining
Gavilan Mining & Milling Comp	U	1891	CA	three miners, one holding sledge hammer.	25	Mining
Gem Hill Silver Mining & Tunnel	IC	1860's		Wm. H. Ladd	330	Mining
Genii Consolidated Mines Co., Ltd.	IU	1930's	NV	Miners	35	Mining
Geronimos Limited	I				50	Mining
Gibraltar Silver Hill Mining	IU	1920's	NV	Mining	35	Mining
Gila Copper Sulphate Co.	I	1910's	AZ	Three	35	Mining
Gila River Mining of New Orleans	U	1800's	NM	Eagle & statue	35	Mining
Gilbert Gold Pan Mining	U	1900's	NV	Mining	15	Mining
Gilpin-Eureka Mines Co.	I	1910's		Figures	15	Mining
Gilpin-Hurricane Gold Mining Co., t	IU	1910's		Mining, gold seal	35	Mining
Gilpin-Mohawk Gold Mining Company	I	1912	AZ	Indian	124	Mining
Girard Gold and Silver	U	1880's	NJ	Miners.	264	Mining
Glen Alden Coal Co.	I	1930's		Scrip certificate	15	Mining
Glen Alden Coal Co.	I	1930's		Miners working	15	Mining
Glen Alden Coal Co.	I	1930's		Bond	15	Mining
Globe Dominion Copper	I	1917	AZ	Green. State seal.	7	Mining
Globe Dominion Copper	I	1918	AZ	Green. State seal.	7	Mining
Globe Dominion Copper Mine	IU	1910's		State seal	35	Mining
Gold & Silver Mining	U	1860's		Mining scene, horses, & wagon	35	Mining
Gold Center Mining & Development	IU	1900's	AZ Terr	Mountain	35	Mining
Gold Cliff Mining & Reduction of Ari	IU	1890's		Eagle	75	Mining
Gold Collar Mining & Milling	I	1900's	AZ	Embossed seal	10	Mining
Gold Cord Mining	I	1902	CO	Mountains	150	Mining
Gold Cord Mining And Smelting Co.	IC	1900's	WY/CO	Stream in the Rocky Mountains.	80	Mining
Gold Creek Nevada Townsite	IU	1898	CO	Surveyors	100	Mining
Gold Development Company of Utah	I	1904	WY	1st Mortgage 5% Gold Loan. Miner with pneumatic drill.	45	Mining
Gold Development Company of Utah	I	1904	WY	1st Mtg 5% Gold Loan. Miner with pneumatic drill.	45	Mining
Gold Dollar Consol Mining	U	1990's	WY		342	Mining
Gold Eagle Mining & Milling	I	1900's		Eagle	35	Mining
Gold Exploration Co.	I	1890's	CO	Mining	35	Mining
Gold Field & Bull Frog Coop Prosp	I	1900's	AZ	Portrait of Lincoln	50	Mining
Gold Hammer Mines & Tunnel	IC	1900's	CO		132	Mining
Gold Hammer Mines & Tunnel Co	I	1909	CO		100	Mining

Gold Hammer Mines & Tunnel Co	I	1909	CO		100	Mining
Gold Hammer Mines & Tunnel Co	I	1911	CO		100	Mining
Gold Hill & Lee Mountain Mining	U	1880's	MT	Mountain & mining scenes	50	Mining
Gold Hill Mining	I	1890	CA	First Mortgage 10% Gold Bond. Miners in tunnel.	95	Mining
Gold Hill Mining	I	1890	CA	First Mortgage 10% Gold Bond. Miners in tunnel.	95	Mining
Gold Hill Mining	U		CA	Large smelting plant in Grass Valley	35	Mining
Gold King Consolidated Mines	I	1900's		Mine smelter with train	50	Mining
Gold Mountain Co.	IU	1880's	NV	1,000 shares to Mark Twain	50	Mining
Gold Park Mining & Milling	I	1902	NV	Green. Miners in circles. Mill, mountain.	18	Mining
Gold Park Mining & Milling	I	1902	NV	Green. Miners in circles. Mill, mountain.	18	Mining
Gold Placer Mining	I	1880's	CT	Man shooting water at mountainside.	60	Mining
Gold Placer Mining	I	1880's	CT	Gold seal. Man shooting water at mountainside	60	Mining
Gold Point Consolidated Mines, Inc	I	1910's		Miners	35	Mining
Gold Reef Consolidated Gold & Silver	U	1900's		Co. logo	15	Mining
Gold Reef Consolidated Mining	I	1900's	NV	Co. logo	35	Mining
Gold Shield Mining Co.	I	1900's	IL	Mining	35	Mining
Gold Syndicate	I	1898	WV	Maroon frame, seal and prospector underprint. Miners.	45	Mining
Gold Syndicate	I	1898	WV	Prospector underprint. Miners.	45	Mining
Gold Tunnel Mining	IU	1900's	AZ Terr	Working miners	100	Mining
Gold Valley Main Tunnel & Mining	U	1860's	CA		35	Mining
Golden Age Number Two Mining	I	1900's	CO		35	Mining
Golden Anchor Mining	IU	1900's	AZ	Woman with wreath	35	Mining
Golden Center Mines	I	1936	DE	Blue. Eagle.	18	Mining
Golden Center Mines	I	1936	DE	Blue. Eagle.	18	Mining
Golden Cycle Mining & Reduction	I	1910's		Large mining plant	35	Mining
Golden Cycle Mining & Reduction	I	1920's		Large mining plant	15	Mining
Golden Cycle Mining & Reduction	I	1930's		Large mining plant	15	Mining
Golden Cycle Mining Co.	I	1910's		Temporary certificate with stamps	15	Mining
Golden Cycle Mining Co.	I	1920's	CO	Cripple Creek mines, embossed seal	35	Mining
Golden Cycle Mining Co.	I	1950's		Milling plant	15	Mining

Golden Cycle Mining Co.	U			Temporary certificate	15	Mining
Golden Stairs Mining & Leasing	I	1890's		Working miners, embossed seal	35	Mining
Golden Sun Mining & Milling	I	1904	WY	Gold. Miners.	35	Mining
Golden Sun Mining & Milling	I	1904	WY	Gold. Miners.	35	Mining
Golden Treasure Co.	I	1900's	AZ	Embossed seal	35	Mining
Goldfield Blue Bell Mining	I	1900	AZ	Mining	35	Mining
Goldfield Combination Fraction Mini	IU	1910	NV	Working miners, with stamps	35	Mining
Goldfield Deep Mines	I	1950	NV		15	Mining
Goldfield Deep Mines	IU	1950	NV		15	Mining
Goldfield Eastern Mining	I	1909-10	NV	Orange. Liberty holds wreath.	25	Mining
Goldfield Eastern Mining	I	1909-10	NV	Orange. Liberty holds wreath.	25	Mining
Goldfield Gold Banner Leasing Min.	IC	1906	NV	Gold Seal. Eagle.	25	Mining
Goldfield Gold Banner Leasing Min.	IU	1906	NV	Gold Seal. Eagle.	25	Mining
Goldfield Panhard Mines Co.	IC	1900's	NV	Underground mining.	70	Mining
Goldfield Ruby Hill Mining	IU	1900's	AZ	Grey seal	15	Mining
Goldfield Treasure Mining	I	1900's	AZ Terr	Two mining	35	Mining
Goldfield-Candelaria Mining	U	1900's		Miners with ore cart	35	Mining
Good Morning Gold Mining Invest.	I	1900's	AZ Terr	Miners with ore car at mine entrance	50	Mining
Gould & Curry Mining	I	1920's			15	Mining
Gould & Curry Mining	I	1930's		With stamps	15	Mining
Governor Low Gold & Silver Mining	U	1860's	NV	Eagle	100	Mining
Grafton Consolidated Mining	I	1900's	CO	Gold borders, green underprint. State seal, eagle, miners.	35	Mining
Grafton Consolidated Mining	I	1900's	CO	State seal, eagle, miners	35	Mining
Granville Gold Co.	I	1880's		Working miners	175	Mining
Grapevine Mining-	IU	1900's	NV	Three mining	35	Mining
Grass Valley Consol Gold Mining	I	1902	AZ	Small form.	20	Mining
Grass Valley Consolidated Gold Min.	I	1902	AZ	Small form.	20	Mining
Great Cariboo Gold Co.	I	1900's	SD	Nine mining plus vials of gold nuggets	1,500	Mining
Great Northern Gold Mining	IC	1897	SD	Four miners work by lamplight underground.	60	Mining
Great Northern Gold Mining	IU	1897	SD	Miners work by lamplight underground.	60	Mining
Great Northern Iron Ore	I	1930's		Mining scene	15	Mining
Great Northern Iron Ore	I	1970's		Mining scene	15	Mining
Great Northern Iron Ore Properties	I	1970's		Western miners at mine shaft, trustee's certificate	35	Mining
Great Republic Gold & Silver Min	I	1860's		Miners at mine head & old railroad engine	100	Mining
Great Republic Gold & Silver Min	I	1860's		Queen Victoria & Lincoln	225	Mining

Company		Date	State	Description	Price	Category
Great Republic Gold & Silver Min	I	1860's		Queen Victoria & Lincoln	500	Mining
Great Western Coal & Transportation	I	1857	PA	Train.	65	Mining
Great Western Coal & Transportation	I	1857	PA	Train.	65	Mining
Great Western Gold Mining & Mill	U			Mining	35	Mining
Greater American Mining Co.	I			Allegorical figures	35	Mining
Green Cananea Copper Co.	I	1930's		Mining	15	Mining
Green Gold-Silver Co.	IU	1900's		Mining	35	Mining
Greene Gold-Silver Co.	I	1900's		Working miners	35	Mining
Grey Eagle Consolidated Mining	I	1880's	CO	Working miners, eagle, seal	100	Mining
Grimes Divide Mining	IU	1910's	NV	Eagle & distant ships	15	Mining
Gruff-Davis Mines	U	1900's	NV	Gold Mining along river	35	Mining
Gruss Mining Co.	I	1920's	CA	Large eagle	15	Mining
Guanajuato Consolidated Mining	I	1890's			50	Mining
Guanajuato Consolidated Mining	I	1900's			40	Mining
Guanajuato Consolidated Mining	I	1920's	VA	American eagle & seal	35	Mining
Guanajuato Consolidated Mining	I	1930's	VA	American eagle & seal	15	Mining
Gunsight Mining	U	1880's	NJ	Miner, flowers.	187	Mining
Guy Silver Mining	I	1880's	ID Terr	Mining scene	175	Mining
Hagan Coal Co.	U			Working miners, plus six men in border	15	Mining
Hailey-Ola Coal	U	1900's	OK Terr	Flying eagle	75	Mining
Hale & Norcross Mining Co.	I	1900's		Comstock lode, miner	50	Mining
Hale & Norcross Mining Co.	U	1900's		Miner	15	Mining
Hale & Norcross Mining Co.	I	1910's		Comstock lode, miner	35	Mining
Hall-Anderson Gold Mining	I	1885	NY	Eagles nest. Miners.	120	Mining
Hall-Anderson Gold Mining	I	1885	NY	Eagles nest. Miners.	120	Mining
Hampshire Coal & Iron	I	1855	VA	Blacksmith, mill, train. Miners. Arm & hammer	250	Mining
Hancock Cons Mining	I	1917	MI	Eagle	192	Mining
Hancock Reorg Gold & Silver	I	1860's		Mining, Quaker	75	Mining
Happ Jack Gold & Silver Mining	I	1890's	CO	Working miners & ore cars	75	Mining
Hartford Zinc	I	1890's		Eagle	35	Mining
Hartford Zinc	U	1890's		Eagle	15	Mining
Haughton Coal of North Carolina	U	1850's	NC	Horseman, small eagle vignette.	165	Mining
Helca Mining & Milling	I	1880's	CO	State seal	100	Mining
Helena Gold Mines	I	1905-8	AZ	Hercules slays lion.	25	Mining
Helena Gold Mines	I	1905-8	AZ	Hercules slays lion.	25	Mining
Helga Gold & Copper Mining	IU	1890's	WA	Smelting plant, gold seal with stamps	35	Mining
Henwood Mines	U	1860's		Old railroad scene	35	Mining
Herbertsville Quartz & Mining	IU	1850's	CA		350	Mining
Hercules Wonder Mining Co.	U	1900's	NV	Eagle	35	Mining
Herkimer County Mining & Petro.NY	IC	1860's	PA	Oil rig, tanks, barrels.	209	Mining

Company		Date	Location	Description	Signer	Price	Category
High Ore Gold Mining	I	1900's	NV	Miners panning for gold, gold seal		35	Mining
Highlander Mill & Mining	IU	1900's		Miners at mine entrance		75	Mining
Hilltop Gold Mines Ltd	I	1934	Canada			58	Mining
Hinds Consolidated Mining	I	1900's		Miner		50	Mining
Hinsdale Horse Co.	U	1900's		Two mining		35	Mining
Hite Gold Quartz Co.	I	1880's		Mountain scenery		125	Mining
Home Stake Mining	I	1980's	CA	Indians watching train		45	Mining
Homestake Mining	I	1899		Native American Soldier	James Ben Ali	50	Mining
Homestake Mining	IC	1905		Blue. Indians overlooking train in valley		45	Mining
Homestake Mining	IC	1870's	NY	Indians, river, bridge.		352	Mining
Homestake Mining	I	1900's		Blue. Indians overlooking train in valley		45	Mining
Honest Gold & Silver Mining Co.	U	1860's	CA	Mining		50	Mining
Horn Silver Mining & Milling	I	1881	NJ	Miners. Light green paper, red 10 underprint.		75	Mining
Horn Silver Mining & Milling	I	1881	NJ	Miners. Light green paper, red 10 underprint.		75	Mining
Hornsilver Mining & Milling	I	1901-4	ID	Boy on winged wheel, flowers. Gold seal.		25	Mining
Hornsilver Mining & Milling	I	1901-4	ID	Boy on winged wheel, flowers. Gold seal.		25	Mining
Hortense Mining & Milling Co.	U	1900's	CO	Mining		35	Mining
Houillere Metallurg & Indust Lomova	IC	1890's	Russia	Underprint of hammers & other tools.		76	Mining
Houilleres D'Irsee	IC	1890's	Germany			32	Mining
Houilleres De Layon Et Loire	IC	1840's	France			130	Mining
Houilleres De Saint-Etienne, S.A.	IC	1920's	France	Coalmines, lovely ladies, Arms of St. Etienne.		80	Mining
Hubbard Silver Mining	IU	1866	MA	Mineshaft, horsedrawn wagons	Oakes Ames	2,900	Mining
Hudson Bay Mining & Smelting	I	1940's		Dogsled, airplane, & mine		35	Mining
Hull Copper Co.	I	1900's	AZ	Miners at work		35	Mining
Hulleras De Ujo-Mieres, Cia. De Las	IC	1900's	Spain	Coal miners at work underground.		48	Mining
Humboldt River Gold Silver Mining	IU	1860's		Working miners		175	Mining
Hunnapah Mining & Smelting	I	1900's				35	Mining
Hupp Motor Car	I	1929		Woman Sitting		94	Mining
Huron Copper Mining	I	1890's	MI	Miners at work, state seal		75	Mining
Huron Gold Ores Co.	I	1910's	CO	Mining		35	Mining
Hurricane Mining	IU	1900's	AZ Terr	Ship		100	Mining
I-X-L Mining & Milling	I	1880's		Gold seal		125	Mining
I.X.L. Tunnel Co. of Wisconsin Mining	I	1880	CO	Miners	R.G. Owens	80	Mining

Name		Date	State	Description	Price	Type
Idaho Mining & Milling	U			Eagle	15	Mining
Idaho-Nevada Consolidated Gold	I	1920's		7.5% gold bond, burning torch	15	Mining
Imperial Consolidated Mining	I	1910's	AZ	Eagle, seal	35	Mining
Indian Queen Mining & Milling	I	1880's		Indian maiden with bow & spear	100	Mining
Indiana Mining Co.	I	1910's		Indians	75	Mining
Indiana Mining Co.	I	1920's	MI	Indian chief	75	Mining
Industry Gold & Silver Mining	U	1870's	NV	Large of miner & ore car	50	Mining
Inferno Mining, Milling, & Power	I	1920's	CO	Gold seal	15	Mining
Inter-Mountain Mining & Industrial	I	1900's	AZ	Embossed seal	35	Mining
Interstate Gold Beach & Bar Mining	I	1900's	CO	Train & buildings	35	Mining
Interstate Mining Co.	U	1890's	MT	Miss Liberty, farmer, train, riverboat & blacksmith	75	Mining
Intl. Minerals & Chemicals	I	1970's		Mining	15	Mining
Intl. Mines Development Co.	I	1910's		Mining	35	Mining
Intl. Syndicate of Mines	IU	1910's		Railroad coal cars	35	Mining
Invincible Gold & Silver Mining Mill	I	1890's	CO	Lake in mountains scene	35	Mining
Invincible Gold & Silver Mining Mill	I	1900's	CO	Lake in mountains scene	35	Mining
Invincible Gold Mining	I	1860's	CO	With stamp	175	Mining
Iowa Gulch Mining of Leadville	I	1880's	CO	Three different mining, plus seals	175	Mining
Iowa Gulch Mining of Leadville	U	1880's	PA	Three mining scenes.	165	Mining
Iron Hills Consolidated Mining	I	1884	CO	Miners	65	Mining
Irwin Coal Co.	I	1850's		Woman with eagle & four corner	350	Mining
Isabella Gold Mining	I	1890's		Large eagle on flag, train, buffalo, & Indian	35	Mining
Isabella Gold Mining	I	1900's		Large eagle on flag, train, buffalo, & Indian	15	Mining
Island Creek Coal Co.	I	1920's		Large mining	35	Mining
Island Creek Coal Co.	I	1930's		Large mining	35	Mining
Ivanhoe Mining	I	1882	CO	Six miners working underground.	75	Mining
Ivanhoe Mining	I	1882	CO	Six miners working underground.	75	Mining
Ivory Coast Goldfields, Ltd	I	1903	Africa	Elephant	75	Mining
J-I-B Mining	I	1920's		Eagle	15	Mining
Jack Boy Mining	I	1917	OK	Miners. Gold seal. Documentary revenue stamps.	25	Mining
Jack Boy Mining	I	1918	OK	Miners. Gold seal. Documentary revenue stamps.	25	Mining
January Jones Leasing & Developing	I	1900's	NV	Miners at work & miners in border, seven	50	Mining
Jay Gould Mining Co.	U	1880's	MT	Working miners	100	Mining
Jefferson & Teton Mining	U	1900's	MT	Eagle with fl	15	Mining
Jefferson Coal Co.	I	1890's		Eagle	35	Mining

Jefferson Mines	IU	1920's	MT	Working miners & mine & mountain	35	Mining
Johnnie Nevada Mining	I	1908	NV		50	Mining
Jumbo Extension Mining	I	1910's	AZ	Gold seal	35	Mining
Jumbo Extension Mining	IU	1920's	AZ	Gold seal	35	Mining
Jumbo Mining & Development	U	1800's		Large eagle, ship, Capitol dome	15	Mining
Juniata Mining & Manufacturing Co.	U	1880's		Eagle, factories, & ship, miners, old train	50	Mining
Kalgoorlie Mint Iron King Gold Mines	IC	1890's	Australia	Mine in the outback.	160	Mining
Kent Mining	I	1880's		Embossed seal	50	Mining
Kentucky Block Cannel Coal Co.	I	1900's		Gold bond	50	Mining
Keweenau Copper	IU	1900's	MI	Elk & eagle	35	Mining
King Edward Silver Mines	I	1900's		King Edward	35	Mining
Kirkland Iron	I	1880's		Beehive	75	Mining
Klamath Placer Mining	I	1900's		Gold bond, Indian on horse, mountain	175	Mining
Klamath River Hydraulic Mining Co	I	1905	CA	Klamath River Hydraulic Mining Co	100	Mining
Kohlen-Bohr-Unternehmens Zukunft	IC	1900's	Germany	Goldprint company name. Crossed hammers.	160	Mining
Komata Reefs Gold Mining Co., Ltd.	IC	1900's	New Zealand		70	Mining
L C O Inc. Nevada Mines	I				15	Mining
La Californienne, Mines D'Or	IC	1850's	CA	Decorative border.	240	Mining
La Fe Mining	U	1900's	TX	Three mining	15	Mining
La Mina de Lalto Gold Silver Mining	IC	1860's	NV	Eagle & baker. William M Stewart	935	Mining
La Reforma Mining	IU	1900's		Surface mining, gold seal	35	Mining
La Ronge Uranium Mines	I	1950			65	Mining
La Rose Mines	I	1920's		Working miners	15	Mining
Lacalifornia Mining & Milling	I	1900's	AZ Terr	Mining	35	Mining
Lake Caswell Mines	IU	1930's			15	Mining
Lake Copper	IC	1917	MI	Reclining woman with miners William A. Paine	495	Mining
Lake Copper	IC	1922	MI	Woman on pedestal, winged wheel William A. Paine	395	Mining
Lake Copper Co.	IC	1910's	MI	Miss Liberty & workers William A. Paine	495	Mining
Lake Copper Co.	IC	1920's	MI	Miss Liberty & workers	35	Mining
Lake Erie, Alliance & Wheeling Coal	U	1900's		Miners with ore car, train, ship, blacksmith	50	Mining
Lake View South Gold Mine (W.A.)	IC	1900's	Australia	Miners at work on a water channel, black swan	210	Mining
Lampazos Silver Mines	I	1918	DE	Green. Miner with pneumatic drill.	25	Mining
Lampazos Silver Mines	I	1918	DE	Green. Miner with pneumatic drill.	25	Mining
Langdon-Henzey Coal Mining	IU	1890's		Bond, miners	75	Mining
Le-Nouveau Mondo Mining	IU	1850's			125	Mining
Lee Bonanza Gold Mining	IC	1900's	SD	Factory, brook, mountains.	154	Mining

Name	Type	Date	State	Description	Price	Category
Legal Tender Gold Mining	I	1900	NM	Green frame and seal. Mill. Miners in circles.	25	Mining
Legal Tender Gold Mining	I	1903	NM	Green frame and seal. Mill. Miners in circles.	25	Mining
Lehigh & Wilkes-Barre Corp.	SP	1920's		Specimen bond	125	Mining
Lehigh Coal & Navigation Co.	I	1860's		Mining village in mountains	125	Mining
Lehigh Coal & Navigation Co.	I	1860's		Building, revenue stamp	100	Mining
Lehigh Coal & Navigation Co.	I	1920's		Two photos & horses with eagle	35	Mining
Lehigh Coal & Navigation Co.	IC	1930's		Portrait of Two founders	15	Mining
Lehigh Coal & Navigation Co.	IC	1940's		Portrait of Two founders	15	Mining
Lehigh Coal & Navigation Co.	IC	1950's		Portrait of Two founders	15	Mining
Lehigh Coal Mine Company	I	1790's	PA		2,970	Mining
Lemon Gold Mining British Columbia	I	1898	NE	Large brown underprint of Nebraska state seal.	45	Mining
Lemon Gold Mining British Columbia	I	1900	NB	Large brown underprint of Nebraska state seal.	45	Mining
Leopard Mining Company	I	1880		Leapord	69	Mining
Lewis Mountain Mining & Milling	I	1910's	CO	Eagle, seal	35	Mining
Lewis Mountain Mining & Milling	I	1920's	CO	Eagle, seal	15	Mining
Lexington Hill Gold Mining	I	1905	ME	Mountains. Miners in circles. Woman below.	20	Mining
Lexington Hill Gold Mining	I	1905	ME	Mountains. Miners in circles. Woman below.	20	Mining
Liberty Mining	I	1850's			125	Mining
Lightning Creek Gold Mines Limited	I	1940			78	Mining
Lime Creek Mining Co.	I	1882	CO	Miners	101	Mining
Lincoln Bessemer Co.	I	1880's	UT	Gold seal, mining scene	125	Mining
Lisbon Valley Uranium	I	1950's	CO	Eagle	15	Mining
Little Bell Consolidated Mining Co.	I	1910's	CO	Working miners	35	Mining
Little Bell Gold Mining	I	1900's	CO	Two mining scenes	35	Mining
Little Butte Extension Mining	IU	1890's		Working miners, gold seal	35	Mining
Little Chief Mining	IU	1902		Large mining	125	Mining
Little Cut Diamond Cons Gold Mine	I	1902	CO	Red-orange. Flowers around title.	75	Mining
Little Cut Diamond Consol. Gold	IU	1900's		Flowers around title.	70	Mining
Little Man Gold Mining Company	I	1901	CO	Flowers	66	Mining
Little Mattie Mining Co	I	1904	ID	Miners	50	Mining
Little Sue Mining Company	I	1880	ME		66	Mining
Logan County Mining & Mfg.	I	1850's		Two ore trains & tunnels, red seal	500	Mining
London Mining	I	1882	NY	Gold Bond	45	Mining

Company	Type	Date	State	Description	Price	Category
London Mining	I	1882	NY	Gold Bond	45	Mining
London Mining	I	1880's	CO	Gold bond	75	Mining
Londonderry Gold Mine Ltd.	IC	1890's	Australia	Mining camp in the bush & two Coats of Arms.	190	Mining
Loretto Mining Co	I	1876	CA		69	Mining
Louise Mining Co.	I	1910's	UT	Three small mining	35	Mining
Lower California Mining	I	1888	CA	Mexican Mines, San Diego offices. Green paper.	25	Mining
Lubec Lead & Zinc Co.	I	1900's	PA	Miners	35	Mining
Lucky Boy Mining	I	1889	PA	Brown. Miners. Embossed seal	35	Mining
Lucky Boy Mining	I	1889		Brown. Miners. Embossed seal	35	Mining
Lucky Mc-Uranium Corp.	I	1950's	NV	Large of mining camp	15	Mining
Lump Gulch Silver Mines Co.	U	1900's	MT	One signature, eagle with flag, gold seal	35	Mining
Luning Consolidated Silver Mines	I	1920's		Unique mining	35	Mining
Lykens Valley Coal	IU	1897	PA	Blacksmith	80	Mining
Lykens Valley Coal	IC	1830's	PA	Forge, locomotive.	121	Mining
Lykens Valley Coal Mine	I	1840's		Working blacksmith, embossed seal	175	Mining
Lynch-Pine Creek Mining	U	1920's	ID	Two mining, one mountain	15	Mining
Macnamara Mining & Milling	IU	1910's	NV	Small certificate	35	Mining
Madeline Mining Co.	I	1920's	UT	Mining	35	Mining
Magma Copper	IC	1920's		Mining	25	Mining
Magma Copper	I	1930's		Large smelter in mountains	20	Mining
Magma Copper	I	1950's		Large smelter in mountains	15	Mining
Magma Silver Lead Mines	U	1900's	WA	Eagle & ships, gold seal	15	Mining
Maid of Orleans Oil, Chemical, Min	I	1900's			15	Mining
Maine & New Hampshire Granite	I	1890's		Train & mountains	50	Mining
Mainnis Mining Co.	U	1920's		Mining	25	Mining
Malachite Mining	I	1870's		Mine scene, Indian maidens	125	Mining
Mameva Mining & Milling	I	1899	CA	Woman	79	Mining
Mammoth Gold Mining	IU	1900's		Mining scene in mountains, with stamp	75	Mining
Manassas Mining	I	1853	VA	Grey borders, red seal. Mill. Eagle below.	175	Mining
Manassas Mining	I	1853	VA	Grey borders, red seal. Mill. Eagle below.	175	Mining
Manchester Gold Mining	I	1897	CO	Grey. Flowers around title.	60	Mining
Manchester Gold Mining	I	1897	CO	Grey. Flowers around title.	60	Mining
Manhattan Giant Mining	I	1906	SD	Grey, gold seal. Factories. Mining scenes in circles.	12	Mining

Name		Year	State	Description	Price	Category
Manhattan Giant Mining	I	1906	SD	Factories. Mining scenes in circles.	12	Mining
Manhattan Gold Mines	IU			Two stamps	35	Mining
Manhattan Silver Mining of Nevada	U	1860's		Mining	75	Mining
Maricopa Mica Mining Co.	U	1890's	AZ Terr	Two mining, plus a female	35	Mining
Marinduque Mining & Industrial	IC	1970's		Miner's helmet and factories.	25	Mining
Marinduque Mining & Industrial	IC	1970's		Miner's helmet and factories.	25	Mining
Mariposa L& & Mining	I	1870's	CA	Unique grizzly bear scene	100	Mining
Mariposa L& & Mining	I	1880's	CA	Unique grizzly bear scene	75	Mining
Marquette Iron	I	1920's		Mining	35	Mining
Maryland & New York Iron & Coal	I	1840's		Bond	500	Mining
Maryland Gold Mining	IU	1860's		Mining scenes	225	Mining
Maryland Smokeless Co.	I	1900's	WV	Gold bond with stamps, miners	125	Mining
Mascot Mining	IU	1900's		Three mining, gold seal	35	Mining
Massachusetts & New Mexico Con	I	1880's		Bonds with coupons, eagle	100	Mining
Massachusetts & New Mexico Con	I	1880's		Miners at mine shaft	75	Mining
Mattie-Bullfrog Mining & Milling	I	1900's		Large Mining scene, gold seal	75	Mining
McKinley Gold Mines	I	1909	AZ	Brown. Justice, woman with torch, man with book.	60	Mining
McKinley Gold Mines	I	1909	AZ	Brown. Justice, woman with torch, man	60	Mining
McLeod River Mining	IU	1930's		Grey seal, Co. logo	15	Mining
McMillan Gold Mines	IU	1930's			15	Mining
Melones Consolidated Mining	I	1876	CA	Eagle	88	Mining
Merced Gold Mining	I	1890's	MT	Mining	50	Mining
Mercer Mining & Manufacturing Co.	I	1860's		Train, revenue stamp	175	Mining
Merrimac Consolidated Mines	I	1900's	CO	Mining, gold seal	35	Mining
Mettacom Silver Mining Reese River	I	1866	NY-NJ	Grey/Black, green seal. State seals.	90	Mining
Mettacom Silver Mining Reese River	I	1866	NY-NJ	Grey/Black, green seal. State seals.	90	Mining
Mexerica Mining Company	U	1924		Mining men	64	Mining
Mexican Gold & Silver Mining	I	1920's			15	Mining
Mexican Premier Mines	I	1920's	ID		15	Mining
Mexico Consolidated Mining & Sme	I	1910's	ME		35	Mining
Mexico Covadonga Mining	I	1900		Mining	70	Mining
Mexico Monterey Mining	U	1904	Mexico	Mountains and building	75	Mining
Middle States Coal & Iron Mines	I	1900's		Large mining flanked by two women	75	Mining
Middlefork Mining Co.	U	1880's	MT	Territory	35	Mining
Midway Gold Minim	IU	1900's	CO	Gold seal	15	Mining
Midway Gold Mining	I	1900's			15	Mining

Name		Date	State	Description		Price	Category
Mildred Gold Mining	I	1910's	AZ	Working miners, embossed seal		35	Mining
Mills Post & White Consolidated Sill	U	1860's	NV	Mining		50	Mining
Milwaukee & New Mexico Mining	I	1905	NM	Miners		50	Mining
Milwaukee Mines	U	1900's	ID	Seal		15	Mining
Milwaukee Mines	IU	1930's				20	Mining
Milwaukee Mines	IU	1940's				15	Mining
Milwaukee Mining & Milling Co.	U	1910's	NM	Large eagle with shield, old seal		15	Mining
Milwaukee Mining & Milling Co.	I	1910's	NM	Two mining		35	Mining
Miner's Hope Gold & Silver Mining	U	1870's	NV	Miners with packs & shovels		75	Mining
Miner's Hope Tunnel Gold & Silver	U	1800's		Several miners, one signature		75	Mining
Mineral Bed Consol Mining of AZ	I	1880-2	NJ	Large red MBCM CO Overprint. Miners. Justice.		110	Mining
Mineral Bed Consol. Mining	I	1880-2	NJ	MBCM CO Overprint. Miners. Justice.		110	Mining
Mineral Spring Mining	I	1860's		Miner at work		225	Mining
Mines D'Or De Gondo Soc. Suisse	IC	1890's	Switzerland			140	Mining
Mines Co. of America	IU	1910's	ME	Miners equipment		35	Mining
Mines D' Heures, S.A. Des	IC	1880's	Belgium			60	Mining
Mines D'Anthracite De Regny S.A.	IC	1900's	Switzerland	Border with miners & underground mining scenes.		120	Mining
Mines D'Or D'Olkhowsk, S.A. Des	IC	1910's	Russia			144	Mining
Mines D'Or D'Ouspendki (Oural)	IC	1890's	Russia	Decorative border.		100	Mining
Mines D'Or La Bretonne (Californie)	IC	1850's	CA	Anchor & cargo.		260	Mining
Mines De Houille De Marles, S.V.	IC	1900's	France	Mines, Miner looking at a lady in a revealing dress		80	Mining
Mines Developing & Operating	U	1900's	NJ	Allegorical figures with state seal		15	Mining
Mining Development Corp.	U		MT	Mine works		15	Mining
Mining Development Corp.	I			Three mining		15	Mining
Minnesota Gold Mining	IU	1866	MN	Miners working	Henry H. Sibley	1,400	Mining
Minnie Gulch Mining & Tunnel	I	1901	CO	Green, gold seal. Factories, mountains. Miners in circles.		65	Mining
Minnie Gulch Mining & Tunnel	I	1901	CO	Factories, mountains. Miners.		65	Mining
Mission Development	I				Facs. J.Paul Getty	35	Mining
Mitchell Mining Co.	IU	1900's	AZ	Large mining scene, with stamps		35	Mining
Mitchell Mining Co.	I	1900's				35	Mining
Mogul Drainage & Trans Tunnel	I	1900's		Seal		35	Mining
Mohawk Mining	I	1919	MI	Indian		76	Mining
Mohawk Mining	I	1910's		Indian chief		50	Mining
Mohawk Mining	I	1920's		Indian chief		50	Mining

Company		Date	State	Description	Signature	Price	Category
Mojave Consolidated Gold & Silver	I	1870's	AZ			175	Mining
Mollie Gibson Consolidated Mining	I	1890's		Mining scene		100	Mining
Mollie Gibson Mining	I	1910's				35	Mining
Molybdenum Mining Co.	I	1900's	CO	Smelting plant in mountains		35	Mining
Montana Clinton Copper	U	1900's	MT			15	Mining
Montana Coal & Coke	I	1900's		Bond, ore train, ovens, & workers		35	Mining
Montana Gold & Gem Mining Co.	U	1890's	MT	Miners & ore cars		75	Mining
Montana Mining	I	1890's	CA			35	Mining
Monte Christo Gold & Silver Mining	IC	1860's	AZ Terr			462	Mining
Monte Cristo Mining	IC	1870's	CA	Shovel & Pick-axe		303	Mining
Montevideo Mining & Milling	I	1890's	CO	Large mining, gold seal		50	Mining
Montezuma Mining Co.	IU	1900's		The beehive		15	Mining
Montgomery County Coal	I	1857	NY	Train. Canal boat. Scarce.		90	Mining
Montgomery County Coal	I	1857	NY	Train. Canal boat. Scarce.		90	Mining
Montgomery Shoshone Consol Mining	IC	1900's	SD	Br borders, security underprint.	Charles Schwab	1,980	Mining
Monument Uranium	I	1970's	UT	Mining, old seal		15	Mining
Moonlight Mining	I	1881	CA	Round silver foil moon, clouds.		200	Mining
Moonlight Mining	I	1881	CA	Round silver foil moon, clouds.		200	Mining
Moraine Mining	IU	1900's	IL	Eagle		15	Mining
Morington Mining	IU	1920's	NV			15	Mining
Morris & Essex Mutual Coal Co.	I	1860's		Indian, ship, train, & 7 figures		125	Mining
Mother Lode Coalition Mines	I	1920's		Working miners		35	Mining
Mother Lode Coalition Mines	I	1940's		Working miners		15	Mining
Mother Lode Gold Mining	I	1900's	WA	Liberty & flag, old seal		35	Mining
Mounier Metallurgical Co.	I	1860's	CO	State seal plus stamp		75	Mining
Mount Hayden Mining & Milling	I	1910's	CO	Mining, gold seal		35	Mining
Mount Pleasant Coal Co.	I	1870's		Bond, old train in mountains		350	Mining
Mount Tritle Copper	I	1900's	AZ	Nice mining		35	Mining
Mountain Oak Gold & Silver Mining	IC	1860's	CA	State arms.	G. H, Parsons	352	Mining
Mountain Queen-Mining	I	1880's	CO	Two mining plus large smelting works, silver seal		125	Mining
Mow Silver Mining	I	1880's		Miner		75	Mining
Murray Mogridge Mining	I	1917	Canada	Blue.		25	Mining
Murray Mooridge Mining	I	1917	Canada	Blue.		25	Mining
Myrtle Gold Mining	I	1900's	AZ Terr	Allegorical figure		100	Mining
Nacimiento Copper Co.	IU	1880's		Gold bond, with all coupons, large mining		175	Mining
Naco Copper Company	I	1906	AZ	Tiger		100	Mining
Nanc Donaldson Mining Co.	IU	1900's	WY	Mines in Nevada		15	Mining
National Anthracite Coal Co.	I	1850's	PA	Train, eagle & so on, eight		500	Mining
National Nickel Co.	IU	1890's		Mining		50	Mining

National Tunnel & Mines	I	1940's		Working miners	15	Mining
Natomas Co.	I		CA	Large gold-dredging	35	Mining
Navarra Coal And Iron Mines Ltd.	IC	1900's	Spain		24	Mining
Nemaha Coal Mining Company	I	1871	NE	Miners	75	Mining
NESHANIC MINING CO	I	1847	NJ		48	Mining
Nevada Belmont Copper	U	1900's	AZ	Train, miner & mules	15	Mining
Nevada Boy Goldfield Mining	IU	1900's	SD	Lady, gold seal	35	Mining
Nevada Eagle Gold Mine & Milling	U	1900's		Eagle	35	Mining
Nevada Hills Florence Mining	I	1890's			35	Mining
Nevada Mines	I	1907	AZ Terr	Triangular red underprint of mill and rising sun.	35	Mining
Nevada Silver Horn Mining	I	1921	NV	Eagle. Orange seal.	25	Mining
Nevada Silver Horn Mining	I	1921	NV	Eagle. Orange seal.	25	Mining
Nevada Silver Horn Mining	I	1920's			35	Mining
Nevada Uranium Company	U	1952	NV		71	Mining
Nevada-Goldfield Lease Co.	I	1900's		Embossed seal	35	Mining
Nevada-Ramona Mining & Milling	I	1900's	NV	Scenic with Indian & harbor	35	Mining
Nevada-Utah Mines & Smelters	I	1907	ME	Blue. Mill.	15	Mining
Nevada-Utah Mines & Smelters	I	1907	ME	Blue. Mill.	15	Mining
New Almaden Quicksilver Mines	I		CA		15	Mining
New Arntfield Mines	U	1948	Canada		58	Mining
New Bedford Silver Mining	I	1880's		Winged eagle	125	Mining
New Comelia Copper Co.	I	1920's	UT	Machine loading ore cars	15	Mining
New Dominion Copper	I		AZ	Mining	15	Mining
New Dominion Copper	U		AZ	Mining	15	Mining
New Emma Silver Mining	I	1880's		Mining, embossed seal	50	Mining
New England & Oaxaca Coffee	IC	1890's	ME	Tropical scene.	242	Mining
New England Mining of Colorado	I	1860's	CO	With revenue stamps	175	Mining
New Gordon Diamond Co. Ltd.	IC	1890's	So. Africa		88	Mining
New Jersey Consolidated Mines	IU			Woman with flag & eagle	15	Mining
New Idria Mining & Chemical	I	1960's	NV	Eagle	15	Mining
New Idria Mining & Chemical	IU	1960's	NV		15	Mining
New Idria Mining & Chemical	I	1970's	NV	Eagle	15	Mining
New Mexico Gold Mine	U	1902	NM	Eagle	300	Mining
New Mexico Minerals	I	1960's		Large eagle	15	Mining
New Mexico Mining	I	1860's	ID	Hole from mining stamp	100	Mining
New Mexico Mining Co.	I	1850's	NM	Small mining town with church in mountains	175	Mining
New Orleans & Concordia Lodge	I	1830's			400	Mining
New Pittsburgh Mining	Proof	1880's	NY	Miners hoist bucket.	165	Mining
New Quincy Mining	I	1920's		Working miners	15	Mining
New Tonopah Dividend Mining Co.	I	1920's		Two mining	35	Mining

Name		Date	State	Description	Price	Category
New Tonopah Dividend Mining Co.	IU	1930's	UT	Lady., gold seal	35	Mining
New York & Boston Gold Mining	Proof	1880's	CA	Miners underground.	209	Mining
New York & Calaveras County	I	1880's		Scenic view	100	Mining
New York & Montana Mining & Disc	I	1860's		Miners, with revenue stamp	225	Mining
New York & Ohio Coal	I	1870's		Bond, miners at work	350	Mining
New York & Ohio Coal	I	1890's		Bond, gold seal, woman	225	Mining
New York & Providence Mining, Mil	IU	1880's		Three mining	100	Mining
New York & Silver Mining	I	1860's		Mining	175	Mining
New York & Utah Prospecting & Mir	IU	1860's	NY	Mining	175	Mining
New York Central Gold Mining	I	1890's		Large mining	50	Mining
New York Central Gold Mining Co.	I	1860's		Bond with stamp	225	Mining
Newark Mining & Milling Co.	IU	1910's	ME	Gold bond, working miners	35	Mining
Newark Mining & Milling Co.	I	1910's		Working miners	75	Mining
Newark Silver Mining Co	U	1877	CA		67	Mining
Newfoundland Consolidated Copper	Proof	1880's		Miner drills, others shovel.	264	Mining
Newfoundland Gold Mining Co.	U	1880's		Working miners in mine with ore car	35	Mining
Newmont Mining	I	1950's	CO	Eagle between two men	15	Mining
Newmont Mining	I	1960's		Eagle between two men	15	Mining
Niagara Mining & Smelting	IU	1891	UT	Niagara Falls, miners	250	Mining
Nipissing Mines Company, Ltd.	U	1929	Canada	Miner	78	Mining
Nixon Nevada Mining	IU	1910's			35	Mining
Nome Exploration Co.	U	1900's	AK	Large mining	35	Mining
Non Pareil Mining & Smelting	IU	1880's			75	Mining
North American _Mines	U	1900's		Eagle with shield, presidents signature	15	Mining
North American Dredging Co.	IU	1900's		Gold bond with coupons, gold mining	35	Mining
North American Gold Placers Co.	I	1905	AZ	Mining Scene	50	Mining
North American Gold Placers Co.	I	1906	AZ	Miners	65	Mining
North American Mining	I	1920's		Eagle	15	Mining
North American Mining	U		CO	Eagle	15	Mining
North Butte Mining	I	1900's		mining scene	15	Mining
North Butte Mining	I	1910's		Mining	15	Mining
North Butte Mining	IC	1920's		Miners drilling underground - green	15	Mining
North Butte Mining	IC	1920's		Miners drilling underground - orange	15	Mining
North Butte Mining	I	1920's		Mining - purple	15	Mining
North Butte Mining	I	1930's		Mining - green	15	Mining
North Fresno Mining Company	I	1880	CA	Miners	100	Mining
North Lake Mining	I	1920's	MI	Working miners	50	Mining

Name		Date	State	Description	Price	Category
North Mexican Mining & Milling	I	1880's			50	Mining
North Span Uranium Mines	IU	1950's		Warrant	15	Mining
North Standard Gold & Silver	I	1870's	CA		75	Mining
North Standard Gold & Silver	I	1880's	CA		50	Mining
North Utah Mining	I	1900's		Large mini n	50	Mining
Northern Mining & Smelting	U	1890's			35	Mining
Northhite & Yosemite Gold Mining	I	1880	CA	Miners	98	Mining
Norwegian Consolidated Mining	U	1900's	AZ Terr		15	Mining
Norwegian Consolidated Mining	I	1900's	CA	Working miners, gold seal	50	Mining
Oakland-Goldfield Mining	IU	1900's	NV		35	Mining
Oatman Combination Mining	I	1910's		Large eagle with shield	15	Mining
Oatman-Combination Mining	I	1916	AZ	Green. Eagle and shield.	12	Mining
Oatman-Combination Mining	I	1916	AZ	Green. Eagle and shield.	12	Mining
Ohio Central Coal	I	1880's		Bond, miners in mine with ore cars	225	Mining
Ohio Copper Co. of Utah	I	1920's		Miners working in tunnel	35	Mining
Ohio Gold Mining Company	I	1896	OH	City Street	50	Mining
Ojibway Mining	I	1910's	MI	Indian chief	100	Mining
Old Gold Mines	I	1909	WY	Gold Title.	35	Mining
Old Gold Mines	I	1900's	WY	Gold Title.	35	Mining
Old Gold Mining	IU	1920's		Co. logo	15	Mining
Old Thirteen Mining	I	1881	CO	Brown. Eagle, shield, flags, cannon.	75	Mining
Old Thirteen Mining	I	1881	CO	Brown. Eagle, shield, flags, cannon.	75	Mining
Olympic Mining	I	1900's	WA	Mountains, mine & stream, gold seal	35	Mining
Omega Mining	I	1900's	AZ Terr	Mining	35	Mining
Onandago Copper	I	1930's	MI		35	Mining
Ontario Silver Mining Co.	I	1910's		Beehive	35	Mining
Opal Mining	IC	1860's	CA	Eagle on flag.	374	Mining
Operator Consolidated Mines	IU	1930's	UT	Three mining, gold seal	35	Mining
Ophir Gold Mines	I	1950's		Lady & Colorado seal	15	Mining
Ophir Gold Mining	U	1909		Miners with picks, miners with shovels, mountain.	35	Mining
Ophir Gold Mining	U	1909		3 vignettes: miners with picks, miners with shovels	35	Mining
Ora Tahoma Mining	U			Three mining, gold seal	15	Mining
Oregon Gold Prospecting & Promot	I	1900's		Bond, eagle	50	Mining
Oriental Gold Mining	I	1880's		Miner & standing woman	100	Mining
Original Bullfrog Mines	U	1900's	AZ	Bullfrog imprint	75	Mining
Original Bullfrog Mines Syndicate	IU	1901	AZ Terr	Bullfrog	495	Mining
Original Bullfrog Mines Syndicate	IC	1900's	AZ Terr	Large green bullfrog.	308	Mining

Original Hidden Treasure Mining	U	1860's	NV	Eagle		50	Mining
Original Hidden Treasure Mining	U	1870's		Eagle		35	Mining
Oro Amigo Platin Mining	IU	1920's		Nice mining		35	Mining
Orphan Bell Mining & Milling Co.	I	1890's	CO	Working miners		50	Mining
Orphan Bell Mining & Milling Co.	U	1900's	CO	Working miners		35	Mining
Orphan Gold Mining_	I	1900's		Railroad plus workers		35	Mining
Osceola Hill Silver Mining & Tunnel	IC	1860's			Wm. H. Ladd	352	Mining
Overland Gold	I	1890's				35	Mining
Owensburg Coal	IU	1920's		Deer in mountains		35	Mining
Pacific Coal & Transportation	I	1900's		Gold bond, miners with ore cars in mine		125	Mining
Pacific Coal & Transportation Co.	IC	1900's	ME	Eagle, underground mining scene.		48	Mining
Pacific Copper	IU	1900's				35	Mining
Pacific Copper Mining Co.	I	1910's	AZ	Two mining		35	Mining
Pacific Smelting & Mining	I	1910's		Eagle		35	Mining
Pacific Smelting & Mining	I	1911-1	ME	Orange or green. Eagle on rock.		25	Mining
Pacific Smelting & Mining	I	1911-15	ME	Orange or green. Eagle on rock.		25	Mining
Palouse Coal	U	1900's		Mining camp		35	Mining
Pan-American Mining & Developing	I	1940's		Mining		35	Mining
Panther Creek Mining	I	1900's				35	Mining
Panuco Gold & Silver Mining Smelting	I	1887	Mexico			99	Mining
Park Tunnel & Mining & Milling	I	1910's		Working miners, seal		15	Mining
Parrot Silver & Copper	I	1899	MY	Yellow paper. Parrot and silver ingot.		35	Mining
Parrot Silver & Copper	I	1903	MY	Yellow paper. Parrot and silver ingot.		35	Mining
Parrot Silver & Copper	IC	1890's	MT	Parrot	Henry H. Rogers	440	Mining
Parrot Silver & Copper	I	1890's	MT			100	Mining
Pasadena Boy Mining	I	1916	AZ	Gold. Miners, mountains.		20	Mining
Pasadena Boy Mining	I	1916	AZ	Gold, Miners, mountains.		20	Mining
Patino Mines & Enterprises	I	1950's	DE	Miners & equipment		15	Mining
Patino Mines & Enterprises Consol	I	1941	DE	Miners drill roof of shaft.		9	Mining
Patino Mines & Enterprises Consol	I	1961	DE	Miners drill roof of shaft.		9	Mining
Patricia Mining	I	1920's	ID	Mining scenes		15	Mining
Patterson Mines, Inc.	IU	1930's	WA	Gold seal, two mining, large mountain scene		15	Mining
Patti-Rosa Gold Mining	U	1890's		Mining		35	Mining
Pay Divide Mining	I	1920's	NV			15	Mining
Paymaster Gold Mining & Milling	U	1900's		Gold seal		35	Mining

Peerless Gold Mine-Development	U	1890's	CA		15	Mining
Pelican & Dives Mining	I	1880's		Working miners scene	100	Mining
Pemberton Hydraulic Gold Mining	I	1870's	CA	Mine scene	125	Mining
Pemberton Hydraulic Gold Mining	I	1880's	CA	Mine scene	100	Mining
Penn Anthracite Coal	I	1889	PA	Orange. Train, mill. Hanging lamps	35	Mining
Penn Anthracite Coal	I	1889	PA	Train, mill. Hanging lamps.	35	Mining
Penn Valle Coal	I	1920's		Bond	15	Mining
Penn-Yan Mining Co.	U	1880's	MT	Gold & silver coins in color	125	Mining
Pennsylvania Anthracite Coal	I	1881		Brown. Four coal miners. Griffins below.	90	Mining
Pennsylvania Anthracite Coal	I	1881		Brown. Four coal miners. Griffins below	90	Mining
Pennsylvania Consolidated Mining	I	1890's	CA		35	Mining
Peruvian Mining, Smelting & Refining	I	1900's		Eagle, justice & llama	15	Mining
Pharmacist Gold Mining Co.	I	1910's	WY		15	Mining
Pharmacist Mining Co Cripple Creek	I	1899	CO	Palm branch	73	Mining
Phelps Dodge Corp.	I	1920's		Working miner	15	Mining
Phelps Dodge Corp.	I	1950's	NY	Seated figure before large open pit mine	15	Mining
Phelps Dodge Corp.	I	1960's		Working miner	15	Mining
Philadelphia-Nevada Mining	I	1900's	AZ	Mining scene plus six individual miners	35	Mining
Phipps Quicksilver Mining	U	1910's	AZ	Mining town, miner, & burro	15	Mining
Phoenix Copper	I	1880's	MI	Winged eagle	75	Mining
Phoenix Gold Mining	I	1890's	AZ	Mining & eagle	35	Mining
Phoenix Mining	IU	1900's	ID	Three mining & goddess	35	Mining
Phoenix Mining & Manufacturing	IU	1850's		Three	350	Mining
Piedmont Mining & Milling	U	1900's		Waterfall	35	Mining
Pigeon River Land & Mining	I	1900's	MN	Large winged eagle with train & ships	100	Mining
Pioneer Coal	U	1900's		Eagle, rare	35	Mining
Pittsburg Johnnie Mining	U		NV		15	Mining
Placers Auriferes Et Travaus Publics	IC	1880's	Switzerland		96	Mining
Plymouth Rock Mining Co.	I	1870's		Large mining	75	Mining
Plymouth Rock Mining Co.	U	1870's		Large mining	50	Mining
Plymouth Rock Mining Co.	I	1880's		Large mining	75	Mining
Plymouth Silver Mining	IC	1860's	NY	Miners in tunnel.	154	Mining
Polk County Copper	IC	1860's	TN	Mining site, log cabin.	110	Mining
Poney Meadows Mining	I	1960's		Three & gold seal	15	Mining
Ponupo Mining & Transportation	U	1890's		Mining	35	Mining
Porcupine Northern Mining	I	1910's			35	Mining
Portage Lake Mining Company	U	1855	MI	Man on horse	300	Mining

Company		Date	State	Description		Price	Category
Portland Gold Mining	I	1930's	WY	Hard rock mining scene		15	Mining
Portland Gold Mining Company	I	1895	CO	Colorado	Burns Peck	97	Mining
Portland Mining	I	1880's				50	Mining
Poto Gold Dredging Co.	IU	1900's		Gold dredging		35	Mining
Prin-Seti Gold Mining	U	1900's	CO	Prince Seti's bust above title.		396	Mining
Princeton Mining	I	1900's	CO	Working miners & seal		35	Mining
Progress Gold Mining	I	1900's	CO	Gold seal		50	Mining
Prosperity Gold Mine	I	1900's	AZ Terr	Mining scene & six miners in border		35	Mining
Providence Tuolumne Gold Mines	I	1940's	CA	Seal & Mining		15	Mining
Provident Coke & Mining	I	1900's		Bond, coke ovens		35	Mining
Pulaski Anthracite Coal	I	1900's		Bond		75	Mining
Queen Mining	IC	1870's	CA	Royal figure.		330	Mining
Quick Silver Mining	I	1910's		Workers pouring molten ore		75	Mining
Quincy Mining	I	1852	MI	Train		49	Mining
Quincy Mining	IC	1920's	MI	Two elks similar to Adventure Mining.		20	Mining
Quincy Mining Co,	IC	1900's	MI	Two moose with antlers (state seal)		50	Mining
Quincy Mining Co.	I	1850's	MI	Ships, trains, ladies & state seal		100	Mining
Quincy Mining Co.	I	1860's	MI	Ships, trains, ladies & state seal		75	Mining
Quincy Mining Co.	I	1890's	MI	Scrip certificate		15	Mining
Quincy Mining Co.	IC	1910's	MI	Two moose with antlers (state seal)		35	Mining
Quincy Mining Co.	IC	1920's	MI	Two moose with antlers (state seal)		35	Mining
Quincy Mining Co.	IC	1920's	MI	Two elks		20	Mining
Quinterro Mining	IU	1860's		Miner, state seal		175	Mining
Quito Gold Mining & Milling	I	1900's	CO	Scenic mountain		35	Mining
Ramsey Wonder Gold Mining	I	1907	OK	Miners		58	Mining
Ramsey-Nevada Mining	IU	1900's	AZ Terr	Miners mountain scene		75	Mining
Rattler Gold Mining	I	1900's	CO			35	Mining
Rawhide Mining	IU	1910's	NV	Mining		35	Mining
Ray Consolidated Gold Dredging	U	1910's		Torch		15	Mining
Ray Hercules Mines	IU	1920's				15	Mining
Raymond-Illinois Mining Co.	IU		UT	Three mining vigs.		35	Mining
Rebecca Mining & Leasing Co	I	1903	CO	Miners		95	Mining
Rebecca Mining & Leasing Co.	I	1903	CO	Miners		49	Mining
Red Cloud Mining Company	I	1890	ID			97	Mining
Red Eagle Gold Mining	I	1897	Canada	Woman		59	Mining
Red Hill Florence Mining	IU	1920's	NV			35	Mining
Reliable Tungsten Mining	I	1916	CO	Green. Miners.		15	Mining
Reliable Tungsten Mining	I	1916	CO	Green. Miners.		15	Mining
Reorganized Cracker Jack Mining	IU	1920's	NV			35	Mining
Reorganized Victory Divide Mining	IU	1920's		Eight _assessments paid, gold seal, two mining		35	Mining
Republic Coal Co.	U	1900's	MT	Mining		15	Mining
Republic Iron Mask Gold Mining	U			Seven mining		35	Mining

Name		Year	State	Description	Price	Category
Republic Mines	I	1900's		Bond, eagle with flag	75	Mining
Requa-Savage Mines	I	1916	CO	Green. Miners with drilling equipments.	15	Mining
Requa-Savage Mines	I	1916	CO	Green. Miners with drilling equipments.	15	Mining
Revenue Leasing & Mining	I	1900's		Miners with wheelbarrow	35	Mining
Revert Mining	IU	1920's	NV	Three assessments paid, gold seal	35	Mining
Revine Gold Mining	U	1900's		Mountains	15	Mining
Rex Mining	U		NV	Eagle	15	Mining
Reynolds & Morris Gold & Silver Min	IC	1860's		Two allegorical women.	363	Mining
Reynolds-Alaska Development	IU	1900's	CA	Train, ship & figures	75	Mining
Rich Evans Haydock Collieries Coal	IC	1899	GB	Very large bond. 7 red embossed revenue stamps.	25	Mining
Richard Evans & Co./Haydock Coll.	IC	1899	GB	Very large bond. 7 red embossed revenue stamps.	25	Mining
Richland Mining Co.	U	1900's		Three mining, gold seal	35	Mining
Richmond Coal & Mining & Manu.	I	1890's	CA	Gold bond, ale ore train loading	15	Mining
Richmond Coal & Mining & Manu.	I	1890's		Working miners	100	Mining
Richmond Coal Mining	I	1890's		Bond	100	Mining
Riddlesburg Coal & Iron	IU	1860's		Miners, & blacksmith, with stamp	100	Mining
Ridge Copper Co.	I	1880's	MI		50	Mining
Rio Delores Copper Co.	I	1900's	AZ	Working miners	35	Mining
Rio Delores Copper Co.	I	1910's	AZ	Working miners	35	Mining
Rio Grande Copper Co.	I	1880's		Two mining plus two miners divided by state seal	175	Mining
Rio Plata _	IU	1900's	AZ	Miners & eagles	35	Mining
Rio Plata Mining	IU	1911		Miners working underground, eagle snake in mouth.	35	Mining
Rising Fawn Iron	IC	1870's	GA	Prospectors, state arms.	385	Mining
Riverside Iron & Co.	U	1800's		Miners, boats, & train	50	Mining
Riverside Iron & Coal Co. of Scrant	U	1800's		Miners, trains & riverboats	100	Mining
Robb-Montbay Mines	I	1930's			35	Mining
Roberta Gold	IU	1930's			15	Mining
Roberts Buena-Vista Mines	I	1900's		Large smelting plant, flatcars, prospector/ burros	15	Mining
Robinson-Victo Mines I	I	1890's	CO	Huge mining operation	100	Mining
Rock Mountain Gold Mining	I	1864	CO	Mortgage Bond. All red.	125	Mining
Rocker Silver Mining	U	1879	NY	Miners	46	Mining
Rocker Silver Mining	I	1880	NY	Miners	48	Mining
Rocky Mountain Gold Mining of Colo	I	1864	CO	Mortgage Bond. All red.	125	Mining
Rodez Coal Co. Ltd.	IC	1912	GB	Debenture	20	Mining

Company		Year	Location	Description		Price	Category
Rodez Coal Co. Ltd. IC	I	1912	GB	Debenture		20	Mining
Roodeplaats (DeBeers) Diamond Mines	IC	1910's	So. Africa			90	Mining
Roosevelt Gold Mining	U	1900's		Miners, gold seal		15	Mining
Rosario Silver Mining	IU	1860's	AZ	Working miners		125	Mining
Rose-Lee Mining & Milling	IU	1890's		Many working miners, gold seal		50	Mining
Rouchleau-Ray Iron L& Co.	I	1890's		Two forest, plus eagle in flight		100	Mining
Rouchleau-Ray Iron L& Co.	U	1890's				35	Mining
Round Mountain Mining & Milling	I	1895	CO	Eagle		50	Mining
Round Mountain Mining Co.	I	1900's	NV	Three mining, old seal		50	Mining
Round Mountain Mining Co.	I	1910's	NV	Three mining, gold seal		35	Mining
Round Mountain Mining Co.	I	1910's		Boy's head		35	Mining
Royal Gold & Silver Mining	IC	1890's	MT	Cherub, rural scenery, prospector.		798	Mining
Royal Tiger Mines	I	1926	CO	Liberty. Gold Seal.		18	Mining
Royal Tiger Mines	I	1920's	CO	Allegorical figures		35	Mining
Royal Tiger Mines	I	1926-33	CO	Liberty. Gold Seal.		18	Mining
Ruby Hill Tunnel &. Mining	I	1880's	NV	Seated goddess		100	Mining
Sacramento Gold & Silver Mining	I	1860's				225	Mining
Saint Croix & Lake Superior Mining	I	1840's				500	Mining
Saint Helena Gold Mine	I	1880's	CA	Bond	Choate, Cushing	75	Mining
Saint Joseph Lead Co.	I	1950's		Large mining, grey seal		15	Mining
Saint Joseph Lead Co.	I	1960's				15	Mining
Saint Joseph Minerals	I	1970's		Mining scene		15	Mining
Salero Mining	U	1800's		Stagecoach portrait		50	Mining
Salido Gold-Copper	IC	1900's	Mexico	AZ,CA Mine in a river valley in mountains.		88	Mining
Sampo Mining & Development Co.	IU	1900's		Three mining		35	Mining
San Andreas Copper Mtn. Mining	IC	1880's	NJ	State arms, train, ferry boat.		121	Mining
San Juan & New Jersey Discovery	I	1880's	CO	Embossed seal		75	Mining
San Juan Smelting & Refining	I	1900's	CO	Gold seal		35	Mining
San Poll Mining & Water Power Co.	I	1900's	WA	Miners		35	Mining
Santa Fe Gold & Copper Mining	I	1920's	NM			35	Mining
Santa Paula Mining & Reduction	I	1900's	CA			50	Mining
Santa Rita Copper & Iron	I	1890's	NM	Miners working in mine		100	Mining
Santa Rita Copper Mining	I	1910's	AZ			35	Mining
Savage Gold & Silver Mining	U	1900's	NV			15	Mining
Savage Gold & Silver Mining	I	1920's	CA	Three mining		35	Mining
Savage Gold & Silver Mining	I	1920's	NV			15	Mining
Scadden Flat Gold Mining	I	1878-9	CA	Grey. State seal, left.		75	Mining
Scadden Flat Gold Mining	I	1878-9	CA	Grey. State seal, left.		75	Mining
Schaffgotsch	IC	1940's	Germany			80	Mining
Schiller Mining of Trenton	IU	1890's	NJ	Working miners		75	Mining
Schuyler Gold & Silver Mining	I	1880's	CO	Mining		100	Mining

Name		Date	State	Description	Price	Category
Seal of Nevada Mining	U	1880's			35	Mining
Selerno Mining & Manufacturing Co	U	1870's	AZ Terr	Large stagecoach	100	Mining
Seneca Copper Corp.	IU	1920's		Bond, mining	35	Mining
Seneca Mining	I	1870's	MI	Mining & woman with horn of plenty	175	Mining
Seneca Mining	I	1900's	MI	Double mining, large state seal	75	Mining
Seneca Mining	I	1910's	MI	Two unique mining	50	Mining
Sequatchie Coal & Iron	I	1890's	TN	Mining	75	Mining
Sequatchie Coal & Iron	U	1890's	TN	Mining	35	Mining
Sequatchie Coal & Iron	I	1910's	TN	Mining	50	Mining
Seven Stars Gold Mining	IU	1890's		Miners	100	Mining
Shannon Copper Co.	I	1930's		Working miners & ore cars	35	Mining
Shasta May Blossom Copper	I	1920's	AZ	Mining	35	Mining
Sheridan Hill Mining & Smelting	I	1870's		Smelting plant	100	Mining
Sheriff Gold Mining	I	1890's		Spread eagle	35	Mining
Shoshone Chief Silver Mining	I	1860's		Sluice box, open pit mining	500	Mining
Silver Bell Mines	I	1950's	CO	Large eagle, gold seal	15	Mining
Silver Bell Mines	U		CO	Woman with lion	15	Mining
Silver Bell Mining	I	1950's	CO	Lion & lady	15	Mining
Silver Cliff Mining & Tunnel	IU	1880's	MT Terr		75	Mining
Silver Consolidated Mining	I	1900's	NV	Embossed seal	15	Mining
Silver Crown Mining	IU	1880's	CO	Embossed seal	75	Mining
Silver Divide Mines	IU	1960's		Large smelting, gold seal	15	Mining
Silver Hills Nevada Mines	I	1920's		Three mining, gold seal	15	Mining
Silver Jacket Mining Co.	U	1870's	NV	Smelting plant, embossed seal	50	Mining
Silver King of Arizona Mining	IU	1910's	CO	Miners in tunnels	35	Mining
Silver Prize No. 2 Gold & Silver Mine	IC	1860's	CA	Eagle on flag.	363	Mining
Silver Rock Mining	I	1880's	CO	Miners in tunnels	100	Mining
Silver Shield Mining & Milling Co.	IU	1920's	NV	Mining scene	35	Mining
Silver Stock	I	1882	NV		99	Mining
Simon South Silver Mines	IU	1910's	NV	Three mining scenes, old seal	35	Mining
Sioux Divide Mining Co.	IU	1910's	NV	Eagle	35	Mining
Small Hopes Consol Mining	I		NY	Wagon	125	Mining
Smuggler Divide Mining	I	1920's	NV	Seven of miners, gold seal, with stamps	35	Mining
Smuggler Mining Co.	I	1930's	NV	Eagle, with stamps	15	Mining
Smuggler Union Mining	I	1920's	CO	State seal	35	Mining
Smuggler Union Mining of Colorado	I	1901	CO	Orange. State seal, bottom center.	60	Mining
Smuggler Union Mining of Colorado	I	1901	CO	Orange. State seal, bottom center.	60	Mining
Sociedad de Minas de la Habana	SP	1840's	Cuba	Sun over mountain top, Cornucopia at base.	242	Mining
Sonora Central Mines	I		AZ	Three mining scenes	35	Mining
South Africa Mining Co.	U	1937		Mining building	60	Mining
South Clear Creek Gold Silver Mining	U	1865		Woman	372	Mining

Name		Date	State	Description	Price	Category
South Eastern Gold Mining	I		AZ	Three mining scenes	25	Mining
South Idaho Consolidated Mining &	I	1890's	CA		35	Mining
South Lake Mining	U	1917	MI	Landscape	59	Mining
South Lake Mining Co	I	1915	MI		69	Mining
South Lake Mining Co.	I	1915	MI		63	Mining
South Lake Mining Co.	I	1915	MI		63	Mining
South Park Mining & Developing	I	1900's		Seven mining	35	Mining
South Park Mining & Development	I	1910's		Seven mining	15	Mining
South Park Mining & Realty	U	1910's	MT	Mountain scene	15	Mining
South Side Milling & Mining	IU	1880's		Large mountain scene & working miners	125	Mining
South Utah Mines & Smelters	I	1920's			50	Mining
South-Western & Arkansas Mining	IC	1850's	AR		121	Mining
Southern Mining	U	1890's	OH	Ship & church	35	Mining
Sovereign Gold Mines	IU	1900's	AZ Terr	Bond	35	Mining
Spearhead Mining	I	1920's		Bond, lake in mountains	35	Mining
Specie Basis Mining	I	1860's		Large mining scene with stamp	350	Mining
Spokane National	I	1960's	NV	Eagle, Indians, train	15	Mining
Spokane Tin Mines	U	1900's	WA	Hill scene	15	Mining
St Louis St Joseph Cripple Creek Mining	I			Miners	79	Mining
St. Croix & Lake Superior Mineral	IC	1840's	MA	Eagle.	143	Mining
Stafford Meadow Coal & Iron	I	1850's	PA	Vignettes	125	Mining
Stafford Meadow Coal Iron City Impr	I	1858	PA	First Mortgage Bond.	45	Mining
Stafford Metal Coal Iron	U	1858		Horses	80	Mining
Standard Mutual Mining of Baltimore	I	1887	MD	Mill on hilltop, tracks leading down to trains loading.	60	Mining
Standard Mutual Mining of Baltimore	I	1887	MD	Metallic gold ink throughout	60	Mining
Star of Nevada Silver Mining	I	1870's		Mill on hilltop	50	Mining
Starmont Mining of Utah	IU	1880's	NV	Train, cherubs, & Liberty seated dollar	250	Mining
State Line Gold Mining	I	1880's	NY	Large scene of workers at mine	100	Mining
State of Arkansas	U	1872	Arkansas	Factory scene	51	Mining
State of Colorado Mining	I	1880's	NY	Miners with picks, miner pushes car.	75	Mining
State of Colorado Mining	I	1900's	CO	Miners with picks, miner pushes cart	75	Mining
Stem-Winder Mining & Leasing	I	1934	DE	Embossed seal	15	Mining
Stone Cabin Consolidated Mines	I	1883	UT	Cabin, mountains	85	Mining
Stone Cabin Consolidated Mines	I	1934	DE	Orange. Cabin, mountains.	50	Mining
Stormont Mining	I	1883	UT	Cherubs, Seated Liberty silver dollars.	85	Mining
Suffold Gold, Silver & Copper Min	U	1860's		Miners & ore car	35	Mining
Sullivan Mining	IU	1880's		Working miners	100	Mining

Name		Date	State	Description	Price	Category
Sun-Hope Mining	U		CO	Three mining	15	Mining
Sunlight Copper Mining	I	1900's	WY	Winged eagle topless women, train & ship	75	Mining
Sunnyside Lead-Silver Mining	U	1920's	NV	Eagle in shield	15	Mining
Sunrise Silver Mine	U	1900's	ID	Lighted torch	15	Mining
Sunset Eclipse Gold Mining	IU	1900's		Black seal	35	Mining
Sunset Mines	IU	1950's	ID		15	Mining
Superior & Boston Copper Co.	IU	1910's	AZ	Miners working	50	Mining
Superior & Boston Copper Co.	IU	1920's	AZ	Three mining	35	Mining
Superior & Globe Copper Co.	IU	1900's	AZ		35	Mining
Superstition Consolidated Mining	I	1910's	AZ		75	Mining
Swanton Coal & Iron	I	1856	MD	Train	70	Mining
Swanton Coal & Iron	I	1856	MD	Train	70	Mining
Swastika Mining & Developing Co.	IU	1910's	UT	Three mining, three swastikas	50	Mining
Syndicate Mines	U	1900's		Large mining	15	Mining
Syndicate Mines, Inc.	U	1920's		Working miners	15	Mining
Tallapoosa L&, Mining & Manufact	IU	1910's		Gold seal, three mining	50	Mining
Tamarack & Chesapeak Mining	I	1907-8	WA	Gold seal. Trackworker, mills.	19	Mining
Tamarack & Chesapeak Mining	I	1907-8	WA	Gold seal. Trackworker, mills.	19	Mining
Tecolote Silver Mining	U	1880's	CO	Owl on tree branch.	154	Mining
Teel Mining	I	1898	WV	Gold seal. Prospectors, miners.	15	Mining
Teel Mining	I	1898	WV	Gold seal. Prospectors, miners.	15	Mining
Tesoro Mining	IU	1901	UT	Two miners	75	Mining
Texas Girl Gold Mining Co	I	1899	CO		49	Mining
Teziutlan Copper Mining & Smelting	I	1920's	NJ	Ladies	75	Mining
The Argus Mines Co	I	1904	CO	Wagon and house	51	Mining
The Arizona Copper Hill Mining	I		AZ	Eagle	50	Mining
The Associated Gold Mining	I			Mountain	80	Mining
The Champagne Mining and Milling	I			House and wagon	50	Mining
The County of Mono	IC	1880's	CA	Three mining scenes.	605	Mining
The Cresson Consolidated Gold Mining	I				51	Mining
The Cripple Creek Drainage and Tunnel	I				57	Mining
The Fort Wayne and Silver Cliff Mining	I				50	Mining
The Gavilan Mining & Milling Co	U	1891	CA	three miners, one holding sledge hammer.	25	Mining
The Gold Chain Mining Company	I			Miners	50	Mining
The Goldsmith Gold Mining	I			Miners	50	Mining
The Gotham Gold Mining and Tunnel	I			Miners	50	Mining
The Highland Mary Mines	I	1916	CO	Elk	140	Mining
The Lemhi Placer Mining Company	I	1893	ID	Woman	100	Mining
The Lucania Tunnel and Mines	I	1909		Boat	130	Mining

The Mohawk Gold Mining Company	I			Miners	70	Mining
The Moore Mining and Smelting	U			Mill and landscape	50	Mining
The Mountain Beauty Mines Company	I				51	Mining
The Navajo Consolidated Mining	I			Native American	50	Mining
The Pearl Gold & Silver Mining	IC	1860's	CA	Young girl, dog.	264	Mining
The Pine Creek Placer Mines Co.	I	1902			100	Mining
The Potsdam Gold Mining Company	I			Miners	50	Mining
The Republic Gold Mining Compan	I			Woman	50	Mining
The Silver State Gold Mining Co	I	1902	CO	Hills	90	Mining
The St. Louis, St. Joseph and Cripple Creek Mining Co.	I			Miners	80	Mining
The Triumph Gold Mining Company	I			Mountain	50	Mining
The United States Gold Mines	I				47	Mining
The Vulcan Mining Company	I	1848	NJ	Man	77	Mining
The Wabash Consolidated Mining Co.	I			Miners	50	Mining
The Washington Mining Co	I	1892	WA		90	Mining
Thomas Laughlin	IU	1900's		State seal	15	Mining
Timberlake Development & Mining	IU	1900's		Eagle, train & ship	15	Mining
Tip Top Gold & Silver Mining	IC	1860's	CA	Sun beyond hills. Frank Cooper	341	Mining
Tippecanoe Lead & Zinc	I	1908	WI	Gold seal, prospector underprint. Miners.	35	Mining
Tippecanoe Lead 8 Zinc	I	1908	WI	Gold seal, prospector underprint. Miners.	35	Mining
Tom Reed Gold Mines	I	1920's		Three mining scenes	35	Mining
Tom Reed Gold Mining Co.	I	1910's		Large, unique mining	35	Mining
Tomas Divide Mining	I	1910's	NV	Two mining, with stamp, gold seal	15	Mining
Tombstone Consolidated Mines	U	1900's	AZ Terr	Two miners & mining camp	50	Mining
Tonapah Divide Mining	I	1910's		Mine entry	35	Mining
Tonapah Divide Mining	I	1920's		Mine entry	35	Mining
Tonopah Belmont Development	I	1919	NJ	Orange. Miners in tunnel.	40	Mining
Tonopah Belmont Development	I	1919	NJ	Orange. Miners in tunnel.	40	Mining
Tonopah Belmont Development	I	1920-24		Brown	40	Mining
Tonopah Belmont Development	I	1920-24		Brown	40	Mining
Tonopah Gold Mountain Mining	IC	1900's	AZ	Woman with star studded hat. Jim Butler	253	Mining
Tonopah Gold Mountain Mining Co.	I	1910's	AZ Terr	Goddess George Wingfield	50	Mining
Tonopah North Star Tunnel & Deve	I	1910's	NV	Miners	35	Mining
Tonopah North Star Tunnel & Deve	I	1940's	NV	Eagle	15	Mining

Name		Date	State	Description	Price	Category
Tonopah North Star Tunnel & Deve	I	1950's	NV	Eagle	15	Mining
Tonopah Oriental Mining	U	1910's	NV	Mining	15	Mining
Total Wreck Mining & Milling	IU	1880's		Miners & mountains scene	75	Mining
Trade Dollar Consolidated Mining	IU	1900's	KY	Three miners	50	Mining
Trail Mines	I	1950's	CO		15	Mining
Tribune Gold Mining & Milling	I	1900's	AZ	Bond, miner at work in mine, gold bond	125	Mining
Trifailer Kohlenwerks-Gesellschaft	IC	1880's	Austria		140	Mining
Trinity Copper Corp.	I	1920's	VA	Co. logo	35	Mining
Trinity Dredging	U	1910's		Large gold dredge	15	Mining
Trinity Dredging	I	1910's		Large old dredge	35	Mining
Trinity Mining	Proof	1880's	NY	Miners, NY arms.	176	Mining
Triunfo Gold & Silver Mining	I	1860's	CA	Mountain mining camp scene	350	Mining
Triunfo Gold & Silver Mining	I	1860's		Two winged eagles, mountain scene	350	Mining
Troy-Manhattan Copper	I	1906-7	ME	1880's aerial view of Manhattan in diamond frame.	35	Mining
Troy-Manhattan Copper	I	1906-7	ME	1880's aerial view of Manhattan in a diamond frame	75	Mining
Trust Mining Co.	U	1800's	WA	Miss Liberty, flag, eagle, & state seal	15	Mining
Trust Mining Co.	I	1890's	WA	Miss Liberty, flag, eagle, & state seal	50	Mining
Tuolumne Copper Mining	I	1910's	AZ	Mining	35	Mining
Tuolumne County Water	I	1850's		Sluice mining	225	Mining
Tuolumne County Water	I	1860's		Huge of methods to mine gold	175	Mining
Twentieth Century Mining	I	1900's		Ship, train, & eagle	50	Mining
Uncas Mining	I	1881	CA	Grey/Black. Indian looks at distant factory.	75	Mining
Uncas Mining	I	1881	CA	Grey/Black. Indian looks at distant factory.	75	Mining
Uncle Ned Gold Mining	I	1890's		Mining plus six miners in border, gold seal	50	Mining
Uncle Ned Gold Mining	U			Mining plus six miners in border, gold seal	15	Mining
Unidilla Mining	I	1880's			75	Mining
Union Consolidated Mining	I	1880's		Embossed seal	50	Mining
Union Copper Mining Smelting of NC	IC	1850's	NC	Blacksmith, train & factory.	253	Mining
Union Hill Mines	I	1910's	CA	Eagle	35	Mining
Unita Tunnel & Mining	I	1910's	WY	Spread eagle	50	Mining
United Coal	IU	1891	CO	Flowers	50	Mining
United Copper	IC	1900's	NJ	Eagle and shield in circle. Frederick Augustus Heinze	880	Mining
United Gold Mining, & Milling	I				15	Mining
United Gold Mining. Co.	I	1900's	CO	Mining with stamps	50	Mining
United Mines of Arizona	I	1900's		Miners in mine	50	Mining

Name		Date	State	Description	Price	Category
United States Gold Corporation	I	1915	CO	Gold. State Seal, Columbia and eagle.	20	Mining
United States Gold Corporation	I	1915	CO	Gold. State Seal, Columbia and eagle.	20	Mining
United States Reduction & Refining	I	1910's		Eagle on shield	50	Mining
United States Smelting	I	1900's		Bond, smelters, seal	50	Mining
United Water & Power Co. of Calif	I	1910's		Three mining	15	Mining
Unity Mining	U	1880's	ME	Mining scene	35	Mining
Universal Mining	IU	1950's	WA	Two mining plus large mountain scene, gold seal	15	Mining
Uspallata, Empresa De Minas De	IC	1820's	Argentina		260	Mining
Utah Consolidated Mining	I	1900's		Drifting rigs	35	Mining
Utah Metal & Tunnel Co.	I	1910's		Mountain mining town	35	Mining
Utah Metal & Tunnel Co.	IU	1930's		Mountain mining town	35	Mining
Utah Metal & Tunnel Co.	I	1940's		Mountain mining town	15	Mining
Utah-Apex Mining Co.	I	1900's		With stamps	35	Mining
Utah-Apex Mining Co.	I	1910's		Eagle atop beehive	15	Mining
Utah-Gingham Mining	I	1900's	CO	Mining	35	Mining
V-I Mining	IU	1920's		Large eagle, gold seal	15	Mining
V.A.M Consolidated Mining	IU	1900's		Large eagle, embossed seal	15	Mining
Van &a Copper & Gold Co.	I	1890's			35	Mining
Van &a Gold Mining	U			Two mining	35	Mining
Van Anda Copper & Gold Co	I	1898			80	Mining
Van Mining Co.	U	1890's	CA	Large of mine entrance & miner pushing mine car	35	Mining
Verde Combination Copper	I	1920	AZ	Prospector sipping coffee, donkey, dog.	35	Mining
Verde Combination Copper	I	1920	AZ	Green. Wonderful vignette of a prospector	35	Mining
Verde Combination Copper Co.	I	1910's	AZ	Miners working in mine, embossed seal	15	Mining
Vermillion Pine & Iron Land	I	1915	MI	Mine	840	Mining
Victor Gold Mining	I	1890's	CO	Mining	50	Mining
Victor Mining	IU	1880's		Two mining	125	Mining
Victoria Chief Copper Mining & Smelt	I	1900's	CO	Indian chief, embossed seal	35	Mining
Victoria Consolidated Mines	I	1910's	UT	Goddess & shield	15	Mining
Victoria Consolidated Mining	I	1910's	UT	Woman with gold shield, gold seal	15	Mining
Village Belle Gold Mining	I	1900	CO	Woman with long hair and cap in circle. Gold eagle	25	Mining
Village Belle Gold Mining	I	1900		Woman with long hair and cap	25	Mining
Virginia Coal & Iron	I	1860's	CO	Train, arm with sledge, with stamp	125	Mining
Virginia Gold Mining	I	1880's			35	Mining
Virginia M. Consolidated Mining	IU	1900's	CO	Eagle	5	Mining

Volcano Gold Mining	I	1910's	CO		35	Mining
Vulcan Mining	I	1848	NJ	Vulcan, anvil, gear, eagle, Neptune, Venus, Ceres, left.	115	Mining
Vulcan Mining	IU	1848	NJ	Men & women	275	Mining
Vulcan Mining	I	1840's		Blacksmith & semi-nudes	175	Mining
Vulture Mining of Arizona	IC	1870's	NY	Mining scene, eagle.	319	Mining
Vznaga Gold Mining	I	1900's	AZ Terr	Mining camp in mountains	100	Mining
Waldorf Metals Co.	I	1910's	AZ Terr		35	Mining
Wall Street Mining	I	1925	ID	Grey, gold. Miners working underground. Prospector.	65	Mining
Wander & Mining	IU	1900's	WY		15	Mining
War Dance Mining	IU	1925	WY		85	Mining
War Eagle Mining	I	1900's	AZ	Working miners, embossed seal	35	Mining
Warrior Copper Co.	I	1900's		Mining	50	Mining
Washington Gold Mining	I	1860's		Miners hauling ore with horses to mill & smelting plant	175	Mining
Washington Mining	I	1880's		Embossed seal	35	Mining
Wayne Coal	I	1910's		Loaded ore train emerging from mine entry	50	Mining
Wellington Mines	I	1910's	AZ		35	Mining
Wells Fargo Express Gold Mining	I	1896	CO	Eagle	54	Mining
Wennerstein Mining	U	1920's		Mining with six miners in border	15	Mining
Wernsberger Erbstolln	IC	1900's	Germany	Underprint of large, & many crossed hammers.	88	Mining
West End Consolidated Mining	IU		NV		15	Mining
West Mariposa Gold Quartz Mine	I	1850's			175	Mining
West Penn & Shenango Coal & Coke	I	1883	PA	Horses and landscape	59	Mining
West Tonopah Consolidated Mining	I	1900's	CA		35	Mining
West Virginia Coal & Coke	SP	1930	WV	Man kneels, shows handful of coal to beautiful woman.	60	Mining
West Virginia Coal & Coke	SP	1930	WV	Muscular semi-nude man kneeling	60	Mining
Western Mines Consolidated	IU	1927	NV	Eagle, flag	20	Mining
Western Nevada Copper Co.	I	1900's	AZ	Mining	50	Mining
Western States Coal	U	1900's	MT	State seal	15	Mining
Wheat Mining	I	1880's	MI	River & mine scenes with seal of Michigan	100	Mining
Wheel of Fortune Gold Mining	I	1890's		Large mining scene	50	Mining
Whipple Gold Mining	I	1860's		With stamp	125	Mining
White Caps Mining	IU	1920's		One paid assessment stamp	15	Mining
White Knob Mining	I	1900's		Mining	35	Mining
White Pine Mill & Mining of Nevada	I	1860's		Miners hauling ore with horses to mill	175	Mining

				&		
White Star Mining	I	1880's		Bond, large white star Co. logo	50	Mining
Whitlatch Union Mining & Milling	U	1880's	CO	Mining scene	35	Mining
Wilkes Barre Coal	U	1910		Miners	50	Mining
Wilkes-Barre Coal Co.	I	1910's		Gold bond, mining scene of mine & jackhammer	75	Mining
Williams Coal Co. of Kanawha	I	1870's		State seal of West Virginia	75	Mining
Williams Coal Co. of Kanawha	I	1880's		Bond	175	Mining
Willow Creek Gold Mining	IU	1910's	NV	of ore train, old prospector with two burros	35	Mining
Winona Copper	I	1918	MI	Brown.	35	Mining
Winona Copper	I	1918		Brown.	35	Mining
Winona Copper Mining	I	1916	MI		62	Mining
Wisconsin Mexico Mining	IU	1903	SD	Miners	65	Mining
Wisdom Silver Mining	I	1920's	MI	Mining	35	Mining
Wiswell Electric Mining Machinery	I	1880's	ME	State seal	75	Mining
Wolverine Copper Mining	I	1910's	MI	Miners	35	Mining
Wolverine Copper Mining	I	1920's	MI	Miners	35	Mining
Wolverine Mining	I	1910's	MI	Miners & equipment	35	Mining
Woman's Gold Mining	I	1894	CO	Brown, gold. Miners underground.	90	Mining
Woman's Gold Mining	I	1894	CO	Brown, gold. Miners underground.	90	Mining
Woman's Gold Mining	I	1899	CO	Grey borders, brown. Liberty, State seal.	90	Mining
Woman's Gold Mining	I	1902	CO	Grey borders, brown. Liberty, State seal.	90	Mining
Wonder Gold Mining	IC	1890's	UT	Eagle, train, Indian. George Q. Cannon	605	Mining
Wonderlandining	IU	1900's	WY	Embossed seal	15	Mining
World Exploration Co.	IU	1920's		Large milling & smelting buildings in mountains	15	Mining
Yaeger Canon Copper Co.	IU	1900's	AZ Terr	Gold Bond	75	Mining
Yankee Girl Gold Mining Co. of Bull	IU	1900's		Three mining	50	Mining
Yellow Metal Mining & Milling	I	1900's	WY	Large mining	35	Mining
Yerlington Mountain Copper Co.	IU	1910's		Working miners	35	Mining
Yguana Smelting & Mining	U	1800's	NV	Mining	35	Mining
Young Helca Mining & Smelting	I	1880's		Working miners with ore car, seal	75	Mining
Yuba Consolidated Gold Fields	I	1940's			15	Mining
Yuma Consolidated Mines & Mill	I	1900's	AZ Terr	Seated lady with winged eagle	50	Mining
Yzerts-Terreinen in Nederlandschindie	IC	1910's	Netherlands	Unique design.	320	Mining
Zapata Producing & Refining	I				35	Mining
Zephyr Mining Co.	I	1880's	CO	Working miners	225	Mining
Zephyr Mining Co.	U	1880's	CO	Working miners	100	Mining

CHAPTER 14 - MISCELLANEOUS CERTIFICATES

Miscellaneous is the catch-all category for those certificates that don't fit into any other category. Many of these are manufacturing companies, service companies, and conglomerates.

… ANTIQUE STOCK & BOND PRICE GUIDE 2014

Name	IU	Date	State	Vignette	Signed by	Value	Category
A & P Co.	I	1920's		Issued to/signed Hartford	George Hartford	150	Misc
A & P Co.	I	1920's			George Hartford	100	Misc
A. M. Byers Co.	I		PA	Man		15	Misc
AbleAuctions.com	I	2003		No vignette		75	Misc
AccessTradeOne.com	SP	1995	NV	Yin Yang symbol		75	Misc
Accurate Specialties	IU	1961	NY			5	Misc
Acieries De Bruges, S.A.	IC	1890's	Belgium	Ironwork, with the arms of the company.		150	Misc
Acieries Reunies De Burbach	IC	1920's	Luxemberg	ARBED works, pouring & rolling process.		520	Misc
Adams Nickel Plating & Mfg	U	1870's				15	Misc
Adirondack Co.	I	1870's	NY	Seven% gold bond, woman, globe with train		350	Misc
African Ostrich Farm Feather	I	1912		Ostriches		250	Misc
African Ostrich Farm Feather	I	1912		Ostriches		250	Misc
Afrique & Congo	I	1924		Dark red. Printed in French.		25	Misc
Afrique & Congo	I	1924		Dark red. Printed in French.		25	Misc
Agnew Automailing Machine Company	I	1906		Press		48	Misc
Agricole & Industrielle Monts Arree	IC	1900's	France	Lady, interior of a paper mill, flowers.		100	Misc
Agricole Du Kouilou, Cie.	IC	1900's	Congo	Coffee & cocoa.		88	Misc
Agricultural Society of N. Chautauqua	IC	1880's	NY	Horses, farmer.		121	Misc
AIgonquin Club	I	1890's	ME	Bond		100	Misc
Air Products & Chemical Inc.	I	1960's		Seminude man, factory, tank, trucks, & train		15	Misc
Air Products & Chemical Inc.	I	1970's		Seated man, tank cars, & modern buildings		15	Misc
Akron Belting Co.	IC	1896	OH	Several rolls of metal		145	Misc
Akzona. Inc.	I	1970's		Seated woman with globe & winged wheel		15	Misc
Alabama-Mississippi Investment	U	1900's		Mining & mountain scenes		15	Misc
Alden Industries, Inc.	I	1960's		Co. building logo		15	Misc
Alden Type Setting & Distrib Mach	I	1860's	NY	Early machine.		275	Misc
Alden Type Setting & Distrib Machine	I	1863	NY	Franklin, Alden, printing press below.		125	Misc
Alden Type Setting & Distributing	I	1860's	NY	Old printing machine & two portraits		395	Misc
Alden Type Setting & Distributing	U	1860's		Old printing machine & two portraits		295	Misc
Alden Type Setting Distrib. Machine	I	1860's	NY	Early machine. Franklin.		160	Misc
Alden Type Setting Distributing Mach	U	1860's	NY	Unissued		35	Misc

130

Company		Year	Location	Description	Signature	Price	Category
Alexander Manufacturing Co.	U	1899	MI	Toilet invention		39	Misc
Algodoes S.A.	IC	1920's	Portugal	Lady spinning cotton, trees & leaves.		80	Misc
All-State Credit Corp.	I	1960's		Woman & two men		15	Misc
Allegheny Corp.	SP			Nude man with wheel		15	Misc
Allen Typewriter Manufacturing Co.	I	1930	PA	Woman		100	Misc
Alles & Fisher, Inc.	I	1920's	MA	Two cigars		15	Misc
Allgemeine Elektricitats-Ges.	IC	1930's	Germany			70	Misc
Allied Chemical	I	1960's		Seated woman, two men, lab equipment		15	Misc
Allied Chemical & Dye	I	1940's				15	Misc
Allied Chemical & Dye	I	1950's		3.5 % bond, seated lady with globe		15	Misc
Allied Kid Co.	I	1940's		Seated ladies & goats		35	Misc
Allied Stores	I	1960's		Seated lad		15	Misc
Alumine Et Ses Derives	IC	1890's	France	Industry & science, a worker, a lion.		108	Misc
Aluminum Co. of Canada	I	1950's		Workmen & world lobe		15	Misc
American & European Crystallized	I	1870's				75	Misc
American & Foreign Power Co.	IU	1930's		Warrant		15	Misc
American Asbestos & Fireproofing	I	1900's		Gold bond, phoenix in flames		35	Misc
American Bank Note Holographics	I	2002		Woman between two globes & hologram		50	Misc
American Book-Stratford Press	I	1970's	NY	Eagle		15	Misc
American Brands, Inc.	U	1970's	NJ	Indian Chief.		60	Misc
American British Home Building Ass.	I	1930		Two women		25	Misc
American British Home Building Ass.	I	1930		Two women		25	Misc
American Can Co.	I	1960's		4.75% bond, four figures winged wheel		15	Misc
American Caramel Co.	U	1890's		Eagle & coat of arms		15	Misc
American Caramel Co.	I	1910's		Eagle & coat of arms		15	Misc
American Centrifugal Concrete Co.	IU	1911		Goddess, Indians & city		75	Misc
American Cigar Company	U	1900	NJ	Woman		46	Misc
American Cities	I	1910's		Topless lady		35	Misc
American Colortype Co.	I	1940's		Warrant		15	Misc
American Commonwealth Power C	IU	1930's		Goddess, power plant, & oil refinery		35	Misc
American Commonwealth Power C	I	1930's		Goddess plus factory & oil refinery		15	Misc
American Construction Co	I	1905	IA	Eagle		91	Misc
American Electric Power	I	1960's	NY	Man with globe, woman with torch		15	Misc
American Express	IC	1850's	NY	Train passing building	H. Wells, W. Fargo	2,000	Misc
American Express	I	1850's		Type III, train	Wells & Fargo	2,500	Misc
American Express	I	1850's		Type II	Wells & Fargo	2,500	Misc
American Express	I	1850's		Type I	Wells & Fargo	3,000	Misc
American Express	I	1860's		Type IV	Wells & Fargo	1,750	Misc

Name	Type	Date	State	Description	Signer	Price	Category
American Express	I	1860's		Type V	Henry Wells	1,500	Misc
American Express	I	1870's		Type VI, of dog	Wells & Fargo	1,250	Misc
American Express	I	1960's	NY	Portrait		15	Misc
American Express	I	1960's		Type VII, Roman soldier		35	Misc
American Express Co.	IC	1970's		Roman Warrior		35	Misc
American Express Co.	IC	1970's		Roman Warrior		35	Misc
American Financial & Home Stead	I	1870's		Eagle, seminude lady, dog, & seal		125	Misc
American Flag House & Betsy Ross.	IC	1890's	PA	Liberty bell, Nations flag.		264	Misc
American Founders Corp.	IC	1929		Washington and Jefferson		35	Misc
American Founders Corp.	IC	1929		Washington and Jefferson		35	Misc
American Founders Corp.	I	1920's	MD	Washington&Jefferson, eagle, Wash.Monument		45	Misc
American Founders Corp.	I	1930's	MD	Washington Jefferson, eagle, Wash. Monument		40	Misc
American General Corp.	I	1930's		Co. logo		40	Misc
American Hay & Cotton Press	I	1860's	NY	Men, horse, & two level working press		350	Misc
American Intl. Corp.	U	1920's	NY	Allegorical figures, western hemisphere		15	Misc
American Light & Traction	I	1940's		Lady with electric torch		15	Misc
American Lock Box and Pouch	I	1880	NY	Illustration of the lock box at left.		75	Misc
American Lock Box and Pouch	I	1880	NY	Eagle on shield. Illustration of the lock box at left.		75	Misc
American Locker Co.	I	1930's		Trustee certificate		15	Misc
American Locker Co.	I	1940's		Outline map of United States, eagle		15	Misc
American Machine & Foundry	I		NJ	Man with gear & sledgehammer		15	Misc
American Merchants Union Express	I	1868		Horses	Fargo	105	Misc
American Merchants Union Express	I	1869		Three expressmen, four horses. Dog in a circle.		265	Misc
American Merchants Union Express	I	1869		Three expressmen drive a team of four horses		265	Misc
American Merchants Union Express	I	1869		Industrial		123	Misc
American Merchants Union Express	I	1860's		William Fargo, president		750	Misc
American Natural Gas	I	1930's		Two ladies		15	Misc
American Natural Gas	I	1950's		Pipeline map from Houston to Detroit		15	Misc
American Natural Resources	I	1960's		Two men with Co. logo		15	Misc
American News Co.	I	1960's		Newsboy between two allegorical figures		15	Misc
American News Corp.	I	1960's		Red. Statue of a newspaper boy holding newspaper.		35	Misc

Company	Type	Date	State/Country	Description	Price	Category
American News Corp.	I	1960's		Statue of a newspaper boy holding newspaper.	35	Misc
American Piano	I	1930	NJ	Blue. Man with trumpet, woman with halo	45	Misc
American Piano	I	1930	NJ	Man with trumpet & woman with halo flank monogram	45	Misc
American Pneumatic Service	I	1920's		Eagle	15	Misc
American Radiator Co.	U	1920's		Specimen, bond, reclining woman	35	Misc
American Reclamation Co.	I	1910's	AZ	Multicolor-Indian, buffalo, eagle	15	Misc
American Safety Device	I	1922	NY	Green. Buildings, construction equip, Brooklyn Bridge.	25	Misc
American Safety Device	I	1922	NY	Buildings, construction equipment, Brooklyn Bridge.	25	Misc
American Safety Device	I	1920's		Building, bridges, & safe items	15	Misc
American Safety Device	I	1930's		Building, bridges, & safety items	15	Misc
American Safety Equipment	I	1970's		Large	15	Misc
American Sugar	I	1960's	NJ	3 figures with tools & equipment	15	Misc
American Superpower Corp.	I	1920's		Old & new power stations & mountains	15	Misc
American Turpentine & Tar	U				15	Misc
American Wood Paper	IC	1890's	RI	Factory grounds, train, and canal scene.	121	Misc
American, British & Continental	I	1920's		Warrior/ sword, figure/ scales, woman	15	Misc
AMF	I	1960's			15	Misc
AMF, Inc.	I	1970's		Factories & seated man with tools	15	Misc
Amiantes De Poschiavo S.A.	IC	1900's	Switzerland	View south from the Bernina pass to the Engadine.	180	Misc
Ampet Carpet	I	1950's		Woman between blacksmith & draftsman	15	Misc
Amsterdamsche Kristal Ijsfabrie	IC	1880's	Netherlands		52	Misc
Analouge Controls	I	1960's			15	Misc
Ancient Accepted Scottish Rite	U	1800's		Emblem of cross, swords	15	Misc
Anderson Management	I				15	Misc
Anglo-French Five Year 5% Ext Loan	SP	1900's	GB	Justice, flanked by British and French arms.	352	Misc
Angola, Companhia De, S.A.	IC	1900's	Angola	Elephant charging out of jungle, ox-wagons	190	Misc
Ansonia Clock Co.	I	1910's	CT	Seal	50	Misc
Appalachian Power Co.	I	1960's		Eagle	15	Misc
Apple Computer	SP	2002		Apple logo printed in rainbow colors	250	Misc

Company	Type	Date	State	Description	Price	Category
Apple Computer	I	2004		Apple logo printed in black	75	Misc
Aracata National Corp.	I	1960's		Lady in clouds	15	Misc
Arastock Potato Co.	U			Eagle, small train	15	Misc
Arcturus Radio Tube Co.	IU	1930's		Man holding radio tube	35	Misc
Art House, Inc.	U	1900's		Two figures, beehive, two globes, & museum	15	Misc
Arvida Corporation	I	1968		Map of Florida	35	Misc
ASA G. Neville Glass Co.	I	1890's		Glassblower at work, state seal	175	Misc
Ashland Industries Corp.	I	1920's		Seated lady with tools, ship & train	15	Misc
Assoc Franc Collection Titres Anciens	IC	1980's	France	Printout from computer, horse, phonograph, worker.	70	Misc
Associated Corp. of America	I	1970's		Eight & one-half% bond, seated man & woman	15	Misc
Associated Dental Products	IU	1926	DE	Eagle holding olive branch	100	Misc
Associated Gas & Electric Co.	IU	1930's		Goddess & two naked children	35	Misc
Associated Gas & Electric Co.	I	1930's			15	Misc
Associated Pharmacists	IU	1920's		Two eagles & world	15	Misc
Associates Investment Co.	I	1960's		Bond, Co. logo between two figures	15	Misc
Association for Mutual Investment	I	1930's	MA		15	Misc
Association Franklin Medal Scholars	IC	1850's	MA	Edward Everett	132	Misc
Astoria Electrical Manufacturing	IC	1890's	WV	Fist with lightening sparks.	176	Misc
Asylum Company	I	1790's	PA		6,160	Misc
Asylum Company	I	1800's	PA		2,970	Misc
Atlantic Department Stores	I	1970's	NY		15	Misc
Atlantic Fruit & Sugar Co.	I	1920's			50	Misc
Atlantic Fruit & Sugar Co.	I	1930's		Bond, lady, globe, wheel, anchor & ship	35	Misc
Atwood Grapefruit Co.	I	1940's		Female & seal	35	Misc
Atwood Grapefruit Co.	I	1950's		Woman	35	Misc
Audobon Society	IC	1880's	NY	James Audubon.	319	Misc
Aug. Van Nylen Editions-Imprim-Publ	IC	1900's	Belgium	Sun, moon, stars, field with flowers & wheat. Van Nylen	33	Misc
Austin Hotel Co.	I	1920's	IL	Eagle	15	Misc
Austin Hotel Co.	I	1930's	IL	Eagle	15	Misc
Auto Train Corp.	I			Train seats	15	Misc
Automatic Retailers of America	I	1960's		Winged gear & allegorical figures	15	Misc
Automatic Traffic Regulator	IU			Eagle & gold seal	15	Misc
Autosonics	I	1960's		Large eagle	15	Misc
Auxiliaire Chimique Et Industrielle	IC	1930's	Belgium		32	Misc
Avon Products	SP	1998	NY	Two angels on either side of logo.	100	Misc
B. F. Goodrich	I	1970's	NY	Plantation & worker	15	Misc
B. Manischewitz Company	IC	1979	OH	Star of David Bern.Manischewitz	195	Misc
B. Manischewitz Company	IC	1970's	OH	Star of David	45	Misc

B. P. O. E.	I	1920's		Bond, elk	35	Misc
B. T. Mortgage Investors	I	1970's		Girl	15	Misc
Babcock & Wilcox Co.	I	1950's		Co. logo	15	Misc
Babcock & Wilcox Co.	I	1960's		Two seated men, Co. logo	15	Misc
Backer, J.B., Inc.	U	1980's		Warrant certificate	15	Misc
Bad Boy Appliances & Furniture	IU	1977	Ontario	Bad Boy cartoon character	45	Misc
Baldwin Piano Company	IC	1909	OH	Eagle	30	Misc
Baltimore & Fredrick-town Road Co	I	1800's			500	Misc
Baltimore & Yorktown Turnpike Road	IC	1880's	MD	Horsedrawn streetcar, dog, wagon.	154	Misc
Baltimore & Yorktown Turnpike Road	I	1880's		Horse trolley covered wagon, farmer, & sailor	125	Misc
Baltimore Refrigerating & Heating	I	1900's		Gold bond, refrigerating & heating plant	35	Misc
Banana Du Rio-Grande	I	1913	Nicaragua	Train, banana plantation and transport, boats, and ship.	30	Misc
Banana Du Rio-Grande	IU	1913	Nicaragua	Train, banana plantation, boats, and ship	30	Misc
Banco de Cartagena	I	1900	Spain	Mercury & Argos after a painting by Velasquez.	45	Misc
Banco Nacional de S. Carlos	SP	1780's	Spain	Crown, squirrel and lion.	1,320	Misc
Banco Peninsular Mexicano	U	1908	Mexico	Two women 'Twin Ladies'	1,495	Misc
Barcelona Traction Light and Power	U	1923	Canada	Train	89	Misc
Barcelona Traction, Light & Power	I	1913	Canada	Red. Streetcar, monument, street scene.	45	Misc
Barnesandnoble.com	I	2003		bn.com logo	35	Misc
Barrows Iron & L& Co.	I	1900's		Eagle	35	Misc
Bartica Company	I	1912	ME	Gold Bond. Workers collect rubber on plantation.	15	Misc
Bartica Company	I	1912	ME	7% 10 Year Gold Bond. Workers, rubber plantation.	15	Misc
Bath Hotel Company	I	1853	NY	Palatial multistoried stone and brick hotel.	165	Misc
Bath Hotel Company	I	1853	NY	Palatial multistoried stone and brick hotel.	165	Misc
Baume-Marpent Et Thirion Reunis	IC	1970's	Belgium		28	Misc
Bausch & Lomb Optical Co.	I	1920's	NY	Six% gold bond, seated lad	75	Misc
Bay Bridge Co.	U	1800's	MD	City	75	Misc
Bay Ridge Company	U	1880	MD	City scenery	50	Misc
Bay State Gas	IU	1900's	MA	State seal	15	Misc
Beacon Chocolate Co.	I			CD, gold bond	15	Misc

Beacon Chocolate Company	I	1924		No vignette. Printed in chocolate brown ink.	10	Misc
Beacon Chocolate Company	I	1924		No vignette. Printed in chocolate brown ink.	10	Misc
Beacon Manufacturing Group	U	1960's		Six% bond, eagle	15	Misc
Beacon Valley Silver Fox Association	I	1920	CT	Large faint underprint of a fox. Foxes and lighthouse.	45	Misc
Beaver Park Land and Water Co.	I			Beaver	106	Misc
Beckman Coulter	SP	1988	DE	Founder of company	30	Misc
Belgica, Fabrique De Plaques Pour	IC	1890's	Belgium	Classical border.	24	Misc
Bell & Howell	U		IL	Specimen, two seated figures with Co. logo	35	Misc
Belmont Iron Works, The	I	1950's		Horse & ship seal, man stamps	15	Misc
Benedict-Manson Marine	I	1911	CT	Grey. Steamship.	100	Misc
Benedict-Manson Marine	I	1911	CT	Grey. Steamship.	100	Misc
Berkeley Canning & Manufacturing	IC	1891	SC	Fort Sumter	250	Misc
Berkshire Gas Co.	I	1960's		Eagle	15	Misc
Berwyn Pharmaceutical	U	1900's	NY	Eagle with wide wingspan, globe.	25	Misc
Bessmer Co.	I	1870's	NJ	Little girl portrait	100	Misc
Bethlehem Steel	SP		NJ	Cannon	500	Misc
Bethlehem Steel Corp.	IU	1930's		Three & one-half% bond, warrant	15	Misc
Bethlehem Steel Corporation	U	1969	DE	Men	70	Misc
Big Horn Timber	I	1900's	ID	Eagle on globe	50	Misc
Big Horn Timber	U	1900's	ID	Eagle on globe	35	Misc
Billings & Spencer Co.	I	1900's	CT	Large building	15	Misc
Bio Recovery Technology	U			Turtle and a large underprint of lab equipment	35	Misc
Bio Recovery Technology	U			Turtle and a large underprint of lab equipment	35	Misc
Bloomfield & Montclair Crystal Ice	I	1890's		Old ice making machine	125	Misc
Bodegas Bilbainas, S.A.	IC	1900's	Spain	Lady holding bottle & glass of Rioja wine.	160	Misc
Bolivia Trading	U	1900's	NJ	Llama, eagle head.	220	Misc
Bolivia Trading Company	I	1902	Bolivia	Llama	109	Misc
Bond Stores	I	1950's		Nude man turning wheel	15	Misc
Bongola Lokundje N'Yong S.A.	IC	1920's	Cameroon	Harvesting rubber & cocoa. Mount Cameron.	72	Misc
Borg Warner	I	1970's	MD	Seated man with wheel	15	Misc
Boston & Worcester Electric Comp	I	1900's		Two angels	35	Misc
Boston Personal Property Trust	I	1960's		Eagle	15	Misc
Boston Rubber Co.	I	1890's	MA		15	Misc

Boston Water Power Co.	I	1860's		Red seal	100	Misc
Boston Water Power Co.	IC	1890's	MA	Coat-of-arms, train, shipping.	28	Misc
Boston Water Power Co.	I	1900's	MA	Two figures with old train & sailboats	75	Misc
Bourne Mills	I	1940's		Portrait	15	Misc
Bradford Hospital	I	1890's		State seal	125	Misc
Brand Assurance Compagnie	IC	1790's	Denmark	Eight page printed form.	880	Misc
Brazilian Traction, Light & Power	I	1955	Canada	Man	50	Misc
Breakfast Brownies Co.	U	1900's	MT	Brownies & cereal box	35	Misc
Bremer Borse	IC	1860's	Germany		40	Misc
Brinker International	SP	1983	DE	Outer space with large radio waves	35	Misc
Bristol-Myers Co.	U			Specimen, bond, Co. logo	15	Misc
Broad Top Improvement	IC	1860's	PA	Canal, train, coal.	127	Misc
Broad Top Improvement Co	I	1864	PA	City	177	Misc
Broadway Joe's	IC	1969	FL	Joe Namath	45	Misc
Bronx Refrigerator	I	1910's		With many stamps, state seal	15	Misc
Brooklyn Tabernacle	I	1890's	NY	Five% bond, three seated figures	500	Misc
Brooklyn Union Gas Co.	I	1960's	NY	Bond, lad with lobe	15	Misc
Brookside Mills	I	1910's	TN	of factories	35	Misc
Brookside Mills	I	1920's	TN	of factories	35	Misc
Brotherhood Investment Co.	IU	1920's			15	Misc
Brown & Bigelow	U			Specimen, two seated ladies with Co. logo	15	Misc
Brown Segmental Tube Wire Gun	IC	1890's	NY	Mounted cannon. JH Brown	154	Misc
Brown Wire Gun	IC	1900's	ME	Gun barrel.	231	Misc
Bruhn Automatic Temp. & Fire Alarm	U	1900's	MN	Three women	45	Misc
Brunswick-Blake-Callender Co.	I			Subscription warrant, no	15	Misc
Bryant & Stratton's Mercantile Collgs	I	1864		Tuition Certificate	300	Misc
Buena Vista Plantation	IU	1900's		Plantation scene, gold seal	35	Misc
Buffalo D Dock Co.	U		WV	of Niagara Falls	15	Misc
Buffalo Iron Co.	I	1900's	TN	Proxy with stamp	15	Misc
Buffalo Niagara Electric Corp.	IU	1800's	NY	2 3/4% bond, buffalos, oil wells, & storage tanks	95	Misc
Buffalo Steam Engine Works	I	1850's		Green seal	175	Misc
Building Products	I	1930's			15	Misc
Bulgaria Textile Co.	U	1919			52	Misc
Bulova Watch Co.	SP		NY	Seminude girl in front of watchface	75	Misc
Bureau Count Minerals	U	1900's		No	50	Misc
Butler Brothers	I	1920's	IL	Co. catalogue, steam engine, & clerks	15	Misc
Butte & Montana Commercial Co.	I	1890's	NJ	Train, ships, & eagle, embossed seal	75	Misc
Butte City Water Co.	I	1890's		Waterfall with city in background	50	Misc

Company	Type	Year	State	Description	Signature	Price	Category
C & C Super Corporation	I	1954	NJ	Company logo, unusual cans with bottle caps		75	Misc
C N A Overseas Capital	I	1970's		Bond		15	Misc
C. Brewer & Company	IC	1927	HI	Ship, warehouse, building, founder, first president.		175	Misc
C. Brewer & Company	SP		HI	Hotels along coast, island, palm trees, mountain		150	Misc
C.I.N.T.A. Centrale Independ Tabacs	IC	1930's	Belgium			70	Misc
Caisse D'Epargnes Et De Bienfaisance	IC	1790's	France		Lafarge	520	Misc
California Controllers Warrant	I	1880's	CA	Train & seated lady & state building		175	Misc
California Culinary Academy	SP	1986	CA	Tiny logo of the CCA		30	Misc
California Fertilizing Co.	U	1870's	CA	Two of fruit & trees, co. logo		50	Misc
Caloris Manufacturing	I	1900's	CA	Two globes with cartridge		75	Misc
Cambridge Garage	I	1930's		Five % income bond, eagle		15	Misc
Camden Land Co.	IU	1902	ME	Boat, pine trees, mountains		100	Misc
Cameroun S.A., Soc. Nationale Du	IC	1920's	Cameroon	Wharf for export of timber.		100	Misc
Canada General Fund	I	1950's		Map of Canada		15	Misc
Canton Building Association, No. 1	U	1870's	OH	Horse-drawn plows.	William McKinley	3,080	Misc
CardioGenesis	SP	1989	CA	Logo		85	Misc
Carolina Power & Light	I	1970's		Dam, woman with globe, & man with turbine		15	Misc
Carregadores Acoreanos-Comp. Naveg	I	1920	Port Azores	Port and town scenes.		100	Misc
Carregadores Acoreanos-Companhia	IU	1920	Portugal	Port and town scenes.		100	Misc
Cartoon & Reynolds, Inc.	I	1930's		Two kneeling women, globes, & Co. logo		15	Misc
Cash Buyers Cooperative Union	I	1907	NJ	Grey, gold underprint and seal. Woman weaving.		25	Misc
Castle & Cooke	IC	1960	HI	Blue. Fancy logo and scrollwork.		75	Misc
Castle & Cooke	IC	1960	HI	Blue. Fancy logo and scrollwork.		75	Misc
Cavanaugh-Dobbs, Inc.	I	1930's		Man & woman with co. logo		15	Misc
CBRL Group Inc. (Cracker Barrel)	SP	1998	TN	Eagle		25	Misc
Cedar Falls Manufacturing	I	1889	NC	Barn	J.M. Worth	100	Misc
Cedar Rapids, Iowa City & Southern	I	1910's		Seated lady with shield & wreath		15	Misc
Celanese Corp. of America	I	1960's		Two men with Co. logo		15	Misc
Central Bridge Corp.	I	1820's	NH	No		175	Misc
Central Farmer's Corp.	U	1900's	FL			15	Misc

Central Gardens Association	IC	1870's	CA	Garden at foot of hill.	352	Misc
Central Mills	I	1940's	OH	Bond, eagle	15	Misc
Central Public Service Corp.	I	1930's	MD	Man	15	Misc
Century Ribbon Mills, Inc.	I	1930's	MD	Bare-breasted seated woman with winged wheel	15	Misc
Champburger Corp	IU	1971	DE		75	Misc
Chapple Publishing Co.	I	1910's		Beehives, gold seal	35	Misc
Charles Lafitte & Company	IU	1866	GB		50	Misc
Charleston Board of Trade S. Carolina	IC	1870's	SC	Coat-of-arms, picking cotton, riverboats, train.	180	Misc
Charleston City Water Works	IC	1880's	SC	People in park with water fountain.	187	Misc
Chemins De Fer Ethiopiens	IC	1890's	Ethiopia	Ethiopian King on horseback, camel.	363	Misc
Chesebrough-Ponds, Inc.	U			Specimen, seated woman & globe	15	Misc
Chicago Cotton Manufacturing	U	1870's		Factory & revenue stamp	75	Misc
Chicago Livestock Exchange	I	1890's		Cows	100	Misc
Chicago Livestock Exchange	I	1900's		Damaged	35	Misc
Chicago Livestock Exchange	I	1900's		Cows	100	Misc
Chicago Realty Shares	I	1930's		City street scene	15	Misc
Chilena De Caracoles (Snail Co.Chile)	I	1875	Chile	National arms of Chile.	100	Misc
Chino Odd Fellows Hall Association	U	1890's	CA		15	Misc
Chocolaterie & Confiserie Fine Saphir	IC	1920's	Belgium	Girl offering chocolates, Antwerp cathedral.	240	Misc
Cimfina, Soc. Financiere Des Ciments	IC	1920's	Belgium	Cement-works beside a river.	36	Misc
Cincinnati Union Stockyard Co.	I	1880's		Stockyards, freight trains, & large cow head	50	Misc
Citizens' Gas Light Co.	I	1890's		Bond, woman with light	35	Misc
Citizens' Light, Heat & Power	I	1890's	VA	Bond, ships in bay, & seal	100	Misc
Citizens' Underwriters	I	1940's		Eagle	15	Misc
City Associates	I	1920's			15	Misc
City Dairy Co.	I	1920's	MD	Eagle	15	Misc
City Investing	IC	1920's	NY	NY City Hall. H.Morgenthau Jr	286	Misc
City of Tokyo	I	1912	Japan	Boat	180	Misc
Claremont Bridge Company	I	1900			450	Misc
Clark Equipment	SP			Bond, seated man with tools	35	Misc
Clifton Iron & Nail	IC	1970's	WV	Riverside factory complex.	220	Misc
Clouterie Et Trefilerie Des Flandres	IC	1900's	Belgium		56	Misc
Co-op Dairy	I	1920's			15	Misc
Co-op Dress Association	I	1880's	NY	Sailor, Indian & eagle	75	Misc
Co. Azucarrera del Paraiso Noviller	IU	1924	Mexico	Map of Veracruz and its surrounding area.	45	Misc
Co. General de Tabacos de Filipina	IU	1882	Philippines	Brown. females, one bare-breasted and cherubs.	75	Misc

Name	Type	Date	State/Country	Description	Signer	Price	Category
Co. General de Tabacos de Filipinas	I	1882	Philippines	Allegorical females, one bare-breasted and cherubs.		75	Misc
Coal Investment	U			Eagle		15	Misc
Cogentag Comptoirs Generaux & Agri	IC	1920's	BelCongo			90	Misc
Cohoes Co.	IU	1860's	NY	Woman & baby sitting on a bale		100	Misc
Cohu Electronics, Inc.	I	1970's		Eagle, globe, & shield		15	Misc
Coldak Corp.	I	1920's	DE	Girl at birdbath		15	Misc
Coleman, J & V	I	1920's		Four % gold bond		15	Misc
Collins & Aikman	I	1960's		Woman standing between seated man & woman		15	Misc
Collins & Aikman	I	1970's		Two women & man		15	Misc
Colonial Beach Improvement	IC	1880's	VA	Gold borders, green underprint.	Melville Bell	242	Misc
Colonial Dairy Co.	I	1950's	IL	Large of dairy, farm, & cows		15	Misc
Coloniale, Co. Generale	IC		BelCongo	Border of coffee, river-port, ship, train		60	Misc
Colorado Southern Irrigation Co.	I	1900's		Gold bond, three ladies		35	Misc
Colt Co.	U	1930		Horse	Ulrich, Nichols	280	Misc
Colt Firearms Factory	I	1955				46	Misc
Colt Gun and Carriage Co. Ltd.	IC	1900's	GB	Soldiers firing machine-guns. Bullets, feed belts, boxes.		995	Misc
Colt Patent Firearms	I	1948		Horse		58	Misc
Colt's Manufacturing	I	1954	CT	Corporate seal with crossed rifles and revolvers.		35	Misc
Colt's Manufacturing	I	1954	CT	Corporate seal with crossed rifles		75	Misc
Colt's Manufacturing	I			Colt		50	Misc
Colt's Patent Fire Arms Manufacturing	I	1947		Horse		67	Misc
Colt's Patent Fire Arms Manufacturing	I	1943-8	CT	Horse catching spear and arrow. Green.		35	Misc
Colt's Patent Fire Arms Manufacturing	I	1943-8	CT	Horse catching spear and arrow. Green.		100	Misc
Columbia College Trustees	I	1899		Man with trumpet, woman with halo flank college seal.		75	Misc
Columbia Turnpike Road	PI	182-	MD		Daniel Carroll	500	Misc
Columbia-Knickerbocker Trust	IC	1900's	NY	Columbia	Edward HR Green	341	Misc
Comet Transport Corp.	I	1970's	NV	Large eagle, gold seal		15	Misc
Commerce Au Congo, Soc.	IC	1890's	BelCongo	Village by a jungle river.		76	Misc
Commerce Colonial, S.A.	IC	1890's	BelCongo	Train & ship.		80	Misc
Commercial Appliance Corp.	I	1960's				15	Misc
Commercial Cable	I	1897		Blue. Map of Cable System.		25	Misc
Commercial Cable	I	1897		Blue. Map of Cable System.		25	Misc
Commercial Cable Co.	I	1890's	NY	Map of Atlantic cable, embossed seal		35	Misc

Commercial Cable Co.	I	1890's		Map of Atlantic Ocean with cables	50	Misc
Commercial Credit	I	1960's		Four & three-fourths% bond, eagle	15	Misc
Commercial Credit	I	1960's		Note	15	Misc
Common Stock Fund	I	1960's		Eagle on mountaintop	15	Misc
Common Stock Fund	I			Ocean liner, trains, truck, & eagle	15	Misc
Comp Centrl Grandes Laiteries Belges	IC	1890's	Belgium		32	Misc
Comp Univ. Canal Maritime De Suez	SP	1860's	Egypt	Tan ornate border.	451	Misc
Comp Univ. Canal Maritime De Suez	IC	1930's	Egypt	Blue frame, lt rose undertint.	231	Misc
Comp Univ. Canal Maritime De Suez	IC	1940's	Egypt	Egyptian obelisks and beam, sphinxes.	495	Misc
Comp. Chilena De Caracoles(Snail)	IU	1875	Chile	National arms of Chile.	100	Misc
Compagnie des Claridges Hotels	I	1921	France	Steamship at left and steam train at right, multicolored	45	Misc
Compagnie des Claridges Hotels	IU	1921	France	steamship, steam train	75	Misc
Compagnie Install. Maritime Bruges	IC	1900's	Belgium	Arms, angel and anchor.	176	Misc
Compan Azucarrera Paraiso Novillero	I	1924	Mexico	Map of Veracruz and its surrounding area.	45	Misc
Companhia Industrial da Beira Alta	I	1920	Portugal	Mountains with tunnels and mining shafts.	60	Misc
Companhia Industrial da Beira Alta	IU	1920	Portugal	mountains with tunnels, mining shafts.	60	Misc
Companhia Leopolding Estrada Ferro	I	1884	Brazil	Fancy title and ornate borders. Small steam train	20	Misc
Compania Industrial Manufactruera	SP	1880's	Mexico	Woman, machinery, wagon.	231	Misc
Comptoir Belge-Persan S.A.	IC	1920's	Iran	Colorful.	16	Misc
Comptoir D' Achat Et De Vente	IC	1920's	Belgium	Belgian soldiers.	320	Misc
Comptoirs Francais D'Oceanie S.A.	IC	1920's	Fr.Polynesia	Tahitian woman, schooner, Tahiti.	100	Misc
Computer Applications, Inc.	I	1960's	DE	Woman with two globes	15	Misc
Comstock Tunnel	I	1880's		Four% gold bond, eagle	75	Misc
Confederate States of America	U	1863			170	Misc
Congo, Soc. Commerciale Miniere	IC	1910's	BelCongo	Mining scene & figure of Justice.	25	Misc
Congo, Soc. Commerciale Miniere	IC	1910's	BelCongo		25	Misc
Connecticut Turnpike	I	1800's	CT		165	Misc
Conserves Aliment Pierre Beziers Fils	IC	1920's	France	Women in Breton dress, carrying sardines	32	Misc
Consolidated Edison Co.	I	1940's		Five% bond, view of New York City	35	Misc

Consolidated Edison Co. of New York	IC	1940's	NY	Light on top of Empire State Building.	35	Misc
Consolidated Edison Co. of New York	IC	1940's	NY	Light on top of Empire State Building.	35	Misc
Consolidated Edison Co. of New York	I	1940's		lighted tower with clocks	15	Misc
Consolidated Edison Co. of New York	I	1950's		Five % bond, of New York	15	Misc
Consolidated Edison Co. of New York	I	1960's		Lighted tower between two figures	15	Misc
Consolidated Investment Trust	I	1960's		Eagle	15	Misc
Consolidated Lake Superior	I	1904	CT	Green. Trains & workers on factory grounds.	28	Misc
Consolidated Lake Superior	I	1904	CT	Green. Trains & workers on factory grounds.	28	Misc
Consolidated Terminal Corp.	U		WA		15	Misc
Consorzio Agrario Vignale Monferr	IC	1920's	Italy	Man holding statue of victory. Consorzio Products	70	Misc
Construction Materials Corp.	I	1930's		Freighter being loaded in ship canal	35	Misc
Consumer Growth Capital, Inc.	U		MN	Eagle	15	Misc
Consumer Ice Co.	I	1910's		No	15	Misc
Consumer Ice Co.	I	1920's		Eagle	35	Misc
Consumers Power Co.	I		ME	bond, generator & power lines	35	Misc
Consumers' Discount Corp.	U		TX	Star & wreath	15	Misc
Continental Express	U	1900's	MT		15	Misc
Continental Gummi-Werke A.G.	IC	1940's	Germany		128	Misc
Continental Shares	I	1932	MD	Gray. Seated allegorical men, globe.	20	Misc
Continental Shares	I	1932	MD	Gray. Seated allegorical men, globe.	20	Misc
Continental Timber Co.	U	1900's		Eagle	35	Misc
Continuous Transit Securities	I	1920's	NY	Co. logo	15	Misc
Controls Co. of America	I	1960's		Man with wheel	15	Misc
CoolSavings	I	2003		Piggy bank	35	Misc
Copeland Commercial Photo	I				15	Misc
Copper Metals Co.	I	1910's		Six% gold bond	35	Misc
Corona Typewriter Co.	I	1920's		Typewriter	50	Misc
Corrugated Container Co.	I	1960's	OH		15	Misc
Cosmopolitan Electric Underground	I	1880's		Lady telegraph operator	100	Misc
Cottaraugus & Buffalo Plank Road	I	1850's		Old stagecoach with four horses	350	Misc
Cox Realization Co. of Houston	IU	1920's		Seal with Texas star	35	Misc
Crawford Equipment & Engineering	SP	1974	FL	Fiery flames	175	Misc
Crescent Corp.	U			Specimen, Winged Mercury, ship, plane, train & cars	15	Misc

Cristal-Chaudfontaine S.A.	SP	1930's	Belgium	Decorative border.	130	Misc
Crown-Zellerbach Corp.	I			Man, woman, & Co. logo	15	Misc
Crusader Industry	I	1970's	NV	Lighted torch	15	Misc
Crystal Ice Manufacturing & Cold	I	1900's		Large of Indian Chief with sailing ship in background	35	Misc
Cuba Co.	I	1920's	NJ	Sugarcane worker	35	Misc
Cuban Cane Products	I	1930's	DE	Gold bond, train	35	Misc
Cudahy Packing	U	1900's		Specimen, portrait of cow, signed	35	Misc
Curtis Manufacturing	I	1932	DE	Mercury seated on lathe, ship, airplane, trucks	75	Misc
Curtis Manufacturing	I	1932	DE	Mercury seated on lathe, ship, airplane, trucks	75	Misc
Cutler Hammer Intl. Finance, Inc.	I	1970's		Bond, electric supplies	15	Misc
Cyro-Therm, Inc.	I	1960's		Woman between two worlds, train & buildings	15	Misc
Czellechowitzer Zuckerfabrik Brunn	IC	1880's	Austria		90	Misc
D. M. Osborne & Co.	U	1800's	NY	Three of farmers working with horses	125	Misc
D'Esterre Estate	I	1910's		Gold bond	15	Misc
Dairy League Co-op Corp.	U		NY	Specimen, cow	50	Misc
Damarra Manufacturing	I	1900's	AZ Terr	Female with electricity	35	Misc
Dane, Stern & Wood, Inc.	I	1930's		Eagle	35	Misc
Data Control Systems	I	1960's		Rocket & tower	15	Misc
Databyte, Inc.	U			Eagle	15	Misc
Davega Stores	I	1960's	NY	Skyline	15	Misc
Davis Sewing Machine Co.	I	1870's		Allegorical figures	100	Misc
Davis Sewing Machine Co. of Water	I	1860's		Two figures with eagle, revenue stamp	125	Misc
Dayco Corp.	I			Orbiting electrons & girl	15	Misc
DeBeukelaer's Fab Biscuits Chocolade	IC	1920's	Belgium		36	Misc
Defiance Light & Power Company	U	1891	OH	Trolly	96	Misc
Delaware & Schuylkill Canal Navigation	I	1792	PA	Robert Morris	2,900	Misc
Delhaize Ferres Et Cie Le Lion S.A.	SP	1960's	Belgium	Lion.	72	Misc
Dennos Food of Portland	I	1915	OR	Gold seal. Unusual photographic litho of a baby.	25	Misc
Denny's Corp.	SP	2002	DE	Logo	75	Misc
Departementale Electrique S.A., La	IC	1890's	France	Elegant lady & electric lighting.	52	Misc
Depew Improvement	IU	1982	NY	Chauncey Depew	250	Misc
Des Moines River Improvement	I	1851	IA	Canal, Early train. Farmer sharpens scythe. Indians.	75	Misc
Des Moines River_ Improvement	I	1851		Canal, Early train. Farmer sharpens scythe. Indians.	75	Misc

Detroit Autocleno Mfg. Co.	IU			Train, gold seal, stamps	35	Misc
Deutsche Pflanzenbutter	IC	1920'a	Germany	A line of cooks, & a cow's head.	104	Misc
Dewey & Alma Chemical	I	1940's	MA	Eagle	15	Misc
Dewey & Alma Chemical	I	1950's		Globe between two ladies	15	Misc
Dewey Portland Cement	I	1940's	WV		15	Misc
Dial Corp	SP	1996	DE	Woman holding torch	35	Misc
Diamond Disc Shop	I	1910's	NY	Charles Edison	125	Misc
Dick's Hamburgers	SP		WA	Skunk	45	Misc
Dickerson Automatic Governor	IU	1920	UT	Photo-vignette of patented engine Arthur Dickerson	250	Misc
Diebold Venture Capitol Corp.	I	1970's		Woman with atoms	15	Misc
Dillingham (Bond)	IC	1970's	HI	Man with scroll, modern factory & dam - brown	35	Misc
Dillingham (Bond)	IC	1970's	HI	Man with scroll, modern factory & dam - green	35	Misc
Dillingham Corp.	I	1970's		9.75% bond, man, dam, bridge, & buildings	15	Misc
District of Richmond	IC	1850's	PA	Liberty, trains, shipyard.	143	Misc
Divco Detroit Corp of Michigan	I	1928	MI	Eagle	50	Misc
Diving & Breathing Apparatus Mfg	IC	1880's	NV	Justice & eagle.	198	Misc
Dixon Chemical Industries	I	1950's	NJ	Tank car, & truck, & factory	15	Misc
Doble Steam Motors Corporation	I	1923	DE		89	Misc
Doers, A. A. Mercantile	U	1900's		Eagle	15	Misc
Domain of Neptunus Rex	IC	1920's		Neptune.	396	Misc
Dominion Diamond Co.	I		NY	Eagle	15	Misc
Dominion Reindeer	IC	1927-31	Canada	Blue, red embossed seal.	20	Misc
Dominion Reindeer	I	1927-31	Canada	Blue, red embossed seal.	20	Misc
DoubleTwist Inc.	SP	2000	DE	Large bubbly DNA	250	Misc
Douglas Monument Association	IC	1860's	IL	Plot, woman with shield and eagle. Leonard W. Volk	231	Misc
Dourte Manufacturing Co.	I	1910's		Gold seal	15	Misc
Dover Corp.	U	1970's		Seated lady with globe, Co. logo	15	Misc
Dow-Corning	I	1970's		Certificate, of research lab	15	Misc
Dow-Corning	I			Bond of research lab	15	Misc
Dreamlife	SP	1999	DE		65	Misc
DrKoop.com	I	2001		Logo	35	Misc
Drugstore.com	I	2003		Logo	35	Misc
Drury's Tailoring	U			Eagle	15	Misc
Dunluth & Dubuque Bridge Co.	I	1860's		Eight% bond, train-crossing bridge	175	Misc
Duquesne Light Co.	U	1950's		Specimen, stock certificate, lady holding light	15	Misc

Duquesne Light Co.	U			Specimen, bond, woman with light & generator	15	Misc
DWG Cigar Corporation	U		OH/MI	Farmer picking tobacco, Mercury & a Goddess.	136	Misc
E. F. Hutton	SP		DE	Woman with Hutton sign	325	Misc
Eagle General Corporation	I	1970's		Eagle	15	Misc
Eagle Lock Co.	I	1890's	NY	Eagle with flag	45	Misc
Eagle Lock Co.	I	1910's		Eagle with flag	35	Misc
Eagle Lock Co.	I	1930's		Eagle with flag	30	Misc
Eames Petroleum Gold & Smelting	I	1880's	NY	Two seated figures with eagle	100	Misc
Eames Petroleum Iron Co.	I	1880's	NY		15	Misc
East-India Company	IC	1840's	India/London		300	Misc
Eastern Cuba Sugar	I	1922		Green. Sugar cane harvest.	35	Misc
Eastern Electric Light & Storage	IU			Stylized light bulb	35	Misc
Eastern Steel Co.	I	1920's		Horses & seal	35	Misc
Eastern Tanning Co.	U		MA	Indian _& harbor	15	Misc
Eastman Kodak Company-8.25%	IC	1984		Astronaut floating in space with camera.	95	Misc
Eastman Kodak Company-8.25% B	IC	1983		Astronaut floating in space with camera.	125	Misc
Easton & Wilkesbarre Turnpike RR	I	1800's	PA		121	Misc
Eaton & Howard Balanced Fund	I	1950's			15	Misc
Eaton Howard	I	1960's		Woman justice between two men	15	Misc
Eaux De Spa S.A.	IC	1920's	Belgium	Pretty border with flowers.	48	Misc
Eaux Minerales Et Thermales De	IC	1920's	France		28	Misc
eBay Inc.	I	2004		Logo & cartoon items	185	Misc
Eckard (Jack) Corp.	I	1970's		Two seated workmen & Co. logo	15	Misc
Eckmar Corp.	I	1960's		Christmas packages, & Co. logo	45	Misc
Eclairage Electrique de St. Petersbourg	I	1897	Russia	Green. St. Petersburg, with street light in the foreground.	65	Misc
Eclairage Electrique St. Petersbourg	IU	1897	Russia	Green. St. Petersburg	65	Misc
Eclairage Electrique St. Petersbourg	IC	1900's	Belgium	Bright electric lights atop ornate poles.	198	Misc
Edison Cement	I	1931	NJ	Blue. Debenture Note. Charles Edison	75	Misc
Edison Cement	I	1931	NJ	Blue. Debenture Note. Charles Edison	75	Misc
Edison Cement Corp.	I	1930's			100	Misc
Edison Electric Illum.New Brunswick	IC	1880's	NJ	Transmission posts and wires.	935	Misc
Edison Electric Illuminating Co.	I	1880's	NJ	Generator with light	175	Misc
Edison Kinetophone Co.	U	1910's		Eagle	35	Misc
Edison New York	I	1940's		Bond	15	Misc

Company	Type	Date	State	Vignette	Signature	Price	Category
Edison Portland Cement	IC	1890's	NJ	Thomas Edison	Thomas Edison	1,535	Misc
Edison Portland Cement Co.	I	1890's		Thomas Edison		100	Misc
Edison Portland Cement Co.	I	1900's		Thomas Edison		95	Misc
Edison Portland Cement Co.	I	1900's		Thomas Edison	Thomas Edison	2,950	Misc
Edison Splitdorf Corp.	IU	1940's				50	Misc
Edison Storage & Battery	IC	1900's	NJ	Woman on clouds, lightning sparks	Thomas A. Edison	798	Misc
Edison Storage Battery	IC	1930's	NJ	Woman amidst clouds.	Charles Edison.	209	Misc
Edison Storage Battery Co.	I	1900's		Woman in clouds, map of North America	Thomas A. Edison	2,000	Misc
Edison Storage Battery Co.	I	1910's		Woman in clouds, map of North America	Thomas A. Edison	2,000	Misc
Edison Storage Battery Co.	I	1910's		Eagle	Thomas A. Edison	2,000	Misc
Edison, Thomas A., Inc.	I	1920's	NJ		Charles Edison	500	Misc
Edison, Thomas A., Inc.	I	1920's			Thomas A. Edison	2,000	Misc
Edouard Hotel	I	1907-8	PA	Gray, gold embossed seal & underprint. Eagle, lightning.		20	Misc
Ego Resources	IU	1979	Ontario	Fancy background		10	Misc
Electric Co. of America	Proof	189-	NJ	Globe with ring		575	Misc
Electric Mfg. & Misc. Stock Exchange	IU	1883	NY	Woman with lightning		700	Misc
Electrique Cie. Gen. Pour L'Exploit	IC	1850's	France	Classical figures, little angels, ship, train & more.		160	Misc
Electro Pneumatic Transit	IU	1900	NJ	Pneumatic mail transit system		395	Misc
Elgin National Watch	I	1903		Angel		100	Misc
Elgin National Watch Co.	IC	1923		Father time holding watch		50	Misc
Elgin National Watch Co.	IC	1920's	IL	Father Time, eagle with watch		50	Misc
Elkhart Bridge Co.	I	1900's		Portraits of Washington & Lincoln, flying eagle		35	Misc
Elston & Wheeling Gravel Road	U	1860's	IL	Peace, Ceres.		154	Misc
Emhart Corp.	I			Specimen Certificate, two figures with building		35	Misc
Emporium Real Estate & Manuf	U	1857		Houses		385	Misc
Emporium Real Estate & Manufact.	I	1850's	IL	Sailing vessel.		385	Misc
Emprestit Gremi Favricants Sabadell	IC	1920's	Spain	Textile industry scenes.		180	Misc
Enron	U			Man		61	Misc
Entrepots Frigorfiques	I	1925	Greece	Blue & brown with green revenue stamps.		35	Misc
Entrepots Frigorfiques	I	1925	Greece	Blue & brown with green revenue stamps.		35	Misc
Equatoriale Congolaise Lulongaike.	IC	1920's	BelCongo			56	Misc
Equity Corp.	I	1960's		Seated lady with books & city skyline		15	Misc
Erdman-Guilder Co.	U	1920's	MI	Eagle		15	Misc

Name		Date	Location	Description		Price	Category
Erie Forge & Steel Corp.	U			Specimen, eagle		15	Misc
Erleme Corp.	I	1930's		Large eagle, two globes, & bolts & lightning		15	Misc
Escalade	SP		IN	Logo		25	Misc
Esperance, Soc. De L'	IC	1820's	Belgium	Logo: anchors, cornucopias with flowers.		140	Misc
Esquire	I	1969-70	DE	Olive. Semi-nude man, quill, scroll.		20	Misc
Ester House	I	1858	IA	Washington. Indian princess, eagle, dog	JEdgar Thompson	75	Misc
Etna Steel & Iron	I	1906	GA	Green. Eagle and shield.		23	Misc
Etna Steel & Iron	I	1906	GA	Green. Eagle and shield.		23	Misc
ETRA Elektromos Transformatorek	IU	1926	Hungary	Skeleton		200	Misc
Eugene Rimmel, Ltd.	IC	1930's	GB	Logo of a lady of the 1920's.		48	Misc
Eureka Smelting Co.	IU	1920's	NV			35	Misc
European Bond & Exchange	IC	1880's	IL	Women, train, dock scene.		633	Misc
Everett Knitting Works	I	1910's	NH	Red seal		50	Misc
Everett, C.F., Inc.	U	1900's				15	Misc
Eversharp	I	1970's	DE	Seated chemist with equipment		15	Misc
Eversharp, Inc.	I					15	Misc
Ex-Soldiers Investment Industrial	IU	1927	AL	African American man		350	Misc
Executone Co.	I	1960's	DE	Lady with book		15	Misc
Explosifs De Clermont Muller & Cie	IC	1900's	Belgium	Deerhunting, cartridges & an exploding mine.		260	Misc
F & W Grand Stores	I	1910's		Seated lady with lion		15	Misc
F. J. Kaldenberg	IU	1887	NY	Pipes, canes, cigars		495	Misc
Faberge Incorporated	IC	1978		Brown. Woman in clouds holding globe.		15	Misc
Faberge Incorporated	IC	1978				15	Misc
Fabrica De Zahar Din Arad S.A.	IC	1920's	Romania	View of the sugar factory with train.		56	Misc
Fabrication D'Allumettes	IC	1890's	Belgium	Coat of arms Belgium & the S. African Rep.		80	Misc
Fabrication De La Soie De Chardonnet	IC	1900's	Hungary	Beautiful girl spinning silk.		60	Misc
Fabrication Des Ciments A Odessa	IC	1890's	Russia			50	Misc
Fabril De Carbones Electricos S.A.	IC	1900's	Spain	Lovely lady with lights, generator, factory, trees, etc.		120	Misc
Fabril Y Comercial De Los Gremios	IC	1840's	Spain	Company's Coat of Arms, Decorative Border.		800	Misc
Fairmount Park Transportation Co	I	1889				48	Misc
Falmouth Turnpike Road	I	1800's	PA			154	Misc
Farmer's Mercantile	U	1900's				15	Misc
Farmers & Shippers Leaf Tobacco	U	1900's	NJ,OH	Warehouses beside the Ohio River.		140	Misc

Company	Type	Year	State	Description	Price	Category
Farmers Co-op Butter & Cheese	IU		MN	Eagle, gold Id seal	15	Misc
Farmers Friend Scale	IU	1908	MN	Old wagon	275	Misc
Farmers Union	IC	1890	CA	Cattle	95	Misc
Fat Man's Shop, Inc	I	1930's		Eagle	35	Misc
Federal -Brandes, Inc.	I	1920's	DE	Eagle	15	Misc
Federal Adding Machine	I	1919	NJ	Green or Orange. Women, beehive, mill.	45	Misc
Federal National Mortgage Assoc	SP		US	Family, home	110	Misc
FedEx	I	2002		Jet flying above woman	150	Misc
Fellow's Co. of New York	I	1900's		Eagles, flag & shield, Indian chief & buffalo in border	75	Misc
Fernandina Manufacturing	IU	1874	FL	Eagle with flag	295	Misc
Fiberglass Homes of America	I	1970's		Eagle	15	Misc
Fidelity Fund, Inc.	I			Statue	15	Misc
Fidelity Investments Associates	U	1960's	MA	Eagle	15	Misc
Fiduciary Mutual Investing, Inc.	U			Specimen, Co. logo	15	Misc
Field, Glore & Co.	IC	1930's	IL	Marshall Field III	341	Misc
Fieldcrest Mills	I	1960's	MD	Seated lady with winged wheel	15	Misc
Fifth Avenue Transportation	I	1881		Horse-drawn coach rendered in red, blue and black.	500	Misc
Fifth Avenue Transportation	I	1881		Red, blue or pink watermarked paper	500	Misc
Fifth Avenue Transportation	IU	1888	NY	Two horses pulling coach	795	Misc
Fifty Five West 19 Inc.	I	19--	NY	Blue. Globe, buildings, airplane, blimp.	10	Misc
Fifty Five West 19 Inc.	I	19--	NY	Blue. Globe, buildings, airplane, blimp.	10	Misc
Filature Du Lin A La Mecanique, S.A.	IC	1800's	Belgium	Spider in it's web.	190	Misc
Filatures & Tissages Sainte-Therese	IC	1920's	France	Weaving looms.	72	Misc
Finck's Bridge Bond	I	1860's	NY	Seven% bond, horse drawn carriage	100	Misc
Finnish Export Credit Ltd.	I	1970's		Note guaranteed by representative of Finland	15	Misc
First Gloucestershire (Bristol) Rifles	IC	1860's	GB	Embossed seal shows the badge of the regiment.	190	Misc
First York Co.	I	1940's		Two men with Co. logo	15	Misc
Five Leaves Cannabis Corp.	U			Marijuana leaves	30	Misc
Florence & Keyport Joint Companies	IC	1850's	NJ	Harbor scene.	451	Misc
Florida Fruit Exchange	I	1890's		Three of Indian, ship, & woman with bird	125	Misc
Florida, State of, Mortgage Co.	I	1920's		Six% gold bond, shield	15	Misc

FMC Corp.	I	1970's		Bond, of science, industry, & farming	35	Misc
Fomento De La Prensa Radicionalista	IC	1900's	Spain	Typesetting, paper-cutting, press. Children	220	Misc
Food Dividend Corp. of America	IU	1960's	FL	Large eagle & houses	15	Misc
Food Fair Stores	I			Girl with horn of plenty, tractor, farm. & factory	15	Misc
Formento De Tarrasa, Asociac Civil	IC	1920's	Spain	Building, arms of the city.	100	Misc
Fort Bragg Electric Co.	I	1900's	CA	Woman holding light, gold seal	45	Misc
Fort Bragg Electric Co.	I	1910's	CA	Woman holding light, gold seal	35	Misc
Fort Wayne Electric Co.	I	1890's	IN	Liberty with lightning	35	Misc
Fou Foong Flour Mill Co. Ltd.	SP	1920's	China	Photovignette of the flour-mill, also flowers.	72	Misc
Four Seasons Nursing Homes	I	1960's			35	Misc
Fox-Borden Manufacturing	I	1907		George Washington	25	Misc
Fox-Borden Manufacturing	I	1907		George Washington	25	Misc
France Elecric Co of Lille	U	1905	France	Woman and child	70	Misc
Franklin Canal Co.	I	1950's	PA	Bond, embossed seal	350	Misc
Franklin Electric Co.	SP		IN	Logo	25	Misc
Fred Rueping Leather	U			Man and woman	294	Misc
Freedom Securities Corp.	SP	1996	DE	Statue of Liberty	35	Misc
Fruit of the Loom, Inc.	I	1930's		Multicolor fruit	15	Misc
Fumades-Les-Baines Development	IC	1900's	France	Art Nouveau Border, scenes at Fumade.	72	Misc
Fusee Vesta Co., Ltd.	IC	1880's	GB	Burning match.	90	Misc
G.E. Overseas Capital Corp.	I	1960's	NY	Bond, man & woman	35	Misc
Galeton Silk Mills	I	1930's	PA	Five% bond	35	Misc
Garden.com	SP	2000	DE	Sunflower	250	Misc
Gardner Denver Co.	I	1960's		Two seated figures with co. logo	15	Misc
Gardner Denver Co.	I	1970's		Man woman with co. logo	15	Misc
Gas & Electric Co. of Bergen Count	I	1900's		Gold bond & state seal	35	Misc
Gaz & D'Electricite Du Hainaut, Soc.	IC	1920's	Belgium	Lady with gasworks, street-lighting & a train.	100	Misc
Gaz & Electricite De La Ville Kazan	IC	1890's	Russia	Electric trains, & shipping on Volga River.	26	Misc
General American Transportation	I	1960's		Four & two-eighths% bond, large eagle	15	Misc
General Aniline & Film Corp.	I	1960's		Man & -woman with Co. logo	15	Misc
General Builders Corp.	I	1950's		Six% bored, eagle	15	Misc
General Electric Co.	I	1950's		Lady with light & man with dynamo	15	Misc
General Foods	I	1968	DE	Brown or Green. Walter Annenberg	100	Misc
General Foods Corp.	I	1940's		Two females with Co. sign	20	Misc

Company	Type	Date	State	Description	Extra	Price	Category
General Foods Corp.	I	1960's		Two females with Co. sign		15	Misc
General Foods (Rockefellers)	I	1960's		Co. logo, allegorical women. Issued to Rockefeller		50	Misc
General Foods (Rockefellers)	I	1960's		Logo, allegorical women. Issued to various Rockefellers		15	Misc
General Investors Fund	I	1950's		Early rifleman		15	Misc
General Investors Trust	I		MA	Minuteman		15	Misc
General Mills, Inc.	I	1960's		Seated couple with globe & horn of plenty, seal		15	Misc
General Precision Equipment	I	1960's		Nude man with wheel		15	Misc
General Water Works & Electric Co,	I	1920's		Six% Bond, power lines		45	Misc
Georgia Pacific Corp.	I	1950's		Bond man reading chart with harbor scene		15	Misc
Georgia Power Co.	I	1960's		Allegorical figures with map of state		15	Misc
Georgia-Alabama Investment & Dev	IC	1890's	AL	Georgia State Arms.		242	Misc
Gesellschaft Fur Linde's Eismaschinen	IC	1920's	Germany		Dr. C. von Linde	224	Misc
Gibbs and Ball Plow	I	1883	OH	Large red underprint of a plow, Ohio state arms.		90	Misc
Gibson Greetings	SP	1982	DE	Eagle on mountaintop		35	Misc
Gil Blas, S.A. Du	IC	1880's	France			140	Misc
Gimbel Brothers	I	1940's	NY	Facsimile signature	Bernard Gimbel	45	Misc
Gitchcrest Co.	U		MA	Eagle		15	Misc
Glass Casket Co.	I	1920's		Eagle, gold seal		35	Misc
Glen Mills	I	1880's	PA	Six% bond, seal		350	Misc
Globe Iron Works	IU	1910's	CA	Gold border, gold seal		35	Misc
Goddard Grooms Drayton Co.	IU	1910's	PA	State seal		15	Misc
Goldman Sachs Trading	SP		DE	Man with motor		325	Misc
Good Hope Steel and Iron Works	IC	1920's	Germany	Woman with beehive, factory, man.		154	Misc
Gouldsboro Land Improvement	I	1891	ME	Eagle on globe, lighthouse, train, ships beyond.		125	Misc
Gouldsboro Land Improvement	I	1891	ME	Eagle on globe, lighthouse, train, ships beyond		125	Misc
Grand Union	I	1950's				15	Misc
Grand Union	I	1960's		Two fen-ale figures		15	Misc
Granite City Steel	I	1960's		Blacksmith with anvil & tools		15	Misc
Granite State Electric Works	U	1900's				45	Misc
Grant, W.T., Co.	I	1920's			W. T. Grant	100	Misc
Gravenwezel Extension, S.A.	IC	1900's	Belgium	Colorful share.		36	Misc
Graves-End & Coney-Island Bridge	IU	1824	NY			500	Misc
Gray & Davis	I		MA	Lady with light & dynamo		15	Misc

Company	Type	Date	State/Country	Description	Signatures	Price	Category
Great America Corp.	SP			Baby on globe & two allegorical figures .		15	Misc
Great America Inc.	I	1970's		Co. logo		15	Misc
Great Western Sugar Co.	I	1910's		Eagle on shield		15	Misc
Green Giant	I	1970's		Olive green border. Green Giant in valley		35	Misc
Green Giant	I	1970's		Orange. Green Giant in valley		45	Misc
Greenwich Development Co.	U	1910's		Eagle		15	Misc
Greger Manufacturing	I	1890's	NJ	Streetcar tracks & seal		35	Misc
Griffiths Electronics	I	1970's				15	Misc
Gronlandet Sodra	IC	1900's	Sweden		Ivar Krueger, P Toll	605	Misc
Guinee Portugaise S.A. Belge, Cie. De	IC	1890's	Port.Guinea	Woman's head, border.		56	Misc
Gustav Stickley The Craftsman	SP	191-	NY	NY seal		650	Misc
Gustelle & Dufour S.A., Ets.	IC	1920's	France	Silk worms on mulberry leaves.		140	Misc
Gyulai Furdo Es Udulo R.T.	IC	1940's	Hungary	City in the corners, underprint of the sun.		52	Misc
H.J. Heinz Company	U	1968	PA	Man		50	Misc
Haines & Slocum Co.	I	1910's		Eagle		15	Misc
Haines & Slocum Co.	U	1910's		Eagle		15	Misc
Hamilton Watch Co.	SP			Two women		75	Misc
Hancock Town Co.	I	1880's		State seal eagle		75	Misc
Handcraft Cooperative Of Bekes	IC	1920's	Hungary	Lovely girl with flowers.		190	Misc
Harpen Mining Corporation	IC	1920's	Germany	Three male allegory of mining.		121	Misc
Harriet Cotton Mills	I		NC			51	Misc
Harsco Corp.	I	1960's		Seated man, factory & Co. logo		15	Misc
Hartford Bridge	IU	1809	CT			300	Misc
Hartford Electric Co.	U			Women, streetcars, boat, & train		35	Misc
Hartford Rayon Corp.	I	1930's		Eagle on rock		15	Misc
Hat Corp. of America	I	1930's		Co. logo angels		15	Misc
Hausbesitzer In Leipzig, Treuhanda.	U	1920's	Germany			56	Misc
Havana Tobacco Company	I	1906		Tobacco Plantation		200	Misc
Havana-American Co.	U		NJ	Woman, cane field		15	Misc
Hawaiian Agricultural Co.	IC	1922	HI		Clarence H Cooke	275	Misc
Hawaiian Agricultural Co.	IC	1922	HI		Clarence H Cooke	275	Misc
Hawaiian Sumatra Plantations	IU	1926	HI Terr.	Hawaiian woman on ladder		1,250	Misc
Heitman Mortgage Investments	I					15	Misc
Henderson Cotton Mills	I		NC	Man and woman		51	Misc
Henninger, A. A., Inc.	I	1930's	NY	Gold bond, eagle		15	Misc
Hermann C. Starck A.G.	IC	1920's	Germany			48	Misc
Hermetical Barrel Co.	I	1860's	NY	Old train. sailor with flag, & anchor		175	Misc
Heska	I	2002		Dog and cat		35	Misc
Highland Valley Power Co.	I	1900's		Bond, river & dam in mountains		75	Misc
Hilaturas Navarro-Cabedo, S.A.	IC	1950's	Spain			40	Misc

ANTIQUE STOCK & BOND PRICE GUIDE 2014

Company	Type	Year	State	Vignette	Price	Category
Hill Top Ice Co.	I			Allegorical	15	Misc
HJ Heinz Company	I	1982		Woman and child	160	Misc
Home Electric Company	I	1904	PA	Lighbulb	75	Misc
Honolulu Plantation Company	U			Horse and wagon	57	Misc
Hope Mills Manufacturing Company	I	1915	NC	Eagle	59	Misc
Horizontal Bore & Drilling Co., Inc.	IC	1980's	NV	Lady by bordello.	180	Misc
Hoster-Columbus Associated Breweries	U	1905	OH		47	Misc
Howard Johnson Co.	I	1967		Orange. Two vignettes of the innkeeper.	15	Misc
Howard Johnson Co.	I	1967		Orange. two vignettes of the innkeeper.	15	Misc
Howe Horseshoe & Machine	IU	1868	NY	Horseshoe machine	450	Misc
Howell Electric Motors	I	1960's			15	Misc
Hoyt's Tree Support Co.	U	1900's	CA	Goddess	35	Misc
Hubbard Ice	I			Hub	35	Misc
Huck Finn Co.	I	1970's		Cartoon Duck fishing	35	Misc
Hughes & Hatcher, Inc.	I	1970's	NY	Gladiator	15	Misc
Huileries & Savonneries De Tunisie	IC	1910's	Tunisia	Harvest at a seaside olive farm in Tunisia	176	Misc
Human Life Publishing	I	1910-11	MA	Orange, co. seal	20	Misc
Human Life Publishing	I	1910-11	MA	Orange, go seal.	20	Misc
Hunt, P. H. Chemical Corp.	I	1970's		Two figures, Co. logo	15	Misc
Hutchinson Sugar Plantation	IC	1909	HI	Green. Oxen pulling cart. Horses/sugar cane wagon.	200	Misc
Hydraulic Press Brick Co.	I	1890's		Train & surveyors	35	Misc
Hydraulic Press Brick Co.	I	1890's		Coat of arms	20	Misc
Hydraulic Press Brick Co.	I	1910's			15	Misc
Hydraulic Press Brick Co.	I	1920's		Gold bond, eagle with shield	15	Misc
Hydraulic Press Brick Co.	I	1940's		Coat of arms	10	Misc
Hygiena-Nova S.A. Franco-Belge	IC	1920's	Belgium	Colorful.	24	Misc
I. Magnin	IC	1929	DE	IMCo crest logo	35	Misc
IBM	U	1957		To god-like figures Thomas J Watson Jr	60	Misc
IBM	IC	1960	NY	Man & globe	35	Misc
ICH Corp.	IU	1997	DE	ICH logo	35	Misc
Illinois & St. Louis Bridge bond	IC	1870		Eads Bridge	350	Misc
Illinois-Kentucky Bridge	I	1940's			15	Misc
ImClone Systems	I	2003		Logo	85	Misc
Immobiliere & Mobiliere Ostendaise	IC	1920's	Belgium		24	Misc
Immobiliere De Bone S.A.	IC	1920's	Algeria	City & Port of Bone.	32	Misc
Immobiliere De La Grande Plage	IC	1920's	France	Statue of woman, centaur, Mediterranean Sea	60	Misc
Immobiliere Des Pyrenees, Soc.	IC	1890's	Belgium	Border with leaves & flowers.	28	Misc
Imperial Paper Co.	I	1970's		Eagle	15	Misc
Imperial Russian Loan	SP	1900's	Russia	Bonds.	176	Misc
Imprimeries Brabo S.A.	IC	1920's	Belgium	Decorative border of flowers.	28	Misc

Company	Type	Date	State	Description	Price	Category
Inair Co.	I	1960's		Large eagle	15	Misc
Incorp. Investors' Equities	I	1930's		scrip certificate	15	Misc
Independence Trust Shares	I	1940's	PA	Independence Hall & Liberty Bell	15	Misc
Independent Ice Co.	IU	1935	CA	Eagle	65	Misc
Independent Packing Co.	I	1920's		6% bond	15	Misc
Indiana Sanitary Potters	I	1920's		Gold bond. Indian	50	Misc
Industria Ceramica Espanola S.A.	IC	1920's	Spain	Design of tiles.	52	Misc
Industrial Exhibition Co of New York	I	1874	NY	Green underprint, red exhibition building.	60	Misc
Industrie Edilizie, Soc. Nazionale	IC	1920's	Italy	Photovignette of company's tile factory in Torino.	40	Misc
Industrielle D'Electricite	IC	1890's	France	Lady, generator, tram, street lighting, lighthouse.	130	Misc
iNetEvents	SP	2000		Logo	75	Misc
Insull Utility Investments	I	1930	IL	Brown. Semi-nude man, dynamo, mills behind.	35	Misc
Insull Utility Investments	I	1930	IL	Brown. semi-nude man, dynamo, mills	35	Misc
Insull Utility Investments	IU	1930's		Gold bond. man, buildings, & generator	35	Misc
Insull Utility Investments bond	IU	1930	IL	Generator, factory, power plant	35	Misc
Insynq Inc.	SP		DE	Logo	35	Misc
Integrity Trust	IU	1930		Men & women	65	Misc
Inter-State Rapid Transit	SP	1906	KS	Elevated railway, horsedrawn streetcar below	25	Misc
Inter-State Rapid Transit	SP	1906	KS-MO	Train on elevated railway, horsedrawn streetcar below.	250	Misc
Interboro Lumber Co.	U	1920's		Lady, seal	25	Misc
International Business Machines	IC	1954	NY	Two women either side of IBM logo Type 1	65	Misc
International Business Machines	IC	1959	NY	Man & woman either side of IBM logo Type 2	45	Misc
International Business Machines IBM	I	1960's		Brown. Topographic map of the world.	35	Misc
International Correspondence Schools	I	1907	PA	Shield	25	Misc
International Linotype Ltd.	IC	1920's	GB	Linotype printing press.	120	Misc
International Pneumatic Tube	IU	1923	ME	Pneumatic tube	125	Misc
Internos, Cooperative Pharmaceutique	IC	1920's	Belgium	Border of stars.	80	Misc
Interstate Department Stores	I	1960's	DE	Lady with lyre	15	Misc
Interstate Equities Corp.	I	1920's		Three allegorical figures with winged wheel	15	Misc
Intertropical-Comfina	IC	1950's	BelCongo		44	Misc
Intl Nickel Co. of Canada	I	1930's		Three workers with anvil & pick	15	Misc
Intl. Bank Note Co.	I	1980's	NY	Globe	35	Misc

Intl. Business Machines	I	1960's		Mercury with map of Northern Hemisphere	35	Misc
Intl. Cellulose Co.	IU	1910's	NV	Woman, electric light with factory & dynamo	15	Misc
Intl. Investors, Inc.	I	1960's		Large eagle	15	Misc
Intl. Match Corp.	I	1930's		Bond, lady with lion	35	Misc
Intl. Money Machine Co.	I	1910's	IN		125	Misc
Intl. Nickel Co., The	I	1910's		Voting trust certificate, woman & lion	15	Misc
Intl. Nickel Co., The	I	1920's		Reeling woman with lion	15	Misc
Intl. Nickel Co., The	I	1930's		Three semi-nude workers	15	Misc
Intl. Paper Co.	I	1920's		Warrants	15	Misc
Intl. Resistance Co.	I	1950's		Eagle	15	Misc
Intl. Resistance Co.	I	1960's	DE	Rocket & railroad radar equipment	15	Misc
Intl. Safety Razor Corp.	I	1920's		Large factory plus six stamps	15	Misc
Intl. Securities Corp. of America	I	1920's		Ship, tugboat, trains, & plane	35	Misc
Intl. Standard Electric	I	1950's		Bond	15	Misc
Intl. Ticket Co.	U		NJ	Allegorical figures with globe	15	Misc
Intl. Western Electric Co.	U	1910's		Eagle	35	Misc
Investigadora Aguas La Villa Cintruen	IC	1860's	Spain	Flowery border with fountains & little angels.	100	Misc
Investment Corp. of Florida	I	1970's		Co. logo	15	Misc
Investment Trust of Boston	I	1960's		Capitol -building	15	Misc
Investors Overseas Services Mgt (IOS)	IU	1969	Toronto	IOS logo 10 shrs	75	Misc
Investors Overseas Services Mgt (IOS)	IU	1969	Toronto	IOS logo 5 shrs	75	Misc
Investors Underwriting Corp.	SP		NY	Seated woman in front of harbor scene.	35	Misc
Investors, Inc.	I	1920's	IN	Green seal	15	Misc
IOS Ltd.	IU	1969	Toronto	Topless woman	75	Misc
Iowa Power & Light	I	1970's	IA	Semi-nude man with gears	15	Misc
Iron City Land Company	I	1871	PA	Train	85	Misc
Ithaca & Geneva Turnpike Corp.	I	1810's			500	Misc
ITT Financial Corp.	I			Bond, woman, globe, skyline, & mountains	15	Misc
J.P. Morgan & Company	U			Two god-like figures	63	Misc
Jack Eckerd Corp.	I	1970's	FL	Chemist_& worker	15	Misc
Jack in the Box	SP	2000	DE	French fries, hamburger	175	Misc
Jamaica Water & Utilities	I	1960's	NY	Bond, eagle on mountaintop	15	Misc
James Dunlap Carpet Co.	I	1900's	PA	State seal	50	Misc
Jamestown Exposition	I	1900's	VA	People celebrating	500	Misc

Jantzen Knitting Mills	I	1930	OR	Green. Young woman in knit swimsuit dives into waves.	75	Misc
Jantzen Knitting Mills	I	1930	OR	Young woman in knit swimsuit dives into waves.	75	Misc
Japanese Tissue Mills	I	1910's	MA	Lad with umbrella	50	Misc
Jefferson Stores	I	1960's		Large eagle	15	Misc
Jersey Central Power & Light Co.	I	1940's		Bond, buildings & woman with light	35	Misc
Jersey Central Power & Light Co.	I	1960's		Bond, woman between generator & power line	15	Misc
Jersey Pines Poultry Farm	I	1909	NJ	Free ranging chickens, basket of eggs, trees beyond.	75	Misc
Jersey Pines Poultry Farm	I	1909	NJ	Chickens, basket of eggs, trees	75	Misc
John B. Stetson	Proof	189-	PA	John B Stetson	250	Misc
John B. Stetson	IC	1960's	PA	John B Stetson	45	Misc
Johnstown Rendering Co.	U		PA	Eagle, streetcar, & tugboat	15	Misc
Jojoba Horizons	IU	1983	AZ	Eagle	35	Misc
Journal Le Matin, S.A. Du	IC	1880's	France	Telegraph poles, logo of the paper.	64	Misc
Judson Manufacturing bond	IU	1887	CA	San Francisco Bay Egbert Judson	495	Misc
Kanes Falls Electric Co.	U	1900's		Gold bond, figure with light bulb	35	Misc
Kanes Falls Electric Co.	U	1900's		Woman on winged wheel	35	Misc
Kansas Water Works & Irrigation	I	1880's		Bond, farm scene with cattle & horses	500	Misc
Kaufman & Broad	I	1970's		Seated -figures, lake & woods	15	Misc
Kentucky Fuel	IU	1890	ME	Child in winter	295	Misc
Kern Incandescent Gas Light Co.	I	1900's	NJ	Portrait of young woman	75	Misc
Keystone Hotel	I	1905	PA	Vintage 4-story hotel rises above Union Station, tracks	175	Misc
Keystone Hotel	I	1905	PA	Four-story hotel, Union Station, tracks, freight car	175	Misc
Keystone Water Works & Electric C	I	1920's		Gold -bond, seminude with torch	50	Misc
Kimball Light, Power & Water	I	1912	WV	Green, gold seal. Woman, dynamo.	20	Misc
Kimball Light, Power & Water	I	1912	WV	Green, gold. seal. Woman, dynamo	35	Misc
Kineo Company of Greenille	U	1890	ME	Building	70	Misc
Kirby Corp	SP	1996	NV	Male & female angel with large wings	25	Misc
Kirk's Mississippi Snag Fender	UI	1840's	MS	Steamboat, eagle, ships.	275	Misc
Kmart	I	2002		Businessmen and woman	25	Misc
Knap Fort Pitt Foundry	IU	1869	PA	Rodman gun	4,500	Misc
Knickerbocker Fund	U			Specimen	15	Misc
Knollwood Cemetery	I	1910's		Large mausoleum	35	Misc

Kohala Sugar Plantation	UC	1899	HI	Workers cutting down sugar cane.	250	Misc
Kohala Sugar Plantation	UC	1899	HI	Workers cutting down sugar cane.	250	Misc
Koniglich Preussische-Staatsanleihe	I	1895	Germany	Brown borders, green underprint. Prussian arms.	25	Misc
Koniglich Preussische-Staatsanleihe	IU	1895	Germany	Text in German, green underprint. Prussian arms.	25	Misc
Koninklijke Stoom-Bontweverij	IC	1860's	Netherlands	Coat of Arms of Sophia.	60	Misc
Kopitzsch Soap	I	1892	PA	6% 1st Mortgage Bond, woman representing Commerce.	35	Misc
Kopitzsch Soap	I	1892	PA	6% 1st Mortgage Bond. Semi nude woman. State arms.	35	Misc
Krueger & Toll Co.	I	1920's		Woman on winged wheel	35	Misc
L N C Corp.	I	1960's		Eagle	15	Misc
L.A. Pulp & Paper	U			Eagle	15	Misc
L' Avenir S.A.	IC	1890's	Belgium	Square format.	48	Misc
L'Ancien Empire Ottoman	IC	1914		Blue & green. Some coupons attached.	25	Misc
L'Ancien Empire Ottoman	IU	1914		Blue green. Some coupons attached.	25	Misc
L'Quest Africain, Soc. Commerciale	IC	1930's	Ivory Coast	Trading station, gov. bldg, & ivory, coffee beans	96	Misc
La Confiance Militaire S.A.	IC	1900's	France	Military motifs, cannon, armour, swords, spears.	200	Misc
La Haute Sangha S.A.	IC	1900's	Congo	African villages, train & river-steamer.	64	Misc
La Turnhoutoise S.A.	IC	1920's	Belgium	Tiger, border.	176	Misc
La Varoise, Soc. Cooperative An.	IC	1940's	France	Different artisans at work, & their tools.	110	Misc
Lackawanna Coal and Lumber	I	1912		Cart building/station	55	Misc
Lake & Export Goal Sales Corp.	IU	1920's		Eagle, gold seal	15	Misc
Lake Keuka Navigation Company	I	1903	NY		50	Misc
Lancaster Caramel Co.	U	1800's	PA	State seal	50	Misc
Law Association of Philadelphia	I	1870's		Woman justice with sword & rearing horses, seal	350	Misc
LCO, Inc.	I	1970's	NV	Eagle, gold seal	15	Misc
Le Depulsor S.A.	IC	1890's	Belgium		20	Misc
Le Ralliement Soc. Cooperative	IC	1920's	Belgium	Train, ship, & 2 workers, railway station at Namur.	110	Misc
Lea Cattle Co.	I	1880's	NM	Six% bond, two cows	500	Misc
Lectro Management Inc.	IC	1979	NY	Abacus	50	Misc
Lederfabriek	IC	1920's	Netherlands	Corner vignettes of company logo.	22	Misc
Lehigh Coal & Navigation	Proof	1867	PA	Train, miners	495	Misc

Lehigh Coal & Navigation	I	1920's		Two portraits & horses	15	Misc
Lehigh Coal & Navigation	I	1940's		Two founders portraits	20	Misc
Lehigh Coal & Navigation	I	1950's		Two founders portraits	15	Misc
Leica	IU	1996	Germany	1913 Leica camera	65	Misc
Leipziger Gummi-Waaren-Fabrik A.G.	IC	1920's	Germany		136	Misc
Lena Horne Beauty Products	I	1960's			35	Misc
Leon B. Allen Fund	I	1960's		Large eagle	15	Misc
Lerner Stores Corp.	I	1950's		Woman & two angels	15	Misc
Letter of Thanks From Rokossovski	IC	1940's	Russia	Stalin with flags, tanks & guns.	90	Misc
Level Club	I	1925-27	NY	Green. Building.	20	Misc
Levi Strauss	I	1984	DE	Levi Strauss	195	Misc
Levi Strauss	SP	1984	DE	Levi Strauss	295	Misc
Lewis Publishing Co.	I	1900's	SD	Many-sided building	100	Misc
Lewiston Suspension Bridge Co.	U	1800's		Bridge over river in mountains	75	Misc
Lewiston Turnpike Co.	IC	1870's	CA	Heavily-laden cart pulled by 8 mules.	140	Misc
Lexington Research Investing Corp	I	1960's		Minuteman with rifle	15	Misc
Lima Cord Sole & Heel Co.	I	1930's		Seated woman by globe & lion, stamp on reverse	15	Misc
Lima Cord Sole and Heel	IC	1930's		Orange. Woman with globe.	25	Misc
Lima Cord Sole and Heel	IC	1930's		Orange. Woman with globe.	25	Misc
Limestone Fertilizer	I	1920's		Seven% gold bond with stamps, eagle	35	Misc
Lincoln Printing Co.	I	1960's		Lincoln Portrait	20	Misc
Lincoln Stores, Inc.	I	1930's	MA		15	Misc
Ling-Temco-Vought, Inc.	I	1960's		Seated man with telescope & books	15	Misc
Ling-Temco-Vought, Inc.	I	1960's		Nude man with globe	15	Misc
Liniere Saint-Pierre S.A. Gand	IC	1920's	Belgium		16	Misc
Lipton, Ltd.	IC	1890's	GB	Offices & warehouses in London.	320	Misc
Lit Brothers	I	1920's	PA	City seal Jacob & Samuel Lit	75	Misc
Lockheed Martin	I	2010		Statue of Liberty	100	Misc
Lockman, W. S., Construction	I	1930's		Six% bond, eagle with shield	15	Misc
Lockwood, Green & Co.	I	1920's		Gold note	15	Misc
Lomas & Nettleton Financial	I			Specimen, Two seated men with Co. logo	35	Misc
Lone Star Flooring	IU	1926	TX	Log on railcar	45	Misc
Long Beach Pleasure Pier	I	1916	CA	Warrior & bear	393	Misc
Long Island Lighting	I	1950's		Bond, seated figure by electric motor with light	15	Misc
Loretta Lynn Western Stores	U			Eagle	25	Misc
Lorillard Corp.	I				15	Misc

Name	Type	Date	State	Description	Price	Category
Lorillard Fire Insurance	IU	1863	NY	Native American overlooking	475	Misc
Lorraine Cemetery Co. of Baltimore	IC	1900's	MD	Hillside cemetery, funeral urn.	180	Misc
Louis Rosenbloom, Inc.	I	1940's		Farm scene, plus stamp	15	Misc
Louisiana Pacific	SP	1998	DE	Worker holding a tiny tree seedling	50	Misc
Lowell Electric Co.	I	1880's		Early electric stock certificate, embossed seal	35	Misc
Lowell Electric Co.	I	1920's		Lad with lightning bolts	15	Misc
Lowell Electric Co.	I	1930's		Lady with lightning bolts	15	Misc
Lowell Electric Light Co.	I	1910's		Lightning bolt	35	Misc
Lukens Steel Co.	I	1930's		Eagle	15	Misc
Lulonga, S.A. La	IC	1890's	BelCongo		120	Misc
Lumena S. A. Lampes Electriques	IC	1920's	Belgium	Pretty border of flowers.	44	Misc
Lundelius & Eccleston Motors	I	1927-28		Blue. Torch.	50	Misc
Lundelius & Eccleston Motors	I	1927-28		Blue. Torch.	50	Misc
Lundstrom Rim Corp.	I	1920's		Portrait of Washington between two figures, eagle	35	Misc
Luthy Storage Battery Co.	I	1910's		Two people & generator	35	Misc
LuthyStorage Battery Co.	I	1920's		Two people & generator	35	Misc
Lyman Cordage Co.	U			Eagle	15	Misc
Lyons Educational Enterprises	IU	1982	DE	Fancy border	10	Misc
M&B Ice Cream	U	1900's	MI	Farm, cows, barn	30	Misc
Machine Calendoli, S.A. Francaise	IC	1900's	France	Elegant border, Calendoli type setting machine.	600	Misc
Mackay Co.	I	1920's		Lightning, transatlantic cable co., embossed seal	35	Misc
Macy Credit Corp.	I	1970's		Eight% bond, seated lady	15	Misc
Madison Park	I	1909	VA	Green underprint. Henry W. Farnam	70	Misc
Madison Square Garden Corporation	U		NY	Mercury	75	Misc
Magnetic Equipment	I	1907	SD	Green. Gold seal. Eagle.	20	Misc
Magnetic Equipment	I	1907	SD	Green. Gold seal. Eagle.	20	Misc
Magnolia Cemetery	U	1880's	SC	Co. logo	15	Misc
Mahrisch-Ostrauer	IC	1900's	Austria		140	Misc
Mammoth Mart, Inc.	I	1960's		Co. logo of Marty (pig).	15	Misc
Manhattan Anti-Sewer Gas	Proof	1883	NY	Two girls' portraits	300	Misc
Manhattan Market of the City of NY	IC	1870's	NY	Grand building.	264	Misc
Manheim, Petersbg Lancaster Turnpk	I	1850's	PA	Ornate borders on blue paper. Horse carriage.	60	Misc

Name	Type	Date	State	Description	Signature	Price	Category
Manheim, Petersburg & Lancaster	I	1850's	PA	Ornate borders on blue paper. Horse carriage		60	Misc
Mansell Heel Machine Co.	I	1880's		Machine		75	Misc
Manshel Ticket Machine Co.	U		RI	Girl with light bulb, dynamo, & factory.		15	Misc
Manufacture De Chaussures Liendard	IC	1920's	Belgium			24	Misc
Manufacture De Tabac	U	1790's	France			594	Misc
Manufacture Lausannoise De Biscuits	IC	1890's	Switzerland	Underprint of the factory, & a passing bus.		160	Misc
Manufactured Rubber Co.	I	1920's		Three seminude seated figures		35	Misc
Marion & Wasco Stock & Wagon Road	I	1881	OR	Mountains		124	Misc
Marion Ice & Cold Storage	I					35	Misc
Mark Ten Suie Trading	I	1899	WA	Green underprint. Freighter.	Mark Ten Suie	150	Misc
Mark Ten Suie Trading	I	1899	WA	Green_underprint. Freighter.	Mark Ten Suie	150	Misc
Martha Stewart Living Omnimedia	I	2003		Large sun style designs		35	Misc
Martin Institute	I	1886	GA	Green. Eagle, train, ship beyond.		35	Misc
Maryland Gas, Light & Coke Co.	I	1880's		Storage tank		100	Misc
Maryland Gas, Light & Coke Co.	I	1890's		Power station		75	Misc
Mason City & Fort Dodge Railroad	I	1889		Proxy. Blank.	James J. Hill	1,200	Misc
Mason City & Fort Dodge Railroad	I	1889		Proxy. Blank.	James J. Hill	1,200	Misc
Mason City & Fort Dodge RR	IC	1880's	IA		James J. Hill	880	Misc
Massachusetts Investor's Second	I	1940's		Old state building		15	Misc
Matawan & Keyport Gas Light Co.	I	1870's	NJ	Two seated ladies with horse head, revenue stamp		100	Misc
Materiaux De Construction De Mosc	IC	1900's	Russia			24	Misc
Matheson Alkali Works	I	1930's	VA	Eagle		15	Misc
Max Factor & Co.	U	1960's		Two seated sexy ladies with world & Co. logo		15	Misc
Maxim Soap Co.	U	1960's		Two seated sexy ladies with world & Co. logo		15	Misc
May Department Stores	I	1950's		Eagle		35	Misc
Mayflower Investors, Inc.	I	1970's		Mayflower		15	Misc
McCloud River Lumber	IC	1957	MN	Large log pulled on cart with big wheels		60	Misc
McDermott & Co., Inc.	I	1970's		Four & three-fourths% bond		15	Misc
Med Com, Inc.	I	1970's	MA			15	Misc
Merchant Calculating Machine	IU	1921	CA	Early mechanical calculator		595	Misc
Merchant's & Miner's Transport Co.	I	1920's	MD	Two men with shield		15	Misc

Merchants Exchange of St. Louis	I	1882		Membership Certificate. Steamboats, train at wharfside.	55	Misc
Merchants Storage & Warehouse bond	IU		NY	Buildings train	25	Misc
Merchants' Dispatch Transportation	U	1880's		Freight dispatcher	75	Misc
Merchants' Exchange of Saint Loui	I	1880's		Horse &wagon, building, train, ships, & waterfront	100	Misc
Merchants' Exchange of Saint Loui	I	1890's		Horse train, ships, & waterfront	75	Misc
Merchants' Transportation Co.	I	1850's		No	100	Misc
Merchants' Union Express	IU	1860's		Galloping horses, railroad station	350	Misc
Mergenthaler Linotype Co.	SP	NY		Man at press logo	35	Misc
Mergenthaler-Horton Basket Machine	I	1902	ME	Brown, Green. Winged woman, allegorical figures.	60	Misc
Mergenthaler-Hortoon Basket Mach	I	1902	ME	Brown, Green. Winged woman, allegorical figures.	60	Misc
Merrill Lynch	IC	1977		New York City skyline	65	Misc
Merrill Lynch & Co. bond	SP	1989	DE	New York City skyline	100	Misc
Merrimack Manufacturing Co.	I	1910's			15	Misc
Metallurgique Des Terres Rouges	SP	1900's	Luxemberg	Large Annule stamp on face.	220	Misc
Metro-Urban Development	I	1970's		Large eagle	15	Misc
Metropolitan Cement Thomas Edison	I	1932		Charles Edison	50	Misc
Metropolitan Errand&Carrier Express	U	1850's	NY	Boy & dog chasing horse drawn freight wagon.	462	Misc
Metropolitan Real Estate	IU	1904	NY	Manhattan cityscape	350	Misc
Mexican Banana Plantation	U			Eagle, shield, train, & ship	35	Misc
Mexico Federal Railway Co	I	1896			170	Misc
Miag Mill Machinery	IC	1920's	Germany	Seated male, gears, factories.	121	Misc
Michigan-Wisconsin Pipe Line	I	1960's		Four & seven-eighths%, seated man & woman	15	Misc
Middlesex Electric	I	1880's			35	Misc
Middlesex Electric	U	1880's			15	Misc
Middlesex Electric Light Co.	I	1880's		Embossed seal	35	Misc
Middletown Point Keyport Gas Light	I	1870's	NJ	Allegorical figures	125	Misc
Middlewest Utilities Co.	I	1930's		Night city scene	35	Misc
Midwest Asbestos Co.	I	1910's	AZ	Young	15	Misc
Milford Marble Company	I				103	Misc
Military Naval Corp.	I	1910's		Gold bond	35	Misc
Milk Row Bleachery	U	1800's			35	Misc
Millerstown Iron Co.	U	1800's		State seal	15	Misc
Millvale Hall Co.	I	1880's	PA	State building, red seal	100	Misc
Milwaukee & St. Paul Rwy	IC	1860's	WI	Train. Russell Sage	286	Misc

Minden Flour Milling Co.	I	1900's	NV	Indian on rock & sailing ships	35	Misc
Minden Flour Milling Co.	U	1900's		Indian on rock & sailing ships	15	Misc
Minehill & Schuylkill Haven RR	IC	1830's	PA	State arms.	165	Misc
Minnesota Mining & Manufacturing	I	1960's		Woman seated in front of city	15	Misc
Mission Equities Corp.	I	1970's		Seated lady with globe	15	Misc
Missouri Meerschaum	IU	1907	MO	Corn cob pipe	350	Misc
Modern Data Techniques	I	1960's		Co. logo	15	Misc
Modern Mexico Cattle & Investment	U	1900's	NM	Man & lion	35	Misc
Monarch Molybdenum	I				15	Misc
Monarch Timber Co.	U		ID	State seal	15	Misc
Monroe Marsh Co.	U	1900's		Flying goose	75	Misc
Monti Della Citta di Firenze	IC	1750's	Italy	Arms, Medici Crest.	605	Misc
Montrose & Harford Plant Co.	I	1850's			350	Misc
Moorkultur, A.G. Fur	IC	1920's	Germany	Ploughing moorland.	70	Misc
Morgan, Stokes & Company	IC	1880's	TX	Portrait of founder.	132	Misc
Morris Canal & Banking	I	1860's		Figures with urns along canal scene	200	Misc
Morris Canal & Banking	I	1870's		Figures with urns along canal scene	150	Misc
Morris Canal & Banking	I	1880's			50	Misc
Morse Underground Conduit	IC	1880's	NJ	Morse, woman, two boys.	176	Misc
Mortgage Finance Co.	I	1920's	FL	Six % bond, eagle with shield	15	Misc
Moslem Cigarette Co., Ltd.	IC	1880's	GB		140	Misc
Mount Rushmore National Memorial	SP			Engraving of George Washington	75	Misc
Multi-Bestos Co.	I	1920's	MA	Old factory building	15	Misc
Murray Hill Allied Corp.	I	1920's		Eagle	15	Misc
Musical Hall Assoc. of Honolulu	IU	1880	HI Terr.	Music book, instruments	995	Misc
Mustang Motor Corp.	U	1944	NV	Eagle on cliff above ocean	30	Misc
Mutual Investment Union	U	1890's			15	Misc
Narco Scientific Industries	SP	1968	DE	Man holding Narco logo	50	Misc
Narragansett Electric Lighting	I	1880's		Viking ship, red seal	100	Misc
Narragansett Mills	I	1890's	MA	Green. Yankee mill workers, eagle and shield.	25	Misc
Narragansett Mills	I	1890's	MA	Green. Yankee mill workers, eagle and shield.	25	Misc
Nashua Corp.	I	1970's		Two men with chemistry equipment	15	Misc
Natco Iron	I				15	Misc
National Alfalfa	I	1960's		Eagle	15	Misc
National Alfalfa Dehydrating Milling	I	1960's		Large eagle	15	Misc
National Color Printing Co.	I	1880's			35	Misc
National Consolidated Power	IU	1900's		Allegorical figures, red seal	35	Misc

National Distributors & Chemical	I	1950's		Bond, chemistry		35	Misc
National Electric Power Co.	I	1920's		Two semi-nude ladies holding Co. banner		35	Misc
National Glass Co.	I	1900's	PA	Gold bond, figure with goblet		35	Misc
National Hat Pouncing Machine	IU	1886	NY	Building		375	Misc
National Lace Paper & Specialty	U			Eagle, capitol building		15	Misc
National Match	I	1901	PA	Brown. Allegorical female. Preferred.		25	Misc
National Match	I	1901		Brown. Allegorical female. Preferred.		25	Misc
National Match	I	1901-2	NJ	Voting Trust Certificate. Series A- olive; Series B- blue.		25	Misc
National Match	I	1901-2	NJ	Voting Trust Certificate, Series A- olive; Series B		25	Misc
National Security Trading Corp.	U	1900's	NY	Eagle		15	Misc
National Steel Corp.	I	1950's		Three & one-half% bond, large eagle		15	Misc
National Steel Corp.	I	1970's		Bond, large eagle		15	Misc
National Stockyard Co.	U	1800's		Cowboys & cows scene		100	Misc
National Storage Co.	U	1860's		State seal, female with eagle		35	Misc
National Sweepstakes	I					15	Misc
National Toll Bridge Co.	I	1930's	MD	Suspension bridge ridge		35	Misc
National Tool Co.	I	1950's	OH	Eagle		15	Misc
National Transit	IC	1899	PA	Eagle	H. H. Rogers	350	Misc
National Transit	IC	1890's	PA	Eagle	Henry H. Rogers	539	Misc
Nauvoo House Association	U	1841		Eagle		456	Misc
Nederland-Duitsche	IC	1910's	Netherlands	Jugendstil border.		70	Misc
Nederland, Rolland Materiaal-Pennock	IC	1900's	Netherlands			44	Misc
Nedick's Corp.	I	1930		Six% bond		50	Misc
Negotiatie Van Plantagien Colon.Sur	IC	1770's	Suriname			300	Misc
Nes Silicon Steel Co.	I	1870's	NY	Indian & Pilgrim		35	Misc
Nevada Irrigation District	I	1930's	CA	Bond		15	Misc
Nevada Power Co.	I	1970's		Lady with light & city scene		15	Misc
New Alban Woolens Mills	I	1890's	IN	Six% gold bond, eagle		75	Misc
New England Alloy Casting Corp.	I	1950's		State seal		15	Misc
New England Cotton Yarn Co.	I	1910's		Eagle with shield		35	Misc
New England Excelsior Manuf	U	1800's				15	Misc
New England Gas & Electric Assoc	I	1940's		Woman, gas tanks, & power lines		15	Misc
New England Manufacturing Works	I	1870's	CT	Two blacksmiths		125	Misc
New England Motive Power	I	1880's	ME	Trains & power plant with seal		50	Misc
New Jersey Patent Co.	I			Eagle		1,450	Misc

New Jersey Zinc Co., The	SP	1900's		State seal	Thomas Edison	15	Misc
New Mercantile Exchange	IC	1820's	So. Africa	Typeset form.		528	Misc
New Orleans Lighting & Wrecking	IU	1860's		Ship		100	Misc
New Paltz Water Works	U	1890's	NY	Waterworks & tower		45	Misc
New York Business Forms	I	1830's	NY		Daniel Phoenix	220	Misc
New York Grape Sugar Co.	I	1880's	NY	Two ladies with eagle & shield		75	Misc
New York Manufacturing Society	I	1780's		Stock share note		750	Misc
New York Produce Exchange	Proof	1880's	NY	Train, grain elevator.		231	Misc
New York Produce Exchange	SP	19--	NY	Ships, docks		250	Misc
New York Quotation bond	SP	1890	NY	Woman		695	Misc
New York Realty Owners	I	1906	NY	Brown/grey. Eagle on shield.		35	Misc
New York Realty Owners	I	1906-13	NY	Brown/grey. Eagle on shield.		35	Misc
New York Siphon	U			Eagle		15	Misc
New Yorker Zeitung Publishing Co.	I	1900's				35	Misc
New Yorker Zeitung Publishing Co.	U					15	Misc
Newark Athletic Club	I	1922	NJ	Pink, orange underprint. State seal.		40	Misc
Newark Ohio Waterworks	I	1880's	NY	Gold bond, waterworks beside lake		175	Misc
Newark Ohio Waterworks Co.	I	1880's	NY	Six% bond, water tower, & prehistoric creatures		100	Misc
Newark Ohio Waterworks Co.	I	1880's		Certificate, water towers		75	Misc
Newburyport Gas & Electric Co.	I	1920's				15	Misc
Newhall Investment Properties	SP	1983	CA	Cowgirl holding a briefcase with fields		195	Misc
Newport & Cincinnati Bridge Co.	I	1890's		Sailboats & steamboats on river under bridge		125	Misc
Newport News & Mississippi Valley	IU	1890		Eagle	C.P. Huntington	395	Misc
Newton Square & Paoli Plank Road	IC	1850's		Sailing vessels, horses		308	Misc
Nickel Holdings Corp.	I	1920's	NJ			75	Misc
Niederosterreichische	IC	1920's	Austria	Powerhouse, fed by pipes		36	Misc
Niengele Soc. Congolaise, LA	IC	1920's	BelCongo	Loading produce on steamer, cutting oil-palms.		44	Misc
Norddeutsche Union Werke	IC	1920's	Germany	Hamburg galleons on stormy seas.		880	Misc
Norddeutsche Union Werke	IC	1920's	Germany	Hamburg galleons on stormy seas.		880	Misc
Norddeutsche Union Werke	IC	1920's	Germany	Galleons, arms, dry dock scene.		523	Misc
Norfolk Hotel	IC	1860's	VA	Hotel, eagle, state arms.		264	Misc

Company	Type	Date	State	Description	Signer	Price	Category
Normal Powder and Ammunition Co.	IC	1890's	GB	Soldiers, cannon & rifles, hunters, shotguns. A. Kinloch		280	Misc
North American Gas & Electric	I	1930's		Indian chief		50	Misc
North American Land Company	IU	1790's	PA		Robert Morris	1,430	Misc
North American Land Company	IC	1790's	PA		Robert Morris	1,320	Misc
North American Lumber	I	18--	NY	Bare-breasted woman. Sailing ship, Washington cherub.		20	Misc
North American Lumber	I	18--	NY	Woman. Sailing ship, Washington cherub		50	Misc
North American Lumber Co.	U	1800's		Woman. Sailing ship, Washington cherub		50	Misc
North American Lumber Co.	I	1830's	NY	Woman. Sailing ship, Washington cherub		225	Misc
North American Rockwell Overseas	I	1970's		Eight & one-half%, topless woman		15	Misc
Northwestern Guaranty Loan Co.	I	1890's		Gold bond, large office building		175	Misc
Northwestern Mutual Life Mortgage	I	1970's		Girl in front of city		15	Misc
Northwestern Portland Cement Co.	I	1900's		Bond, factory		35	Misc
Norton Co.	I	1920's		Male & female with Co. logo		15	Misc
Norwich Water & Power	U	1850's	CT			35	Misc
Norwood Heights Co.	I	1900's	OH	Embossed seal		15	Misc
Nostra, Handels-A.G.	IC	1920's	Czech	Peacocks, underprint of sailing-ship & peacock-tails.		100	Misc
Noval, S.A.	IC	1920's	Luxemberg	Logo in border & underprint.		110	Misc
Oak Park Shop	IU	1910's		Eagle, shield, train, & ship		15	Misc
Odd Fellows Assoc of Sacramento	U	1860's				75	Misc
Odd Fellows Hall Assoc Sacramento	I	1871	CA	Grey. Three rings. U.S. flag.		45	Misc
Odd Fellows Hall Association Sac.	I	1871	CA	Grey. Three rings. U.S. flag.		45	Misc
Odorless Rubber	U	1870's	CT	Engineers, state arms.		138	Misc
Oesterreichisch-Alpine Montanges	IC	1920's	Austria	Mining & industry, underprint of alpine flowers.		150	Misc
Office Central De Pompes Funebries	IC	1930's	France	Gravestone, grieving family.		56	Misc
Ohio Cold Storage	U			Factory		15	Misc
Ohio Edison Electric Installation	IU	1883	KY	Electric generator		595	Misc
Ohio Union Loan	I	1860's		Ben Franklin, dog, & safe		350	Misc
Old Briar Co., N.V.	IC	1920's	Belgium			80	Misc
Old Welch Co. Inc.	I	1950's		Eagle		15	Misc

Name		Date	Location	Description	Price	Category
Oliver Typewriter Manufacturing Co.	IC	1930's	GB	Early Oliver Typewriter.	80	Misc
Onderneming Latour N.V.	IC	1920's	Netherlands		16	Misc
Oregon Smelting and Refining	I	1902	OR	Mill	150	Misc
Orr Paper Co.	I	1900's		Five% gold bond, waterfall & seal	75	Misc
Ostpreuszische	IC	1920's	Lithuania		100	Misc
Oswego & Ithica Trunpike	I	1811			90	Misc
Oueme-Dahomey S.A., Cie. De L'	IC	1890's		River & village scenes.	100	Misc
Outer Space Savings Bonds	U	1964		Unissued.	350	Misc
Overland Traction Engine.	I	1865	NY	Grey/black. Eagle on shield.	175	Misc
Overseas Fin. Corp.	I	1910's		Large eagles	10	Misc
Owensboro Water Works	I	1880's		Six% finking fund bond, large eagle	125	Misc
P. Lorillard Co.	U	1900's	NY		39	Misc
P. Lorillard Co.	SP		NJ	Two seated ladies in tobacco field	50	Misc
Pacific Coast Redwood Co.	I	1900's	CA	Eagle, gold seal	35	Misc
Pacific Coast Redwood Co.	I	1910's	CA	Eagle, gold seal	15	Misc
Pacific Gas & Electric	I	1940's		Two & seven-eighths% bond, generator & woman	15	Misc
Pacific Gas & Electric	I	1940's		Ladies & generator	15	Misc
Pacific Guano Co.	U	1850's	CA	Eagle	75	Misc
Pacific Pearl	IC	1860's	NY	Woman and pearl necklace.	995	Misc
Pacific Press Syndicate	U	1920's	CA	Two women & man	15	Misc
Pacific Sugar Construction Co.	I	1900's	CA	Eagle	15	Misc
Pacific-Ohio Electric	I	1920's		Woman with lamp, dynamo, & streetcar	35	Misc
Pacific-Ohio Electric	U	1920's		Woman with lamp, dynamo, & streetcar	15	Misc
Palmer Mountain Tunnel & Power	I	1900's		Seminude between rushing river & tunnel	100	Misc
Pamida, Inc.	I	1970's	NE		15	Misc
Pan-American Exposition Co.	I	1900's		Western Hemisphere, gold seal	685	Misc
Panama Canal Founder	U	1881			180	Misc
Panhandle Eastern Pipeline	I			Bond, oil derricks, valves tanks, city skyline	15	Misc
Paper Company of Tsver	IC	1850's	Russia	Immense factory building at top.	231	Misc
Pare Marquette Light & Power	U	1900's	MI	Gold bond, Co. logo	15	Misc
Parfumerie Ramses S.A.	IC	1910's	France	Egyptian lady ancient Egyptian perfume bottle. Sphinx	200	Misc
Parfumerie Thorel A. Sergent Fils	IC	1890's	France	Logo of a golden crown.	52	Misc
Parfums Des Fourrures Weil S.A.	IC	1920's	France	Company logo.	80	Misc
Parke-Davis Co.	I	1960's		Bare-breasted ladies with Co. logo	15	Misc
Parkersburg Aetna Corp.	I	1960's	WV	Oil well & ship	15	Misc

Patapsco Female Institute	I	1830's			350	Misc
Pates De Bois L'Eure, S.A. Des	IC	1900's	France	Colorful, pretty flowery border.	40	Misc
Patron Corp.	I	1960's		Standing woman between two men	15	Misc
Patrons Peintres Federes De Belgique	IC	1940's	Belgium		56	Misc
Patterson Dental	SP		MN	Eagle	45	Misc
Pavelle Corp.	I	1970's	NY	Large eagle & seal	15	Misc
PCCW Ltd.	I	2003	Hong Kong	Color blocks	25	Misc
Peel-Elder	I	1960's		Mercury globe	15	Misc
Pemberton & Pennsylvania	I	1920's	VA		15	Misc
Pennsylvania Canal Co.	I	1870's		Six% bond, canal scene	225	Misc
Pennsylvania Canal Co.	I	1870's		Bond, train on bridge	225	Misc
Pennsylvania Land Company	I	1790's	PA		5,170	Misc
Pennsylvania Military & Collegiate In	IC	1880's	PA		83	Misc
Pennsylvania Population Company	I	1790's	PA		3,080	Misc
Pennsylvania Power Co.	I	1940's		Bond, chariot scene	35	Misc
Pennsylvania Salt Manufacturing	I	1888	PA	Eagle on shield.	50	Misc
Pennsylvania Salt Manufacturing	I	1870's	PA	Grey/Black. Eagle on shield.	45	Misc
Pennsylvania Salt Manufacturing	I	1870's	PA	Eagle on shield.	50	Misc
Pennsylvania Salt Manufacturing	I	1940's		Green. William Penn silhouette in keystone below.	10	Misc
Pennsylvania Seaboard Steel Corp	I	1920's	NY		15	Misc
Pensalt Chemicals Corp.	I	1960's	PA	Two chemists & Co. logo	15	Misc
PeopleSoft	I	2003		Logo	85	Misc
Pequea Fishing Club	I	1910	PA	Eagle.	60	Misc
Perfumeria Gal S.A.	IC	1950's	Spain		32	Misc
Perfumes Y Cosmeticos	IC	1956	Cuba	Flowers, winged head	40	Misc
Perkin-Elmer Corp.	I	1970's		Engineer, blueprints with carpenter & rockets	15	Misc
Perkins Co.	IU	1920	LA	Pelican with four chicks	35	Misc
Permeator Corp.	I	1970's		Reduction unit & towers	15	Misc
Philadelphia & Lancaster Turnpike	IU	1790's	PA	Covered wagon at tollbooth	William Bingham 1,500	Misc
Philadelphia & Lancaster Turnpike	IC	1790's	PA	Covered wagon at tollbooth	William Bingham 1,400	Misc
Philadelphia Arms Company	I	1905	PA	Eagle	189	Misc
Philadelphia Bourse	I	1908	PA	Allegorical figures represent Commerce, ship, train	45	Misc
Philadelphia Bourse	I	1908	PA	Allegorical figures Commerce, ship, train on bridge	70	Misc
Philadelphia Bourse	UC	1900's	PA	Woman with sailor, farmer	39	Misc
Philadelphia Co.	I			Registered note, eagle	15	Misc

Name		Date	State	Description	Signer	Price	Category
Philadelphia Co.	I			Specimen, bond		15	Misc
Philadelphia College of Pharmacy	I	1860's		Six percent bond		350	Misc
Philadelphia Electric Co.	I	1960's		Woman with dynamo		15	Misc
Philadelphia Electric Co.	I	1970's		Woman with dynamo		15	Misc
Philadelphia Fire Extinguisher	U	1870's	PA	Fireman		143	Misc
Philadelphia Lodge Number Two B.	I	1920's		Six% bond, elk		50	Misc
Philadelphia-Warwick Co.	I	1940's		Voting trust certificate, no		15	Misc
Philip Morris Incorporated	U			god-like figures flanking a corporate logo		75	Misc
Phillip Hunt Chemical	I	1970's		Two chemists with Co. logo		15	Misc
Phillip Morris	I	1950's		Bond, reclining woman with lamp		15	Misc
Phillips & Phillips	U	1900's		Large eagle & harbor scene		15	Misc
Phoenix Whaling & Manufacturing	I	1900's				50	Misc
Pig'n Whistle	IC	1927	DE	little pig blowing on a flute		75	Misc
Pike Corp. of America	I	1960's		Woman with globe		15	Misc
Pike's Peak Cottage City Corp.	U	1920's	CO	Gold bond		15	Misc
Pillsbury	SP			Giant farmer		150	Misc
Pillsbury Co., The	I	1960's		Man & woman		35	Misc
Pittsburgh American China Co.	I	1920's		Eagle		15	Misc
Pittsburgh Ice Co.	I	1910's		State seal, of polar bear		35	Misc
Pittsburgh Screw & Bolt	I	1940's		Screw & bolt piercing the world		35	Misc
Pittsburgh, McKeesport Youghio RR	IC	1880's	PA	Coal miners, train.	Geo W Vanderbilt	363	Misc
Plantagie Annasburg Te Suriname	IC	1820's	Suriname		Jacob H. Luden	144	Misc
Plantations & D'Elevage Du Kivu	IC	1920's	Bel.Congo	Africans picking coffee & herding cattle.		130	Misc
Planter's Cotton Seed Co.	U	1800's	DE	Cotton pickers & bales		35	Misc
Planters Bank of the State of Mississ	I	1830's	MS			275	Misc
Playboy Enterprises, Inc.	I			Reclining nude		395	Misc
Pneumatic Gun Carriage	IU	1897	WV	Cannon		750	Misc
Pneumatic Pulverizer	I	1881	NY	Black. Close top margin.		150	Misc
Pneumatic Pulverizer	I	1881	NY	Black. Close top margin.		150	Misc
Pneumatic Scale	IC	1927	MA	Woman holding scale and sword		45	Misc
Pneumatic Scale Corp.	I	1920's		Justice with hemispheres & seal		35	Misc
Pneumatic Scale Corp.	I	1930's		Justice with hemispheres & seal		35	Misc
Pneumatic Scale Corp.	I	1950's		Woman holding scale & sword with two globes		15	Misc
Point Pleasant Bridge	I	1886	WV			200	Misc

Name	Type	Date	Location	Vignette	Signatures	Price	Category
Polyplane Packaging Co.	I	1960's		Eagle		15	Misc
Pont De La Mulatiere	IC	1790's	France			340	Misc
Pont-A-Mousson, Cie. De	IC	1950's	France	Design of engineering & metal-working themes.		480	Misc
Portage Fish & Game Co.	IU	1920's	OH	Indian tent at shore of lake		35	Misc
Poteries D'Art Se Sars-La-Bruyere	U	1920's	Belgium	Logo of a house.		32	Misc
Poulsen Wireless Corp.	U	1910's	CA			15	Misc
Pratt & Whitney	I	1896	CT	Man with winged hat machinery behind.	Francis A. Pratt	250	Misc
Pratt & Whitney	I	1896		Orange. Semi nude man with winged hat	Francis A. Pratt	250	Misc
Pratt & Whitney	IC	1890's	CT	Mercury, compass, drafting table.	Pratt, Rockefeller	1,540	Misc
Precision Polymers, Inc.	I	1970's	CT	Woman between two globes & train		15	Misc
Prestan-Moss Fund	I	1960's		Large eagle		15	Misc
Priceline.com	U	2001	DE			50	Misc
Princeton & Kingston Branch Turn	I	1850's		No, embossed seal		225	Misc
Products Chimiques De La Manufact	IC	1880's	France			32	Misc
Products Refractaires & Ceramicques	IC	1890's	Russia	Border of vases & dishes & other ceramic products.		40	Misc
Proprietors of the Woman's Journal	IC	1870	MA		Henry B. Blackwell	395	Misc
Providence Securities Co.	I	1900's	CT	Four% bond, three seated seminude figures		75	Misc
Providence Securities Co.	U	1900's		Gold bond, lady & two men		35	Misc
Providence Washington Insurance	I	1890's		Portrait of George Washington		125	Misc
Provinzial-Loge Von Niedersach Ham	IC	1940's	Germany	The badge of the Lodge, with Masonic symbols.		120	Misc
Public Service Electric & Gas	I	1960's		Gold bond, two men & woman		15	Misc
Public Service Gas & Electric	I	1970's		Three figures with winged wheel		15	Misc
Publiker Industries	I	1960's		Four allegorical figures & large winged wheel		15	Misc
Puget Sound Commercial Co.	I	1870's	WA	Eagle		125	Misc
Puget Sound Power & Light	SP	1994	WA	Dam		45	Misc
Pullman's Palace Car	IC	1900's	IL	George Pullman	Robert T. Lincoln	385	Misc
Quail Extract Co.	I	1930's		Eagle		15	Misc
Quaker Alloy Casting	I	1960's		Eagle		15	Misc
Quizno's Corp.	SP		CO	Logo		50	Misc
R. E. Rodda Candy Co.	I	1910's		Eagle with shield		15	Misc
R. J. Reynolds Tobacco Co.	SP			Eagle		50	Misc
Raccoon Coal & Fuel	IU	1901	WV	Raccoon		95	Misc
Ralston-Purina Corp.	I	1950's		Bond		15	Misc
Ransome's Patent Stone Co.	I	1860's	NJ	Stoneworker, state seal, eagle, with revenue		175	Misc

Company	Type	Date	Location	Description	Signature	Price	Category
Rapid Transit Subway Construction	I	1900	NY	Brown. State arms.	August Belmont	300	Misc
Reading Water Co,	I	1850's		No logo		100	Misc
Real Co. de Commercio Estab Barcel	IU	1758	Spain	Fancy Barcelona harbor		12,500	Misc
Real Property Investment	U	1930's	CA	Large building, street corner.	Rudolph Spreckels	165	Misc
Real Silk Hosiery, Inc.	SP			Woman with lion		75	Misc
Red Cross bond	IC	1882	Hungary	Red Cross workers, soldier		150	Misc
Red Hook Building Co.	I	1830's		Blacksmith		175	Misc
Red Square Upper Levels Trading	IC	1900's	Russia	Kremlin tower, imperial eagle.		2,750	Misc
Red Wing Carriers, Inc.	U		FL	Specimen, Red bird		35	Misc
Regia Cointeressata Dei Tabacchi S.A.	IC	1860's	Italy	Little angels. Arms of Italy, cigars & oriental pipes.		60	Misc
Reliance Intl. Corp.	I	1920's		Woman, globe, two topless seated women & man		15	Misc
Remington Rand, Inc.	I	1920's		Warrant		15	Misc
Replogle Steel Co.	I	1910's		Temporary certificate		15	Misc
Republic of Texas	I	1840	TX	Ship & Soldier		1,430	Misc
Research Investing Corp.	I	1960's		Eagle with Co. logo		15	Misc
Rex Manufacturing Co	IU	1911	DE	Woman with steam engine on left		35	Misc
Rexall Drug	I	1940's		Bowl between bare-breasted figures		35	Misc
Rexall Drug	I	1950's		Bowl between bare-breasted figures		30	Misc
Rexall Drug & Chemical	IC	1963		Brown. Mortar and pestle, flask		25	Misc
Rexall Drug & Chemical	IC	1963		Brown. Mortar and pestle, flask		25	Misc
Rexall Drug & Chemical	I	1960's		Two men & chemical		25	Misc
Rheinische Stahlwerke Zu Suisburgm	IC	1910's	Germany			130	Misc
Rich's, Inc.	U		GA	Two god-like figures		51	Misc
Richie Mineral Resin & Oil Co.	I	1860's	WV	Bond, state seal, & state products		125	Misc
Ridgway Farm & Land	U	1850's	PA	Trains, Farmers.		165	Misc
Rigaer Papierfabriken, A.G.	IC	1920's	Lativa	Seal with a lion.		80	Misc
RJ Reynolds Tobacco	IC	1910's	NJ	Embossed seal.	RS Reynolds	1,430	Misc
Rock Manufacturing Co.	I	1830's				125	Misc
Rodgers-Brown Co.	I	1920's		Gold bond		15	Misc
Rogers-Brown Iron	I	1922	NY	Brown. Woman flanked by two semi-nude men.		10	Misc
Rolex	U	1950's		Crown		613	Misc
Roltabakfabriek Kentucky N.V.	IC	1900's	Netherlands			120	Misc
Romania Industrial Farm Machinery	U	1898	Romania	Woman		80	Misc
Rome Turnpike Co.	I	1800's		No		75	Misc
Rotary Ring Spinning	U	1909-12	DE	Green. Woman and spinning wheel.		60	Misc
Rouissages Belges Legrand & Co.	IC	1900's	Belgium			24	Misc
Royal Axminster Carpet Co.	IU	1890's		Factory by river		50	Misc

Name	Type	Date	State/Country	Vignette	Signer	Price	Category
Royal Baking Powder	I	1922	NJ	Orange. Justice, sleeping lion, company books.		15	Misc
Royal Baking Powder	I	1922		Orange. Justice, sleeping lion, company		15	Misc
Royal Cercle Equestre De Bruxelles	IC	1880's	Belgium	Logo of the Cercle - a horse on it's back legs.		36	Misc
Royal Co. of St. Ferdinand of Seville	IU	1749	Spain	Port of Seville, ship, Neptune		12,500	Misc
Royal Co. of the Philippines	IU	1785	Spain	Lion, fruit, elephant, ships, rabbit, turtle		3,000	Misc
Royal McBee Corporation	U		OH	Woman		100	Misc
Roycrofters	IC	1900's	NY	Company logo.	Elbert Hubbard	572	Misc
Ruhr Housing Corporation	IC	1920's	Germany	Seated female within columns.		165	Misc
Russian 5% loan of 1822	IC	1820's	Russia	Imperial eagle at top.	Nathan Rothschild	299	Misc
Russian-American Trade & Industry	U	1910's		Eagle, shield, & anchor		15	Misc
Rust International	SP	1994	DE	Workers, office, building		39	Misc
Rutherford Drug Co.	I	1920's				15	Misc
S.S. White Dental Manufacturing	SP		PA	Logo		65	Misc
Sacramento Gas	U	1850's	CA	Allegorical woman.		143	Misc
Saint Joe Minerals	I	1970's	NJ	State seal		15	Misc
Salaisons Ardennaises S.A., Ets.	SP	1930's	Belgium			32	Misc
Salmon Falls Manufacturing Co.	I	1920's	MA			15	Misc
Salt Lake Rock	IC	1880's	UT	Quarry scene.	John W. Young	176	Misc
Samuel Blodget Jr. of Boston	I	1790's	DC			1,320	Misc
San Diego Land and Town Co.	U	1900's	ME	Indian on hill, watching train, ship, farming.		120	Misc
San Juan Portland Cement Co.	I	1900's		Mission & figures		35	Misc
San Luis Valley Irrigation Land Power	I	1907	CO	Train	S.S. Bernard	75	Misc
Sandgate Corp.	I	1970's		Seated woman, two globes, train, & city		15	Misc
Sandra Post, Inc.	I	1950's	NY	Eagle		15	Misc
Sandy Rock Investment	IU	1930's		State seal		15	Misc
Santol Products Co.	I	1920's	OR	Seven% gold bond		15	Misc
SAP Aktiengesellscaft	I	2004				45	Misc
Sara Lee Corp.	SP		MD	Brand logos		50	Misc
Savana S.A. De Filature Tissage Mec	IC	1920's	India	Elephants, Hindu Gods, Ceremonies.		240	Misc
Savannah Exchange	I	1790's	GA			2,640	Misc
Savonnerie Produits Chimiques Alger	IC	1900's	Algeria	Arab, camel, mosque, palm trees		130	Misc
Schaaf & Good Co.	I	1920's	OH	Allegorical figure & harbor scene		15	Misc
Schering Corp.	I	1960's		Man & woman with lab equipment & world		35	Misc
Schimpf & Keim Boiler & Mfg	I	1889	PA	Boiler		119	Misc
Schuldverschreibung der Stadt Koln	I	1923	Germany	Text in German. Brown with coupons.	Konrad Adenauer	30	Misc

Schuldverschreibung der Stadt Koln	I	1923	Germany	Text in German. Brown with coupons.	35	Misc
Schultze Gunpowder Co., Ltd.	IC	1900's	GB	Logo: Hand holding lightning.	140	Misc
Schuylkill River Bridge	U	1810's			175	Misc
Schuylkill Water Co.	U	1880's		Hunter with rifle, stream, & waterfall	35	Misc
Science Resources, Inc.	I	1960's	PA	Lady with two globes	15	Misc
Scientific American Compiling De	I	1910's	NJ	Eagle	75	Misc
Scudder, Stevens & Clark	I			Sailor at wheel	15	Misc
Sears, Roebuck and Co.	U	1966	NY	Large building	50	Misc
Security-Columbian Banknote Co.	SP	1950's		Seated woman with cherub	35	Misc
Seneca Falls Machine Co.	I	1940's	MA	Eagle	15	Misc
Sentinel Manufacturing	IU	1915	CT	Cooking clocks	150	Misc
Shannon Manufacturing Co.	U	1890's	MA	Girl	15	Misc
Sharaf, R. M., Machine	I		MA		15	Misc
Shering-Plough	I	1960's			15	Misc
Shortwave Television Corporation TV	I	1932			200	Misc
Shoshoni Power & Irrigation Co.	I	1910's	WY	Dam with open floodgate	35	Misc
Shoshoni Power and Irrigation Co.	IC	1910's	WY	Dam with gates open.	24	Misc
Shrine of Our Lady of La Salette	I	1960's		Five% bond, eagle	15	Misc
Shulton, Inc.	I	1960's		Sailing ship & woman holding globe	15	Misc
Sierra Nevada Water and Power	I		CA	Pictures of California	199	Misc
Signode Steel Strapping Corp.	I	1960's		Man at forge	15	Misc
Silicon Graphics	I	2002		SGI logo	20	Misc
Silox Pure Water of Philadelphia	U			Shield & ship	15	Misc
Simco Stores	I	1970's		Lady between two globes	15	Misc
Simpson, J., & Co.	U	1920's	NY	Commercial building	15	Misc
Sizzler International	SP	2000	DE	Woman, horn of plenty	35	Misc
Skouheagan Bridge	I	1820's			300	Misc
Smith, D. A. & Sons, Inc.	IU	1920's		Eagle on rock	15	Misc
Smith, D. A. & Sons, Inc.	IU	1920's			15	Misc
Social Insurance Co.	U	1800's	MA		75	Misc
Societe Du Luxemborg	IC	1820's	Luxemberg		760	Misc
Society for Establishing Useful Manuf	I	1790's	NJ		2,915	Misc
Society for Establishing Useful Manuf	I	1790's	NJ		825	Misc
Society for Establishing Useful Manuf	I	1790's	NJ		440	Misc
Society for Establishing Useful Manuf	I	1790's	NJ		187	Misc
Solitude, Manufacture Draps Livonie	IC	1890's	Russia		80	Misc
Somerset Lighting Co.	I	1890's	NJ	State seal with stamp	35	Misc
Somerset Lighting Co.	I	1900's	NJ	State seal with stamp	15	Misc

Name	Type	Date	State	Vignette	Signer	Price	Category
Soprano Waste Management	U	2003		Eagle on Garbage truck		35	Misc
South Gila Canal	I	1892	AZ Terr	Orchards, fields, mountain in the distance.		35	Misc
South Nevada Power Co.	I	1960's		Large eagle, river, & factory		15	Misc
South Porto Rico Sugar	IC	1950's	NJ	Purple. Workers at sugar plantation.		25	Misc
South Puerto Rico Sugar Co.	IC	1960's	NJ	Vignette of workers at sugar plantation.		25	Misc
South Sea Letter of Authority	IC	1720's		South Sea Bubble	Halifax	242	Misc
Southern Art Exhibition Co.	I	1880's		Embossed seal		175	Misc
Southern Art Exhibition Co.	U	1880's		Embossed seal		35	Misc
Southern Calif. Gas Co.	IC	1988		Nude woman		45	Misc
Southern Calif. Gas Co.	IC	1988		Nude woman		45	Misc
Southern California Water Co.	U			Filtration plant		35	Misc
Southern Improvement Co.	I	1880's		Gold bond, beehive & portrait of lady		35	Misc
Sparky's Virgin Islands, Inc.	I	1970's		Seal		15	Misc
Spencer Arms Co.	I	1880's	NY	Three hunters with o under two long rifles		50	Misc
Spencer Shoe Corp.	I	1950's		Eagle		15	Misc
Sperry-Rand Corp.	SP	1950's		Specimen, Bond, chemist with machinery		35	Misc
Sperry-Rand Corp.	I	1950's		Seated chemist with machinery		35	Misc
Spic & Span Markets, Inc.	U	1920's	DE	Lady, two hemispheres, & a beehive.		36	Misc
Spinks, Wm. A.	I	1920's	IL	Eight% bond		15	Misc
Splitdorf-Bethlehem Electric Co.	I	1920's	NJ	Woman, electricity, facsimile of Charles Edison sig		120	Misc
Splitdorf-Bethlehem Electric Co.	I	1930's	NJ	Woman, electricity, facsimile of Charles Edison sig		100	Misc
Squirrel Hunter's Discharge	IC	1860's	OH			358	Misc
SRA International	SP	2002	DE	Man and woman at computer		25	Misc
St Louis Suburban Teachers' Assoc	I	1960's		Ten-dollar debenture		15	Misc
St. Louis Bridge	IC	1881		Eads Bridge	J. P. Morgan	1,500	Misc
St. Louis Bridge Co.	I	1884		Bridge	J P Morgan	77	Misc
St. Louis Bridge Company	I	1881		Road	JPMorgan,JSMorgan	406	Misc
St. Louis Bridge Company	I	1884		Bridge	JP Morgan	167	Misc
St. Louis Exposition & Music Hall	IC	1900's	MO	Grizzly bear.		165	Misc
Stadt Essen	IC	1920's	Germany	Three modernistic industrial scenes.		198	Misc
Stadt Koln	IC	1920's	Germany	Loan.		231	Misc
Stafford Meadow Coal & Iron	I	1850's		Bond, navy		100	Misc
Stafford Meadow Coal, Iron City	I	1850's				100	Misc
Stafford Meadow Coal, Iron City Im	IU	1850's		Bond, with seven vignettes		125	Misc
Stamps.com	I	2003		Logo		35	Misc
Standard Cattle Co.	I	1880's	IL	Cowboy on horse		225	Misc

Name	Type	Year	State	Description	Signature	Price	Category
Standard Cordage	I	1906	NY	Green/purple. Women hold ships.		35	Misc
Standard Cordage	I	1906	NY	Green/purple. Women hold ships.		35	Misc
Standard Rope & Twine	I	1898	NJ	Green. Steamships and sailing vessels.	John M. Forbes	85	Misc
Standard Rope & Twine	I	1898	NJ	Green. Steamships and sailing vessels.	John M. Forbes	85	Misc
Standard Rope & Twine Co.	I	1890's	NJ	Waterfront		100	Misc
Standard Rope & Twine Co.	I	1900's		of ships		75	Misc
Standard Wholesale Phosphate Acid	IC	1920's	MD	Indian chief, & cotton.		64	Misc
Stanislaus Central Bridge	IU	1853	CA	Steamboat, bridge, train		495	Misc
Stanislaus Central Bridge Co.	IC	1850's	CA	The bridge, side-wheel boat, train.		760	Misc
Stanley Co. of America	SP		DE	Eagle.		50	Misc
Stanley Co. of America	SP		DE	Eagle.		50	Misc
Stanley Works	I	1863-7		Printed on blue paper.	Frederick Stanley	200	Misc
Stanley Works	I	1863-7		Printed on blue paper.	Frederick Stanley	100	Misc
State of Arkansas	U	1872	Arkansas	Ships		66	Misc
Stauffer Chemical Co.	I	1970's		Seated lady chemist		15	Misc
Stellum Intl.	IU					15	Misc
Sterling Energy Systems	IU	1980	DE	Eagle	John De Lorean	1,250	Misc
Sterling Precision Corp.	I	1960's		Large eagle & seal		15	Misc
Stetson, John B., Co.	I	1920's		Portrait of John B. Stetson		60	Misc
Stevens' Patent Bread Machinery Co.	IC	1860's	GB	Breadmaking machinery, & wheat. Border of wheat.		200	Misc
Stewart Medicine	IU	1884	NJ	Dr. Stewart		375	Misc
Stock Exchange, London	IC	1930's	GB			220	Misc
Stoll Werck Chocolate Co.	I	1920's				15	Misc
Strand Bridge	IC	1800's	GB	Gold seal.		407	Misc
Studebaker Watch Fob	U	1954	NY	Shed		75	Misc
Sucre Engram S.A. Holding, Centrale	IC	1930's	Luxemberg	Colorful.		100	Misc
Sucriere Europeenne & Coloniale Cie.	IC	1890's	BelCongo	Arms.		170	Misc
Suetepec Electric Light & Power	I	1910's	NY	Embossed seal		15	Misc
Suetepec Electric Light & Power	I	1920's	NY	Embossed seal		15	Misc
Suetepec Electric Light & Power	I	1920's		Seven% bond		15	Misc
Suisun & Fairfield Water	IU	1868	CA	Lake		225	Misc
Sullivan Machinery Co.	I			Eagle with mountains & ship		15	Misc
Sumatra Caoutchouc Plantagen Mij	IC	1900's	Indonesia	Rubber Estate, rubber trees.		60	Misc
Summit Branch RR	IC	1880's	PA	Coal train leaves mill.		242	Misc
Sun Microsystems	I	2002		Sun logo		20	Misc
Supervised Shares, Inc.,	I	1910's		Two men with world & dollar sign		15	Misc
Susquehannah & Lehigh Turnpike	I	1800's	CT			154	Misc
Susquehannah Bridge Co.	IC	1820's	NY			160	Misc

Company	Type	Date	Location	Description	Price	Category
Sutro Mortgage investment Trust	I			Co. logo	15	Misc
Swanee Paper Corp.	U	1970's		Specimen, Two globes, lady, city, & train	15	Misc
Swedish Ball Bearing	U			Specimen, Two seated men with Co. logo	15	Misc
Swedish Shipping Shares	IC	1900's	Sweden	Ships.	88	Misc
Syntavco, Inc.	I			Large eagle & gold seal	15	Misc
Tabasco & Chiapas Trading & Trans	IU	1906	NJ	Arm & hammer with train, ship	50	Misc
Tacoma Ice Corp.	U	1960's	WA		15	Misc
Talking Clock Manufacturing	U	1900's	MO	Grandfather clock, elk	35	Misc
Teaching Machines Inc.	SP	1961	NM	Portable collapsible computer	395	Misc
Tele-Market	IU	1996	Russia	3 large green diamonds	45	Misc
Telepost	I	1910-11	ME	Blue. Woman holds lightning.	20	Misc
Telstar, Inc.	I	1900's		Woman between two globes & train	15	Misc
Tennessee Electric Power Co.	U			Specimen, Woman on winged wheel & eagle	35	Misc
Terminal Ice & Fuel Co.	U			Government building	25	Misc
Terminal Ice Co.	I	1920's		Horse & buggies in front of buildings	15	Misc
Terminal Refrigerating & Warehouse	U	1930's		Bond	15	Misc
Territorial Company	I	1790's	PA		6,270	Misc
Texas Association	I	1840's	TX	Indian spearing bison.	385	Misc
Texas First Mortgage Reit	IU	1970's		Warrant	15	Misc
Texas Salt Co.	U				15	Misc
Textielgroothandel Voorheen	IC	1920's	Netherlands		52	Misc
Textile Croon S.A., LA	IC	1930's	Belgium		32	Misc
Textilwerke Johann Hernych & Sohn	IC	1940's	Czech	Textile workers showing cloth & a woman spinning.	80	Misc
Thayer West Point Hotel Corp.	I	1920's			35	Misc
The Cuba Company	IC	1927		Oxen pulling sugarcane cart.	25	Misc
The Cuba Company	IC	1927		Oxen pulling sugarcane cart.	25	Misc
The Genoa & District Water Works	I	1908	Italy	Port of Genoa	220	Misc
The Genoa & District Water Works Co	I	1908	Italy	Port of Genoa, from which Columbus sailed to America.	220	Misc
The Georgian Inc.	IU	1833	MA	Woman standing behind a food counter	300	Misc
The Mexican Telephone Co.	I	1892		Paine Webber	77	Misc
The National Avenue Company	U	1880	OH	Carriage and horses	49	Misc
The Piston Ring Company	I	1921	MI		45	Misc
The Valley Turnpike	I	1848	VA	Conostoga Wagon	136	Misc

Company						
The Wardcorn Corp.	IU	1902	DC	Lockbox with lightning bolts	300	Misc
Their Majesties Treasure, Loan 1693	IC	1693	GB	Part printed form.	473	Misc
Thermal De Bagnoles De L'Orne S.A.	IC		France	Decorative modern border.	30	Misc
Thermal De La Motte-Les-Bains, Ets.	IC	1840's	France		120	Misc
Thermal De Mont-Fore S.A.	IC	1950's	France		24	Misc
Thermal De Vichy, Cie. Fermiere De	IC	1890's	France	Spa at Vichy, fountains, roses etc.	120	Misc
Thermale Des Abatilles, S.A.	IC	1920's	France	Sea through the pine forests, fountain in forest.	196	Misc
Thermatomic Corp.	I	1920's	VA	Large of machinery	35	Misc
Thermes D'Enghien, S.A. Des	IC	1870's	France	Town of Enghien.	300	Misc
Thermes Salins De Biarritz, S.A., Cie	IC	1920's	France	Thermes Salins.	160	Misc
Thiokal Chemical	I	1960's		Allegorical figures with gear	15	Misc
Thiokal Chemical	I	1970's		Man with chemical equipment	15	Misc
Third Moravian Church School	U	1850's	PA	Old church building	125	Misc
Third National Corp.	I			Eagle	15	Misc
Thomas Cusack Company	I	1917	CO	Cusack	69	Misc
Three Flags	IU				15	Misc
Tientsin Land Investment Co. Ltd.	IC	1920's	Hong Kong	Color blocks	120	Misc
Tippecanoe Securities	IU	1910	NJ	President Harrison	125	Misc
Tissages & Dentelles S.A.	IC	1920's	Belgium	Old lady making lace, border of lace.	52	Misc
TMP Worldwide (monster.com)	I	2003		Multicolor vignette of a monster.	50	Misc
Tobacco Producing Co-op	I	1926	Bulgaria	Tobacco Producers	114	Misc
Tobacco Products	I	1924-31	VA	Workers pick tobacco.	5	Misc
Tobacco Products	I	1924-31	VA	Workers pick tobacco.	5	Misc
Tobacco Products Corp.	I	1920's	VA	Workers in tobacco field ~	15	Misc
Tobacco Products Corp.	I	1930's		Five & one half% bond, two seated ladies	125	Misc
Tom Moore Distillery Co.	U		MI	Specimen, Two seated ladies with Co. logo	50	Misc
Topper Corp.	I		NY	City	15	Misc
Torre Pellice	IC	1890's	Italy	Topless girl bringing hydro-electric power to Alps.	240	Misc
Tot-Lam S.A.	IC	1900's	Indochine	Local gentleman enjoying tea.	280	Misc
Transit Warehouse Co.	I			Seven% bond, eagle	15	Misc
Transportation Corp. of America	U	1960's		Bond, eagle	15	Misc
Trenton Institute	I	1860's	NJ	State seal	100	Misc
Tri-plex Safety Razor Co.	U	1900's		Eagle	15	Misc
Tri-State Stamp Vending	IC	1900's	DE	Early stamp vending machine.	176	Misc

Company	Type	Date	State/Country	Description	Price	Category
Triangle Industry, Inc	I	1970's		Man holding triangle	15	Misc
Trow City Director Co.	I	1870's	NY	Cherub with directory	100	Misc
Trow City Director Co.	I	1880's	NY	Cherub with directory	100	Misc
Trustees of Francis	I			Green 10,000 underprint, blue seals.	225	Misc
Trustees of Francis Ellershansen	I			Green 10,000 underprint, blue seals.	225	Misc
Try-Utilities Corp.	I	1920's		Bond	15	Misc
Tube City Brewing	IU	1950's		Eagle, brewery & farm scene	35	Misc
Tuolumne County Water	I	1852		Grey/Black. Men building sluices.	95	Misc
Tuolumne County Water	I	1852		Grey/Black. Men building sluices.	95	Misc
Turkish Bath & Laundry Co., Ltd.	IC	1860's	GB	Decorative border.	120	Misc
Twentieth Century Market	I	1920's		Eagle	15	Misc
Typo-Et-Lithographie Anversoise S.A.	IC	1900's	Belgium	Superb, flowery border.	56	Misc
U.S. Reformed Church-Reformed Mis	IC	1880's		Foreign missionaries.	231	Misc
Union Acieries Charleroi Et Luxemb	IC	1900's	Luxemberg	Underprint of flowers, & a great lion.	130	Misc
Union Bag-Camp Paper Co.	I	1950's		Winged goddess with sword & horn & Co. logo	15	Misc
Union Cattle Co.	I	1880's	WY	Seven% gold bond, bust of horned cow	500	Misc
Union Cement Co.	U	1860's		Portrait	15	Misc
Union Centrale Des Grandes Mauques	IC		France	Mercury, warrior lady, lion with globe, garlands	72	Misc
Union Metallurgique De France S.A.	IC	1870's	France	Factory by the sea, workers, more scenes.	80	Misc
Union Miniere Du Haut-Katanga	IC	1930's	BelCongo		80	Misc
Union Textil Exportadora S.A.	IC	1920's	Spain	Company's textile-mill, loading on ship.	180	Misc
United Drug Inc.	IC	1934		Mortar & pestle, male & female angel	25	Misc
United Drug Inc.	IC	1934		Mortar & pestle, male & female angel	25	Misc
United Kingdom Great Britain Ireland	SP	1900's	GB	Lion head at top.	550	Misc
United Lumber	SP	1900's	Canada	Forest scene.	110	Misc
United Parcel Service (UPS)	I	2002		Workers, globe, train, truck	125	Misc
United States Express	IC	1870's	NY	Eagle on top of circle.	407	Misc
United States Leather	I	1937-42	NJ	Olive. Steer.	20	Misc
United States Steel	I	1912	NJ	Orange. Steelmakers.	20	Misc
United States Worsted	I	1914		Sheep	50	Misc
United Stores	I	1931-44	DE	Shares.	5	Misc

Universal Lock-Tip	I	1929	MA	Preferred. Gold. Eagle on dome.	65	Misc
Universal Lock-Tip	I	1929	MA	Green. Liberty, flag, eagle.	50	Misc
US Colonial Fiscal Paper	I	1791	VA		100	Misc
US Internal Revenue Tax Receipt	IU	1870	NH	Check size receipt	20	Misc
US Steel	I	1940's		Workers in steel mill.	30	Misc
US Treasury War Bond	U	1940's		Disney Characters.	475	Misc
US Treasury War Fin Cmttee (Disney)	I	1940's		Disney Characters	475	Misc
Utah & Salt Lake Canal	I	1893	UT	Blue. Farmer plowing.	60	Misc
Utah Book & Stationery	IU	1891	UT Terr	Mormon Tabernacle	395	Misc
Utica Burial Case	I	1898-08	NY	Shares.	30	Misc
Vaughn Machine Company	I	1903		Topless Woman	90	Misc
Verein Naturgemasse Lebens Heilwei	IC	1910's	Germany	Two young ladies in the open air.	72	Misc
Vereinigte Gluhlampen Und Electricit	IC	1900's	Hungary	Factory at Budapest.	60	Misc
Verreries De Dampremy	IC	1830's	Belgium		280	Misc
Verreries De L' Hermitage S.A.	IC	1920's	Belgium		52	Misc
Verreries De Moutier, S.A. Des	IC	1900's	Switzerland	Colorful share.	110	Misc
Verres Speciaux De Bonne-Esperamce	IC	1920's	Belgium		24	Misc
Vicksburg National Military Park	IC	1890's	MS	Eagle, train, ship.	176	Misc
Victory for America in 1964	U	1964		Goldwater	30	Misc
Villapark 'T Motje N.V.	IC	1930's	Belgium	Three workmen's houses.	22	Misc
Vim Tractor	I	1919	WI	Two men	56	Misc
Virginia, Tennessee Carolina Steel	SP	1889	NJ	Green. Locomotive, farmer, wife, miners below.	100	Misc
VistaCare	SP	2003	DE	Heart shaped logo	35	Misc
W. E. Hendricks	I		CO	Man on unusual bicycle.	85	Misc
W. T. Grant Co.	IC	1923	MA	Brown	W.T. Grant	100	Misc
W.T. Grant Company	IC	1920's		Orange	W.T. Grant	100	Misc
Wage Earners Emergency Hospital	IU	1903	RI	Elk	65	Misc
Waialua Agricultural Company	SP		HI	Very large plantation.	150	Misc
Waialua Agricultural Company	I		HI	Very large plantation.	150	Misc
Walkill Stump & Land Clearing Dist	I	1920	FL	Green.	5	Misc
Waltham Watch	I	1927	MA	7% Prior preference. Eagle holds watch. Silver overprint.	50	Misc
Waltham Watch	I	1927	MA	7% Prior preference. Eagle holds watch	50	Misc
Welde & Thomas Brewing	I	1893-4	PA	Gray. Company plant. Founders.	90	Misc
Western Atlas	SP	1994	DE	Woman with wings between two globes	35	Misc
Western Building and Investment Co	IU	1911		Home	75	Misc

Westford Cemetery Association	IC	1870's	CT	Widow and child. Dog, safe and key.	121	Misc
Westinghouse Electric	SP	1930	PA	Large gear with wings, three women	35	Misc
Westinghouse Electric & Manufact	I	1910's		Brown. Semi-nude woman	10	Misc
Westinghouse Electric & Manufact.	I	1910's		Brown. Semi-nude woman.	35	Misc
Westley Richards & Co. Ltd.	IC	1900's	GB		140	Misc
Westmahrische	IC	1930's	Czech	Man & electrical equipment.	96	Misc
Wey & Arun Junction Canal	IC	1830's	GB	Company arms, white seal.	352	Misc
Wheelabrator Technologies	V	1985	DE	Man holding a garbage can	45	Misc
White Cross Copper	I	1917	DE	Blue. White cross.	20	Misc
Whitemarsh Valley Country Club	I	1923	PA		89	Misc
Widescope Camera & Film Corp	I	1923	DE	Man	50	Misc
Williams Valley Railroad & Mining	I	1830's	PA	Mining scene.	209	Misc
Wilmington & Philadelphia Turnpike	I	1814	PA		104	Misc
Wilmington Steam Fire Engine	IC	1870's	NC	Early steam fire engine.	650	Misc
Winchester Repeating Arms	I	1929	DE	Orange borders & security underprint.	40	Misc
Wind River Producing & Refining	I	1919	ME	Brown.	35	Misc
WIRED Inc.	SP			Fancy color designs	175	Misc
Wisconsin Cabinet and Panel Co	IC	1917	NJ	Issued to/signed twice by Thomas Edison	2,975	Misc
Wisconsin Cabinet and Panel Co	IC	1917	NJ	Signed once by Thomas Edison	2,395	Misc
Woman's Land Syndicate bond	IU	1893	IL	Mrs. Emmons	295	Misc
Woodstream Corp.	Proof		PA	Native American Indian and beaver	40	Misc
Woodward Undergd Elec Light Cable	SP	1890's	NE	Electric Parlor	209	Misc
World's Columbian Commission	IC	1890's		Globe, women, eagle.	660	Misc
World's Columbian Exposition	I	1892	IL	Woman on wheel races eagle. Trains.	450	Misc
WorldCom	I	2002			40	Misc
Worldwide Restaurant Concepts	SP	2003	DE	Woman holding wheat	40	Misc
WPL Holdings	SP		WI	Four workers, computer disk	40	Misc
Wrigley Pharmaceutical	I	1927	DE	Orange. W.W. Wrigley	125	Misc
Wrigley Pharmaceutical	IU	1929	DE	Spearmint Toothpaste	175	Misc
Youssef & Ahmed El-Gammal Soc.	IC	1920's	Egypt	Egyptian ladies.	36	Misc
Zellwood Florida Farms	I	1915	DE	Green. Eagle.	15	Misc
Zion's Co-operative Mercantile Instit	IC	1860's	UT	Lion & key. Brigham Young	8,140	Misc
Zion's Co-operative Mercantile Instit	IC	1880's	UT	Young at center. John Taylor	1,430	Misc

Zion's Co-operative Mercantile Instit	IC	1890's	UT	Portrait of Young.	Wilford Woodruff	880	Misc
Zion's Co-operative Mercantile Instit	IC	1900's	UT	Portrait of Young.	Lorenzo Snow	671	Misc
Zion's Co-operative Mercantile Instit	IC	1900's	UT	Portrait of Young.	Joseph H. Smith	578	Misc
Zion's Co-operative Mercantile Instit	IC	1900's	UT	Portrait of Young.	H.J. Grant	330	Misc
Zion's Co-operative Mercantile Instit	IC	1940's	UT	Portrait of Young.	George A. Smith	253	Misc
Zion's Co-operative Mercantile Instit	IC	1950's	UT	Portrait of Young.	David O. McKay	248	Misc
Zions Investment Corp.	U	1955	UT	Family pulling cart		25	Misc
Zuckerfabrik Pelplin A.G.	IC	1940's	Germany			70	Misc

CHAPTER 15 - OIL & GAS CERTIFICATES

Oil and gas drilling certificates usually have interesting vignette of oil fields with derricks and gushers. Pennsylvania certificates are highly desirable.

Name	IU	Date	State	Vignette	Signed by	Value	Category
Alaska Petroleum Company	I	1898	AK	Alaska		115	Oil & Gas
Albany Petroleum & Coal	IC	1860's	NY	Men, tanks & barrels.		176	Oil & Gas
Amber Petroleum	IC	1860's	PA	Dog on safe.		297	Oil & Gas
Anita Oil Association	I	1920-21	TX	Green. Oil rigs.		15	Oil & Gas
Barnett Oil & Gas	I	1919	DE	Brown. Oil rigs, gushers.		12	Oil & Gas
Bawang-Petroleum Maatsch	IC	1890's	Indonesia			60	Oil & Gas
Bay State Gas	I	1896-97	DE	Green. State arms. Ornate title.		20	Oil & Gas
Berry Petroleum	I	2003		Oil men standing next to dinosaurs		50	Oil & Gas
Big Three Oil	I	1922-3	CO	Gray. Eagle, shield.		20	Oil & Gas
Boone Oil and Gas Co.	U	1920's	CO	Oilfield.		40	Oil & Gas
Brooklyn Petroleum	IC	1860's	NY	Oil depot, steamboat, barge.		341	Oil & Gas
Buchanan Farm Oil	IC	1870's	NY	Train, men, barges.	W.W. Rose	330	Oil & Gas
Buffalo Pipe Line Co.	IU	1800's	NY			45	Oil & Gas
Buick Oil	IU	1912	CA	Train, oil derricks, tanks	David D. Buick	750	Oil & Gas
Buick Oil	IC	1900's	CA	Oil field, torch.	David D. Buick	660	Oil & Gas
Bull Creek Oil	IC	1860's	WV	Oil depot, steamboat, factory.		297	Oil & Gas
Bull Creek Oil Co.	IC	1860's	WV/PA	Oilfield.		140	Oil & Gas
Bunker Hill Petroleum	I	1865	PA	Grey. Spread eagle flanked by sailing ships.		125	Oil & Gas
Burk Pipe Lines & Refining	I	1920's	TX			15	Oil & Gas
Bush Service Corp.	I	1930's	TX	Woman, winged wheel, port city, railroad		15	Oil & Gas
Central States Electric Corporation	I	1930-31	VA	Olive. Seated allegorical male holding a compass.		15	Oil & Gas
Charles Pratt & Co.	IC	1880's	NY		C. Pratt	2,310	Oil & Gas
Cochran Cotton Seed Oil	I	1891	PA	Cotton wagon, field hands and an overseer		75	Oil & Gas
Colonial Oil	I	1922-3	CO			15	Oil & Gas
Colonial Oil	I	1922-3	CO			15	Oil & Gas
Columbia Gas System Inc., The	I	1970's		Seminude lady with torch, oil derricks in rear		15	Oil & Gas
Compass Oil	I	1922-3	WY	Orange. Oil rigs, circles.		15	Oil & Gas

Connecticut Gas & Coke Securities	I	1930-37	CT	Blue. Eagle.	12	Oil & Gas
Consolidated Gas	I	1960's			15	Oil & Gas
Consolidated Oil Fields of South Afr	IC	1910's	S. Africa	Cape Town & oil tanker.	70	Oil & Gas
Curtin Oil	IC	1875	PA	Railcar, oil barrels	350	Oil & Gas
Davis Oil	I	1917	WY	Grey/Black, gold seal. Miners drilling underground.	20	Oil & Gas
December Oil	U	1860's	PA	Oil rigs, tanks, train.	297	Oil & Gas
Densmore Oil	IC	1865	PA	Train, oil barrels	295	Oil & Gas
Desert Oil & Gas Co.	U	1920	NV	Circular vignette of oil field and refinery in background	35	Oil & Gas
Dunkard Creek Oil	U	1860's	PA	PA State Arms.	253	Oil & Gas
East Oil Creek Petroleum	IU	1865	NY	Lakeside oil depot	595	Oil & Gas
Eclairage & De Chauffage Gaz Madril	IC	1880's	Spain	Gas works, machinery, Madrid, arms of the city	36	Oil & Gas
Electric Illuminating of New York	I	1910	NY	Brown. Lamps, dynamo, telephone, electric streetcar.	175	Oil & Gas
Ennis Petroleum	I	1920	DE	Brown. Eagle.	15	Oil & Gas
Enron	U	1998		Industrial	125	Oil & Gas
Enron	U	2001		Industrial Kenneth Lay	95	Oil & Gas
Enron	I	2003			100	Oil & Gas
Enron	I	2004		Man with oil refinery, Crooked E logo	100	Oil & Gas
Enron	U				70	Oil & Gas
Enron	U			Man	51	Oil & Gas
Enron	U			Construction man	50	Oil & Gas
Enron Corp.	I	2003	OR	Crooked E logo Ken Lay facsimile	150	Oil & Gas
Essok Oil	I	1927	CO	Brown. Oil rig, tanks.	15	Oil & Gas
Eureka Oil	IC	1860's	WV	Tanks, barrels, oil rigs.	220	Oil & Gas
Eureka S.A. Petrolera	IC	1900's	Mexico	Oil workers, tanker & oil well.	90	Oil & Gas
Exploitation De L'Acetylene, S.A.	IC	1890's	Belgium	Figures bringing light to world, & world underprint.	170	Oil & Gas
Farnsworth Oil of West Virginia	U	1860's	WV	Steamer, oil towers, tanks.	154	Oil & Gas
Fox Head Brewing Co.	U	1957	WI	Fox	75	Oil & Gas
Frazier Oil	IU	1866	NY	Oil depot	495	Oil & Gas
Freeport Gas Works	IU	1870's	PA	State seal	75	Oil & Gas

Name	Type	Date	State	Description	Price	Category
G. M. B. Oil	I	1929	KS	Green. Oil depot, gusher.	20	Oil & Gas
Getty Oil Co.	SP			3 Vignettes of Oil Co. Workers	50	Oil & Gas
Glenrock Oil Co.	U	1910's	VA	Oilfield, oil train, & little angel.	100	Oil & Gas
Government Oil & Mining W Virginia	U	1860's	PA	Loading barrels of oil into a rail car.	180	Oil & Gas
Green Mount Water Supply	I	1905	PA	Red-brown. Allegorical females.	40	Oil & Gas
Guardian Coal & Oil	I	1934	WV	Orange or green. State Arms.	20	Oil & Gas
Hoboken City Water Scrip	I	1872	NJ	Grey. Orange, red. State Arms. Allegorical females.	40	Oil & Gas
Houston Oil Company of Texas	IC	1930		Woman between two oil derricks.	35	Oil & Gas
Humboldt Oil	U	1860's	PA	Oil towers, tanks, barrels.	319	Oil & Gas
Internationale Des Petroles S.A.	IC	1900's	Austria	View of oilfield & globe.	50	Oil & Gas
Jackson Exploration	IC	1981	TX	Star with TEXAS around it.	10	Oil & Gas
Jacob Creek Oil	IU	1865	PA	Oil derricks, tanks	300	Oil & Gas
King Resources	IU	1970	ME	Blue eagle	45	Oil & Gas
Kingsland Oil	IU	1864	PA	Oil derricks, tanks	300	Oil & Gas
La Compagnie Francaise Des Petroles	IC	1930's	France	Team of oil workers.	80	Oil & Gas
Leading Petroleum of West Virginia	IC	1860's	NY	Eagle, men working.	154	Oil & Gas
Little Kanawha & Elk River Petroleum	IU	1865	NY	Oil depot by river	375	Oil & Gas
LJ Priest Texas Well	IU	1930	TX	Oil field	35	Oil & Gas
Maple Shade Oil	IC	1860's	PA	State arms.	253	Oil & Gas
Mc Clintockville Petroleum	I	1860's	PA	Mc Clintock House. Eagle.	135	Oil & Gas
Mid-Continental Oil	I	1915-17	CO	Lakeside oil site, derricks. Oil gusher along side borders.	20	Oil & Gas
Mike Henry Oil	I	1921-2	WY	Green. Spread eagle on dome, ship, terminal.	15	Oil & Gas
Minerva Oil Co. Ltd.	IC	1920's	Romania	Oilwell.	56	Oil & Gas
Mission Development	I	1950-58		Brown. Woman with shield and sword.	25	Oil & Gas
Mission Development	I	1950's		Brown. Woman with shield and sword.	25	Oil & Gas
Mississippi River Corp.	IC	1965		Train, pipe, derrick.	20	Oil & Gas
Mississippi River Fuel	IC	1964		Oval vignette of fuel refinery, oil derrick on left, valves	20	Oil & Gas
Monitor Oil	IC	1860's	PA	Train, oil depot.	297	Oil & Gas

Name		Date	State	Description	Signature	Price	Category
Mud Creek Valley Oil	IC	1860's	NY	Oil depots, train and wagon.		297	Oil & Gas
National Mecca Oil	IU	1865	OH	Liberty		575	Oil & Gas
New England Petroleum	IU	1866	NY	Oil derricks, tanks		275	Oil & Gas
New York & Philadelphia Petroleum	IC	1860's	NY	Oil towers.		308	Oil & Gas
New York Cable Railway	I	1884		Bond with coupons.	W.C. Andrews	150	Oil & Gas
Newark Gas Co.	I	1890's		Storage tanks, factories, stokers, & Ms Liberty		75	Oil & Gas
Newark, Ohio Water Works	I	1885	NY	Grey/Black. Work site.		35	Oil & Gas
Niagara & Eastern Power	I	1926	NY	Blue. Large dynamo fronting Niagara Falls.		15	Oil & Gas
North American Oil	I	1922	DE	Orange or Brown. Ornate temporary certificates.		12	Oil & Gas
O-i-l Drilling	I	1922-24	WY	Grey/Black, go security underprints. Woman top left.		12	Oil & Gas
Ohio & California Refining Oil Co.	U	1900's	WV	Oilfield.		112	Oil & Gas
Ohio Petroleum	IC	1860's	OH	3 vignettes.		297	Oil & Gas
Oil Run Petroleum	IC	1860's	NY	Train and horse-drawn carts.		220	Oil & Gas
Oklahoma Oil	IC	1928	AZ	Oil field	J. Paul Getty	1,970	Oil & Gas
Oklahoma Oil	IC	1920's	AZ	Oil towers and tanks.	Jean Paul Getty	1,500	Oil & Gas
One Hundred% Special Oil Trust	IU	1920's	WA			15	Oil & Gas
Oporto Oil Co.	IC	1920's	Portugal	Porto & New York. Arabesques border.		200	Oil & Gas
Organic Oil	IU	1865	PA	Oil depot by river		300	Oil & Gas
Panonia Petroleum Co. Ltd.	IC	1930's	Jugoslavia	Elephant.		100	Oil & Gas
Penn-Louisiana Natural Gas	U			Windmill		46	Oil & Gas
Pennsylvania Imperial Oil	I	1865	PA	State arms, ships, train on bridge.		150	Oil & Gas
Pennsylvania Imperial Oil	I	1865	PA	State arms, ships, train on bridge.		140	Oil & Gas
Petrolera Mexicana Faros De Aztlan	IC	1870's	Mexico	Oil wells & Aztec temples.		120	Oil & Gas
Petroleum A-G Kaukaz	IC	1920's	Poland	Oilfield.		80	Oil & Gas
Petrolifera Fratia S.A. Romana	IC	1920's	Romania	Oilwell, refinery, sunrays.		90	Oil & Gas
Philadelphia Mutual Petroleum	IU	1865	PA	Oil depot by river		300	Oil & Gas
Philipsburg Coal Iron & Oil Company	U	1867	PA	Train on bridge		50	Oil & Gas
Phoenix Oil	IC	1860's	AZ	Eagle.		286	Oil & Gas
Pittsburgh & Westmoreland Oil	IU	1864	PA	Oil derricks, tanks		350	Oil & Gas

Name	Type	Date	State	Description	Signed	Price	Category
Public Utility Holding Corp of Amer	I	1930's	DE	Semi-nude male in front of industrial complex.		35	Oil & Gas
Ranger Comanche Oil	I	1921	DE	Green. Title against oil field.		25	Oil & Gas
Rathbone Petroleum of Pennsylvania	U	1860's	PA	Oil towers, tanks, eagle.		132	Oil & Gas
Red Rose Oil	IU	1931	AZ	Red rose with green leaves		275	Oil & Gas
Reiter-Foster Oil Corp.	IC	1939		Train going by gusher in oil field.		35	Oil & Gas
Rice Oil Company	I	1917	DE	Orange. Eagle.		50	Oil & Gas
Ritchie Mineral Resin Oil WV	I	1869	VA	Grey. State Seal.		95	Oil & Gas
Round Mountain Central	I	1908	AZ	Grey, gold. Woman with a star-studded cap.		25	Oil & Gas
Royal Dutch Co.	IC	1920's	Netherlands			70	Oil & Gas
Russell Farm Oil	IC	1860's	PA	Men working at oil depot.		330	Oil & Gas
Seaboard Oil & Transit	I	1912	CA	Grey, gold. Hillside oil site, train, derricks.		25	Oil & Gas
Seneca Oil	IC	1865	PA	Barrels being loaded into boxcar		300	Oil & Gas
Shell Transport & Trading	IC	1920's		Large oil tanks, shipping scene.		231	Oil & Gas
Shell Transport & Trading Ltd.	I	1944	GB	Striking bond featuring an oil site and depot, and ships.		300	Oil & Gas
Shell Transport & Trading Ltd.	I	1944	GB	Blue. Oil site and depot, and ships.		300	Oil & Gas
Sherman & Barnsdall Oil	IC	1860's	NY	Men working on oil tanks and barrels.		110	Oil & Gas
Sinclair Oil Company		1967		Man and Woman		60	Oil & Gas
Sohio, B. P. Trans Alaska Pipeline	I	1970's		Bond		15	Oil & Gas
Sources Petroeiferes De L'Italie	IC	1870's	Italy	Coats of Arms of Italy, France & Paris		80	Oil & Gas
Southwest Gas Utilities	I	1932	DE	Green. Men at base of a large oil tower, globes.		18	Oil & Gas
Standard Hydro-Carbon Fuel	IU	1884	WY	Factory		295	Oil & Gas
Standard Oil Co.	IC	1881	OH	Government building, woman, flag	John Rockefeller	9,000	Oil & Gas
Standard Oil Trust	IC	1882	OH	Government building	John Rockefeller	4,500	Oil & Gas
Star Oil	U	1860's	PA	Stars surround oil field vignette.		297	Oil & Gas
Steaua Romana Industrial Petroleum	I	1923		Brown. 3 languages.		15	Oil & Gas
Steaua Romana Industrial Petroleum	I	1923		Brown. 3 languages.		15	Oil & Gas
Sterling Oil	I	1865	PA	Gray/Black. Spread eagle, ax.		170	Oil & Gas
Sterling Oil	IC	1860's	PA	Eagle.		143	Oil & Gas

Sycamore Oil	IC	1860's	MA	Men working, steamboat, barges.	330	Oil & Gas
Texana Oil & Refining	I	1920-22	DE	Green. Gusher, flanked by oil fields.	20	Oil & Gas
Texas Atlantic M Oil Co.	I	1920	TX	Eagle	60	Oil & Gas
Texiana Petroleum	I	1923-4	CO	Tricolor border decors. Green, grey, orange. Eagle flag.	20	Oil & Gas
The Middlesex Valley Oil	I	1856			99	Oil & Gas
The Pueblo Gas & Oil Well Company	I	1888		Tower	78	Oil & Gas
Thomasson Panhandle	I	1941-3	CO	Brown. Riverside oil site, derricks, oil geyser.	15	Oil & Gas
Trans Ocean Gulf Oil	I	1970's		Bond	15	Oil & Gas
Transport Oil	I	1903	CA	Green. Oil rig. Flowers.	35	Oil & Gas
Uncle Sam Oil	IU	1914	KS,OK	Uncle Sam & gusher	45	Oil & Gas
Union Refining	IU	1882	AL	Riverboat, train	250	Oil & Gas
United Cuban Oil	IU	1960	DE	Photo-vignette of oil tanks	45	Oil & Gas
Venture Oil & Refining	I	1922	CO	Spread eagle on shield, farmer plowing, train & ships.	20	Oil & Gas
Vulcan Oil & Mining of West Virginia	U	1860's	WV	Oil towers, miners.	165	Oil & Gas
Wayne County Beaty Oil Well	IC	1860's	KY	Oil depots.	660	Oil & Gas
West Canadian Oil & Gas	IC	1958	Alberta	Truck going over bridge to large oil field.	30	Oil & Gas
West Virginia Oil City	I	1867		Oil rigs, tanks, horse-drawn wagon.	200	Oil & Gas
Wyoming Illuminating Oil Co.	IC	1900's	CA	Oilfield, dog & safe.	120	Oil & Gas

CHAPTER 16 - RAILROAD CERTIFICATES

Railroads are probably the most popular type of stock certificates collected by scripophilists. Many of these are signed by famous industrialists and most of the certificates feature great vignettes of locomotives.

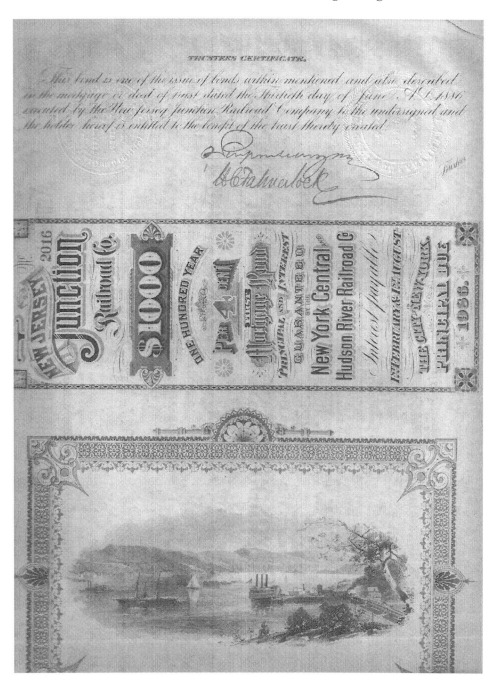

ANTIQUE STOCK & BOND PRICE GUIDE 2014

Name	IU	Date	State	Vignette　　　　　Signed by	Value	Category
Acme Magnetic Traction	I	1907	WA	Gold embossed seal and underprint. Horseshoe.	20	Railroad
Alabama & Vicksburg Rwy	SP	1880's	MS	Train at station.	187	Railroad
Alabama and Vicksburg Railway	IC	1920's	MS, LA	Train.	110	Railroad
Alaska Anthracite Rail Road Co	I	1917	WA	Train	90	Railroad
Alaska Midland Railway	I	1911		Brown borders. Preferred.	40	Railroad
Albany & Susquehanna RR	I	1906	NY	Printed corporate seal featuring a vintage locomotive.	25	Railroad
Albany & Susquehanna RR	I	1945	NY	Brown. Locomotive and tender. Specimen.	25	Railroad
Albany & Susquehanna RR	I	1945	NY	Red. Spread eagle.	20	Railroad
Albany & Susquehanna RR	I	1945		Brown. Eagle.	20	Railroad
Albany & Susquehanna RR	SP		NY	Printed corporate seal featuring a vintage locomotive.	25	Railroad
Aldrich Passenger Recorder Co.	IC	1880's	NY	Train by a harbor.	144	Railroad
Allegheny Valley Street Rwy	IC	1900's	PA	Woman in an ornate circle.	798	Railroad
Altoona & Phillipsburg Connect RR	IC	1890's	PA	Trains on bridges.	385	Railroad
American Locomotive	IC	1947	NY	Globe, logo	70	Railroad
American Niagara Railroad Co.	IC	1920's	NY	Passenger train leaving station.	110	Railroad
Arkansas Valley Rwy	U	1870's	CO Terr	Train, steamers, mountain and mill.	286	Railroad
Atchison & Nebraska RR	IC	1877		Train at station	575	Railroad
Atchison, Topeka & Santa Fe Railroad	I	1889		Train, boats in the distance. Egyptian busts below.	50	Railroad
Atlantic & Pacific Railroad West Div	I	1880		Forest green.	30	Railroad
Atlantic & Pacific Railroad Western	I	1880		Brown. Surveyors, trains.	30	Railroad
Atlantic City & Shore Railroad	I	1900's	NJ	Green. Surf bathers, trolley.	100	Railroad
Atlantic Coast Line Railroad	I	1929	VA		50	Railroad
Atlantic Mississippi and Ohio RR Co.	U	1870's	VA	Train in mountain country.　　William Mahone	436	Railroad
Atlantic Mississippi and Ohio RR Co.	IC	1870's	VA	Train, ships.	360	Railroad
Atlantic Mississippi Ohio RR	IU	1871	VA	Locomotive　　　William Mahone	225	Railroad
Augusta & Summerville RR	IC	1868	GA	Horse drawn streetcar	295	Railroad
Auto Motive Tractor Corp of America	I	1919		Tractor	90	Railroad
Baldwin & Rowland Switch & Signal	I	1904	CT	Tan underprint. Gold seal. Eagle.	25	Railroad
Baltimore & Drum Point Railroad	I	1888	MD	Green.	75	Railroad
Baltimore & Ohio Railroad	IC	1920's		Very old stagecoach type train.	25	Railroad
Baltimore & Ohio RR	IC	1890's	MD	Locomotive.　　　J.W. Gates	495	Railroad

Name	Type	Date	State	Description	Signer	Price	Category
Baltimore & Ohio RR	IC	1900's	MD	Columbia, flag, capitol.	E.H. Harriman	385	Railroad
Baltimore & Ohio RR	IC	1900's	MD	Antique train.	Murry Guggenheim	550	Railroad
Baltimore and Ohio Railroad Co.	IC	1860's	MD	Train, allegorical ladies.	Johns Hopkins	256	Railroad
Baltimore Ohio Southwestern Railway	IC	1894	MD,OH	Locomotive & dog		25	Railroad
Bangor & Aroostook RR	SP	1900's	ME	Moose, men in canoes, locomotive.		198	Railroad
Barney & Smith Car Company	I	1906	WV	Orange. Lantern and flowers.		75	Railroad
Beech Creek Extension	I	1907-22	PA	Gold seal and underprint. Eagle. With stubs at left.		30	Railroad
Beech Creek Railroad	I	1890's	PA	Green. Allegorical women flank title. Train.		15	Railroad
Bellaire, Zanesville & Cincinnati RW	I	1885-90	OH	Owl. Train, mill.		20	Railroad
Bellingham Bay & Eastern RR	SP	1900's		Little girl, locomotive		132	Railroad
Bickford Railway Electric Co.	IC	1880's	ME	Train.		90	Railroad
Bloomsburg and Sullivan Railroad	U	1890's	PA	Train.	Charles Buckalew	170	Railroad
Blue Ridge RR	I	1869	NC,SC,TN	Purple. State Arms.		95	Railroad
Bossard Railway Signal Corporation	IC	1920's	NY	Train, Statue of Liberty.	G.L. Bossard	56	Railroad
Boston Worcester Railroad	I	1861		Industrial		150	Railroad
Boston & Albany Railroad	I	1890's	MA-NY	Indian on shield in circle. Harbor with train & ships.		30	Railroad
Boston Hartford Erie Railroad Railway	U	1860		Train		50	Railroad
Bradford, Bordell & Kinzua RR	IC	1880's	PA	Train station, horse carriages.		396	Railroad
Brasso (Kronstadt) Haro.	IC	1890's	Austria			120	Railroad
Broadway & Seventh Avenue RR	I	1893	NY	Reclining nude allegorical figures, lamp.		80	Railroad
Broadway and Seventh Ave Railroad	I	1912				50	Railroad
Brooklyn & Queens Transit	I	1930's	NY	Woman holds globe, man holds lightning rod, gear		15	Railroad
Brooklyn Prospect Park Flatbush RR	IU	1860's	NY	Streetcar		250	Railroad
Brooklyn Rapid Transit	I	1896	NY	Grey/Black, orange underprint. Eagle.		35	Railroad
Brooklyn, Fort Hamilton Coney Isl RR	IC	1860's	NY	Streetcar, woman, state arms.		308	Railroad
Brunswick & Albany RR	IU	1869	GA	Train, mansion		475	Railroad
Buenos Ayres Lacroze Tramways	I	1913	Argentina	Trolley, horse-drawn streetcar flanking a bust engraving		45	Railroad
Buffalo & Jamestown RR	IU	1873	NY	Train at station		250	Railroad
Buffalo & Lake Erie Traction	IC	1900's	NY	3 vignettes		60	Railroad
Buffalo & State Line RR	IC	1850's	NY	Train, steamship.		3,960	Railroad
Buffalo & Susquehanna Rwy	I	1903	NY	Red. Train passing by factories.		45	Railroad

Name	Type	Date	State	Description	Price	Category
Buffalo and Lake Erie Traction Co.	U	1900's	PA	Electric streetcar, Arms, Eagle.	70	Railroad
Buffalo Thousand Islands Portland RR	U	1890's	NY	Building	50	Railroad
Buffalo, Bradford & Pittsburgh RR	SP	1860's		Erie related.	143	Railroad
Burlington & Northwestern Railway	I	1877	IA	Black, red embossed seal. Busy train station.	35	Railroad
Burlington, Cedar Rapids North RW	IC	1880's	IA	Beehive, eagle.	40	Railroad
Burton Stock Car	I	1882	ME	Black on pink paper, gold seal. Railcar.	150	Railroad
Burton Stock Car	I	1886	ME	Black on pink paper. Company railcar. Star at corners.	110	Railroad
C.D.F. Armavir-Tuapse	IC	1900's	Russia		100	Railroad
C.D.F. Belgies	IC	1960's	Belgium	Modern trains.	52	Railroad
C.D.F. De Braine	IC	1860's	Belgium	Locomotive, decorative border.	260	Railroad
C.D.F. De L'Orne	IC	1860's	France	View of train.	112	Railroad
C.D.F. De La Banlieue Reims Extens	IC	1920's	France	Steam-trams & arms	112	Railroad
C.D.F. Dept.	IC	1930's	France	Eight coat of arms, locomotive.	120	Railroad
C.D.F. Electriques de Catane S.A.	IC	1900's	Italy		40	Railroad
C.D.F. Ethiopiens	IC	1890's	Ethiopia	Camel caravan, train.	400	Railroad
C.D.F. Secondaires Russes	IC	1890's	Russia		380	Railroad
C.D.F. Vic. De Liege	IC	1900's	Belgium		52	Railroad
Cairo & Norfolk RR	I	1908	KY	A fast steam locomotive races a steamboat. Orange.	25	Railroad
California & Nevada Railroad	I	1884	CA	Brown. Train.	300	Railroad
Campbell Hall Connecting RR	SP	1880's	NY	Locomotive near station in a circle.	165	Railroad
Canon City & Cripple Creek Elec RW	IC	1890's	CO	Mills, mountains.	187	Railroad
Cape May & Millville Rail Road	I	1864		Beach	125	Railroad
Capital Traction	I	1900	DC	Olive green. The Capitol Building.	19	Railroad
Carl Ludwig-Bahn	IC	1900's	Austria	Austrian arms, woman, child.	100	Railroad
Carolina Central RR	I	1881	NC	Grey/black. Train, cows drinking water under bridge.	40	Railroad
Carthagene	IC	1890's	Spain	Arms of Spain & Belgium.	64	Railroad
Central Car S.A.	IC	1890's	Belgium	Views of Brussels.	180	Railroad
Central Iowa Railway Co.	IC	1880's	IA, NY	Train.	240	Railroad
Central of Georgia Rwy	SP	1890's	GA	Train, women, ship.	132	Railroad
Central Ohio Railroad	IC	1854	OH	Train, farmer, two women	75	Railroad

Company	Type	Date	State	Description	Signature	Price	Category
Central RR & Banking	I	1865	GA	Train, riverside oil depot. Train, woman, lower corners.		175	Railroad
Charleston & Savannah RR	IC	1870's	SC-GA	Train, sailboat.	Thomas Drayton	319	Railroad
Charleston & Western Carolina Rwy	I	1914	MD	Orange. Series B. Train, factory in the distance.		45	Railroad
Chemins de Fer Ethiopiens	IU	1899	France	Emperor on horseback, camels		500	Railroad
Chesapeake & Ohio Coal & Lumber	IC	1870's	NY	Man cutting tree, coal mining site, lumber mill.		165	Railroad
Chesapeake & Ohio Rwy	SP	18--	NY	Specimen. Shares set.		175	Railroad
Chesapeake, Ohio & Southwestern RR	U	1880's		Train at busy rural station.	C. P. Huntington	352	Railroad
Chester Street Rwys	I	1921-28	PA	Grey. Streetcar.		25	Railroad
Chicago & Alton Railroad	I	1899	IL	Green. Locomotive. Eagle.		35	Railroad
Chicago & Great Western RR	IC	1870's	IL	Cargo train.		462	Railroad
Chicago & Illinois River RR bond	IU	1875	IL	Train, farmers, miners		475	Railroad
Chicago & Rock Island RR	IC	1850's			John B. Jarvis	165	Railroad
Chicago and Alton Railroad Co.	IC	1920's	IL			80	Railroad
Chicago and Alton Railroad Gold	I	1899		Locomotive on a turntable.		100	Railroad
Chicago and Northwestern Railway	IC	1880's	IL	Train, Coats of Arms.		90	Railroad
Chicago and Rock Island Railroad	I	1850's			Henry Farnam	100	Railroad
Chicago Burlington & Quincy RR	I	1890	IL	Orange. Train, steamship in the distance.		25	Railroad
Chicago Rock Island & Pacific RW	IC	1915	IL&IA	Locomotive and tender	Louis Sonnenberg	35	Railroad
Chicago Subway	I	1903		Gold bond. Red. Woman holds sparking torch.		200	Railroad
Chicago Terminal Transfer Railroad	I	1898	IL		John D. Rockefeller	905	Railroad
Chicago Terminal Transfer Railroad	U	1898	IL	Woman	John D. Rockefeller	995	Railroad
Chicago, Burlington & Quincy RR	IC	1880's	IL	Locomotive, passengers, ferry.		2,200	Railroad
Chicago, Danville & Vincennes RR	IC	1870's	IL-IN	Coal train, state arms, mining scene.		231	Railroad
Chicago, Freeport & St. Paul RR	Proof	1800's	IL,WI,MN	Train, cherubs, lyre.		121	Railroad
Chicago, Rock Island & Pacific RR	I	1902		Blue. Busy train station.		35	Railroad
Chicago, Rock Island & Pacific RR	IC	1900's	IL-LA	Locomotive, ship.	J.W. Thompson	1,100	Railroad
Chicago, Rock Island & Pacific RW	IC	1900's	IL-IA	Locomotive	Bernard M Baruch	990	Railroad
Chinese Imper. Canton Kowloon RW	IU	1907	China	5% Government Guaranteed Gold bond		1,595	Railroad
Cincinnati Lafayette & Chicago RR		1871	IL	Train		80	Railroad
Cincinnati RW Tunnel	IU	1872	OH	City, train, woman	J. C. Fremont	485	Railroad

Name	Type	Date	State	Description	Signer	Price	Category
Cincinnati Rwy Tunnel	U	1870's	OH	Woman and Train.		319	Railroad
Cincinnati, Indianap, St Louis Chicago	U			Train	Collis P. Huntington	200	Railroad
Cincinnati, Lebanon & Northern Rwy	I	1880's	OH	Eagle and shield.		35	Railroad
Cincinnati, Lebanon & Northern Rwy	I	1880's	OH	Eagle and shield.		15	Railroad
Cincinnati, Portsmouth & Ohio RR	IC	1850's	OH	Train, sail and ferry boats.		264	Railroad
Cincinnati, Sandusky & Cleaveland	IC	1888		Old Western Steam Engine		70	Railroad
Cinn, Indianap, St. Louis Chicago RR	IC	1880's	IN	Train, steamboat.	Collis P. Huntington	275	Railroad
Cinn, Indianapolis, St Louis Chicago	I	18--		Green. View at North Bend Ohio		15	Railroad
City RW of Pasadena	IC	1888	CA	Horse drawn streetcar		365	Railroad
Claremont University & Ferries St. RR	IC	1891	CA	Horse drawn streetcar		325	Railroad
Cleveland Cincinnati Chicago St. Lou	IC	1950's	OH,IL,MO	Railyard		60	Railroad
Cleveland, Akron & Cincinnati Railway	I	1911	OH	Train		50	Railroad
Cleveland, Cinn, Chicago & St. Louis	I			Green. Steam train. Griffins.		35	Railroad
Cleveland, Lorain & Wheeling Rwy	SP	1890's	OH	Train.		165	Railroad
Cleveland, Youngstown & Pittsburgh	Proof	1880's	OH	Train, state arms.		198	Railroad
Clinton Line RR	IC	1850's	OH	River and trains, bridge.		308	Railroad
Co. Imperiale des Chemins de Fer	IU	1899	Estonia	Servants, camels, crowned king on horseback.		350	Railroad
Colorado Central	U		CO	Train		250	Railroad
Colorado Central Railroad	I	1873	CO	Train		129	Railroad
Colorado Central Railroad Company	I		WY	Mountain		218	Railroad
Colorado Midland RW bond	IC	1897	CO	Train by river		350	Railroad
Columbus & Indiana Central Railway	I	1868	OH-IN	Royal blue throughout!		22	Railroad
Columbus & Indiana Central RW	IC	1868	OH,IN	Train		100	Railroad
Columbus & Ninth Avenue Railroad	I	1893	NY	Gold Bond. Brown.		25	Railroad
Columbus & Xenia RR	I	1914	OH	Train.		9	Railroad
Columbus & Xenia RR	I	1902-12	OH	Gray. Trains.		20	Railroad
Columbus Chicago Indiana Central	IC	1871	OH,IN,IL	Three state seals	Jay Cooke	800	Railroad
Columbus Southern Railway	I	1890's	GA	Brown. Steam train at station.		35	Railroad
Columbus, London & Springfield	I	1903	OH	Brown. Steam train at station.		35	Railroad
Comp Imperiale Chemins de Fer Ethio	I	1899	Estonia	Camels surrounding a crowned king on horseback		350	Railroad
Companhia Leopolding Estrada Ferro	IU	1884	Brazil	Orange. Small steam train.		20	Railroad
Concord & Claremont Rail Road	I	1849				75	Railroad

Company	Type	Date	State	Description	Price	Category
Concord & Montreal RR	I	1913-9	NH	Brown or Green. Train, town in the distance.	20	Railroad
Connecticut Rwy & Lighting	I	19--	CT	Brown. State arms flanked by allegorical women.	12	Railroad
Connecting Rwy	I	1911	PA	Olive. Large portrait of J. Edgar Thompson.	120	Railroad
Consolidated Rolling Stock	I	1880's	CT	Grey/black. Train loads passengers, stagecoach.	35	Railroad
Consolidated Traction	U	1899	PA	Electric trolley.	20	Railroad
Consolidated Traction Co.	IC	1890's	PA	Electric streetcar. Andrew Mellon	760	Railroad
Cooperstown & Susquehanna Vly RR	I	1888		Vintage steam locomotive in an oval.	50	Railroad
Cornwall & Lebanon Rail Road	I	1910	PA	Train	50	Railroad
Cornwall & Lebanon Rail Road Co.	I	1891	PA	Train	75	Railroad
Costa Rica Railway	I	1889	Costa Rica	President Don Bernardo in military uniform.	25	Railroad
Covington Street RW	IU	1868		Bridge, steamboats	300	Railroad
Dallas Consolidated Traction Rwy	IC	1890's	TX	Streetcar. State arms.	209	Railroad
Danbury and Norwalk Railroad	IC	1880's	CT	Train.	150	Railroad
Dayton Springfield & Urbana Electric	I	1908		Brown.	15	Railroad
Deer Creek & Susquehanna RR	I	1889	MD	Stag. Steam engine - S in Susquehanna.	150	Railroad
Delaware & Atlantic RR	I	1838	DE		75	Railroad
Delaware & Hudson	I	1916-56	NY	Orange. Locomotive #1054.	35	Railroad
Denver & Rio Grande Railroad	I	1906	CO	Miners	47	Railroad
Detroit and Lima Northern Railway	U	1890's	MI	Trains, topless lady, flowers.	220	Railroad
Docks Connecting RW	IC	1888	NJ	Train	125	Railroad
Docks Connecting RW	U	1888	NJ	Train	50	Railroad
Dover & Rockaway Railroad	I	1937	NJ	Two women Edward Scheer	100	Railroad
Duluth St Cloud Glencoe & Mankato RW	I	1904	MI	Train	54	Railroad
Duquesne Traction of Pittsburgh	I	1891-5	PA	Green or brown. Bare-breasted woman, machineries.	18	Railroad
Dutch Rhenish Railway	IC	1870's	Netherlands		90	Railroad
Dux-Bode. Eise.	IC	1890's	Austria		36	Railroad
Eagle RR & Slate	IU	1875	VT	Eagle, train, ship	250	Railroad
East Chicago Belt RR	IC	1896	IN	Woman	85	Railroad
East Mahanoy RR	IC	1910's	PA	6 vignettes	95	Railroad
East Pennsylvania Railroad	I	1881-5	PA	Steam locomotive waits at station.	25	Railroad
East Pennsylvania Railroad Co.	IC	1880's	PA	Train, coal mine entrance. Austin Corbin.	80	Railroad
Electro Pneumatic Transit	I	1900	NJ	Air pressure system for mail through tubes.	250	Railroad
Elizabethtown & Paducah RR	IC	1870's	KY	Train station.	176	Railroad
Elkhart & Western RR	U	189-	IN	Train	45	Railroad
Elkton & Guthrie RR	IU	1957	KY	Train	100	Railroad
Ellenville & Kingston RR	IC	1938	NY	Train	75	Railroad

Name	Type	Date	State	Description	Price	Category
Elmira & Williamsport RR	I	1930	PA-NY	Green, brown or orange. Locomotive and tender.	28	Railroad
Elmira, Jefferson & Canandaiqua RR	IC	1860's	NY	Train	150	Railroad
Erie Railroad	IC	1950's		Green. Man and woman, Erie logo.	10	Railroad
Erie Railroad	IC	1950's		Blue. Man and woman, Erie logo.	10	Railroad
Erie RR	SP	1890's		Freight train, passenger train.	165	Railroad
Erie Rwy	SP	1860's	NY	Train, cities.	286	Railroad
Erie-Lackawanna Railroad	IC	1960's		Red. Man and woman, tools, logo in center.	10	Railroad
Erie-Lackawanna Railroad	IC	1960's		Brown. Man & woman holding tools, logo	10	Railroad
Erste Ungar. Galiz.	IC	1870's	Hungary	Coat of arms of Galicia.	180	Railroad
Espagne, Soc. D'Etudes	IC	1890's	Spain	Border of rosettes.	48	Railroad
Eureka & Palisade RR	IC	1870's	NV	Trains, blacksmith, farmer.	385	Railroad
Fayoum Light Railways Co.	IC	1890's	Egypt	Pharaoh & servants.	380	Railroad
Ferrocarril Entre San Fernando Curico	SP	1860's	Chile	Train.	132	Railroad
Findlay Ohio Street Railroad	I	1889	OH	Trolly Carriage	50	Railroad
Findlay, Fort Wayne & Western Rwy	I	1894	OH-IN	Reddish brown. Woman. Sphinxes.	75	Railroad
Fitchburg & Worcester RR	IU	1854	MA		90	Railroad
Flint & Pere Marquette Railway	I	1868	MI	Land Grant Bond, green $1000. Train town.	75	Railroad
Flint and Pere Marquette Railroad	I	1880	MI	Train on bridge	50	Railroad
Florida Central & Peninsular RR	SP	1890's	FL	Train, woman.	253	Railroad
Florida Central RR	IC	1870's	FL	Train, workers, locomotive.	330	Railroad
Florida RR	IC	1858	FL	Train, bridge	495	Railroad
Florida RR	IC	1866	FL	Train, steamboat	495	Railroad
Florida Rwy & Navigation	Proof	1880's	FL	Locomotive, cows, trees.	264	Railroad
Fort Pitt Traction	U	1899		Electric streetcar.	20	Railroad
Fort Wayne & Belle Isle RW	IU	1895	MI	Streetcar	100	Railroad
Franklin Canal	I	1858	PA	Grey/black. Liberty, train, sailing ship.	120	Railroad
Franklin RR	I	1830's	PA		363	Railroad
Fredericksburg & Potomac Railroad Co	I	1895	VA	Train	75	Railroad
Fredericksburg, Orange & Charlottes	IC	1870's	VA	State arms.	715	Railroad
Ft. Wayne & Southern Rail Road	I	1856	IN	Train Parker	100	Railroad
Gagnier Griffin Suspended RWBridge	IU	1894	IL	Suspended rail car crossing a river	495	Railroad
Galveston Houston & Henderson RR	IU	1857	TX	Fancy border	1,000	Railroad
Galveston, Houston & Henderson	I	1853		Vintage steam locomotive pulls a string of cars	150	Railroad

Name		Year	State	Description	Price	Category
Galveston, Houston & Henderson RR	I	1855		Bond. Green.	1,000	Railroad
Geldersch-Westfaalsche Stoomtram	IC	1900's	Netherlands		80	Railroad
Georgetown RR	IC	1870's	TX	Men loading cart with hay wagon and train.	242	Railroad
Georgia & Florida RW	IU	1910	GA	3 vignettes	125	Railroad
Georgia RR & Banking	IC	1840's	GA	Train	135	Railroad
Gilpin Tramway	IC	1880's	CO	Train.	198	Railroad
Grand Canyon Railway Company	I	1902		Train	90	Railroad
Grand Gulf & Port Gibson RR	U	1870	MS	Train	75	Railroad
Grantsburg, Rush City & St. Cloud	I	1900		Train	62	Railroad
Great Falls & Conway RR	U	1800's		House	410	Railroad
Great Southern of Spain Railway Co.	IC	1900's	Spain		100	Railroad
Guadarrama, Ferrocarril Electrico	IC	1920's	Spain	Electric train, snowy Guadarramas	160	Railroad
Guatemala Central Railroad	I	1886		Sphinx. Trains. Seated bare-breasted woman below.	200	Railroad
Guatemala Central RR	IC	1880's		Ornate frame. CP Huntington	660	Railroad
Gulf & Ship Island RR	IU	1913	MS	Train	120	Railroad
Gulf Mobile & Ohio Railroad	IC	1950's		Brown. Two women, locomotive.	25	Railroad
Gulf Mobile & Ohio Railroad	IC	1950's		Blue. Two women, locomotive.	25	Railroad
Hackensack & Lodi RR	U	1910	NJ	Eagle	40	Railroad
Hamburg Railroad Bond	I	1891	Germany	Green borders, brown underprint. City arms.	60	Railroad
Hannibal & St. Joseph RR	U	18--	MO	Train	75	Railroad
Harlem River & Portchester RR	I	1877	NY	Orange. Train.	95	Railroad
Harrisburg, Portsmth, Mt Joy Lanc RR	I	1860's	PA	Two steam locomotives, eagles, Wm Penn, Ben Franklin	375	Railroad
Harrisburg, Portsmth, Mt Joy Lanc RR	IC	1870's	PA	Trains, eagles. JEdgarThompson	385	Railroad
Hartford & Connecticut Western RR	IU	1920's	CT	Train	75	Railroad
Hartford & Wethersfield RW	IC	1860's	CT	Trolley	85	Railroad
Havana Rantoul & Eastern RR	U	1870's	IL	Train	50	Railroad
Head Ski Co.	U	1970	DE	Skiing people Howard Head	50	Railroad
Helena & Red Mountain Railroad	SP	1887	MT	Sphinxes, train, cows resting, busy harbor scene.	250	Railroad
Herkimer & Mohawk St. RR	IC	1871	NY	Horse drawn trolley	175	Railroad
Herkimer & Mohawk St. RR	U	1871	NY	Horse drawn trolley	60	Railroad
Herkimer, Mohawk & Frankfort Elect	IC	1897	NY	Clouds	65	Railroad
Herkimer, Mohawk & Frankfort Elect	U	1897	NY	Clouds	35	Railroad
Hestonville, Mantua Fairmount Pass	IC	1900's	PA	State, bridge, canal.	80	Railroad
High Bridge Railroad Co.	U	1890's	NJ	Train.	200	Railroad
Holly, Wayne & Monroe Rwy	IC	1870's	MI	Train.	264	Railroad
Hot Springs RR	IC	1901	AR	Train	95	Railroad
Hot Springs RR	U	188-	AR	Train	45	Railroad

Name	Type	Date	State	Description	Price	Category
Houston & Texas Central RR	IC	1900's	TX	Locomotive, freight cars.	132	Railroad
Houston & Texas RR	SP	1900's	TX	Locomotive, switch, trackworkers, tower.	176	Railroad
Houston East & West Texas	I	1889	TX	Workers, cotton bales, loaded horsecarts. Train.	150	Railroad
Houston, Tap & Brazoria Rwy	IC	1860's	TX	Train, cargo.	176	Railroad
Hudson & Berkshire RR	IC	1840's	NY	Millard Fillmore	1,100	Railroad
Hudson & Manhattan Railroad	U	1913		Shoreline, Subway & Railway	40	Railroad
Hudson & Manhattan Railroad	I	1928	NJ	Train tunnel	50	Railroad
Hudson & Manhattan RR	U	19--	NY	Head end view of train in tunnel	50	Railroad
Hudson & Manhattan RR	IC	1930's	NY,NJ	Train in underground tunnel	120	Railroad
Hudson & St. Lawrence RR	IC	1870's	NY	State arms, train, steamboat.	165	Railroad
Hudson River RR	IC	1860's	NY	Stock power on blue paper. Pierre Lorillard	220	Railroad
Huntingdon Car & Car-Wheel Works	IC	1880's	PA	Company plant.	110	Railroad
Idaho & Washington Northern RR	IC	1900's	ID	Woman with flag	70	Railroad
Idaho & Washington Northern RR	U	1900's	ID	Woman with flag	40	Railroad
Illinois Central RR	IU	1873	IL	Train. Blue	135	Railroad
Illinois Central RR	U	1880's	IL	RR map	45	Railroad
Illinois Central RR	IC	1900's	IL	RR map	80	Railroad
Imperial Gov of Russia Nicolas RR	IU	1869	Russia	Two headed eagle Russian crest	85	Railroad
Indian motocycle Company	U	1933		Eagle	164	Railroad
Indiana, Bloomington & Western Rwy	SP	1870's	IN	Locomotive.	110	Railroad
Indiana, Illinois & Iowa RR	IC	1900's	IN	Train	60	Railroad
Indianapolis & Cincinnati RR	IC	1860's	IN	Train	90	Railroad
Indianapolis & Cincinnati RR	U	1860's	IN	Train	50	Railroad
Indianapolis & Martinsville Rapid Tr	IU	1900's	IN	Streetcar	50	Railroad
Indianapolis & Vincennes RR	IC	1860's	IN	Ambrose Burnside	110	Railroad
Inter-State Car Trust Equipment Co.	IC	1920		Railroad Passenger Car	45	Railroad
International & Great Northern RR	I	1874	TX	Green. Cowboys roping cattle.	100	Railroad
International RR of Texas bond	IU	1874	TX	Train Galusha Grow	350	Railroad
International RW Tie	U	188-	NY	Railway tie	50	Railroad
Iowa Falls & Sioux City RR	IC	1880's	IA	Train, factories	95	Railroad
Iowa Falls & Sioux City RR	U	1880's	IA	Train, factories	50	Railroad
Iowa Southern & Missouri Northern	U	187-	IA	Train	50	Railroad
Irun y Lesaca y Ferrocarril Bidasoa	IC	1900's	Spain	Views of mines & railways.	320	Railroad
Jackson & Cincinnati RW	U	189-	MI	Eagle	50	Railroad
Jackson & Eastern RW	U	19--	MS	Eagle	45	Railroad
Jacksonville, Tampa & Key West Rwy	SP	1890's	FL	Steam locomotive	341	Railroad
Jamestown & Franklin RR	IC	1870's	NY	4 vignettes	85	Railroad
Jamestown & Franklin RR	U	1870's	NY	4 vignettes	45	Railroad
Jamestown, Westfield Northwest RR	U	19--	NY	Streetcar	50	Railroad
Jeffersonville City RW	U	189-	IN	Clouds	35	Railroad

Name	Type	Date	State	Description	Price	Category
Jeffersonville Madison Indianapolis	IC	1871	IN	Thomas A. Scott	125	Railroad
Jersey City Locomotive Works	I	1858	NJ	Grey/black, orange embossed seal. Train.	100	Railroad
Jersey City, Hoboken, Patterson Street	SP	1890's	NJ	Streetcar.	165	Railroad
Jersey Shore, Pine Creek & Buffalo	I	1882	PA	Green. Riverside coal factory.	200	Railroad
Jersey Shore, Pine Creek, & Buffalo	IC	1882	PA	Mountains, valley Vanderbilts	895	Railroad
Johnston Electric Train Signal Co.	U	1890's	ME	Train.	130	Railroad
Johnstown and Somerset Railway	I	1930		Train	80	Railroad
Joliet & Chicago RR	IU	1879	IL	Train	100	Railroad
Joliet & Chicago RR	IU	1886	IL	Train	110	Railroad
Joliet & Chicago RR	IU	1930's	IL	Train	95	Railroad
JP Morgan	I	1896			128	Railroad
Junction City & Fort Kearney Rwy.	IC	1890's	KS	Train, ferry boat.	231	Railroad
Kaaterskill RR	U	18--	NY	Train	45	Railroad
Kalamazoo & White Pigeon RR	SP	1890's	MI	State arms of Michigan.	154	Railroad
Kanawha & Michigan Rwy	SP	1890's	MI	Indian maiden. Cherub, trains, switchmen.	121	Railroad
Kansas City & Eastern RW	IU	1879	MO	Train	160	Railroad
Kansas City & Pacific RR	SP	1890's	KS	Freight train, passenger train.	143	Railroad
Kansas City & Southwestern RR	SP	1890's	KS	Locomotive, porter, Indians.	154	Railroad
Kansas City Southern Industries	SP	1960's	MO	2 men, logo	75	Railroad
Kansas City, Fort Scott & Gulf RR	SP	1870's	KS	Kansas State Arms, train, ship.	132	Railroad
Kearney & Black Hills Rwy	IC	1890's	NE	Go embossed seal.	231	Railroad
Kentucky & Great Eastern Railway	I	1872		Daniel Boone's rescue. Steam locomotive. Tobacco planter.	265	Railroad
Kentucky & Indiana Car Trust	SP	1880's	KY	Locomotive.	110	Railroad
Kentucky Western RW	U	1890's	KY	Train	45	Railroad
Keokun & Des Moines Rwy	Proof	1870's	IA	Surveyors, train.	176	Railroad
Kilby Frog & Switch	IC	1906	AL	Train	165	Railroad
Kona & Kau Railway-6% Gold Bond	I	1902	HI	Old train	250	Railroad
L'Ouest-Oural Railroad	I	1912		Green. Russian and French. A few coupons attached.	35	Railroad
La Crosse and Milwaukee Railroad	IC	1850's	NY	Trains & riverboat.	240	Railroad
Lackawanna RR Co. of New Jersey	IC	1900's	NJ	Florence Twombly	264	Railroad
LaGrange Connecting RR	U	19--	IL	Eagle	50	Railroad
Lake Erie, Alliance & Wheeling RR	I	1875	OH	Brown. Train.	125	Railroad
Lake Erie, Evansville & South W Rwy	IC	1870's	OH-IN	Trains, sailing vessel.	220	Railroad

Company	Type	Date	State	Description	Price	Category
Lake Erie, Evansville & Southw Rwy	I	1872	OH-IN	Train, sailboat. River scene. Bison, man cutting tree.	150	Railroad
Lake Erie, Youngstown, & Southern	IC	1907	OH	Train	65	Railroad
Lake Erie, Youngstown, & Southern	U	1907	OH	Train	40	Railroad
Lake Shore & Michigan Southern	SP	1903	NY	Olive. $1k bond Harbor scene, ships, warehouse, train .	35	Railroad
Lake Shore & Michigan Southern	SP	1903	NY	Brown. $5k bond Harbor scene, ships warehouse train	35	Railroad
Lake Shore & Michigan Southern	SP	190-	NY	Steam train trackworkers. View of train below.	25	Railroad
Lake Shore Michigan Southern Railroad	U	1911	MI	Sub	75	Railroad
Lake Shore RW	IC	1868	OH	Train Devereux	195	Railroad
Lawrenceburgh & Indianapolis RR	IC	1830's	IN	Locomotive, double-decker coach	375	Railroad
Lawrenceburgh & Indianapolis RR	U	1830's	IN	Locomotive, double-decker coach	250	Railroad
Leavenworth, Lawrence & Galveston	U	1870's	KS	Farmers, train.	374	Railroad
Lebanon Springs Railroad	I	1867	NY	Train steamboat.	35	Railroad
Lehigh & Hudson River RR	I	1881-99	NY-NJ	Grey/Black. Train.	35	Railroad
Lisbon Electric Tramways Ltd.	IC	1920's	Portugal	Allegorical ladies, street scenes in Lisbon.	120	Railroad
Little Rock, Mississippi River Texas	IC	1880's	AR	Passenger train.	154	Railroad
Locomotive Cooperative Loan Fund	IC	1930's	Bulgaria	Locomotive.	80	Railroad
Louisiana Western RR	IC	1880's	LA	Train, state arms.	132	Railroad
Louisville & Nashville RR	Proof	1850's	KY	Locomotive, riverboat.	275	Railroad
Louisville & Northern Rwy & Light	IC	1900's	IN	Trolley, light bulbs. Samuel Insull.	121	Railroad
Louisville and Nashville Railroad Co.	IC	1890's	KY	Indian chief, woman, train, beehive.	170	Railroad
Louisville Bridge	IC	1890's	KY	Bridge	60	Railroad
Louisville Southern Railroad Co	I	1894	KY	Train Bennett H Young	129	Railroad
Louisville, Cincinnati & Lexington RR	IC	1870's	KY	Woman reading John Echols book, globe.	429	Railroad
Lykens Valley RR & Coal	IC	1940's	PA	Train	65	Railroad
Macon & Brunswick	IC	1870's	GA	Train, factory, sloop.	352	Railroad
Macon & Brunswick Railroad	I	1868	GA	Trains. Workers pick cotton. Farm boy with scythe.	120	Railroad
Madrid to Zaragoza RW	U	1883	Spain	Train	50	Railroad
Madrid y Zaragoza	IC	1880's	Spain	Bridges, tunnel, trains, city arms.	160	Railroad
Maine Central Railroad	IC	1920's		Two trains at station, men working between	35	Railroad
Maine Central RR	I	1935	ME	Purple. Series A. Trains, trackworkers.	50	Railroad
Maine Central RR	I	1944	ME	Blue. Series B. Trains, trackworkers.	35	Railroad

Name	Type	Date	State	Description	Signer	Price	Category
Manhattan Rwy	Proof	1880's	NY	Railway map of Manhattan, sailor, Indian.		275	Railroad
Market Street Railway	IC	1921	CA	Eagle		35	Railroad
Memphis Branch RR of Georgia	Proof	1870's	GA	Train.		242	Railroad
Memphis, El Paso & Pacific RR	IC	1860's	TX	Trains.		132	Railroad
Metropolitan Cross-Town Railway	U	1890		Tolly Carriage		50	Railroad
Metropolitan Cross-Town Railway	U	1890				50	Railroad
Mexican International Railroad	U		Mexico	Train		100	Railroad
Mexico Federal Railway Co	I	1896	Mexico	Multiple Pictures		100	Railroad
Mexico Tramways Co.	IC	1910's	Mexico	Tram in a city street.		44	Railroad
Miami Valley RR	IU	1876	OH	Train		350	Railroad
Michigan Air Line Railroad	I	1880-99	MI,IN	Train loads at station. Blacksmith.		60	Railroad
Michigan Central RR	I	1854	MI	White paper, green embossed corporate seal. Small train.		35	Railroad
Midway & Oakdale Rwy	I	1907-09	PA	Grey/black, orange seal and underprint. Eagle on shield.		20	Railroad
Millstone & New-Brunswick RR	I	1880's	NJ	Train.		30	Railroad
Milwaukee & Horicon RR	IC	1850's	WI	Train, ferry boat.		231	Railroad
Milwaukee & Prairie du Chien RW	IC	1866		Train	Russell Sage	350	Railroad
Minneapolis St Paul Rochester Dubuque	I	1910	MN	Horse head		95	Railroad
Mississippi Railroad	IC	1830's	MS	Cotton, train, ship.		220	Railroad
Missouri Kansas and Texas Railroad	I	1881	MO,KS,TX	Cows	Jay Gould	204	Railroad
Missouri Kansas Texas Railway	IC	1880	NY	Cattle & sheep	Russell Sage	250	Railroad
Missouri Kansas Texas Railway	IC	1881		Cattle & sheep	Jay Gould	395	Railroad
Missouri Kansas Texas Railway	IC	1892	NY	Train roundhouse	John D. Rockefeller	1,750	Railroad
Missouri Kansas Texas Railway	IC	1890's	NY	Train roundhouse		35	Railroad
Missouri River & Northwestern RR	U	1904	MO	Train		58	Railroad
Missouri, Kansas & Texas Railway	I	1880	MO,KS,TX	Cattle	Jay Gould	306	Railroad
Missouri, Kansas & Texas Railway Co	U	1881	MO,KS,TX	Cattle		329	Railroad
Missouri, Kansas & Texas Rwy	IC	1890's		Trains at terminal.	John D. Rockefeller	1,375	Railroad
Missouri, Kansas & Texas Rwy.	IC	1880's		Horseman, cattle & sheep.	Jay Gould	341	Railroad
MKT RR	I	1886		Cows	Jay Gould	150	Railroad
Mobile & Alabama Grand Trunk RR	IC	1870's	AL	Cotton bales, oil barrels.		209	Railroad
Mohawk & Hudson RR	I	1839	NY	Small, very early typeset certificate.		200	Railroad
Mohawk & Hudson RR	IC	1839	NY			200	Railroad
Morgan's Louisiana & Texas Steamsh	Proof	1880's	LA	Morgan portrait in oval.		198	Railroad
Mount Vernon RR	IC	1850's	IL	Columbia, eagle and globe.		429	Railroad
Mount Washington RW	IC	1890's	NH	Climbing train		300	Railroad
Mt. Tamalpais & Muir Woods Rwy	IC	1900's	CA	Redwoods, city skyline.		750	Railroad

Name	Type	Year	State	Description	Price	Category
Nashville Chattanooga & St Louis RW	I	1880	TN	Train	46	Railroad
Nashville, Chattanooga & St. Louis	I	1881	TN	Grey, brown. Locomotive.	35	Railroad
Nassau Electric RR	I	1894	NY	Orange. Temporary Certificate, printed across in red.	12	Railroad
Nassau Electric RR	IC	1894	NY		45	Railroad
Nassau Electric RR	U	1900's	NY	Trolley	45	Railroad
Nevada Central Railroad	I	1902	NV	All green. Train, harvest scene, dog chasing bull.	450	Railroad
Nevada Copper Belt RR	I	1909	ME	Green, brown.	30	Railroad
Nevada-California-Oregon Rwy	SP	1890's		Train, cowboys.	253	Railroad
New Jersey & New York RR	U	1892	NJ&NY	Train	56	Railroad
New Jersey & New York RR	U	188-	NJ,NY	Train	65	Railroad
New Jersey and New York RR	Proof	1880's	NJ, NY	Train, telegraph pole.	220	Railroad
New Jersey Junction Railroad bond	IU	1886	NJ	Harbor J.P. Morgan	895	Railroad
New Jersey Junction Railroad Co.	IC	1880's	NJ	Train.	168	Railroad
New Jersey Junction RR	IC	1880's	NJ	Busy harbor scene. J.P. Morgan	506	Railroad
New Lackawanna & Western RW	IC	1930's	NY	3 vignettes	50	Railroad
New Orleans, Mobile & Texas RR	I	1872		Eagle, shield, steam locomotive, red 1000.	110	Railroad
New Orleans, Mobile & Texas RR	IC	1870's	AL	Eagle on shield. O.Ames, F.Ames	1,100	Railroad
New York & Atlantic RR	Proof	1880's	NY	Cherubs, state arms.	231	Railroad
New York & Erie RR	IC	1847	NY	Early train Millard Fillmore	1,500	Railroad
New York & Harlem RR	IC	1870's	NY	Locomotive, carriage. H. Vanderbilt, C. Vanderbilt	396	Railroad
New York & North Shore Rwy	SP	1890's	NY	Electric streetcar, sailors	154	Railroad
New York & Oswego Midland RR	IU	1872	NY	Train, steamboat	300	Railroad
New York & Ottawa RR	SP	1890's	NY	Locomotive.	121	Railroad
New York & Pennsylvania Blue Stone	IC	1870's	NY	Track workers, state arms.	154	Railroad
New York and Boston Rapid Transit	IC	1880's	NJ	Train.	160	Railroad
New York Central	I	1909	NY	Train	63	Railroad
New York Central Railroad	IC	1913		Face of a man. Gold bond.	20	Railroad
New York Central RR	IC	1850's	NY	State arms, train & ship. Erastus Corning	396	Railroad
New York Central Sleeping Car	I	1880	NY	Train, steamboat. Shields at corners.	50	Railroad
New York Central Sleeping Car	I	1880	NY	Steam locomotive, station and steamboat in the distance.	45	Railroad
New York City & Northern RR	Proof	1880's	NY	Train, NY City Arms.	198	Railroad
New York City & Northern RR	Proof	1880's	NY	Eagle and shield.	165	Railroad

New York State Rwys	I	1912-34	NY	Blue or olive. State arms. Streetcar, factory.	25	Railroad
New York, Lake Erie & Western RR	Proof	1890's	NY	Workmen, freightcar.	385	Railroad
New York, Ontario & Western RW	I	1906	NY	Cattle, train. Head-on view of locomotive. Canal barges	75	Railroad
New York, Ontario & Western RW	IC	1940's	NY	Train	60	Railroad
New York, Ontario & Western RW	SP	1940's	NY	Train	100	Railroad
New York, Ontario & Western RW	U	1940's	NY	Train	35	Railroad
New York, Ontario & Western Rwy	IC	1880's	NY	Route map, train and ship.	330	Railroad
New York, Woodhaven & Rockaway	Proof	1880's	NY	Train, trees, cow, steamer, state arms.	275	Railroad
Newfoundland Railway	I	1881	Canada	Train	100	Railroad
Niagara Falls Branch Railroad	I	1893	NY	Train Chauncey Depew	66	Railroad
Nied. Land. Anle.	IC	1900's	Austria	Arms, train.	160	Railroad
Nord-Est De L'Espagne	IC	1900's	Spain	Train, ladies arms of Spain & Catalunya.	220	Railroad
Norfolk & Western RR	IC	1887	VA	Train	95	Railroad
Norfolk & Western RR	Proof	1880's	VA, WV	Virginia State Arms, locomotive.	220	Railroad
Norfolk & Western RR	Proof	1880's	VA, WV	Head-on view of locomotive.	440	Railroad
Norfolk and Western Railroad Co.	IC	1880's	VA	Train in country station.	100	Railroad
North Western RR	U	1850's	PA	Train, factories.	275	Railroad
Northern Pacific Railroad	I	1880		Train Frederick Billings	125	Railroad
Northern Pacific Railroad	U	1896		Woman	100	Railroad
Northern Pacific Railroad	U	1896		Woman	100	Railroad
Northern Pacific RR	IU	1897		Train, telephone poles	450	Railroad
Northern Pacific RR	Proof	1870's		Train.	429	Railroad
Northern Pacific RR	IC	1870's		Train Jay Cooke	750	Railroad
Northern Pacific RR	IC	1870's		Train Cooke, Cooke Jr.	900	Railroad
Northern Pacific RR-J.P. Morgan	I	1896		Green. Education, sailing ship.	75	Railroad
Northern Refrigerator Line	U	1930's		Blue. Man & partially topless woman, alter.	25	Railroad
Northern RR	I	1866-69	NH	Red printed seal. Pen cancelled revenue stamp.	23	Railroad
Northwestern Pacific RR	IC	1900's	CA	State arms, train, ship.	330	Railroad
Norwich & Worcester RR	I	1877	CT	Gray/black, orange. Train, pier scene.	60	Railroad
NY Central Railroad	IC	1930's		Brown. Commodore Vanderbilt.	15	Railroad
Ocean City Railroad Company	I	1901	NJ	Train	85	Railroad
Old Colony Railroad	IC	1896		Train at busy harbor	30	Railroad
Olot & Gerona	IC	1900's	Spain		130	Railroad
Olot & Gerona Railway Co. Ltd.	IC	1890's	Spain		600	Railroad
Omaha & Elkhorn Valley Rwy	IC	1890's			220	Railroad

Name	Type	Date	State	Description	Signer	Price	Category
Omaha & Republican Valley Rwy	IC	1890's	NE	All light blue.		220	Railroad
Oregon And Transcontinental Railroad	I	1882	OR	Indian	Henry Villard	105	Railroad
Oregon Pacific RR	IC	1880's	OR	Train, canal, barges, ships.		220	Railroad
Ost. Nord. Verb.	IC	1900's	Austria	Austrian coat of arms.		244	Railroad
Ottumwa, Cedar Falls and St. Paul	Proof	1880's	IA	Miners push coal cars.		198	Railroad
Owensboro, Falls Rough Green Riv	IC	1890's	KY		John Ecols	220	Railroad
Pacific RR	IC	1865	CA	Globe, train		350	Railroad
Painesville & Hudson RR	IC	1850's	OH	Coal train, factory.		308	Railroad
Pan Handle Railway	I	1868	PA		J.Edgar Thompson	150	Railroad
Panama Rail Road Co	I	1871				47	Railroad
Panama Railroad	U	1860 & 1870				1,600	Railroad
Panama Railroad	U	1865 & 1871	NY			415	Railroad
Panama Railroad Co.	IC	1870's	Panama			140	Railroad
Paterson & Little Falls Horse RR	IC	1870's	NJ	Embossed seal.		176	Railroad
Paterson & Passaic Horse RR	IC	1870's	NJ	Horse-drawn streetcar.		132	Railroad
Patterson and Passaic Horse RR Co.	IC	1870's	NJ	Horse tram, tramcar on seal.		220	Railroad
Peach Botom Rwy	U	1870's	PA	Train & steam ship.		396	Railroad
Penn Central	IC	1960's		Man running in front of train, truck, plane		15	Railroad
Penn Central Mtg. bond	IC					10	Railroad
Penn Central Transportation	I	1969	PA	Green.		20	Railroad
Penn Yan & New York RW	IC	1885	NY	Train		80	Railroad
Pennsylvania Canal	I	1870		Canal barge, bridge, train.		95	Railroad
Pennsylvania Railroad	I			Railroad Tracks		150	Railroad
Pennsylvania Railroad (New)	IC	1960's		Green. Two trains going around curve.		15	Railroad
Pennsylvania Railroad (Old)	IC	1910's		Orange. Two horses, shield.		15	Railroad
Pere Marquette RR Co.	U	1900's	MI	Train.		90	Railroad
Petaluma & Sebastopol RR	IU	1889	CA	Train		500	Railroad
Philadelphia & Easton Railway	I	1904	PA	Green. Man walks his dog, trolley.		25	Railroad
Philadelphia & Sunbury RR	IC	1850's	PA	Liberty, coal train.		187	Railroad
Philadelphia Rapid Transit	I	1925-6	PA	Orange. Double-decker bus, train & trolley.		20	Railroad
Philadelphia, Baltimore & Wash RR	I	1924		Orange. Portrait of George B. Roberts.		25	Railroad
Pine Creek Railway Company	I			Woman	Vanderbilt&Depew	90	Railroad
Pittsburgh & Lake Erie RR	IC	1900's	PA	View of Pittsburgh.	JP Morgan	963	Railroad
Pittsburgh & Lake Erie RR	IC	1920's			A. Felix Du Pont	352	Railroad
Pittsburgh & Moon Run RR	I	1900	PA	Typeset. Geometric borders.		18	Railroad
Pittsburgh Cincinnati Chicago St. Lou	IC	1899	PA,WV	Train	Russell Sage	195	Railroad
Pittsburgh Traction	I	1891-5	PA	Green. Fancy letter P in title. Company trolley.		28	Railroad
Pittsburgh Virginia Charleston RW	IC	1891		Train	Henry Clay Frick	1,500	Railroad

Name		Year	State	Description		Price	Category
Pittsburgh Virginia Charleston RW	IC	1895		Train	Andrew Mellon	750	Railroad
Pittsburgh, Cinn, Chicago and St. Lou	IC	1900's	PA	Train, track layers		70	Railroad
Pittsburgh, Cinn, Chicago St. Louis	I	1930's		Steam locomotive and trackworkers.		12	Railroad
Pittsburgh, Fort Wayne & Chicago RR	I	1857	PA	Train at station. Bust engravings. Farm and foundry		50	Railroad
Pittsburgh, Fort Wayne & Chicago RR	I	1869	NY	Gray/black. Train, steamboat. Small locomotive below.		45	Railroad
Pittsburgh, McKeesport Youghioghen	IC	1900's		Men, railcars.		209	Railroad
Pittsburgh, Youngtown & Ashtabula	I	1923-49	PA-OH	Man on horse stops for locomotive, town in the distance.		15	Railroad
Placerville & Sacramento Valley RR	IC	1860's	CA	Train, state arms.		528	Railroad
Plymouth, Kankakee and Pacific RR	I	1871	IL-IN	Train at top center and lower right.		75	Railroad
Podolie Railroad	I	1914		Purple. Russian and French.		35	Railroad
Portage Lake & Lake Superior Ship	IC	1860's	MI	Sailing vessels, busy harbor scene.		231	Railroad
Portland & Ogdensburg Railway	I	1909	ME-NH	Train, stagecoach and steamer.		75	Railroad
Portland & Rumford Falls Rwy	I	1896	ME	Grey/black. Train, sailboat.		15	Railroad
Portugal Royal Co or Railways	U	1884				55	Railroad
Poughkeepsie City Railroad Co.	IC	1870's	NY	Horse tram, tramcar on the seal.		220	Railroad
Providence & Worcester RR	IC	1870's	RI	Decorative left border.		110	Railroad
Puerto Rico Railway	U	1888	PR	Anchor		80	Railroad
Puerto Rico Railway	U	1888	PR	Anchor		80	Railroad
Pullman	I	1900	NY	Green or blue.		35	Railroad
Pullman	I	1905	IL	Grey.George M. Pullman vignette	Robert T. Lincoln	500	Railroad
Pullman's Palace Car	I	1898	IL	Cherub, St Pancras Station, London, Pullman Car Works		125	Railroad
Pullman's Palace Car	IC	1870's	IL	Illuminated first letters in title.	George M. Pullman	253	Railroad
Pullman's Palace Car	I	1896-8	IL	St. Pancras Stn in London, Pullman Car Works in Detroit.		100	Railroad
Pullman's Palace Car Co.	IC	1870's	IL		George M. Pullman	560	Railroad
Railroad Lighting & Manufacturing	U	1890's	PA	Passenger car.		209	Railroad
Railroad Pan Am	U					1,000	Railroad
Railway of Northern Spain	U	1876				50	Railroad
Raleigh & Gaston RR	IC	1870's	NC	Train station.		165	Railroad
Rensselaer & Saratoga Railroad	I	1862		Smoking Train		50	Railroad
Rensselaer & Saratoga RR	I	1854	NY	Ships		70	Railroad
Rhinebeck and Connecticut Railroad	U	1870's	NY	Trains crossing river bridge.		240	Railroad
Richmond, Fredericksburg & Potomac RR	U	1859	VA			75	Railroad

Name	Type	Date	State	Description	Price	Category
Rio Grande Junction Railway Co.	IC	1900's	CO	Train emerging from tunnel.	110	Railroad
Rjasan-Uralsk Eisenbahn	IC	1890's	Russia		160	Railroad
ROBINSON DEEP	U	1936		Mill	50	Railroad
ROBINSON DEEP	U	1937		Mill	50	Railroad
Rockford, Rock Island & St. Louis RR	I	1868	IL	Grey, red, green. Trains.	70	Railroad
Rome and Decatur Railroad Company	U	1886		Train	53	Railroad
Roya Railways of Portugal	U	1879	Portugal	Two children	70	Railroad
Royal Tiger Mining Company	I	1908	NV		49	Railroad
Rutland & Washington RR	I	1852	VT-NY	Train. Erastus Corning	75	Railroad
Rutland Railroad Company	U	1900's	VT	Arms of Vermont, trains & steamboat.	260	Railroad
Sacket's Harbor & Saratoga RR	I	1854	NY	Grey, orange $1000. Locomotive, deer & bear.	120	Railroad
Sacket's Harbor & Saratoga RR	IC	1850's	NY	Train, deer and bear by lake.	121	Railroad
Saint Joseph Union Depot	IU	1888	MO	Train	175	Railroad
Saint Paul Eastern Grand Trunk RR	IC	1880's	WI	Floating mass of logs.	180	Railroad
Salina, Sterling & El Paso RR	SP	1880's	KS	Train in circle.	121	Railroad
Salt Lake & Western RR	U	1880's	NV		220	Railroad
San Francisco & San Joaquin Valley	IC	1890's	CA	Passenger train. Claus Spreckels	375	Railroad
San Francisco and San Joaquin Valley	U	1900's	CA	Passenger train. Claus Spreckels	320	Railroad
San Francisco Railway bond	IC	1950	CA	Electric streetcar	50	Railroad
Sandy River & Rangley Lakes RR	U	1908		Train	50	Railroad
Sandy River RR	IU	1892	ME	Train	250	Railroad
Santiago Al Puerto Del Carril	IC	1860's	Spain	Coat of Arms of Santiago, railway scenes.	600	Railroad
Savannah and Northwestern Railway	IC	1900's	GA	Passenger train at speed.	92	Railroad
Savannah, Florida & Western Rwy	SP	1890's	GA/FL	Train, little girl.	297	Railroad
Scioto & Hocking Valley Railroad	I	1856		Coal train. Sheep shearing. Corn harvesting. Henry Clay	125	Railroad
Scioto Valley and New England RR	IC	1890's	OH	Trains.	120	Railroad
Sciotto Valley & New England RR	U	18--	OH	Train	50	Railroad
Seaboard Air Line RW	IC	1920's	NY	Woman	60	Railroad
Seaboard Air Line RW	IC	1940's	NY	Train	50	Railroad
Seaboard Air Line RW	SP	1940's	NY	Train	100	Railroad
Second Avenue RR in the City of NY	I	1898	NY	Olive. Cherubs flank title.	80	Railroad
Selma & Gulf RR	IC	1870's	AL	Trains, steamboat.	308	Railroad
Selma, Marion & Memphis RR	IC	1860's	AL	Train. Nathan B. Forrest	1,155	Railroad
Semiretchensk Railroad	I	1913		Green. Russian and French. Coupons.	35	Railroad
Sharon Railway	IC	1911	PA	Locomotive in rail yard	45	Railroad

Name		Date	State	Description	Price	Category
Shenandoah Valley Railroad Co.	U	1870's	VA	Speeding train, state arms.	80	Railroad
Shenandoah Valley RR	I	1883	VA	Steam locomotive	63	Railroad
Shenango Valley RR	I	1889	PA	Grey/black. Eagle on shield	25	Railroad
Shenango Valley RR	I	1900	PA	Grey/black. Eagle on shield	20	Railroad
Short Route Railway Transfer	U	18--	KY	Train	60	Railroad
Short Route Rwy Transfer of Louis	I	1886-87	KY	Grey/black. Train, passengers, boxcar.	35	Railroad
Short Route Rwy Transfer of Louis	IC	1890's	KY	Train leaves city. John Echols	231	Railroad
Sioux City & Pacific RR	U	18--	IA	Train	60	Railroad
Sixth Ave. RR	IC	1920's	NY	Train	50	Railroad
Sixth Ave. RR	U	1920's	NY	Train	35	Railroad
Slate Belt Electric Street Rwy	I	1912	PA	Green. Streetcar. Benson & Son Lith.	25	Railroad
Slate Belt Electric Street Rwy	I	1912	PA	Red. Streetcar. Benson & Son Lith.	25	Railroad
Somerset Railway Co.	I	1906	ME	Train	64	Railroad
Sop.-Poz. Loc.	IC	1890's	Hungary	Soporon, train.	110	Railroad
South Carolina Rwy	I	1881	SC	Grey/black. Negroes picking cotton.	75	Railroad
South Manchuria Railway	U		Japan	Train	57	Railroad
South Manchuria Railway			Japan	Train	104	Railroad
South Manchuria Railway			Japan	Train	82	Railroad
South Manchuria Railway	U			Train	50	Railroad
South Pennsylvania RR	IC	1880's	PA	Train, miners.	209	Railroad
South Side RR of Long Island	IC	1870's	NY	Train, state arms.	286	Railroad
South Spain RailroAd	U	1889	Spain	Queens crown	60	Railroad
South Spain Railroad	U	1910	Spain	Queen crown	60	Railroad
South West Connecting Rwy	I	1897	PA	Eagle, train, Capitol, fort.	20	Railroad
South Winnipeg, Ltd.	IC	1900's	Canada	Mercury, trains, city skyline.	84	Railroad
Southern Art Exhibition	I	1885	IL	Man with compass teaching youngster, globe, telescope	50	Railroad
Southern Central RR Tompkins Cty	I	1867	NY	Grey borders, Two trains	50	Railroad
Southern Minnesota RR	I	1850	MN	Train, farm scene, pier in the distance.	200	Railroad
Southern Pacific Company	U			Men	85	Railroad
Southern Pacific Company	U			Women	85	Railroad
Southern Pacific RR	IC	1870's	TX	Indians, train.	132	Railroad
St. Croix & Lake Superior	I	1866	WI	Land Grant Bond, green, red. Train. Sheaves of wheat.	125	Railroad
St. Louis & Cairo RR	SP	1880's		Train on bridge.	132	Railroad
St. Louis Alton & Belleview Electric	IU	1900's	IL	Woman with flag	75	Railroad
St. Louis Alton & Terre Haute RR	IC	1897	IL,IN	Train. Green border	95	Railroad
St. Louis Alton & Terre Haute RR	U	188-	IL,IN	Train	45	Railroad
St. Louis Alton & Terre Haute RR	IC	1890's	IL,IN	Train. Green border	45	Railroad
St. Louis Bridge	U	19--	MO	Bridge	50	Railroad
St. Louis Southern RR	U	188-	MO	Train	60	Railroad
St. Louis Terminal RW	IC	1920	MO	Eagle	50	Railroad

Name	Type	Date	State	Description	Price	Category
St. Louis Terminal RW	U	1920	MO	Eagle	50	Railroad
St. Louis, Alton & Terre Haute	I	1892-3	IL-IN	Train load passengers at a rural station. George F. Peabody	180	Railroad
St. Louis, Lawrence & Denver RR	I	1871	KS	Orange. Train, another crossing bridge.	120	Railroad
Staten Island Railroad	I	1864	NY	Train, sloop. Steamboat RICHMOND. Wm H. Vanderbilt	2,000	Railroad
Staten Island RR	U	1870's	NY	Train, sailboat. J. H. Vanderbilt	1,100	Railroad
Stillwater and St. Paul Railroad	I	1905		Bridge	74	Railroad
Streator & Clinton RR	U	1910	IL	Woman with flag	45	Railroad
Stroudsburg Passenger Rwy	I	1871	PA	Grey/black. Green central denomination. State arms.	90	Railroad
Sturgis, Goshen & St. Louis Railway	IC	1880's	IN	Trains, eagle.	121	Railroad
Sturgis, Goshen & St. Louis RW	IC	1910's	MI,IN		50	Railroad
Sturgis, Goshen & St. Louis RW	U	1910's	MI,IN		35	Railroad
Sullivan RR	IU	1849	MA	Woman, train	195	Railroad
Sussex Rail Road Co.	I	1870	NJ	Bridge	67	Railroad
Swedesboro RR	IC	1860's	NJ	Train	125	Railroad
Syracuse & Chenango RR	U	18--	NY	Train	45	Railroad
Syracuse & East Side Rwy	IC	1890's	NY	Woman holding lightning bolts.	121	Railroad
Syracuse Rapid Transit Rwy	I	189-	NY	Orange. Streetcar, horse carriage.	22	Railroad
Syracuse, Chenango & New York RR	U	18--	NY	Train	45	Railroad
Syracuse, Ontario & New York	Proof	1880's	NY	Train on bridge.	165	Railroad
Syracuse, Ontario & New York Railway	U	1880	NY	Train	50	Railroad
Taunton Branch RR	IU	1835	MA		295	Railroad
Taunton Branch RR	IU	1870	MA	Train, stamp	175	Railroad
Tennessee Coal, Iron, Railroad	IC	1900	TN	Train, miners, ore cart - brown	100	Railroad
Tennessee Coal, Iron, Railroad	IC	1900	TN	Train, miners, ore cart - green	100	Railroad
Tennessee Coal, Iron, Railroad	U	18--	TN	Train, miners	75	Railroad
Tenth & Twenty-Third Street Ferry	SP	1880's	NY	Ferry, ships in harbor.	165	Railroad
Terre Haute & Indianapolis RR	IC	1887	IN	Train	200	Railroad
Terre Haute & Indianapolis RR	I	1900	IN	Freight agents load steam locomotive at station.	12	Railroad
Terre Haute & Indianapolis RR	I	1870's	IN	Grey/black. Train unloads freight.	32	Railroad
Terre Haute and Indianapolis RR Co.	U	1870's	IN	Train in busy station.	112	Railroad
Terre Haute, Indianapolis & Eastern	IU	1930	IN	Streetcar	90	Railroad
Terre Haute, Indianapolis & Richmond	IU	1870's	IN	Revenue stamp	95	Railroad
Texas & New Orleans RR	SP	1890's		Engine, cotton pickers.	176	Railroad
Texas & New Orleans RR	IC	1900's	TX	Locomotive.	341	Railroad

Name	Type	Date	State	Description	Price	Category
Texas & New Orleans RR of 1874	Proof	1880's	TX	Frontiersman, train and buffalo.	330	Railroad
Texas Santa Fe & Northern RR	Proof	1800's	TX	Woman, plants, volcano.	231	Railroad
Texas Short Line Railway $1000 Gold	IU	1902	TX	Train leaving station Henry M. Strong	295	Railroad
The City Railway Co.	IC	1893		Cablecar	30	Railroad
The Denver, Cripple Creek and Southwestern Railroad Co	I	1896	CO		138	Railroad
The Railway if Northern Spain	U	1870	Spain		60	Railroad
Thirty Fourth Street Railway	IC	1890's	NY	Woman with caduceus.	121	Railroad
Tioga RR	U	18--	NY	Man	45	Railroad
Toledo Logansport & Burlington RW	I	1865		Train Morris Jessup	50	Railroad
Toledo, Ann Arbor & Mt. Pleasant	I	1886	MI	Brown. State arms, commercial and agricultural scenes.	45	Railroad
Toledo, Logansport & Burlington RR	IC	1859	OH	3 vignettes	165	Railroad
Toledo, Norwalk & Cleveland Railroad	I	1852	OH	Train	114	Railroad
Toledo, Peoria & Western Railway	I	1887	IL	Gold Bond, brown.	55	Railroad
Toledo, St. Louis & Western RR	IC	1910's	OH,MO	Train	65	Railroad
Topeka & Northwestern RR	IC	1900's	KS	Woman, eagle.	209	Railroad
Tramvie Vicentine, Societa	IC	1910's	Italy	Mercury, winged wheel, leaves & flowers.	130	Railroad
Tramway Co. of the Rive Gauch	U	1899	France	Trolly	70	Railroad
Tramway Electrique De Rome	IC	1900's	Italy		112	Railroad
Tramways & Ominbus De Genes, Soc.	IC	1870's	Italy		160	Railroad
Tramways D'Anvers, Cie. Generale	IC	1900's	Belgium	View of the City of Antwerp, river Scheldt.	130	Railroad
Tramways De Barsovie S.A.	IC	1880's	Russia	Classical border.	80	Railroad
Tramways Neerlandais Harlem Ext	IC	1890's	Netherlands	Arms of Holland, two towns, trams in the street.	150	Railroad
Tramways Provinciaux De Naples	IC	1880's	Italy		28	Railroad
Tramways Vervietois S.A.	IC	1900's	Belgium	A Tram in front of the Hotel de Ville.	56	Railroad
Trenton Traction	IC	1890's	NJ		125	Railroad
Trenton Traction	U	1890's	NJ		30	Railroad
Troy & Bennington RR	IC	1940's	NY	Train	50	Railroad
Tuckerton Rail Road Company	I	1872	NJ	Bridge	123	Railroad
Tunnel RR of St. Louis	IC	1900's	MO	Train	90	Railroad
Ulster & Delaware RR	IC	1890's	NY	Train	75	Railroad
Ulster & Delaware RR	U	1890's	NY	Train	40	Railroad
Union Freight Railroad	U	1880	MA	Train	88	Railroad
Union Freight RR	U	18--	MA	Train	95	Railroad
Union RR & Transfer & Stockyard	U	1870's	IN	Aerial view	60	Railroad
United Light & RW	SP	1950's	IA	Woman	75	Railroad
United Railways & Electric of Balt	I	1901	MD	Brown. State arms, top left.	12	Railroad
United Railways Terminal	U	18--	OH	Underprint	50	Railroad

Company	Type	Year	State	Description	Signer	Price	Category
United States Land & Investment	IC	1880's	NY	US Capitol and busy grounds.		220	Railroad
United Traction Co.	U	1899	PA	Trolley with govt. building in back.		20	Railroad
United Traction Co.	U	1899		Cable Car & Buildings		25	Railroad
Ussuri Railway	IC	1930's	Russia			440	Railroad
Utica & Belt Line St. RR	IC	1891	NY	Horse drawn streetcar		100	Railroad
Utica & Black River RR	IC	1880's	NY	Train, steamboat and sailboats.		660	Railroad
Utica & Schenectady RR	U	18--	NY	Train		60	Railroad
Utica & Schenectady RR	U	184-	NY			50	Railroad
Utica & Waterville RR	I	1866		Trolley	John W Butterfield	67	Railroad
Utica & Waterville RR	IC	1860's	NY	Streetcar.	John Butterfield	330	Railroad
Utica & Waterville RR	IC	1860's	NY	Streetcar.		352	Railroad
Utica & Watervillle RR	U	18--	NY	Streetcar		50	Railroad
Utica Clinton & Binghamton RR	IC	1936	NY	Train		65	Railroad
Utica Clinton & Binghamton RR	U	1936	NY	Train		35	Railroad
Utica Ithaca & Elmira RW	IU	1880	NY	Train, station		295	Railroad
Utica, Ithaca & Elmira RR	IC	1870's	NY	Train, underpass, workers, ferry.		286	Railroad
Utica, Ithaca & Elmira Rwy	IC	1880's	NY	Train.		275	Railroad
Valence A Liria	IC	1880's	Spain	Railway scenes.		180	Railroad
Vera Cruz & Pacific RR	IC	1900's	WV-Mex.	Train, ship.		110	Railroad
Vernon, Greensburg & Rushville RR	U	188-	IN	Train		50	Railroad
Vernon, Greensburgh & Rushville	I	1880	IN	Green. Train. Large attractive certificate.		60	Railroad
Vicinaux En Espagne Generale Tram	IC	1900's	Spain	Underprint of winged wheel.		72	Railroad
Vineland Railroad	I	1880	NJ	Ornate borders.	Jay Gould	700	Railroad
Virginia & Truckee RR	IU	1874	NV	Train, mills	William Sharon	495	Railroad
Virginia & Truckee RR	IC	1870's	NV	Indians, miners and train.	William Sharon	396	Railroad
Virginia and Tennessee Railroad Co.	IC	1850's	NY	Train & allegorical scenes.	Abram S. Hewitt	160	Railroad
Virginian Railway Company	U		VA	Train		75	Railroad
Virginian Terminal RW bond	IC	1907	VA	Woman, two men		250	Railroad
Vtg Indiana Northwestern Traction RR	U	1940	IN	Locomotive		46	Railroad
Wabash RR	IC	1908	OH,MI,IN	Train		100	Railroad
Wabash RR	IC	1910	OH,MI,IN	2 vignettes		100	Railroad
Wagner Palace Car	I	1880	NY	Brown. Train. Magnificent building in circle		35	Railroad
Wagner Palace Car	IC	1890	NY	Union Stn, Grand Central	W.S. Webb	50	Railroad
Waldumer Electric Magnetic Brake	U	1880's	OH	Train, cherubs		165	Railroad
Wallkill Valley Railroad Co.	IC	1880's	NY	Long freight train.		160	Railroad
Warschau-Wiener	IC	1900's	Russia			200	Railroad
Warwick Valley RR	I	1880	NY	Grey. Cattle resting. State arms. Train. Harvest scene.		40	Railroad
Washington & Idaho RR	SP	1880's		Train.		231	Railroad

Name		Date	State	Description	Price	Category
Washington, Baltimore Annapolis Elec	U	19--	MD	Streetcar	35	Railroad
West End Traction	U	1899	PA	Streetcar with bridge in background	20	Railroad
West Jersey Railroad	I	1879-88	NJ		8	Railroad
Western Maryland RR	IC	1900's	NY	Train. J. D. Rockefeller Jr.	908	Railroad
Western RR	IU	1840	MA		175	Railroad
Western RR	IU	1850	MA	3 vignettes	165	Railroad
Western RR	IU	1860's	MA	3 vignettes	150	Railroad
Western Spanish Railroad		1888	Spain	Man	80	Railroad
Western Vermont Rail Road	I	1854	VT	Train	100	Railroad
White Water RR	IC	1878	IN	Scrip. No vig.	65	Railroad
White Water RR	U	1878	IN	Scrip. No vig.	30	Railroad
White Water RR	IU	1878	IN	Train	100	Railroad
White Water RR	U	1878	IN	Train	40	Railroad
White Water RR	IC	1900's	IN	Train	75	Railroad
White Water RR	U	1900's	IN	Train	35	Railroad
WI. Milwaukee and Northern Railroad	U	1881		Cattle	250	Railroad
Wildwood & Delaware Bay Short Line	I	1915	NJ	Train	100	Railroad
Wildwood & Delaware Bay Shrt Line	IC	1913	NJ	Train	85	Railroad
Wildwood & Delaware Bay Shrt Line	I	1914-30	NJ	Green or orange. Train beneath semaphore signals.	35	Railroad
Wilkes-Barre & Eastern RR	I	1898		Train	50	Railroad
Wilmington & Northern RR	I	1881-2	NJ,PA	Busy pier scene. State arms, either side. H.A. du Pont	400	Railroad
Wilmington & Northern RR	IC	1890's	PA,DE	Dockyard, state arms. H.A. du Pont	198	Railroad
Wilmington New Castle & Delaware City	I	1912	DE		57	Railroad
Woodruff Sleeping & Parlor Coach	I	1870's	PA	Indian with rifle on cliff, train, riverboats. Jonah Woodruff	95	Railroad
Woodstown & Swedesboro RR	IC	1880's	NJ	Train	75	Railroad
Worcester RR	IC	1870's	MD-VA	Harbor scene, trains, village.	121	Railroad
Wyandotte & Detroit River RW	U	189-	MI	Train	50	Railroad
Yazoo & Mississippi Valley RR	IC	1913	MS	Train	150	Railroad
Yazoo & Mississippi Valley RR	U	1913	MS	Train	65	Railroad
Youngstown-Sharon Rwy	IC	1901	NY	Woman	50	Railroad
Zanesville & Western RW	U	190-	OH	Eagle	35	Railroad
Zaragosa a Escatron	IC	1870's	Spain	Small coat of arms.	88	Railroad

CHAPTER 17 - SHIP CERTIFICATES

The ship category also includes boats, submarines, deep sea diving, wharfs, yachts, and under water treasure recovery.

Name	IU	Date	State	Vignette	Signed by	Value	Category
Adria, S.A. Di Navigazioni Maritima	IC	1920's	Italy	Anchor, Eagle, Mercury & a Goddess.		100	Ship
Agence Maritime Walford S.A.	IC	1900's	Belgium			44	Ship
Aguan Navigation & Improvement	IU	1886	NY	Steamship		300	Ship
American Hawaiian Steam Ship	I	1913		Ship		130	Ship
American Nautilus Submarine	IU	1856	NY	Ships, diving bell		3,900	Ship
American Salvage	IU	1917	NJ	Diving bell, sunken ship		750	Ship
American Submarine	I	1871	NY	State arms flanked by trains. Ships. Revenue stamp		140	Ship
American Submarine	I	1871	NY	Red-orange embossed seal. State arms		140	Ship
Anchor Co.	IU	1925	VA	Woman with wings holding lightbulb		35	Ship
Arctic Alaska Fisheries	U	1987	WA	Shoreline with wave and boats		100	Ship
Argonaut Salvage	IU	1920	ME	Two women, ship	Simon Lake	150	Ship
Astilleros De Tarragona, S.A.	IC	1900's	Spain			170	Ship
Atlantic Royal Mail Steam Navigation	IC	1860's	GB	Steamers at sea.		220	Ship
Ayuntiamiento de la Habana	SP	1880's	Cuba	Boat, lighthouse.		176	Ship
Boston, Newport & New York Steamb	IC	1866		Ship	Oliver Ames	200	Ship
California Navigation & Improvement	IC	1906	CA	Steamships		250	Ship
California Navigation & Improvement	I	1910	CA	Boats		75	Ship
Camden & Philadelphia Steamboat	I	1849		Steam ferry. Train, cows. Steamboat Philadelphia.		75	Ship
Camden And Phila Steam Boat Ferry	IC	1880's	PA	Ferry boat on a stormy Delaware River.		120	Ship
Canal & Lake Steamboat	I	1880's	NY	Embossed corporate seal. Low numbers.		50	Ship
Canal De Blaton	IC	1860's	Belgium			28	Ship
Canal De Jonction Sambre A L'Oise	IC	1830's	France	Two Coats of Arms.		80	Ship
Canales Imper.Real Tauste Reynos Ar	IC	1800's	Spain	Garlands of Roses.		220	Ship
Chargeurs Francais S.A.	IC	1920's	France	Cargo liners, smaller vessels.		120	Ship
Codorus Navigation	I	1843		Corp seal featuring the sun rising behind the hills		55	Ship
Commercial Wharf	IC	1870's	MA	Ship		100	Ship
Commerical Wharf	I	1830's	MA	Ship, long wharf.		374	Ship
Compagnie Maritime De La Seine	I	1899	France	Brown. Romantic scenes of Paris along the Seine.		30	Ship
Concordia, Soc. Comerciale Pe Actii	IC	1890's	Romania	Shipping, train, freight, lighthouse.		300	Ship
Dampfschiffahrts-Ges.	IC	1920's	Germany			140	Ship
Delta Canal	U	18--	FL	2 dredging boats		65	Ship

Delta Canal Co.	IC	1890's	FL	Dredgers at work.		110	Ship
Detroit & Cleveland Navigation	I	1925	MI	Orange. Steamship.		25	Ship
Detroit & Cleveland Navigation	I	1927	MI	Blue. Steamship.		25	Ship
Deutsche Ost-Afrika-Linie	IC	1930's	Germany			112	Ship
Doctor Gray's Great Eastern Bitters	IU	1880	NJ	Steamship		500	Ship
East Boston Dry Dock	I	1853	MA	Unusual stern quarter view of a square rigger in a dry dock.		150	Ship
East Boston Dry Dock	I	1853	MA	Squae rigger in a floating dry dock.		150	Ship
East Boston Dry Dock	I	1871		Ship		48	Ship
East Boston Dry Dock	IC	1850's	MA	Sailing ship, dock scene.		143	Ship
Erie Rwy	IC	1870's		Covered terminal.		605	Ship
Georgia Steam Packet	IC	1830's	GA	Steamship.		440	Ship
Hartford & NY Transportation	U	1887	NY	Steamboat		70	Ship
Henslee Sinking Sip Saver Patent	IU	1923	TN	Ship with large hole in hull	Conrad S. Henslee	250	Ship
Hernodia, N.V. Scheepvaartmij	IC	1900's	Netherlands			56	Ship
Hlutafjelagid Eimskipafjel AG Islands	IC	1910's	Iceland	Decorative border. Whale catching ship		900	Ship
Hoboken Ferry	IC	1897	NJ	Ferry	Emanuel Lehman	350	Ship
Hoboken Ferry	I	1897		Ferry	LehmanBros issued	100	Ship
Hoboken Ferry Co.	I	1896		Ferry		80	Ship
Hope Mills Manufacturing	IU	1907	NC	Anchor		60	Ship
Hydro-Glisseurs Dumond Galvin, S.A.	IC	1920's	France	Hydro-glisseur, border of leaves.		70	Ship
Industrial Maritima	IC	1940's	Morocco	Whale.		92	Ship
International Mercantile Marine	IC	1910's	NJ	Huge passenger ship		75	Ship
International Mercantile Marine	IC	1920's	NJ	Ocean liner, tugboats.	Philip F. Du Pont	105	Ship
International Mercantile Marine	IC	1920's	NJ	Huge passenger ship		60	Ship
International Mercantile Marine	IC	1920's		Ship in harbor, tugboats		50	Ship
International Mercantile Marine	IC	1930's	NJ	Huge passenger ship		45	Ship
Iron Steamboat	SP	1880's	NJ	Steamboat.		198	Ship
Isle of Man Steam Packet Co. Ltd.	IC	1930's	GB	Ship at sea, coats of arms of the Island		160	Ship
Junta De Obras Del Puerto De Tarra.	IC	1900's	Spain	Harbor, old coins, arms of the city.		120	Ship
Kennet and Avon Canal Navigation	IC	1800's	GB	Blue seal.		308	Ship
Kroatische Flusschiffahrt A.G.	IC	1940's	Croatia			100	Ship
Lake Sub-Marine	IC	1901	NJ	Eagle	Simon Lake	150	Ship
Land And River Co.	U	1890's	WI	Harbor scene, ship, arms of Wisconsin.		100	Ship
Leerer Heringsfischerei A.-G.	IC	1920's	Germany	Decorative border.		96	Ship
Lewis Clark Centen Amer Pac Expo	U	1900's	OR	Ships in harbor.		660	Ship
Manchester Ship Canal Co.	IC	1890's	GB	Steamship, large embossed seal.		140	Ship
Martins Cigar Shippers	I	1925				66	Ship
Mercantile Wharf Co Wellfleet	I	1870	MA	Soldier		69	Ship
Messageries Maritimes S.A.	IC	1920's	France	Liner, home ports, animals, company arms		100	Ship
Moosehead Lake Yacht Club	IU	1908	ME	Eagle		85	Ship

Name		Year	Location	Description	Signature	Price	Category
Mount Vernon Hotel	IC	1850's	NJ	Sailing vessels. Allegorical women.		220	Ship
Navigation Fluviale Du Nord, Cie.	IC	1890's	France	Map with river & canal routes.		140	Ship
New York Steam	I	1888		Brooklyn Bridge. Light tan underprint.		150	Ship
Oregon Steam Navigation	I	1874	OR	Side-wheel steamship.		180	Ship
Oregon Steam Navigation	IU	1874	OR	Side wheel steamship		350	Ship
Orinoco Steam Navigation of NY	I	1852	NY	Steamboat, horses pull a loaded wagon. Commerce		110	Ship
Pacific Land	IC	1860's	CA	Ocean steamer.		132	Ship
Pacific Mail Steamship	IU	1867	NY	Side wheel steamship		450	Ship
Pacific Mail Steamship	SP	19--	NY	Brown. Beautiful sailing steamer.		225	Ship
Pacific Mail Steamship	SP	19--	NY	Brown. Beautiful sailing steamer.		225	Ship
Pan-American Fisheries	I	1930's	CA	Ship in harbor		15	Ship
Panama Canal bond	I	1884				90	Ship
Panama Canal bond	IU	1886	France	Canal		195	Ship
People's Transportation	I	1860	OR	Boat		200	Ship
Peoples Transportation	I	1865		Boat		229	Ship
Pioneer Steamship	I	1913	OH	Orange underprint. Great Lakes Steamer.		20	Ship
Porpoise Fishing	IC	1880's	NJ	Porpoise.		330	Ship
Portage Lake & Lake Superior Ship	IC	1870's	MI	Indian warrior, sailing vessels.		253	Ship
Potomac Steam Boat	U	1880's	MD	Side wheel steamboat.	Charles C. Savage	352	Ship
Puerto De Pasajes S.A., Soc General	IC	1920's	Spain	Harbor scene.		48	Ship
Real Eight Co.	U	1975				49	Ship
RMS Titanic	I	2002		Titanic		35	Ship
Robert Stephenson & Co. Ltd.	IC	1890's	GB			80	Ship
Romania Navigation of the Danube	I		Canada			70	Ship
Romania Navigation of the Danube	I			Ships		60	Ship
Romania Navigation of the Danube	I			Two men with anchors		55	Ship
Romano Marine Salvage	IC	1930's	WA	Ship. Vig. on reverse.	EH Romano	550	Ship
Russo-Baltic Shipbuilding and Engin	IC	1920's	Estonia			110	Ship
San Francisco Fire Protection	U	1908	CA	Ships		70	Ship
Savannah & Charleston Steam Packet	IC	1830's	GA	Steamship.	Gazaway B. Lamar	578	Ship
Schuykill Navigation	I	1879	PA	Preferred Stock.		50	Ship
Schuylkill & Susquehanna Navigation	I	1790's	PA		Robert Morris	1,980	Ship
Schuylkill Navigation	IC	1886	NY	Ship		125	Ship
Shangai City Ferry Co. Ltd.	IC		China	Ferry boat.		150	Ship
South Dock Capital	I	1889	Argentina	Woman		100	Ship
South Gila Canal Co.	IC	1890's	AZ	The Canal & Farmland.		80	Ship

Southwestern Transportation	U	1880's	LA	Steamboat.	220	Ship
Standard Rope And Twine Co.	U	1900's	NJ	Ships at sea.	112	Ship
Steam-Boat Helen	I	1834	NY	Steamboat shares.	45	Ship
Submarine Signal	I	1940-5	ME	Green. Steamer with sails.	25	Ship
The American Ship Building Co.	I			Two god-like figures	65	Ship
The William Cramp & Sons	U		PA	Boats	90	Ship
Transport Et La Navigation	IC	1920's	Egypt	Ships, coat of arms of Egypt.	180	Ship
Union Canal Company of Pennsylv	U	1860's	PA	Women, train and steamship.	143	Ship
Union Navigation	IU	1867	NY	Three masted ship	350	Ship
United States & Brazil Mail Steamship	IC	1890's	NY	Ships.	143	Ship
United States and Brazil Mail Stmship	IC	1880's	NY	Company ship on stormy sea.	300	Ship
United States Lines	IC	1939	NV	Photo-vignette of ship	100	Ship
United States Lines	IC	1960's		Ocean Liner.	35	Ship
United States Lines, Inc.	IC	1930's	DE	Company liner in the port of New York.	100	Ship
United States of Brazil - Port of Para	I	1906	Brazil	Panoramic vignette of the town and port.	60	Ship
United States of Brazil - Port of Para	I	1906	ME	Panoramic vignette of the town and port.	60	Ship
United States Ship Corp	IU	1921	ME		25	Ship
Western Transit Co.	IC	1880's	NY	Sailing ship at sea.	80	Ship
White Star Line, Ltd.	IC	1920's	GB	Company flag.	44	Ship
Wiggins Ferry	IC	1870's	IL	Ferry Boat.	121	Ship
Williamson Submarine	IU	1912	VA	Eagle	100	Ship
Zodiac Steamship	U	1860's	NY	Zodiac Signs	1,155	Ship

CHAPTER 18 - TELECOMMUNICATIONS CERTIFICATES

Telecom includes telephone, telegraph and other telecommunications companies.

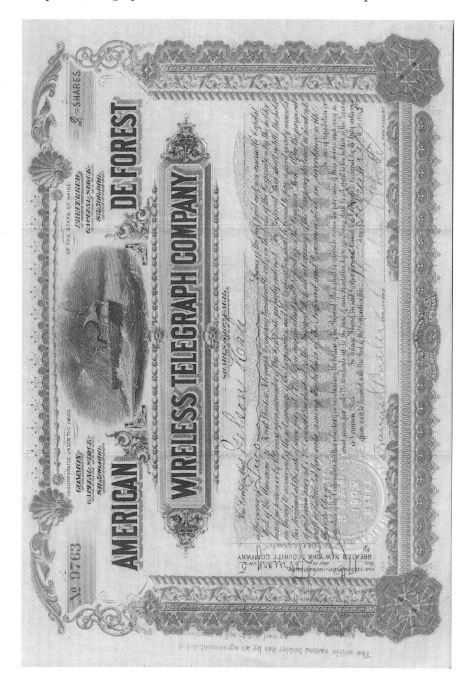

Name	IU	Date	State	Vignette	Signed by	Value	Category
American Telegraph-Typewriter Co.	U	1910's	DE	Mercury using a telegraph machine.		260	Telecom
American Telegraphone	I	1907	DC	Fancy title in clouds. Red embossed seal.		25	Telecom
AT & T	I	1950's		Green. World encircled by old telephone receivers.		35	Telecom
Automatic Telephone Exchg Wash.	U	1890's	WVA	Building, horse drawn traffic, lion with wings.		160	Telecom
Automatic Telephone of Key West	SP	1915	FL	State seal		300	Telecom
Bodie & Hawthorne Telephone & Tel	IU	1892	CA	Bodie Mine		250	Telecom
Bridges Telephone	I	1900's	OK	Lightning, red seal		100	Telecom
Broadcast Relay Service	IC	1950's			Handsigned	10	Telecom
Cartridge Television	I	1970's		TV screen with CTV logo printed in red white blue green		15	Telecom
Clark Wireless Telephone & Telegr	I	1910's	AZ	Eagle		100	Telecom
Clay Commercial Telephone Co.	I	1890's	NJ	Lady with two cherubs, brown seal		175	Telecom
Collins Wireless Telephone Co.	IC	1900's	DC	Radio equipment, ferry on Lake Erie.		260	Telecom
Colorado Telephone	I	1883	CO	Landscape		48	Telecom
Commercial Telegram	U	1880's	NY	Woman with two children.		242	Telecom
Connecticut Telephone	IC	1881	CT	Early phone speaker	Marshall Jewell	500	Telecom
Connecticut Telephone	I	1881		Early telephone earpiece.		60	Telecom
Consolidated Telephone Co.	I	1880's		Eagle		125	Telecom
Consolidated Telephone Co. of Pen	I	1900's		Female with telephone five% gold bond		125	Telecom
Continental Wireless Telephone Teleg	IC	1900's	NY			20	Telecom
Cumberland Telephone & Telegraph	I	1884	KY	Green telegraph poles. Antique telephone.		100	Telecom
Cumberland Telephone and Telegraph	IC	1884	KY	Early wall phone		300	Telecom
De Forest Radio Company	I	1931		People		85	Telecom
Deutsche Telecom	I	2004		Eye, ear, lips		85	Telecom
Drachtloser Ubersee-Verkehr A.G.	IC	1920's	Germany	Four continents, telegraph-post.		110	Telecom
Farnsworth Television & Radio	U	1946		Man		68	Telecom
Foreign Electric Date & Time Stamp	IC	1890'a	GB	Telegraph-wires & machine, locomotives.		80	Telecom
Global Crossing	IU	2003	Bermuda	Map of the world		49	Telecom
Halma Telephone Co.	IC	1900's	MN	Classical lady, telephone & telegraph-posts.		64	Telecom
Hawaiian Bell Telephone	IC	1880's	HI	Palm trees, tropical birds & plants		275	Telecom
Hawaiian Telegraph & Telephone	I	1909	HI	Green.		70	Telecom

Hawk-Eye Telegraph of Iowa	IC	1870's	IA	Train, cattle, eagle.	209	Telecom
Home Telephone Co. of New Albany	IC	1890's	IN	Statue, trees, leaves, globe.	56	Telecom
International Ocean Telegraph	Proof	1880's		American & Spanish Shields	209	Telecom
Irish Submarine Telegraph Co.	IC	1850's	Ireland	Britannia & a Girl representing Ireland.	400	Telecom
Long Distance Telephone & Telegraph	I	1905	AL	Woman holds antique wall phone mouthpiece	25	Telecom
Marconi Wireless Telegraph	I	1920's		Blue. Woman between globes and towers.	45	Telecom
Mediterranean Electric Telegraph	IC	1850's	France	Coats of Arms of the three countries.	60	Telecom
Nebraska Telephone Company	I	1887		Woman Flying	125	Telecom
New Orleans & Ohio Telegraph	IC	1858		Three women, train, barge	325	Telecom
New Orleans & Ohio Telegraph Co.	I	1850's	KY	Bond	225	Telecom
New Orleans & Ohio Telegraph Co.	I	1850's		Train & three ladies	175	Telecom
New Orleans & Ohio Telegraph Less	IC	1850's	KY	Train & canal.	187	Telecom
New York Telephone	U	1920's	NY	Operator, telephone.	264	Telecom
Nortel Networks		1977		Man	65	Telecom
Pacific Telephone & Telegraph bond	IC	1965	CA	Phone worker four rolls of wires	50	Telecom
Pacific Wireless Telephone & Teleg	I	1900's		Embossed seal	35	Telecom
Paterson District Telegraph	IC	1880's	NJ	Eagle on shield.	198	Telecom
People's Telephone	I	1887	NY	Grey/Black. Science. Allegorical figures.	125	Telecom
Societe Des Telephones Erickson	I	1910	France	Blue, tan underprint. Globe, telephone wires	80	Telecom
Societe Des Telephones Erickson	I	1911	France	Globe, telephone wires and antique telephones.	80	Telecom
Southern New England Telephone	SP	1936	CT	Phoneman in storm	300	Telecom
Southern Telegraph	Proof	1880's		Telegraph sending messages across the globe	165	Telecom
Southern Time Telegraph	I	188-	TN	Clock, Roman numerals in diamond. Hand holds lightning	300	Telecom
Telegraphies Publics de Dour & Nuit	IU	1832	France	River scene, forts	6,000	Telecom
Telephone Rentals	IC	1950's		Earliest dial phone printed in red ink.	35	Telecom
Telepost	I	1910-11	ME	Blue. Woman holds lightning.	35	Telecom
Telepost Co.	IU			Woman holding lightning	35	Telecom
Time Telegraph	IU	1883	NY	Watch face	495	Telecom
Typewriting Telegraph Corporation	IC	1900's	GB	Equipment.	100	Telecom
Virgin Express Holdings Company	U	2001	GB		68	Telecom

Western Union Telegraph	Proof	1880's	NY	Woman sits by telegraph and instructs youths.	209	Telecom
Western Union Telegraph	SP	1880's	NY	Woman seated by telegraph.	231	Telecom

ABOUT THE AUTHOR

Fred Fuld III, a former executive in the financial services industry, started collecting antique stock certificates many years ago, then started selling certificates through his firm, Investment Research Institute, and later, antiquestocks.com, one of the first online scripophily dealers. He has written numerous article on the hobby for various publications, including Friends of Financial History Magazine, the Bond and Share Society Journal, and Scripophily Magazine.

Printed in Great Britain
by Amazon